"Steve wanted to be James Dean. He wanted to be Paul Newman. Most of all, he wanted to be me. But he became Steve McQueen."

Marlon Brando

"The motor revved, the clutch went in, the gears shifted, the brake was off, foot on the accelerator, fasten your seatbelts. Look out, honey! Steve McQueen was about to kiss me."

Faye Dunaway, referring to the kiss
in *The Thomas Crown Affair* that became
the longest and most famous kiss in screen history

"The first time I watched Steve McQueen in a movie, I got a hard-on. I knew Marlon Brando and Paul Newman as David knew Bathsheba. But Steve was a mystery. I thought he was unobtainable and that made him a tantalizing specimen. I've had nights when I used to dream about, first, Fidel Castro and second, Steve McQueen. Alas, so many dreams are meant only to be dreamed."

Tennessee Williams

"He climbed the heights of fame, and plumbed the depths of depravity."

Christopher Sanford

"Steve McQueen ended as he began, a rebel outside the establishment, a man who had preserved his fierce sense of unwavering integrity against all odds, who had gone through the fire, and who had found, at the end, a deep personal peace within himself. He died as he had lived--with courage."

William F. Nolan

"Steve was the world's champ at getting laid in the bathroom of an airplane."

Elmer Valentine

"Steve McQueen, Clint Eastwood, and Sean Connery are Hollywood's three greatest ball-clankers."

Joan Crawford

"He was a good father, a bad husband, an unfaithful lover, and he lived for himself. He told me that himself on the set of *The Cincinnatti Kid.* He also told me that he screwed everybody from Paul Newman to Barbra Streisand and had them begging for more. 'Regrets?' he said. 'I've had a few. Elizabeth Taylor should have asked me to marry her. The bitch lost out there.'"

Joan Blondell

"Most of his professional life, Steve spent trying to catch up to me. Then, one fine, sunny day, he found out I wasn't running anywhere."

Paul Newman

"He was a fascinating, crazy, irascible, lovable, roguish, likable, dislikable guy."

David Foster

"He was the biggest asshole who ever walked down Hollywood Boulevard. Chalk me up as his enemy no. 1"

Bobby Darin

"McQueen liked having sex with more than one woman at a time. He also enjoyed it when several males--including himself--had sex with the same woman at once. As one close friend said, 'He enjoyed making love to a woman who was still warm, as it were, from sex with his buddies.'"

Mart Martin

"One thing about Steve. He didn't like for the women in his life to have balls."

Ali McGraw

"At a time when the word is that Hollywood is no more, that there are no more stars, Steve McQueen, characteristically, flies in the face of popular opinion."

Malachy McCoy

"Steve liked to fuck blondes, but he married brunettes."

Neile Adams McQueen

"Our last night together was sexy and romantic. Steve and I had dinner, smoked a joint, drank a few beers, had some tequila, and then sweated the night away with nonstop sex. Steve usually slept in the nude, and insisted that I do the same."

Barbara Leigh

STEVE MCQUEEN

"You know the day I realized I was a star? It was the day I learned I was on the enemies list of both Charles Manson and Richard Nixon."

Steve McQueen

OTHER BOOKS BY DARWIN PORTER

Biographies
Paul Newman, The Man Behind the Baby Blues
Merv Griffin, A Life in the Closet
Brando Unzipped
The Secret Life of Humphrey Bogart
Katharine the Great: Hepburn, Secrets of a Life Revealed
Howard Hughes: Hell's Angel
Jacko, His Rise and Fall (The Social and Sexual History
of Michael Jackson)
And Coming Soon:
Humphrey Bogart, the Making of a Legend

Film Criticism
Blood Moon's Guides to Gay & Lesbian Film (Volumes One & Two)
And Coming Soon:
Fifty Years of Queer Cinema (500 of the Best GLBTQ Films Ever Made)

Non-Fiction
Hollywood Babylon-It's Back!
And Coming Soon:
Hollywood Babylon Strikes Again!

Novels
Butterflies in Heat
Marika
Venus (a roman à clef based on the life of Anaïs Nin)
Razzle-Dazzle
Midnight in Savannah
Rhinestone Country
Blood Moon
Hollywood's Silent Closet

Travel Guides
Many editions of *The Frommer Guides* to Europe, the Caribbean,
California, Georgia, and The Carolinas

STEVE McQUEEN

King of Cool

TALES OF A LURID LIFE

Another Hot, Startling, and Unauthorized Celebrity Biography by

Darwin Porter

BLOOD
MOON
Productions, Ltd.

Steve McQueen King of Cool
Tales of a Lurid Life

Manufactured in the United States of America

ISBN 978-1-936003-05-1

First Edition, First Printing, December, 2009

Cover designs by Richard Leeds (Bigwigdesign.com)
Distributed in North America and Australia
through The National Book Network (www.NBNbooks.com)
and in the UK through Turnaround (www.turnaround-uk.com)

CONTENTS

STEVE McQUEEN, KING OF COOL

1930-1980

HOW CRITICS FROM THE BOOK INDUSTRY
INTERPRETED THIS TITLE

"With astonishing focus and intensity, Darwin Porter shows how Steve McQueen arrived in New York City as a poor and obscure twenty-something determined to carve out a path to fame and fortune. His close-up of McQueen, along with his overview of the icon's psychology and sources of creativity, should prove endlessly fascinating for his fans.

Porter approaches Steve McQueen through his cinematic image: 'A man's man and a woman's dream' to his admirers, or a star saddled with a face that 'looked like a Botticelli angel who had been crossed with a chimp' to those less enchanted with his Bad Boy appeal.

Exhibiting a tabloid reporter's enthusiasm, Porter investigates how McQueen developed the unique persona that captivated audiences in such movies as *The Magnificent Seven* and *Bullitt*.

McQueen's early years were a nightmare of abandonment, neglect, abuse, and exploitation. His mother was an alcoholic; purportedly one of his 'stepfathers' put him on the street as a child prostitute; he spent time in reform school and ran away to kick around brothels as a towel-boy. All that was a nasty prelude to a direction-changing three-year stint with the Marines (he enlisted at 17) and acting classes in Greenwich Village.

If McQueen was secure in anything, Porter assures us, it was his physical appeal and sexual allure. Notorious for having the morals of an alley cat (according to many sources), he admitted to one of his girlfriends that he would do anything with any-body—men, women, acting coaches, co-stars, competitors, idols—if it landed him a part. He told Rod Steiger, 'I became a slut in New York looking for sluts.' There are no complaints on record.

McQueen may have wanted to remain a tantalizing mystery to everyone, but even women he bedded suspected his competitive friendships with James Dean, Montgomery Clift, Marlon Brando, Rock Hudson, George Peppard, and others went beyond a few beers and shop talk. Lee Strasberg and Shelley Winters shared their own theories about McQueen's sexuality with Porter, and they are suitably lurid.

To his credit, Porter, although at times tarnishing McQueen's luster, celebrates his star to the heavens and miraculously, brings us closer to him."

JOHN McFARLAND
www.SHELF-AWARENESS.com
October 31, 2009

Prologue

Steve McQueen was an expert on Death Valley. He made a claim that he'd explored every geographical oddity in the whole valley, from the fantastically eroded golden badlands of Zabriskie Point to Dante's View, from which he could look down at bleak Badwater, the lowest point in Death Valley.

In 1973, after five "wild nights" in Las Vegas, he'd ridden his motorcycle 140 miles west of Las Vegas to this National Monument in the Mojave Desert. It was summer, and temperatures at noon had reached a scorching 120°F. "I can take the heat," Steve told his fellow bikers, thirty-two-year-old Darron McDonald and twenty-four-year-old Casey Perkins.

That night, however, even Steve didn't want to camp out. He'd booked the three of them into a rustic cottage in a large resort that called itself a "ranch," although it really wasn't. Once inside the air-conditioned cottage, all three men stripped down. Since Steve was the movie star, he got to take the first cold shower, and he remained there for nearly half an hour, washing away the sweat of the badlands.

When he came out toweling himself, he didn't bother to put on clothes, but paraded around nude. "There's one thing you could say about my buddy Steve," Casey recalled. "There was no false modesty about him. He never minded flashing his dick in front of people. If he wanted to take a piss along the road somewhere, he got off his bike and whipped it out. 'When a man's gotta go, he's gotta go,' he always said."

Over dinner that night and after a few drinks, Steve entertained his buddies with a great dream of his. He pulled out three maps to show his friends. One of these maps, he was convinced, was going to lead him to one of the legendary gold mines said to exist in Death Valley.

He was enthralled with the many legends about the fabulous lost mines of Death Valley, which had been the site of some of the country's richest mines. Steve felt that his best chance of finding one of these caves was within a few miles of two former boomtowns named "Skidoo" and "Bullfrog." In the morning, he announced to Casey and Darron that he would head for Skidoo with them.

1

The waitress who was serving drinks that night was an attractive woman in her mid-twenties. Steve told his buddies that she reminded him of his mother, Jullian Crawford. "She has blonde hair and blue eyes like my mother, a real looker," Steve told his friends. "I'm going to have her before the night is over, and I want you boys to enjoy her too."

"I found it odd that Steve was attracted to someone who looked like his mother, but I was horny and ready, willing and able," Casey later said. "Steve was always picking up somebody from along the highway, often teenage runaways. He especially liked teenage runaways."

"Steve told us that his mom was a teenage runaway, and he'd become one, too," Darron said.

"I like to fuck blondes, but, if I must get hitched, it would be to a brunette, never a blonde," Steve always said.

"He never explained why," Casey said. "Darron and I figured that he associated blonde hair with whores because of his mother."

The waitress had introduced herself only by the name of "Dolores," and she'd been flirting with Steve all evening, signaling that she was available. Steve kept calling her "baby," and privately at the bar he arranged to hook up with her when she got off work at midnight.

Steve told his buddies that he'd made a deal with Dolores. "She wants me," he said, "and I mean real bad. But I told her that she would have to satisfy you boys first before she got the mother lode. She protested at first but finally agreed, especially when I told her there was a hundred in it for her."

"That makes her a whore," Steve said. "I've found that all women, deep down, are nothing but whores. My mother was a whore. My earliest memory of her was when she came and rescued me from the family farm in Slater, Missouri, and took me to Indianapolis."

Death Valley

"Once, while I was playing on the floor in this walk-up, I looked up and watched as this fat sailor fucked her. I didn't really know what was going on, but I learned quick. She was getting twenty dollars for every john who hopped on her, back when gals was settling for ten dollars, or even five."

"Jullian put up with me for only two weeks before sending me back home to the farm in Missouri," Steve said. "It would

2

be a hell of a long time before I saw the bitch again."

After work, the waitress, Dolores, kept her word and joined the three men in the cottage. Since Steve wanted an early morning start, he was eager for the action to begin.

"I went first," Cascy said. "Steve huddled over us wanting to see all the action. I didn't mind. So he was a voyeur. Darron was next. The gal didn't get really turned on until Steve mounted her. He put on quite a show for us. When it was all over, he slapped the whore on the ass, gave her a hundred dollar bill, and sent her on her way, although the bitch wanted to spend the night."

After Dolores had gone, Steven locked the door behind her. He turned to Casey and Darron. "Now get your asses over here and crawl in bed with me. We've got to get an early start. The desert is always at its most beautiful at dawn."

Chapter One
Rebel Without a Cause

Just as the Great Depression was lengthening its mighty shadow across the American landscape, a blond-haired, blue-eyed baby boy was born on March 24, 1930, in Beech Grove, Indiana, a blighted suburb of Indianapolis.

In ancient Rome, no mother ever wanted her child to be born on March 24, the "Day of Blood." According to ancient tradition, any baby that came into the world on that day would face death early in life.

Other than being the birthplace of Steve McQueen, Beech Grove had another claim to fame. The flamboyant gay actor, Clifton Webb, had also been born there, on November 19, 1889.

The tiny baby that came into the world that day was named Steven Terrence McQueen. The Steven in the boy's name came from Steve Hall, a one-armed bookie and a crony of the baby's father.

"The only thing my father ever gave me was a name," a mature Steve McQueen, the movie star, would recall. "I was born a bastard. No marriage certificate between my father and my mother ever surfaced."

Steven's mother, Jullian Crawford, was blonde, beautiful, and nineteen years old. His father, Terrence William McQueen, was something of a mysterious figure.

A stunt pilot, he flew what was called "spit-and-polish crates," which were very dangerous planes not really safe to become airborne. Before Sunday carnival crowds, he performed barrel rolls and Immelmanns, a particularly

The unwanted "bastard" child, left only a name by his father.

risky stunt considering the limitations of his aircraft. An Immelmann is a showy but dangerous undertaking, usually impractical during warfare, in which an airplane in flight first completes an ascending half-loop followed by a half-roll, a maneuver resulting in level flight in the exact opposite direction but at a higher altitude. When McQueen couldn't find carnival work, he "hedge-hopped," as it was called, through the Middle West, performing equally dangerous aeronautics as a crop-duster.

In addition to his success as a stunt pilot, McQueen thrilled crowds as a "wing walker," pulling off a stunt that could have hurled him to the ground and his death at any minute.

Performing these death-defying feats allowed McQueen to scrap together enough cash to open an illegal gambling joint in Indianapolis. It was called "Wild Bill's," and it was installed in the basement of a bordello on Illinois Street on the darker side of the city.

Through word of mouth, the bordello secretly advertised itself as having a "gal of every nationality—black, African, Indian, Chinese, and a blonde and busty German." Some of the girls working in the joint were said to be twelve years old.

The farms in the Middle West provided plenty of new recruits, as girls left their homesteads when the banks seized their property for failure to pay mortgages. "These gals arrived daily at the train station," McQueen once said. "The pluckings are easy. Some of these wretches have only a dollar bill stuffed in their bras."

Such was the case with Jullian Crawford when she arrived trying to get hired by the bordello. According to all reports, McQueen was the first customer to "sample Jullian's wares" when she was hired by the madam of the bordello. Jullian found her first client "dashing and handsome" and was thrilled to have been seduced by an airplane pilot, fancying him as a sort of Howard Hughes type.

Steve's mysterious pilot father, hedge-hopping in the Middle West as a crop duster.

For a few months, both the bordello and McQueen's casino flourished until the police raided the building, shutting down both operations. Neither the madam nor McQueen had paid off the right people in the police department.

Thrown out onto the street, McQueen rented a small room in Indianapolis' seedy Hotel Sequoia, which was filled with hookers, bums, and drunks. It was in this ratty room that Steven was conceived.

Jullian was alarmed that the health of her new boyfriend seemed to be deteriorating. He would go into coughing spasms at night, and he feared something had gone wrong with his lungs. He never seemed to get enough money together to see a doctor. McQueen told Jullian that he felt he'd infected his lungs with all that crop-dusting. "If you breathe it, that stuff is lethal," he claimed.

Jullian later told her family that her baby spent the first day of his life crying. He had good reason to. Outside his window, the sprawl of dust-blown Indianapolis was staggering from the shock of the onslaught of the Depression. The hospital where Steven was born stood next to the Conrail Depot.

Shabbily dressed hobos got off there, having ridden the rails from the eastern industrial cities, heading West with dreams about how they'd find relief from their hunger in the "land of milk and honey," California.

The stench from the stockyards where cattle was brought to be slaughtered assailed one's nostrils, as did pollution from the coal-fueled factories. The morning Steven was born, it had rained all night, carrying raw sewage along the city gutters.

Steven's young mother and her handsome pilot were alcoholics. Money was scarce, and most of it was spent on liquor. Milk was cheap and Steven survived mainly on store-bought liquids since Jullian refused to nurse him, "not wanting to ruin my beautiful breasts."

When the money that Jullian had been given by her family disappeared, so did her boyfriend. When she came home with bootleg liquor one afternoon, she found him gone, her soiled baby crying for milk.

Although Steve McQueen in later years would spend thousands of dollars in fruitless searches, he never met his runaway father.

In his fantasy, Steve, as he grew older, told friends that his flier dad was one of the pilots in General Chennault's Flying Tigers in China, and that he was shot down by Japanese aircraft in 1939.

In the 1960s, Steve claimed that "my life was fucked up while I was still in the womb. What chance did a bastard child born on the wrong side of the tracks in Indianapolis have in 1930?" He also liked to brag, "Who would have believed that I came from such low lives to become the

General Chennault and a Flying Tiger: Steve's fantasy version of his missing father

highest-paid movie star in the world, making $5 million per picture."

As she walked the streets of Indianapolis, shiftless, out-of-work men whistled at Jullian, catcalling promises of their prowess in bed. Her blonde hair, prominent breasts, and sexy figure turned many a male eye. She always wore her brown stockings rolled down, revealing almost pasty white but shapely calves, and she was said to be the best hoochy-koochy dancer in Indianapolis.

With no permanent man in her life, it was obvious to her how she was going to survive. But her new profession didn't allow for any baby. Burdened with a child and full of blossoming life, she wasn't going to retire with an unwanted baby to a family farm in a hick town in Missouri with only 2,500 people.

It was a hard decision for her to make, but Jullian and her baby, broke and abandoned, once again rode the train to Slater, from which she'd fled.

Founded in 1878, Slater was a small Midwestern farming community lying about 102 miles northeast of Kansas City. In the 1920s it had flourished as a railroad town and was a major repair junction of the old Chicago & Alton Railway Company. By the time the Depression hit, the railway had moved on. Two factories, one making bib overalls, another "shoes for clodhoppers," had shut down and would remain idle until World War II, when they were revived to make components for the B2-9 bomber.

With her baby, Jullian arrived on the doorstep of her parents, Victor and Lillian Crawford, in Slater. Lillian and Victor could have posed for Grant Wood's *American Gothic*.

The runaway Jullian was welcomed back. Her mother reached for the baby boy. "I'll raise him," she said, looking with stern disapproval at her errant daughter. "Maybe this time

The home in Slater, Missouri. Steve grew up here with "Gothic" proxy parents

one of my offspring will turn out right."

She stared at her grandson. "He has the bluest eyes God ever gave any baby boy." A similar remark had been made by the mother of Paul Newman in Shaker Heights, Ohio, only five years earlier.

A devout Catholic, Lillian had raised her daughter to be an image of herself—church-going, properly mannered, God-fearing. But the rebellious Jullian had grown up to be the very opposite. She'd seen pictures of flappers in the newspapers, and she wanted to be one herself—fully accessorized with bootleg gin, promiscuous sex, and bobbed hair. She fled the rigid confines of her Bible-thumping rural home for Indianapolis "for the good times," which in her case meant lots of handsome, horny men.

After delivering her baby to the farmstead in Slater, Jullian returned to the seedy Hotel Sequoia. She later told her son that on her first night back, seven men entered her hotel room and held her down while they brutally gang-raped her. She had to be taken to the hospital to stem the bleeding.

After her release two days later, she took the first train to Chicago, 130 miles to the north. There she would begin her new life as a full-time prostitute, in spite of the brutal experiences she'd already suffered at the hands of men. Months would go by before she ever saw her baby again.

Slater, Missouri, with the bleakest Main Street in the Middle West.
Steve McQueen is Slater's only claim to fame.

In Slater, one of Steven's earliest memories involved watching the black hearses come and go with the dead at a funeral parlor across the street from where he lived with his grandparents. His devoutly religious grandmother always predicted his own mother would be arriving one day in one of those dark and foreboding hearses. "God will strike her dead in her prime from the life she's living," Lillian repeatedly told Steven.

Just after Steven turned four years old, on a wild impulse, Jullian unexpectedly returned to Slater to reclaim her baby boy. She told her parents that she was doing well in Indianapolis and wanted Steven back with her. "A boy's place is with his mother."

"And with a father," Lillian pointed out.

Back in Indianapolis, Jullian took Steven to a boarding house run by a "Mrs. Rhodes," who took care of Steven at night.

Jullian had explained to Mrs. Rhodes that she worked at nights in a factory on the far side of town. In fact, she was turning tricks until the early morning hours.

Steven had nothing but good memories of the kindly Mrs. Rhodes, who had met an American soldier in Germany and had married him. He took her back to his home in the Midwest. After he died, she'd converted the home into a boarding house. "For most of my boyhood, I never got enough to eat. Except when I lived with Mrs. Rhodes. She was a good German cook, and she liked to stuff me. I learned to like sauerkraut and pig sausages."

When Mrs. Rhodes died of a heart attack, Jullian once again packed up Steven's belongings and once again boarded the train for Slater. She dropped him off with Victor and Lillian, and told him "to be a good boy." She was able to catch a night train heading back to Indianapolis at eight o'clock.

A hog farm in Slater.
Hog for breakfast, lunch, and dinner.

In Slater, Steven told his grandparents about all the toys that "strange men" gave to him when he was allowed to meet some of them. They moved quickly through Jullian's life. She defined these men to Mrs. Rhodes as "dates." Whenever Jullian ran low on cash, she gathered up Steven's toys and sold them to a kindergarten.

A lost, lonely kid, Steven confronted dire circumstances at the Crawford household. An aging Victor had lost his job as a salesman, and his health was failing. Lillian turned more and more to prayer, and was rarely seen around the house without her Bible. She was moving deeper and deeper into religious fanaticism.

With no money coming in, Lillian appealed to her estranged brother, Claude Thomson, to take her in. A hog baron, he lived on a 320-acre farm down Thomson Lane, three miles outside of Slater along muddy Buck Creek.

Although they were brother and sister, Claude and Lillian were a study in contrast. He'd been known as a hell-raiser in his youth, and it was rumored that he'd "deflowered" most of the young girls in the county, with several unwanted pregnancies resulting.

Steven's great-uncle, Claude, took an almost instant liking to the young boy and would become the only surrogate father he ever had. Later, in recalling his stay at Claude's farm, Steven said, "We had hog for breakfast, hog for dinner, and hog for supper."

Claude always came to breakfast with his revolver, and was never seen without it. "I'd no more leave my bedroom without my revolver than I would without my pants," he told Steven. "I shot my own brother when he started messin' around with my gal. Served him right."

In 1904 Claude had married a nurse, Lecho McFall, but he divorced her in 1918, alleging spousal abuse and citing her violent attacks on him with objects ranging from a bronze lamp to an axe on one occasion. The court awarded her their son, Pike McFall Thomson, and twenty dollars a month in child support.

Claude never remarried but filled the house with a series of young, pretty girls he hired as housekeepers. In one year alone, Steven witnessed the arrival and departure of four different girls.

Claude began to look upon Steven as the son he'd lost to his wife. He knocked on Steven's door before dawn, yelling, "Rise and shine, boy." He taught the young boy to milk cows and chop wood. On journeys into town to purchase supplies, Steven was always seen riding in the front seat. At the local drugstore, he always bought the boy an ice cream sundae.

When Steven did something wrong, like not closing the gate and therefore letting the farm animals out, he felt the sting of a hickory switch. Claude always had the boy take off his overalls and strip down so the sting of the switch would be felt more strongly against the boy's tender skin.

With that same switch, Claude also beat his housekeeper of the moment for any alleged infraction on her part. After beating the hapless girl, Claude would always haul her off to his bedroom for more "punishment." In the room next door, Steven could hear the girl's pleas for mercy. It was later said that Steven used Claude for his role model in handling women.

On Saturday at three o'clock in the afternoon, Claude always drove

Steven to the matinee at the Kiva Grand. The picture, sometimes starring Gene Autry, was invariably a Western. With his cap pistol, Steven fired at the villains on the screen, little knowing that one day he'd be the hero on that screen tangling with the bad men.

In the autumn of his sixth year, Steven had to walk two miles a day to the one-room Orearville School where grades one to twelve were taught. "I don't take to learning," he later told his uncle. What held Steven back was his dyslexia, which would not be discovered or even defined until years later. He also was hard of hearing in his left ear because of a mastoid infection that was never treated. This loss of hearing would plague him for the rest of his life. Consequently, he learned to listen to people with his right ear.

The movie star, Steve McQueen, remembered that "my racing fever began when Uncle Claude presented me with a shiny red tricycle. I'd take it up a hill, and then race down. I sometimes tumbled in the briar patch. I had a lot of close encounters with blackberries, and even a rattlesnake, that year."

Saturday afternoons were a special treat for Steven, beginning when he was only eight years old. Loading the family rifle with only one shot, Claude turned it over to Steven and sent him into the woods "to kill something. You've got just this one shot to get your prey so don't waste it."

Sometimes Steven turned up empty-handed, but on some occasions he brought back game, everything from a rabbit to a pigeon. In later years, Steve cited his time hunting in the woods as the beginning of his love of the outdoors.

During his early years in Slater, Steven had always suffered abuse from his classmates because of his mother. He was often mocked as a "bastard," his mother called a "whore." Quick to offend, Steven fought his attackers, even if some of these bullies were far bigger than he was. He returned to Uncle Claude's hog farm many a late afternoon with a bloody nose.

"Steven kept to himself," said Claire Lemmon, his classmate. "He was a loner and didn't mix in with the other kids. One or two girls found him attractive, but decided he was too much trouble to bother with. Besides, he was so short. One look into Steven's steely blue eyes and I wanted to run the other way."

The last picture show in Slater. Young Steven "killed" the onscreen villians.

"His biggest hero at the time was that gangster, John Dillinger," Claire said. "He kept a picture of him in his desk. I always figured that Steven would grow up to become a gangster himself. I think that was what he was dreaming about in class. He never paid any attention to the teacher—that is, if he showed up in school at all. Most often he didn't."

Without even a letter to announce that she was coming back to Slater, Jullian showed up at Claude's doorstep to reclaim her son. He was just a few days short of his ninth birthday.

Before he left Slater, Uncle Claude presented Steven with a gold pocket watch. The inscription read: *To Steven, who has been a son to me.*

***

Once back in Indianapolis, Jullian walked from the station to another old rambling boarding house, so common in those days. Steven followed her, climbing with her to the cheapest room in the house, which was virtually up in the attic.

There he met his new "Daddy," who was lying drunk and unshaven in bed, clad only in his underwear. Jullian claimed she'd gotten married to him, but Steve was never sure of that.

Larson Ward, if that was his real name, was a tall, very dark, well-built man with a strong jaw and thick lips. Steven later found out he was from Chicago. The gossip around the boarding house, as Steven was to learn, was that Ward was a mulatto, although he merely shrugged off that suggestion, telling Steven that his mother came "from one of the islands," with the suggestion that he might be part Puerto Rican.

All three of them were forced to share a tiny room under the eaves. Jullian had curtained off a corner of the room, installing within it a small cot just adequate to sleep on.

Ward had little to say to his newly acquired son and ordered Steven to go to bed behind that curtain. That night as he lay awake on the verge of tears, Steven heard Ward trying to force Jullian to go down on him. She kept resisting, claiming it was disgusting, but he punched her out and forced her to do it anyway. Steven buried his good ear into the pillow, hoping to blot out the noises.

Steven could not stand to be in the same room with his mother and Ward. He skipped school on most days and took up with a gang that roamed through slum like sections of Indianapolis. He and his buddies broke into stores and stole hubcaps. Amazingly, they never got arrested. Some nights he didn't bother to go home at all but slept on a soiled blanket with the hobos near the railroad tracks.

Deep into their alcoholic haze, Jullian and Steven's new "Daddy" didn't seem to care where he was or what he did. As headlines were filled with the breakout of World War II, Steven roamed the streets of Indianapolis, looking for trouble.

When he had no money for food, he found that he could go to the back of a restaurant and beg for bones from the plates of diners inside. Often they left enough meat on a chicken leg or sirloin steak to provide nourishment for him. "It was a shit world back then," he later proclaimed. "On second thought, it still is."

Like all of Jullian's men, Ward eventually left her, taking all the money they had. That was the day she discovered she was a month behind in the rent. She and Steven were forced to move into a dangerous "hot bed" hotel where Jullian resumed her trade of prostitution.

If Steven ever came home too early, she told him to wait out on the sidewalk. Over a period of several weeks, he saw a parade of men of all ages, sizes, and descriptions descending from their bedroom.

Most often a sailor or a military man bounded down the steps of the hotel and out the door, after enjoying thirty minutes to an hour locked in an embrace with Steven's mother. Sometimes a well-dressed businessman descended those stairs, after enjoying an off-the-record tryst before heading home to his wife and kids, who lived on the right side of the railroad tracks.

Jullian never went to a restaurant, but Steve brought her food, mostly fried

chicken or Chinese from a take-out joint. Since there was only one bed, she invited him to share it with her. She slept nude and crawled in with him "to cuddle" against the cold of the night. He would later tell his biking buddies that he often got an erection sleeping in such intimacy with his mother. "One night," Steven confessed, "I felt her tits when she was drunk to the world. But nothing really sexual happened between us. That would come much later."

When not hanging out with his gang, Steven wandered alone to the neighborhood Roxy Theatre. Child molesters often took the seat next to him, but he'd brush their hands away and move elsewhere to safety.

Bogart, in the shadow of *The Maltese Falcon*. Steve would eventually be called the screen's "second Bogie."

Any picture with Humphrey Bogart intrigued him. He could sit through a Bogie movie four or five times and never tire of watching it. In a day

14

far away, some critics would compare his presence on the screen to that of Bogart's. Those comparisons thrilled him more than any others.

Steven was always the last to leave when the Roxy closed for the evening. One time he slipped behind a curtain and spent the entire night in the theater on an old mattress he found backstage. To him, the theater was a magical place.

When he woke up the next morning, and the theater had not yet opened for its noon-day business, Steven stood in the middle of the stage and imitated Bogie doing a scene.

Back at the communal bathroom at his hotel, he would stand in front of the shaving mirror and practice his Bogart sneer until one of the boarders pounded on the door demanding that he vacate the place. Even though he was much too young, he hung out with gang members at seedy pool halls. He became skilled at the game, imagining himself a pint-sized Minnesota Fats.

To one of his early biking buddies, Steven admitted a dark secret. "When I got bored, I indulged in a little playful arson. Often the fires were put out. But I think I burned three claptrap buildings to the ground. When two kids were killed in one fire in a tenement, I felt guilty and gave up arson. I had to take up something else. That's when I became adept at the art of the circle jerk."

A guy named "Buddy" was the leader of Steven's gang in Indianapolis. No more than sixteen years old, he was also the school bully. Every school has a hunky stud like Buddy. He had good looks, charm, and sex appeal, and he took a skinny, short, and underaged Steven under his arm and protected him from the other guys. If asked why, he claimed, "The guy is my mascot." Buddy was the only one in his class who revealed a day's growth of beard at school.

He was the first to acquire pornographic pictures, and he invited the members of his gang to join him for a circle jerk. Steven had never done anything like that before, and he joined in for the fun, although at his age he couldn't produce a spectacular climax like Buddy.

Sometimes when looting had been good, Buddy hired two or three prostitutes, often black, to service his boys in an abandoned shack outside of town. Steven felt too insecure to join in that kind of maneuver and always bowed out. Buddy assured him that, "I understand. Some guys mature faster than others." He grabbed his crotch. "I got my first piece of ass when I was only nine years old. My old man's second wife."

Steven often felt like a farm boy hick from Missouri and not really capable of keeping up with the other guys. Still, he stayed with the gang and felt secure with him. At least no one made fun of him the way the kids had done back in Slater.

15

In the gang that he ran with in Indiana, most of the members didn't even know who their fathers were, so nobody called anybody else a bastard.

Buddy shocked Steven when he took him for a ride one night. On the way to a house outside of town, he revealed to Steven that he often sold himself to older men for "big bucks." All you have to do is stand there, unbutton yourself, and let one of these queers do all the work."

This horrified Steven and marred his image of Buddy, but he went along for the ride, especially when Buddy told him that one of the guys liked real young boys. Shaking and nervous, he entered the house where Buddy's patron awaited him along with a man who looked in his late 50s. Buddy disappeared into a front bedroom with the owner of the house, and Steven very reluctantly went along to the back bedroom. The older man assured him that, "I have a son about your age."

The older man was arrested eight years later and charged with pedophilia. A cache of naked pictures of young boys from nine to thirteen years old was discovered in his private office when a young boy's mother went to the police and told of her son's molestation.

But long before that happened, the pedophile patronized Steven on many an afternoon, providing him with a crisp ten dollar bill for every time Steven would let him fellate him. Those bills were crisp because the middle-aged man was the president of a small bank.

Steven told Buddy that allowing the man to "get his kicks is a painless way to make money."

But this sexual liaison wasn't made to last. One night when Jullian wasn't at home, Ward discovered nearly one hundred dollars hidden in Steven's mattress. When he ran out of liquor money, he often searched the hotel room to see if Jullian or her son were hiding any money from him.

When Steven came into the room, Ward confronted him with the money and demanded to know where he'd gotten it. After a severe beating, Steven broke down and confessed the source and what he did to earn it.

That confession seemed to excite Ward that night, and he demanded that Steven have sex with him, too. When Steven refused, Ward beat him into submission. The young boy fellated Ward, something Jullian had not wanted to do. Even though "it made me sick at my stomach, I knew that something worse awaited me if I didn't do a good job," Steven told Buddy. Once or twice, Ward slapped him when Steven used "too much teeth."

When he'd finished, Ward began to fellate the young boy like the pedophile had done. Another biographer, Christopher Sandford, also learned of this seduction. In his exploration of the life of Steve McQueen, he quotes a childhood friend, Teri Gahl, who learned of Ward's attack on his "son."

"Steven would always remember the beads of ice dripping from the ceiling like the sweat on the geek's lips and how he, Steven, had tried to focus on the sound of the water and the wind flapping the hotel sign around outside the door to avoid thinking about what was going on."

This horrendous introduction to sex led Steven, at least in his comments to friends, to become the leading homophobe in Hollywood in the years to come. Actually, it was more complicated than that. He divided men who engaged in homosexual sex into two categories., First, came the "queers," whom he despised, although not to the extent that he wouldn't get involved with them to take advantage of them, or to enter into some sort of agreement.

The other category of men, of which he included himself, were straight but a thrill-seeker at heart, a man who indulged in homosexual acts as a change of pace. Steven could hang out with men in the latter category and not feel threatened.

One day when he came in from school, one of the few classes he'd actually attended, he noticed Jullian packing. "Where are we moving now?" he asked.

"I'm moving," she said. "To California. With the war about to come, I heard there's a lot of money to be made in both San Francisco and Los Angeles. I bought a ticket for you to back to Slater."

***

Life at the family compound in Slater had changed drastically since Steven had gone away with his gold pocket watch from his Uncle Claude. His grandmother Lillian had become a complete "religious nut," according to Claude. He could no longer put up with her zeal and "Bible-thumping," and she could no longer endure the "Godless life" he led in the main house. Although she had almost no money, and Claude was hog rich, he asked her to move off his property.

As if to defy him, she moved to a point a few feet from the border of his sprawling farmstead into an unused cook shack, which was actually an abandoned railroad vehicle resting on cement blocks. The one-room shack—a former chuck wagon of sorts—had no heat and no toilet facilities except for a chamber pot.

Deep into his seventies, Victor, her husband, spent most of his days in bed complaining of stomach trouble. As it turned out, he was dying of cancer which would reclaim his life in June of 1943.

Lillian took to walking barefoot up and down Thomson Lane, carrying her rosary and her crucifix. "She'd completely lost her mind," Steven remembered. "My Uncle Claude had to have her committed to an insane asylum, where she spent the rest of her life."

After his grandmother had been committed to the Fulton State Hospital for the insane—a ward of the state—Claude told Steven the real reason Jullian had fled Slater as a teenage runaway. "Lillian one night tried to kill your mother. I had to put her away back then. She might have killed you, too."

At the main house on Thomson Lane, Steven encountered a very different Uncle Claude. Although in his seventies, he'd married a former showgirl from St. Louis who was half his age. He later found out her name was Nellie Bullis, although she'd used various names during the course of her career, once billing her act as "Zorita" and appearing with a boa constrictor.

After she became too old to be a showgirl, she'd drifted into Slater where she'd become one of the many "housekeepers" employed by Claude. In another act at a strip joint in St. Louis, Nellie had billed herself as "The Lady Eve," again employing a snake (the older reptile had died). By the time she went to work for Claude, "Eve" had become Eva Anderson. She claimed that she'd married a George Anderson at one point and had had a baby girl with him.

She was different from all of Claude's other housekeepers. She managed to get "the lovesick old fool" (Steven's words) to marry her. It was obvious that she wanted Claude's money.

Some old-time Slaterians still remembered Eva driving around the countryside in a buttercup yellow Cadillac Claude had bought for her. A flashy dresser, she wore a diamond on every finger.

During this time in Slater, Steven noticed that his uncle had become "insanely jealous" of Nellie (or Eva). Her shiny Cadillac was seen parked at various places around town, or out in the country, even late at night.

Steve's new aunt was once "The Lady Eve," working the strip joints of St. Louis.

By June of 1942 all the news reaching Slater was from the outside world and dealt with how badly the war was going for the Americans. There was even talk in Missouri of a possible Japanese invasion of the coast of California. That's why Claude was very concerned when he received a letter from Jullian, asking that Steven be "shipped" to Los Angeles. She falsely claimed that she was "happily married to a wonderful man" and that she and her new husband could provide a happy home life for her growing boy.

Since Steven was her son, Claude gave in to her request, but warned Steven that "the Japs might attack any night. Los Angeles is not a safe place." Steven promised him that "if any Japs attack, I'll shoot at least thirty of them before they take me down."

18

With that bravado promise, Steven, with a packed lunch and a bag of apples and smoked meat from Claude's hogs, boarded the train and rode across half a continent. Along the way, many soldiers and sailors shared their smokes with him, urging him to join up as soon as he was old enough.

At the time, he was only twelve years old.

***

Two hours late, Jullian arrived at Union Station in Los Angeles to retrieve her son. When she didn't show up at first, he thought she'd forgotten about him. In a battered 1933 Ford, she drove Steven to a decaying apartment house in Silver Lake. The building was filled mostly with out-of-work actors or film people who lived on the fringe of the industry, hoping that each new day would bring work and a paycheck.

The complex was called The Shady Arms, the shady perhaps coming from its inhabitants. In the bright California sun, Steven noticed that his mother looked older and a bit beat up, and was using more bleach than ever. She had obviously tried to fashion herself into a Betty Grable look-alike.

As Steven climbed to the third floor with his mother, he noticed a large rat scurrying across the garbage-strewn hallway. Before going into the tacky apartment, Jullian warned her son, "Be extra good around Berry. He doesn't take any sass from anybody."

The man who greeted them looked like he was recovering from a drunk. He was unshaven and in his underwear, evoking Jullian's so-called husband in Indianapolis. He looked as if he'd been handsome in the 1930s, but those good looks were fast fading. He appeared sullen and hostile. His first words, "So this is the punk son you've been raving about?"

"This is your stepfather, Berry Berri," Jullian said. "Shake his hand."

Steven extended his hand but Berry didn't offer to shake it. "That's a funny name. Berry Berri. "Sounds like a disease."

Angered at the remark, Berry slapped Steven so hard he fell down.

"Don't hurt the kid," Jullian said, pleading with

Sonja Henie (left) and Ilona Massey. Blonde goddesses and conquests of Steve's abusive stepfather.

19

him. "He didn't mean anything."

"Smartass kid," Berry said, reaching for his pants. "I'm going out. I need a drink."

At the door, Jullian asked him when he was coming home.

"Maybe never, bitch," he said, slamming the door behind him.

Across the hallway, Steven could hear what sounded like domestic violence. He later recalled he was heartsick, in spite of Jullian's assurances that Berry was a great guy once you got to know him. "Are you really married to this bastard?" Steven asked.

"Of course, I am," she said. "He's your new stepfather. You should call him Daddy."

"That I'll never do." In the days ahead, Steven never got to know Berry Berri nor did he want to.

His last name may have been Berri, but "Berry" was just a nickname. When he occasionally got film work, his co-workers had named him "beriberi" after the disease.

His claim to fame, and he bragged about it constantly, was that he'd had a brief affair with the Hungarian singing sensation, Ilona Massey, when she was added to MGM's musical stable in the late 30s. Berry had worked on her 1939 film, *Balalaika*, in which she'd co-starred with Nelson Eddy. Berri had also seduced the Norwegian ice-skating champion, Sonja Henie. An Olympic star, she made several skating films in Hollywood. Berri had become involved very briefly with her when she'd filmed *Thin Ice* in 1937.

Apparently, Jullian was still plying her trade as a prostitute. Whenever she didn't bring home enough money, Berri beat her. Young Steven wondered why she'd sent for him in the first place, since having any semblance of a home life was obviously out of the question.

In spite of his young age, Berri constantly hounded Steven urging him to seek work. "You need to bring home a paycheck, kid," Berri said. "Even if you have to hustle to get it. A lot of queers live out here. Walk along Hollywood Boulevard or Santa Monica Boulevard during the day. Some asshole will pick you up and give you ten bucks. But, remember, those ten bucks belong to me. After all, I'm the one who keeps a roof over your head. On some days I think I'll kick out both you and that no-good rotten whore you call a mother."

Steven later admitted that Berri "beat me with his fists until I agreed to let him drive me to Hollywood Boulevard." He was let out of the car and warned that he'd better bring home some money that night—"or else."

Against his wishes, he was launched early into a career of prostitution, just like his mother. "I got picked up a lot," he later confessed. "I had to let the creeps do what they wanted to do to me."

At the lowest point of his life, he was picked up by a middle-aged man who drove him to a secluded home in Laurel Canyon. There four other men awaited him. Reports are sketchy, but apparently Steven was held down and gang raped. Afterward, he was driven back to Hollywood Boulevard and let out of the car. He was bleeding.

Part of his later hatred of homosexuals stemmed from incidents such as this.

When he could stand this form of torture no more, Steven quit walking the boulevards waiting for men to pick him up. He fell in with a gang who operated near Pershing Square in downtown Los Angeles. In less than a week, he was earning more money than he did at prostitution. "We were one hell of a gang of tough guys," Steven later recalled. "We stole purses from old ladies, broke into stores, ripped off hubcaps, and even hotwired a car or two."

Steven had completely dropped out of school, and truancy officers from Los Angeles came to call, informing Jullian of her son's delinquency. When Steven was caught shoplifting in a store near the bottom end of Sunset Boulevard, he was arrested and detained at the police station. Jullian was called.

The police hauled him before a judge who seemed to want to send him to reform school. Jullian intervened and begged for mercy since this was her son's first offense. She told the judge that she would send him back to work on his uncle's farm, claiming that her boy would be of help to the war effort, since Claude Thomson was raising pork to feed hungry American soldiers fighting overseas. The judge bought that.

That night Jullian drove Steven to Union Station. She'd already notified Claude that he was on his way back to Missouri.

At the station, he told his mother good-bye.

She didn't kiss him or hug him, but shook his hand.

"I guess I didn't work out," he said to her.

"You're a bad boy, kid, and I fear that's all you'll ever be."

He remembered her walking away from him without looking back. In the distance, he saw her approach two soldiers and engage them in conversation.

This time he turned his back on her and boarded the train.

A shirtless, beer-swilling movie star: Steve recalls his boyhood home of Slater

* * *

Steven resumed the life he'd led before being shipped off to California.

The major difference in the Thomson household had involved the arrival of Eva's daughter from East St. Louis. Eva was never sure who the father was, but she'd given birth to Jackie Anderson when she was only eighteen and dancing at the Follies in St. Louis. After she was firmly entrenched in Slater, Eva, in her Cadillac, drove to St. Louis where she picked up her daughter who had been raised by her sister.

Back home in Slater, Eva introduced her fifteen-year-old daughter as her niece. On the farmstead, Steven and Jackie didn't get along, fighting like siblings and getting into arguments, especially when Jackie stole Steven's jeans to wear.

Nellie (or Eva) took Steven in and treated him like her own son. She was a good cook and put plenty of fried chicken and biscuits on the table. At one sitting, she cooked eight different vegetables, including corn on the cob. He could always go to the cookie jar and find it filled with his favorite, chocolate chip. He was eating well once again and putting on some weight.

Even though she'd been a stripper, Eva took to farm chores like she'd been born to slop hogs, feed chickens, and milk goats. She even became adept at castrating hogs, which she did with her mouth. "It's less painful on the poor critters," she told Steven.

"The idea of some woman biting off my nuts is disgusting," he said.

"I bet those nuts of yours are growing bigger every day," she said flirtatiously.

Eva wasn't the only one to notice that Steven was on the road to becoming a fully developed male. One night, as Uncle Claude sat in his favorite rocking chair on his front porch, he called Steven out for a man-to-man talk. Eva had driven to Indianapolis with Jackie to buy her some new clothes.

"With Eva's good cooking," Claude told Steven, "I noticed you're growing up. Probably thinking a lot about girls these days."

"Not so much," Steven said.

"I'm not so sure about that," Claude said, studying him carefully. "I got some good news for you. When the cat's away, the mice will play. Tonight's our night to indulge in some tomfoolery."

Claude asked Steven to get into his car for a ride into town to a house on one of the back streets of Slater. En route there, his uncle explained that with the influx of men into town to work at the munitions factory, some women from Indianapolis had come to Slater and opened up a bawdy house. "I'm gonna take you there tonight," Claude told Steven. "Tonight you're gonna get your first taste of pussy, and I bet you'll be as happy as a pig in shit."

Steven was never clear about what exactly happened at the bordello that night. But reportedly, Uncle Claude, even though in his mid-seventies, occupied one room and Steven the next. The young boy was introduced to heterosexual sex by a prostitute.

All he would later tell his friends was, "She must have been past forty if a day. But she sure knew her business. I left that whorehouse that night a man of the world. She even complimented me on the size of my dick. I liked that."

Some reports suggest that when Steven and Jackie weren't bickering over something, the teenagers enjoyed a sexual relationship. But this cannot be confirmed. What is known is a bit more shocking than that.

Aware of Steven's burgeoning manhood, good looks, and easy-going charm, Eva began to pay special attention to him. Once or twice, she barged in on him when he was taking a bath, pretending she was just bringing some towels.

The first time that happened, he yelled at her to get out.

"Don't be embarrassed, kid," she told him. "You've got nothing to be ashamed of."

In a few weeks, the inevitable happened. When Claude went on one of his frequent trips to New Orleans, Eva seduced young Steven. Since his seduction at the hand of a prostitute in Slater, he at least had some experience in making love to an older woman.

If he felt any guilt about seducing his uncle's wife, he didn't show it. Eva and Steven made love every chance they got before Claude's return. They entered a pact to continue to make love even after Claude came back from Louisiana, except they've have to be far more discreet. Eva warned Steven that if Claude caught the two of them in bed together, he was liable to shoot both of them.

Perhaps Steven did experience some guilt or grew tired of being Eva's boy, satisfying her sexually when Claude was getting too feeble to perform his marital duties.

Details are slim, but Steven mysteriously deserted the Thomson farm one night and wasn't seen again for years. Getting the law after him after shooting out the window panes of a café window, he disappeared with a traveling circus on its way to California.

No one is sure how such a young boy got the job, but it was speculated that the manager of the circus had a fondness for teenage boys. Even though he shared the manager's living quarters at night, Steven was assigned the day job of "mopping up elephant dumps," as he later recalled.

The circus folded before it reached California. The manager escaped with the receipts, owing his workers their

TRAVELING CIRCUS

GRAND OPENING june 6th

23

wages. The Bearded Lady and the Lion Tamer, as well as all the others, had to make it to California on their own.

Steven later said he hitchhiked all the way to Los Angeles in a series of cars with very strange men. He shared their beds at night, their cars by day, and he stayed well fed. "I learned early in life," he told a biker friend, "that pretty boys don't have to go hungry."

***

Once in Los Angeles, he had a reunion with Jullian, who was still living with Berri. His so-called "stepfather" seemed to like Steven even less than before, and viewed his second arrival with even more disdain.

"I became acquainted with that guy's fist on many a drunken night," Steven said. "Jullian just stood by as he beat the crap out of me."

One night Steven went to bed with a butcher knife under his pillow. If Berri attacked him one more time in his sleep, he was going to stab that knife into the man's heart.

Once again, Steven took up with one of the gangs roaming the streets of Los Angeles, trying to hustle a quick buck. He tried to avoid returning home whenever he could. Desperate and lonely, he turned to gang members for some semblance of "family" life, however remote.

His passion was cars, and he found that he was quite adept at repairing them. He and a nineteen-year-old male friend, whose father had been a mechanic, joined a Model A frame with a Ford 60 engine. Steven pronounced it "a real jumper." They rode all over Los Angeles in it at top speed. Once they were forced to outrun a squad car hot on their trail.

When a gang from East Los Angeles invaded the territory of Steven's gang, there was a rumble that led to his arrest. Because of his age, the judge let him off with a warning.

Steve's first of many machines was a Model A Ford accessorized with a Ford 60 Engine. "A real jumper."

He arrived back at the Berri household with a police escort. Only Berri was at home, and the police, assuming that the man was Steven's father, informed him of what had happened. In the rumble, Steven, along with the other boys, had used knives and two rival gang members had been seriously slashed.

Berri didn't do anything to

punish Steven right away. But that night when Steven was asleep in the apartment, Berri attacked him, pounding him viciously with his fists and bashing in his nose to the point that it gushed blood.

In that weakened condition, Berri hauled a kicking and screaming Steven into the hallway. Still clad in his underwear, the boy was tossed down the steps. Picking himself up, Steven threatened Berri. "You try to pull that shit on me again, and I swear I'll kill you."

Berri must have sensed the fierce determination in Steven's steel-blue eyes. The next day he signed the papers to commit him to California Junior Boys Republic at Chino. His enrollment papers, in which he was identified as "Steven Berri," claimed that he was "incorrigible."

***

In the middle of farmland and cow pastures, Chino is a small city in San Bernardino County. "A dirtbag town," Steven proclaimed upon seeing Chino for the first time.

Chino was the site of the dreaded California Institution for Men, filled with hardened criminals. Opened in 1941, its reputation was more horrendous than that of San Quentin. CIM, as it was called, was the first major maximum security institution built and operated in the United States.

The reform school to which Steven was sent was almost the opposite of CIM. It was a minimum security facility with no fences to keep the delinquent boys in. Instead of cellblocks, the boys lived in dormitories.

It rained all day on February 6, 1945 when Steven was checked into the Boys Republic at Chino. He was assigned #3188, a designation he would remember for the rest of his life.

Even older than Father Flanagan's Boys Town, launched in Omaha, Nebraska in 1917, Boys Republic had been established with roughly equivalent ideals by Mrs. Margaret Fowler, in cooperation with the California juvenile courts, in 1907.

Steven hated the school and his fellow juvenile delinquents. They didn't like Steven

Boys Republic founding matriarch **Margaret Fowler.**
Saving juvenile delinquents from the streets.

either.

Frank Graves, the principal of the school, remembered Steven as "being hostile and alone. He didn't mix with the other boys. All the boys were given work assignments. Steven almost never fulfilled his and was constantly being reprimanded. He also got in a lot of fights because he angered some of the bigger boys. He was a rather small, skinny guy and was often beaten up. He landed in the infirmary with a lot of black eyes and bruises. But that didn't teach him a lesson. As soon as he recovered, he was in another fight."

When Steven could take it no more, he escaped. For two days, he hid, surviving on a loaf of bread he'd stolen before running away. Policemen finally nabbed him in a hayloft of a horse stable and brought him back in handcuffs to the reform school. In the past, Steven had been assigned to the laundry room. To punish him for his escape, Graves assigned him to cleaning out the latrines.

Faced with the threat of being shipped off to a much rougher reform school, Steven buckled down and performed his duties, regardless of how odious. At night the boys talked about other kids who'd been "sent away." Tales spread that in the rougher schools they were held down and gang raped, sometimes by as many as ten older boys a night.

The superintendent of the school, Leonard Panther, met Steven upon his return to school and took a fatherly interest in him. Reports that that interest was more than fatherly cannot be confirmed. Steven later recalled that "Mr. Panther reminded me of my Uncle Claude and also of Spencer Tracy in *Boys Town*."

In the days and weeks ahead, Steven spent a lot of time with Mr. Panther, who, as superintendent, outranked the principal. The boys were rounded up every Saturday afternoon and hauled into town to see a movie. Sometimes Mr. Panther personally escorted Steven to the movies. He also got special gifts such as candy bars and chewing gum.

"Steven also walked around in the best athletic shoes at school," said Johnnie Freedhold, another inmate. "Mr. Panther bought them for him. One time, Mr. Panther took Steven on a two-week vacation to his family retreat in Oregon. All of us envied Steven. With such a strong protector, no kid ever tangled with Steven again. He became the golden boy of the reform school, God's anointed. It pays to have friends in high places."

Mr. Panther ended Steven's chores, especially latrine duty. He was no longer assigned hard work like digging ditches and mixing cement. Instead he was given a pad of yellow paper. His new job was to inspect the various bungalows and worksites to see if the other boys were performing their duties properly. "All of us were afraid of him, fearing we'd get a bad report," said Freedhold.

At Christmas the boys sold Della Robbia-style wreaths to raise money for food and supplies at the school. These wreaths became so popular that they were eventually shipped all over America. They were fashioned from pine cones, eucalyptus, apples, redwood foliage, and other local materials. On the streets of town, Steven sold more wreaths than the other boys and was elected to Boys Council.

By buckling down with hard work and lowering his hostility level, Steven slowly had begun to gain the respect of his fellow inmates. "I had become a man among boys," he later recalled with a smug smile. "All my life, I'd been treated like a piece of shit, but I was slowly gaining respect from others. Much more important than that, I was beginning to respect myself. The Boys Republic saved my life."

Around April of 1946, after Steven had served an eighteen-month sentence, a letter arrived from Jullian. It was postmarked New York City. He read the letter slowly, learning that Berri had died. She didn't list the cause of his death.

"I'm working in New York City now," she wrote. "I've decided to make a new start of it. You are going to be let out of school this month, and I've enclosed a bus ticket. I want you to come and live with me. Both of us will make a new start of it. Let's forget that the past ever happened."

Folding the letter, he couldn't help but note that she had never come to visit him, not even for a single day, during his incarceration.

***

"I got off the bus in New York, and I felt like Lil' Abner," Steven later recalled. "There I was in my reform school high shoes, Levi's, and a Levi jacket. A California suntan and a square-cut juvenile delinquent haircut. I remember standing on 34th Street, and that was a bad crowd I was seeing."

This time he had to wait one lonely, bewildering hour before Jullian turned up late. She didn't kiss him but shook his hand instead. Up that close, he smelled whiskey on her breath.

In a taxi en route to his new home in Greenwich Village, there was an unspoken tension between them. It was not a happy reunion. Finally, she explained that after Berri's funeral, attended by no one but herself, she'd taken the train to New York.

Once here, she'd met a new boyfriend in a bar on Third Avenue. His name was Victor Lukens. She informed Steven that she was going to marry him. "He'll be your new stepfather."

"The other one was enough," Steven told her, not disguising his hostility.

Before arriving at a decaying apartment building from the turn of the century, Jullian explained that she and Victor would live in a top-floor apartment, and that he would live with a male friend of hers in the apartment below.

Upstairs, Victor shook his hand but was obviously unhappy at seeing him. He didn't seem as hostile as Berry Berri, but Steven felt definitely unwelcome.

"All I remember about Victor," Steven later recalled, "was that after shaking my hand he walked into the toilet and took a big horse piss without shutting the door."

Jullian ushered Steven downstairs to the apartment of her friend, Dean Jeffrey, who had been a Broadway chorus boy in the 1930s. Many reports claim that Steven walked into his new apartment and found his host making love to another man.

Steven later told close friends that that was not what happened. First, he wouldn't just walk into a strange apartment unannounced. And assuming that Jeffrey had been making love to another man, he would have undone the embrace to answer a knock on the door.

"Reports that I fled that very day from that apartment house aren't true," Steven later claimed. "My break with Jullian came but it would be weeks later, not on my first day in the city."

Already an outspoken homophobe at sixteen, Steven had mixed reactions to homosexuals. He wasn't above using them if he felt there was something to gain. After all, by the time he'd arrived at Jeffrey's apartment, he'd been introduced to childhood prostitution through Berri.

The street in Greenwich Village where Steve lived as the kept boy of a local psychologist.

"I saw Dean as an easy mark," Steven later said. "I knew if I played my cards right, I'd be living on Easy Street."

He never provided details about how he'd hustled Jeffrey, who had inherited money when his mother died in Ohio. Soon Steven was seen about the Village in a new suit of clothes and new shoes. "I even got the fucker to buy me a watch."

Steven had been extra horny after those months lodged in the reform school. He'd perhaps welcomed the sexual release that Jeffrey so willingly provided. As he'd later tell a biker buddy, "I learned it was the easiest way I knew to make quick money. All you had to do was lie on your back and dream of some pretty gal while the cocksucker did all the work. I got my jollies, and he got his. For about fifteen minutes work at night—if you'd call it that—I was free to roam all day in my new clothes discovering New York City."

He visited Jullian and Victor only rarely, doubting very seriously if Victor would ever place a wedding band on her finger. Jullian never asked him how he'd gotten the new clothes and watch.

Steven later recalled that he felt this arrangement with Jeffrey could have continued as long as his host had money to spend on him. He took him to some of the best restaurants in New York and more or less bought him what he wanted. "I knew the geezer didn't have all that much more to spend, but I didn't really give a damn," Steven said.

And then one day his world came to an end. He returned home early with a slight headache. He just wanted to rest and catch up on his sleep. He found Jeffrey in bed with another man, a young one at that. They were engaged in sex, which they broke off when Steven came into the apartment.

"What in the fuck's going on here?" Steven shouted at Jeffrey.

He grabbed his robe and confronted Steven in the living room. "The kid's name is David. I've been seeing him when you're gone all day, God knows where. I've decided I prefer him to you. You just lie in bed like you're dead or something. David knows how to give me more of what I want."

Steven slugged Jeffrey in the face, knocking him down. He threw all his new possessions in a suitcase. Before leaving, and right in front of the hapless Jeffrey, he removed all the money in his wallet, counting out eighty dollars.

Upstairs he confronted Jullian. Victor was nowhere to be seen. He told his mother that he'd had a fight with Jeffrey and needed to use their spare room for a few nights.

"You can't stay here," Jullian shouted at him. "Victor won't stand for it, and he pays the rent. He thinks you're a faggot, and he won't live with a guy like you under the same roof."

"Ok," he said. "Bye, bye, Mom, it's been great knowing you."

"Where are you going?" she asked. "A kid like you won't survive for one day on the streets of New York."

"What do you have in mind?"

"I could raise the money to send you back to Slater," she said.

"Forget it!" he said.

"Will you write?" she asked. "So I can know what's happening."

He looked at her with a smirk on his face. "I was never much for writing letters," he said. "Can't spell. Goodbye, gal, and I hope you and that Victor have a hot time together before he dumps you like all the others. When you get too old to sell it, what are you going to do then?"

He walked toward the door and opened it, putting down his suitcase in the hallway. For one final time, he looked back at her bewildered face. "I think she wanted to do something to rescue me," he later said. "But she was too afraid of Victor. We said good-bye with our eyes. I think I might have detected a tear or two. When I looked at her one final time, I fully expected I'd never meet up with her again. I slammed the door in her face and very slowly walked down four flights of steps."

Once on the street, he realized he had no place to go. He pondered his options for a minute.

"The sun was shining real bright that day," he remembered. "It was shining down just on me. It was at that very moment that I buried the boy in me and became a man."

***

A Dr. Matthew Dennehy was a psychologist who practiced in Greenwich Village, treating teenage boys struggling with their homosexuality. The court sent him troubled teens, some of whom were suicidal over their sexual preference. What the judges didn't know was that Dr. Dennehy often seduced his young patients once he'd won their trust.

For years until his death in Florida in 1973, he dined out on how he met Steven McQueen. It was at the Port Authority Terminal in New York. Perhaps when he was roaming the streets of New York, Steven learned that the Port Authority was a prime pick-up spot for homosexuals, many of whom went here to ensnare young men just getting off a Greyhound from the Middle West.

Apparently, Steven had decided to find another mark like Jeffrey who would pay his bills and keep him in style, to which he'd become accustomed. When he wasn't seducing his clients, Dr. Dennehy often hung out at the bus station, hoping to score.

As he later claimed, when he first met Steven, he believed his story that he'd just arrived on the bus all the way from Missouri. "The boy was well dressed and carried a suitcase," Dr. Dennehy later said. "I had no idea he was pulling a scam. I believed his story even though I considered myself pretty good at realizing when a boy was telling me a lie. Even back then, Steven was a good actor."

Dr. Dennehy approached the young boy and offered his assistance. Steven told him that he was looking for a hotel but didn't have much money to spend on a room. That was music to Dr. Dennehy's ears, who told him he had a good, comfortable bedroom to rent in his townhouse on Jane Street in Greenwich Village. "It's only ten dollars a month."

"I had seduced far more beautiful boys than this future movie star," Dr. Dennehy later said. "But there was a sexiness about him that really attracted me. There was also a latent hostility about him, but that made him all the more enticing."

Dr. Dennehy claimed that with Steven he felt he'd have to go slow and move in on him gradually. "But when he came out of the bathroom nude after taking a shower, and when he blatantly exhibited himself to me, I realized this farm boy from Missouri wasn't as inexperienced as I'd thought. It was only weeks later that I learned he'd engaged in childhood prostitution."

"Steven lived with me for about six weeks, and I must say I took advantage of the kid every chance I got," Dr. Dennehy claimed. "I was giving him room and board, and also presenting him with gifts, so I wanted my money's worth and for the most part I got it."

"I used to have these Sunday afternoon gatherings of other psychologists at my townhouse," he said. "All of them were gay. "Steven was a star attraction at these gatherings. All of my friends were sexually attracted to him. It was only when Steven left me that I found out that he was making dates with some of them and hustling them behind my back. I didn't have a clue at the time, and I thought I was so smart back then. The little devil outfoxed me."

"Steven was a bundle of contradictions," Dr. Dennehy said. "He could both submit to being used by men while at the same time finding the whole experience disgusting. He expressed hostility toward gays yet moved in their circles. I have no doubt he was fucking plenty of girls outside the house. A few nights he didn't come home. He and I had bitter fights about that. Sometimes he'd disappear for an entire weekend and not tell me where he was. On one occasion he got the clap, and I had to get a doctor friend of mine to treat him."

"Sometimes he talked about his past, but rarely," the doctor said. "When I brought up the subject, he'd grow morbidly depressed. I gathered that his mother extended love but then suddenly withdrew it. The men in her life were obviously more important to her than her own son. Steven was virtually an orphan, a tumbling tumbleweed. Sometimes he'd have a tender moment, but these were rare events. Mostly he seemed to use people for his own selfish ends. He trusted no one. In fact, he seemed to feel that everybody was out to get him. As my father used to say, he walked through life with a chip on his shoulder. He had a mercurial personality. Within five minutes, he could go through incredible shifts in his moods. A Jekyll and Hyde transformation. I felt there was a mean, cruel streak in him. I wondered if he'd ever find someone to love, and I doubted if he ever would. To love someone, you've got to trust. Steven McQueen couldn't trust anyone."

"The inevitable happened," the doctor proclaimed. "I came home one day after shopping to find the house in disarray. I always kept money in my desk drawer. I didn't bother to look there because I knew he'd taken it. He'd also stolen two or three of my most valuable objects, which I knew he was planning to hock. I more or less expected that something like that would happen. I had set myself up for it."

"Even so, on looking back, I count the days and nights I spent with the future movie star, Steve McQueen, as the most memorable of my life," the doctor said. "Nothing like that streak of lightning had ever come into my life before and nothing like him would ever appear again."

***

Within three weeks, all of Steven's money was gone. He never explained what he did with his stolen money and possessions, although he later recalled "I lived the high life. For the first time in my life, I was the king, dependent on nobody."

Down and out, he had only the clothes on his back when he wandered into a bar on Tenth Avenue. Someone had stolen his clothes the night before. Although underage, he was still served a beer, as he had a baseball cap on his head and two day's growth of beard.

It was in this bar that he met two old salty seadogs, Ted Ford and Tinker, who was nicknamed "Tinker Bell." This pair of swabbies was about to sail out on a ship called the SS *Alpha*. The Greek tanker was sailing that night for the West Indies, and Ford and Tinker enthralled Steven with the adventures that awaited him in the Caribbean—first stop, Havana.

To Steven, Havana sounded like the most glamorous place in the world. He'd heard stories about the beautiful girls and the hot nightlife there.

Two hours later, Steven was drunk when Ford and Tinker hauled him aboard the SS *Alpha*. It was docked in Yonkers and set to sail within the hour. "I was shanghaied," Steven said when he woke up with a splitting headache the next morning.

Teenaged Steve: Shanghaied as a slave laborer aboard a rusty tub to Havana.

He found himself sailing aboard a rusty tub that wasn't even seaworthy. "The God damn thing looked like it should have been sunk years ago. I was brought on as slave labor and assigned the filthiest jobs aboard, like cleaning out the urinals. The stench the first time I breathed the air down in that hole made me vomit. There was no shower aboard. I smelled like a harbor rat. I had to carry chamber pots and dump the sailors' shit overboard. There wasn't even a working toilet. After emptying my first shitpot, I learned never to do that in the wind. Of all the asshole jobs I've done in my life, sailing aboard the SS *Alpha* was the pits for me."

"The captain was drunk most of the day and all the night." Steven said. "He'd brought some thirteen-year-old black gal aboard that the crew had picked up in Harlem. The poor creature was gang-banged all the way to Havana. I could forego the sex but not my money. I went to the captain when he staggered on deck one day around noon and confronted him about my wages. He was a mean son-of-a-bitch. He looked like something from a pirate movie, no doubt Blackbeard. He'd also had one leg amputated somewhere along the way. The guy looked at me like he could have killed me. He knocked me across the deck. Nearly split my head open. So much for my wages. I knew I was in for the duration."

When the SS *Alpha* sailed into the port of Havana, Steven plotted his next move. The old tub was supposed to pick up a load of Cuban molasses for shipment to Ciudad Trujillo, the capital of the Dominican Republic. "All that gooey stuff, once it arrived in the Dominican Republic, was to be shipped to a factory where it would be turned into rum," Steven said.

Planning to abandon ship, Steven waited until all the crew, including the captain and the black girl, had gone ashore before he went into action. The horny sailors wanted to patronize some of the dens of prostitution that flourished in Havana at the time. The black girl was turned loose on the streets to fend for herself. Steven was ordered to stay on deck to prevent anyone from boarding the tanker.

When the crew was safely out of sight, Steven invaded the captain's bedroom where, after a thorough search, he found nearly two hundred dollars. Stealing the money, he also searched through the captain's possessions where he uncovered a gold watch that he'd managed to pick up somewhere in the world. It wasn't in working order but Steven stole it too.

There was absolutely nothing else of value he knew on the ship. Before leaving and in lieu of wages, he took a large glass jug of kerosene. Pouring it across the deck, he struck a match to it.

As the flames spread across the rotting wood, Steven with only a little handbag of possessions ran down the gangplank to freedom.

***

A tip from a shoeshine boy led Steven to check into Havana Nocturne, which was actually a bordello that rented rooms on its top floor. Twenty-eight beautiful girls, of various shapes, sizes, and colors, worked the bordello, some having other nighttime jobs in the casino showrooms of Havana.

Some American tourists, often businessmen, checked into Havana

33

Nocturne for days at a time. If a client wished, the madam made it possible for one of her guests to sample each girl who worked there, but that took a few days.

"All my girls wanted young Steven, who was cute, blond haired, and blue eyed," said Olga Tamayo, the madam of Havana Nocturne. After she fled to Miami in the wake of the Castro revolution, when her bordello was set on fire by revolutionaries, she attempted but failed to sell her memoirs of *gangsterismo* and prostitution in Old Havana.

She remains the only source for information about Steven's brief stay in Havana.

"My girls would have done Steven for free," Olga claimed. "He was adorable. I wanted to make love to him myself. But I think I was a little too old and a bit too fat for this young man. He didn't make love to all the gals in my house—not at all. Very early he fell for one of my smallest gals, Rosa Quiroga. She was very short and very cute, with little perky breasts. She was about twenty but looked fourteen. She spent many a night in Steven's upper floor bedroom which was painted all purple and red."

"Because I liked Steven and knew he didn't have much money, like most of my gangster clients from America, I charged him only fifty dollars a week," Olga said. "When his money ran really low, Rosa suggested he perform in a show with her at night. The manager was looking for a new boy."

Olga claimed she attended the show one night, "and I thought Steven was wonderful." In the Barrio Chino, Steven was hired to do three shows a night at the notorious Shanghai Theatre, which dated from 1930. It was famous for its kinky sex shows and nude theater. Both nude young men and nude young women were a feature. The men were stripped down when management realized that it was attracting a large contingent of homosexuals from the United States.

Wild nights in pre-Castro Havana:
Steve breaks into show biz doing live porn.

Between the live acts, pornographic movies, shot locally in Havana, were shown to amuse the audience of both women and men.

The theater held nearly eight

hundred spectators who were charged anywhere from 75¢ to $1.50 for a seat. Raunchy shows followed the film screening. The most popular act—billed as El Toro—featured an African-Cubano with a thick penis that extended more than a foot, measuring seven inches in circumference. He would penetrate at least three young girls on stage. Although the girls were used to accommodating El Toro's girth, they still screamed during penetration, their cries stimulating the audience, at least the more sadistic contingent.

Steven's skit began its first show at 9:30 at night. The red curtain opened onto a scene in a café where a man was seated with a beautiful woman, Rosa herself. They were both well dressed. The waiter appeared.

"It was Steven," Olga claimed, "making his first stage appearance." She had a front row seat.

"Where is the silver?" the seated man demanded. From his pockets, Steven removed knives and forks. "Where is the salt and pepper?" the man asked. From each of his hip pockets, Steven removed a salt and pepper shaker.

"I want some coffee," Rosa demanded of Steven. He briefly went off stage and returned with a cup of coffee. "Sugar!" Rosa said. He reached into his pocket and produced a packet of sugar. After she sprinkled it into her coffee cup, she angrily said, "You forgot the cream."

To the delight of the audience, Steven unbuttoned his trousers and produced his flaccid penis. Like the skilled fellatio artist she was, Rosa performed oral sex on him until he produced an erection. Withdrawing from her suction pump of a mouth, he masturbated himself to climax, his "cream" shooting into her coffee. Rosa then proceeded to drink all of the coffee as the curtain went down to thunderous applause.

Steven had to perform another show at 12:30am, and yet another at 3:30am. After two weeks of this work, he told both Olga and Rosa that he was tired of performing every night. "I've got nothing left to have any fun with, although the pay is good."

As was perhaps inevitable, it was eventually arranged for Steven to appear in a "blue movie," which would be shown between acts. When Steven arrived one Saturday afternoon for the filming, he was surprised to find the other cast of characters, which consisted of three women and a young, blond-haired English boy. The plot was simple. Steven had to penetrate and have intercourse with all four, beginning with the three women and "climaxing" with the young boy.

"Rosa told me he was a natural performer," Olga said. "Even with the boy. To my knowledge, this film called *Quartet* was the first bit of cinema the future star ever made. If the film still exists today, it would surely be a collector's gem."

Rosa also arranged for Steven to do some nude studies for an American photographer shooting porno in Havana. Their distribution and sale in the United States was illegal, and the photographer had to slip them by Customs. Pictures of a nude Steven with a semi-erect penis still exist today, and can be viewed by those talented at searching the Internet. Although not of El Toro dimensions, his penis is impressive.

***

Finally, Steven had had it with Havana. He'd grown bored with his night job. After performing three shows a night, he spent the rest of the day sleeping them off. He told Olga that, "I don't plan to spend the rest of my life jerking off in front of a lot of voyeurs. I want to move on."

The question was where. Olga had a half-sister who ran another bordello in Santo Domingo (then called Ciudad Trujillo) in the Dominican Republic. She agreed to call her and get Steven a job working for her, promising him that it would be a very glamorous place, and he'd be thrilled at the beautiful young girls he'd meet there.

After a night spent in Rosa's arms, Steven departed the next morning on a tanker headed for Ciudad Trujillo. On this tanker he was a paying customer, and the crew waited on him. No more latrine duty. He'd saved nearly a thousand dollars from his performances in Havana.

***

He disembarked at the port of Ciudad Trujillo, and hired a taxi to take him to Los Carnavales, the bordello operated by Lita Valachi, a shadowy figure who sometimes used the name Lina Hostos. Formerly a showgirl in Havana, Olga's half-sister was said to operate her exclusive bordello under the personal patronage of Rafael Trujillo, the dictator of the Dominican Republic.

Though long past her prime, Lita still retained vestiges of her fading beauty. Her whorehouse, or so it was rumored, was actually owned by Trujillo himself.

Lita took a liking to Steven, and hired him as her new towel boy. "The job's easy," she said. "You just see that the customers are supplied with plenty of white towels. Since many of my clients are married men, they like to do a bit of freshening up before heading home to their wives. Also, my girls need to freshen up before receiving their next customer."

She informed him that he'd make no salary but could on some weeks expect nearly a hundred dollars in tips. "My clients are most generous because they like to keep things quiet."

Lita also explained that the job had fringe benefits. When one of the girls wasn't occupied during the day, he could "sample the merchandise—but not at night. After dark we're too busy around here."

At first Steven was worried he'd also be assigned laundry duty, just as he was at the reform school. But he found that in a cottage out back, a large woman, called Mamá Altagracia, did the laundry, drying the sheets in the sun and trade winds of the Caribbean.

Now old and fat, she too had been a popular prostitute in her heyday. As rumor had it, a sixteen-year-old Trujillo, then working as a Morse code telegraph operator, lost his virginity at the experienced hands of Mamá Altagracia.

Steven's favorite prostitute was a striking brunette, Aminita Meriño, who was five years older than him. When he made love to her, he found her the most responsive of all of Lita's girls. During the day when she was not working, she showed him the sights of Santo Domingo, even taking him to his first cockfight.

It was during one placid, hot afternoon, while sipping *cerveza* in a park, that Aminita told him that Lita's Los Carnavales wasn't like a regular bordello. "We are spies for Trujillo," she said.

She explained that the bordello was patronized mainly by generals or other high officials in the Trujillo administration. Camera equipment had been secretly installed to take pictures of some of Trujillo's top brass having intercourse with one or another of Lita's girls.

She called Trujillo *El Cabrito* or "The Goat." "If *El Cabrito* wants to blackmail a member of his staff, he might find some of our evidence very useful to him."

As Aminita explained, Lita's girls were instructed to obtain any information they could glean from pillow talk with any of these high-placed officials.

Far from being repulsed by all this blackmail and espionage, Steven found it "very intriguing."

He also learned that two famous guests showed up at least once a week at Lita's place, both Flor de Oro, the daughter of the dictator, and Porfirio Rubirosa, Flor's former husband. Of course, Lita was careful to keep these cheating former spouses from showing up together.

Three days later, Steven got to meet Flor

Dominican dictator *"El Cabrito,"* **Rafael Trujillo**. A plumed and embroidered mass murderer

de Oro, the most famous woman in the Dominican Republic. Dressed in a costume so frilly it appeared to be for a carnival celebration, she was immediately intrigued by this blond-haired *gringo*. "Your eyes," she said, "so blue. All the men down here have brown or very dark eyes. But your eyes are as blue as the sky."

She explained to him that she was entertaining a general in the Dominican army, a man under the direct command of her father. But she told him, "After he leaves, I want you to come to my room. I will entertain you, too."

"Her eyes were black as midnight," Steven later recalled. "She was a regular little spitfire, but I felt I could tame her. I also felt I could provide her better sex than some pot-bellied Dominican general in a white jacket with gold braid."

Lita told him that between 1932 and 1937 Flor de Oro had been married to Rubirosa. "She's still friends with her former husband," Lita told Steven. "Trujillo still has an on-again, off-again relationship with his former son-in-law."

After the general left Flor de Oro's room, Steven, with towels, knocked on the door and discreetly entered. Flor de Oro was lying nude on top of the bed, wearing a flowery hat and still retaining her stiletto high heels. Inviting him to come and join her, he pulled off his clothes and lay on top of her.

On a visit to New York in 1940, dictator **Rafael Trujillo** and his whorish daughter, **Flor de Oro**, Rubirosa's first wife.

As he remembered it, she was still warm from the recent invasion of the general. This didn't bother him. He was eager to seduce her, and he plunged in. "She was a tigress," he would recall. "She clawed my back. She bit my tongue. A hellcat with its tail on fire."

Steven would later claim that sex with Flor de Oro was "the hottest, the best of my life." From that experience he developed a life-long passion not fully explained or even understood by him.

He found he liked making love to women who were still warm from having had intercourse with another man.

"I dig sloppy seconds,"

Steve McQueen, the movie star, would often say in later life, particularly to his biking or racing car buddies. On some occasions he invited two or three men to enjoy a prostitute he'd secured for them, with him going last. "Nothing is better than having a woman who's already enjoyed my buddies. She's more relaxed, all tension gone. It's the most sensational sexual feeling I've known. If there's anything that I hate, it's a dry fuck."

During the two months Steven spent in the Dominican Republic, Flor de Oro asked for him at least once a week.

Because of this intimacy, he was a bit nervous one day when he knocked on the bordello door of her former husband, the notorious playboy, Porfirio Rubirosa himself.

At first there was no answer. He knocked harder. Finally, he heard Rubirosa calling him to enter the boudoir bedroom suite.

When Steven identified who he was, Rubirosa called for him to come into the bathroom. Rising from the sudsy water was "The Playboy of the Western World," a darkly handsome man whose international reputation as the world's greatest lover had spread to three continents.

"Good," he said. "You've brought plenty of towels. I'm Rubi. It'll take one whole towel just to dry off 'The Terror.'" He looked down at the most monstrous weapon Steven had ever seen.

"I'm Steven," he said with hesitancy, almost fear.

"Don't worry, *gringo* boy," Rubi said. "I'm not going to stick it in you. It wouldn't fit anyway."

Steven was about to embark on one of the strangest, but also one of the most secretive, relationships of his life.

Chapter Two
American Rebel at Large

A diplomat and sportsman, Porfirio Rubirosa was a man of mystery. All the *putas* at the bordello talked about him and his sexual prowess. The girls practically fought with each other for the honor of servicing him when he visited Lita's bordello.

He was about thirty-six when he first met Steven. At the time, Rubirosa was freeing himself from a marriage to the highest paid movie star in France, Danielle Darrieux, called "the most beautiful woman in the world."

As Steven helped Rubirosa dress—the Dominican playboy always liked a valet—he was in awe of this world-class lover, who was already on the road to becoming a legend. He gave Steven permission to address him as "Rubi—all my friends call me that." He told Steven that, "a day in which I make love only once is virtually wasted. It is very common for me to take on two or three women in a night. After midnight when I'm good and drunk, I don't give a damn what kind of legs open for me."

For some odd reason, Rubi took a liking to Steven and hired him to drive him to visit some relatives in the Dominican Republic's Cibao valley, from which Rubi still had roots, with some family members remaining.

Eagerly accepting the job, Steven helped Rubi load down his sedan with gifts for his family and many acquaintances. "When I get there, they'll think I'm Santa Claus," he said.

In the town of San Francisco de Macorís, Rubi

San Francisco de Macorís:
The simple town in the D.R. where Rubirosa was born. "No newly born baby ever had such an appendage."

41

was welcomed like a conquering hero. Checking into a seedy inn, Rubi told Steven, "This is the town where I was born. It was back in 1909. So I'm told, all the nurses at the hospital came to see my appendage. One of them said, 'I've seen grown men with less than that.' I was a very popular boy."

"The girls lined up outside Rubi's hotel at night," Steven later recalled. "He could have his pick of the litter. Those he didn't like so much, he tossed my way. But I would never take a gal that Rubi had had, even though on most occasions, I sorta liked doing that. But the way I figured it, once a gal has had Rubi, he ruined her for all other men."

On the way back to Ciudad Trujillo, Rubi told Steven that he was flying out of the country to marry Doris Duke. Steven didn't know who that was.

"She's the heiress to the Duke tobacco fortune. The richest woman in the world. She's got a face like a horse, but when you've got all the money in the world, what does it matter? Besides, as a polo player, I adore horses."

Rubi confided that he'd once borrowed money from Flor de Oro to buy an obsolete dredge in New Orleans. "That didn't work out," he claimed. "But there's big money to be made, and I'm going to try it again. I borrowed money from Doris this time, and I'm buying this old dredge in Port Arthur, Texas. It's going to be transported to Ciudad Trujillo to build a new port here. The Generalíssimo himself approved the deal."

Before arriving back in Ciudad Trujillo, Steven learned that the equipment was going to be loaded upon Dominican vessels in Port Arthur for shipment

Porfirio Rubirosa (left) after his marriage to tobacco heiress **Doris Duke**. (Right photo) The Dominican playboy in a tuxedo later given as a cast-off to Steven.

to the Dominican Republic. Impulsively, Steven asked Rubi if he could be hired to sail on that tanker. He'd never been to Texas and wanted to try his luck there.

Rubi promised he'd get him a job sailing aboard yet another tanker. For his final night in Ciudad Trujillo, Rubi invited Steven to attend a dinner party that he was sponsoring at the Hotel El Embajador.

It was on that night that Steven got to see the dictator himself. He almost laughed as Trujillo paraded through the vast lobby of the hotel in a gold-braided white uniform topped by a plumed bicorne hat. Steven felt that the Generalíssimo looked like a singer from a comic operetta—"not that I'd ever seen a comic operetta."

At around 2am, Steven and Rubi retired to the presidential suite upstairs, with three of the most beautiful women in the hotel. Each of them was from Havana and had been brought to the hotel to dance at the casino show.

As Steven later confessed, "I got over my fear that night, and took each of the gals after Rubi had finished with them. It takes a real man to do that. One gal told me that Rubi's thing actually hurt her. She said, 'His thing is long, pointed, and hurt like hell. It never got hard and it never got soft. And once he tops you, he never seems to want to get off. He just goes and goes.' After all that, she welcomed my gentler love-making."

At 4am, Rubi ordered a special Japanese mushroom tea from room service. Earlier he'd dropped into the kitchen and given the cook the ingredients for making this brew. When he drank a cup, he told Steven and the showgirls, "It makes me virile." To demonstrate, he masturbated himself in front of them, then on his erection balanced a chair with a telephone book on it. Steven, along with the chorines, applauded.

At dawn, when Rubi told Steven goodbye, he gave him ten one-hundred dollar bills and thanked him for his services. Even though he planned to marry Doris Duke, he told Steven that he was going to Buenos Aires.

"*El Caudillo* has named me Ambassador to Argentina," he said. "My first diplomatic goal will be to fuck Evita Perón."

Aboard that dismal tanker headed for Port Arthur, Steven speculated that he might have missed one of the greatest opportunities in his life. "I should have asked Rubi to hire me as his traveling valet. At least that way, I could see the world in style. But there would be a drawback to living in such close intimacy with Rubi. On that rare night when he couldn't get a gal, he might descend on this cute little blond boy. Sticking that tree trunk up me would have ruined me for life."

***

After saying good-bye to the crew aboard the Dominican tanker, Steven disembarked at Port Arthur. He was fifteen years old. It was the bleakest docklands he'd ever seen in his short life.

An influx of African-Americans into the port city had led to white flight. Many whites relocated in neighboring towns, selling out to black families taking over the neighborhood.

The wind was blowing in from the Gulf of Mexico but the noonday sun was broiling. Steven planned to find a cheap hotel where he wanted to crash for two days and two nights before even leaving his room. He was exhausted. For food, he hoped he could call for take-out.

The Hotel Neches, named for a river, had never seen better days. Since its birth in 1920, it had never had a heyday. He was assigned a room on an upper floor that was blistering hot since it was close to the roof. A little fan on a nightstand provided some comfort.

The next day was a Sunday, and against his earlier commitment to himself, he ventured out of that hot, boxy room and went downstairs to the lobby where a motley crew sat smoking and drinking Cokes from a battered old machine that dispensed them.

He struck up a conversation with a leather-faced man who was leaving the next day to work at an oil refinery in Corpus Christi. He talked for an hour about that kind of work and told Steven he should consider taking up such a job.

At that point in his life, Steven was intrigued but felt the work sounded too rigorous.

"What experience have you had before coming here?" the middle-aged man asked.

Steven decided to be both blunt and truthful. "My last two jobs were in a whorehouse—one in Havana. The merchandise the house sold was free to employees like me."

"What kind of job would a boy like you have in a whorehouse?" the oil man asked.

"I was a towel boy."

The man suggested that if the whorehouse business was his game, he might find employment at a bordello right here in Port Arthur. "I visited it last night. Lots of hot women there . . . and young."

Two hours later, after Steven had splurged on a Texas T-bone, he walked ten blocks to the whorehouse to knock on the red door at an address provided by the oilman.

A large, fat woman answered the door. "We close on Sunday," she said. "Go away."

"You don't understand," he said. "I want to see the madam. About a job."

"Okay, wait in the hall."

After about fifteen awkward minutes, a woman clad in a flowery house-coat, and way past fifty, came out to see what he wanted. At first she seemed hostile, but after encountering such a good-looking blond-haired boy, she became intrigued with him in a flirtatious kind of way.

Directing him to a little Victorian style sitting room off the corridor, she offered him a seat. "Estrella told me you need a job, and you may have come at the right time. Our waiter quit last week, and I haven't found a replacement. His job was to deliver whiskey and ice cubes to the rooms—or whatever supplies one of our clients want."

"That sounds like a job with my name written on it," he said. "I was a towel boy at this house in Havana and also in Ciudad Trujillo. Here I could list my profession as room service waiter."

"I must warn you," she said. "The job comes with no salary but you get free room and board. Don't worry about the money. The Texans and the dock-workers from God knows where who drop in here are big tippers."

"Sounds fine to me."

"I own a dormitory build-ing next door," she said. "There's an empty room for you on the top floor. Room C1."

"I'd be most grateful," he said. "When do I move in?"

"This afternoon," she said. "I'm Sadie Barnhill. What's your name?"

"Steven McQueen."

Congressman **Lyndon Johnson** (above) campaigning by day in Port Arthur (lower photo) and visiting the local bordello after dark.

Although obviously hung over from the night before, her face brightened at his presence. He feared that part of his new job would involve servicing her. "If all of my clients looked like you, the girls would do them for free and I wouldn't make any money."

He went back to the Neches. The man who tipped him off about the whorehouse was still in the lobby. "I got a job thanks to you," Steven said.

"It's really not a place for a kid like you," the man said, finally introducing himself as Leroy Calder. "I still think you should go into the oil business. Tell you what. I'll write down my name and address in Corpus Christi. If you decide you want a job, I can perhaps get you in. You look like a fine and decent kid who got into the wrong business."

By the end of the first week, Steven had learned a lot about the whorehouse business, which on a good night employed ten girls. He learned that on the other side of the river, beyond the KCS Railroad tracks, Sadie operated another whorehouse reserved just for her black trade.

Sadie told Steven that nearly all the girls who worked the African-American market were blondes. "They don't want any other kind." To his surprise, half of the prostitutes in her main house that catered to white men were black. "They've got vanilla at home," Sadie told him. "When they go out, they like a taste of chocolate."

Steven learned that one of the Port Arthur brothel's most famous customers was Congressman Lyndon Johnson.

After only the first week had gone by, the inevitable happened. He'd seen it coming.

One night Sadie invited him to her private quarters, where she'd dressed in a black negligée. He knew he'd have to perform for her before the night was over.

"I've got some rotgut whiskey here," she told him. "You look old enough to drink."

As he'd later recall to his buddies, "It wasn't as bad as I thought it would be—in fact, I ended up enjoying it. It was a completely different experience than with a young girl. I can't explain the attraction. For one thing, these old bitches heap praise on you, and they seem so God damn grateful that you fucked them. Sadie didn't just give a blow-job, she went around the world, as she called it. She discovered hot spots on my body I didn't know existed."

His experience during his eight weeks in Port Arthur changed his life in that he discovered an occasional passion for older women way past their prime. "I mean, I'd spend most of my life with beautiful young women, but I liked to slip off every now and then and hook up with one of the older broads. Sometimes I'd beat the shit out of them and take their money, but they were always so grateful to get plowed they shut up and took what I dished out."

***

After a month at the bordello, Steven was growing bored. He'd sampled every one of Sadie's girls, including the black ones, but that wasn't enough. He wanted something more exciting than bringing whiskey to already drunken Texans who arrived in ten-gallon hats. Sometimes he'd hear a girl scream, but Sadie warned him never to investigate. "Sometimes our clients get a little carried away with a girl," she told him, "but boys will be boys."

After he'd been at the bordello a month, he became captivated by a beautiful young girl who looked no more than fifteen. She seemed shy and didn't mix with the other girls but sat in the corner, smoking a Philip Morris cigarette and drinking Coca-Cola. He was immediately attracted to the lovely face of this towheaded girl with cornflower blue eyes.

"Aren't you a little young to be smoking?" he asked, coming over in the rear lounge of the bordello and sitting down beside her. "What's your name?"

"Wanda Ferguson," she said. "But people call me Wa-Wa, 'cause I was always begging for cold water when I was a baby."

"I'm Steven and I work here," he told her.

She looked surprised. "Are you a whore, too? I guess some of Sadie's clients like cute young boys."

"Not that," he said. "I'm the waiter."

It was a Sunday, when the bordello was closed, so he sat late into the night talking with Wanda and smoking some of her Philip Morris cigarettes. After about an hour, she finally broke down and told him of the desperation that had propelled her to Port Arthur.

After her mother died, she had been repeatedly raped by her father. One night he brought in three of his friends who also raped her. Early the next morning, when her attackers were sleeping, she put her meager possessions into a battered suitcase, stole one of the men's wallets, and fled. "I got on the first bus I could," she told him. "It didn't matter where it was going. When it pulled into the station, I found myself in Port Arthur. Since my daddy had already made a whore of me, I decided that would be the way for me to make a living."

Before midnight, he asked her if he could come to her room, and she agreed. "You've known all the wrong men, including your papa," he told her. "Men can be gentle too."

As she sat on her bed, she looked up at him with a kind of popeyed terror as he took off his clothes. "You won't hurt me?" she said.

"I won't hurt you," he promised.

In the middle of intercourse, Wanda called out in a faint voice, "Help me!"

47

He withdrew and noticed to his horror that she was going into an epileptic seizure. He'd once seen a woman in that condition on a Greyhound bus ride. Feeling helpless to deal with this crisis, he summoned both Sadie and Estrella to the bedroom of the hapless girl. Sadie assured him she could handle the situation and ordered him to his own room.

The sun was high in the sky when he woke up the next morning. He went immediately to check on Wanda, finding her room empty, the bed freshly made. Her closet was also empty. He headed to the main parlor where he confronted Sadie.

"She's gone," Sadie said.

"She's not able to work at my place." Even though he pressed her hard, Sadie wouldn't tell him any more. He suspected she knew something she didn't want him to find out.

Later that day, Steven asked one of the black prostitutes what happened to Wanda.

"Sold down the river," she told him.

He didn't know what that meant and pressed her for more information. He learned that sometimes young girls were "sold," as a form of slavery, to service men on a tanker making a long haul to ports in the south. A tanker had left that morning from Port Arthur, heading for Trinidad.

"While these men are at sea, they like to keep a young gal locked in her room to service the crew during those seemingly endless days away from port," the girl said. "Sometimes they've even been known to take a young boy instead of a gal."

He was haunted for days about Wanda's disappearance, and he even had a nightmare that he might be sold himself as a slave on one of those tankers. Waking up in a cold sweat, he packed his suitcase and headed for the Greyhound bus station. At six o'clock, he boarded a bus that would eventually take him the three hundred or so miles southwest to Corpus Christi.

He decided that he didn't want to work anymore in bordellos. In his wallet he still had the address of that oil worker whom he planned to look up on the slim chance he might find a job for him working the oil fields.

Even though Steven would probably start out in a lowly job, he had dreams of working his way to the top to become the richest oilman in the State of Texas.

Renting a pillow, he slept most of the way to Corpus Christi, dreaming of Wanda. Later he'd tell friends that she was the only girl he ever loved until he met his first wife.

***

48

In Corpus Christi, when the taxi pulled up in front of Leroy Calder's home, Steven's heart sank. It was small and made of cement blocks. A lone cactus grew in a front yard which was littered with rubbish. Leroy was not the successful oilman Steven had envisioned.

When he knocked on the door, there was no answer at first. Eventually Leroy, obviously recovering from a hangover, answered the door in his boxer shorts and with a two-day growth of beard. At first he didn't remember Steven until his memory was goaded.

Leroy invited him in and went toward the back to get Steven a cold beer. Surveying the living room, Steven realized that a beer blast had occurred the previous night and no one had bothered to clean up.

Taking a chair opposite Steven, Leroy said, "So you decided to give up whoring and come into the oil business?"

Steven related in detail his experiences, and especially his aborted and too short involvement with Wanda.

"Forget her," Leroy advised. "This town is slimy with pussy. The gals line up for us at the gate to the refinery every Saturday afternoon. That's pay day. The grunts have money to spend, and the whores know how to help them get rid of it. Speaking of whores, that's one pulling into the driveway now."

Edna Mae Purdue barged into the living room with take-out hamburgers for all. Leroy introduced her as "my roommate."

In some ways she reminded Steven of Uncle Claude's burlesque queen wife, Eva. Over a case of beer that afternoon, Steven learned that Edna Mae's professional name had been "Dixie Daisy," before she got too old and flabby to put on a G-string. A faded blonde, Edna Mae had breasts that looked like they could have nourished a herd of homeless calves. She was a cliché of the gum-twanging, smart-talking showgirl who lived on the fringe of strip clubs

A Corpus Christi roughneck (left) and a "nodding donkey" (right) silhouetted against the Texas sky.

with prostitution thrown in after the curtain went down.

The very next day Steven was hired as a roughneck, an unskilled laborer. The tough old man who hired him still used the 19th century term of "roustabout."

Steven wasn't exactly sure what a roughneck did, but he soon learned. His main job was as a "worm," a derogatory term used by the more experienced roughnecks. The worm—more formally known as a leadhand—was the lowest in the pecking order at any drilling site, moving and setting up equipment, digging ditches, mixing or cleaning up drilling fluids, and all kinds of grubby, muscular labor.

Some days, the temperature rose above 100°F in the shade. As the sun set, he would stand and look at pumpjacks, sometimes known as "nodding donkeys," silhouetted against the darkening sky.

At night, in seedy taverns, he hung out with rugged wildcatters who talked about the "romance" of oil exploration. These men seemed a part of the final days of the Old West. The way Steven figured it, any big strike would be immediately commandeered by one of the big oil industry companies. He later told some friends in Hollywood that the oil business was peopled with men "with empty pockets and big dreams."

If he'd been old enough, he'd have been tempted to enlist in the Navy, where he'd have wanted to be stationed at the Corpus Christi Naval Air Station, which had been established the year the Japanese attacked Pearl Harbor.

"For six fucking weeks, I was bathed in oil," Steven later recalled. Of all the future movie roles that got away from him, the one he most regretted losing was that given to James Dean in *Giant* opposite Elizabeth Taylor and Rock Hudson. "That scene with Dean blackened with oil was made for me," Steven said. "It was like ripped from my own life."

James Dean strikes "black gold" in the film *Giant*.

Leroy invited Steven to move in, but he turned out to be not the ideal landlord. On some drunken nights "he beat the shit out of Edna Mae, accusing her of sleeping around," Steven claimed. "Believe it or not, he was horribly jealous of this gal whose heyday was a long time ago."

Joining the rest of the grunts on Saturday payday, Steven took up with one of the girls who waited outside the gates. He told Leroy she was Mexican. "I don't know her name. I call her Cha-Cha. I don't know where she was brought up, but she is a regular spitfire. I've never heard of, much less experienced, some of the tricks she performs. She'd once worked in Tijuana, so I guess that explains it."

One afternoon when he came home early, he found Edna Mae trying on some of her old show business costumes. He couldn't believe it, but she was thinking of getting her act together and going back to work at a nearby strip club. "Of course, I've got to get into shape, perhaps take off a few pounds," she told him.

She went into the bathroom and emerged fifteen minutes later dressed in a G-string with pasties to which she'd attached tassels. As part of her performance, she twirled the tassels in opposite directions.

Once again, as with Sadie, the inevitable happened. Although he'd been running around with an underage prostitute, his occasional lust for an older woman asserted itself.

His affair with Edna Mae lasted two weeks until Leroy returned home unexpectedly and caught them in bed naked and drunk.

"I escaped with my life that day," Steven said. "No time to gather up my clothes. I think I made it out of the house just with my pants."

En route to town, a mostly undressed Steven hitched a ride. Although he expressed his disgust with "queers" when hanging out with fellow rough necks, he was glad that the man who picked him up was an obvious homosexual.

That very night Steven was moved into a comfortable home in the suburbs and bought a suit of clothes. He didn't plan to live with the guy forever, only until he got enough money off him to make a break out of Texas. Leroy was the kind of man who held grudges.

Two weeks later an opportunity arose when a traveling circus passed through Corpus Christi. Steven went to see it and met Ralph Porter, whom he had known briefly when he had hooked up with another circus, which had provided him with his escape route from Slater.

Steven asked Ralph to get him a job, and he did. It wasn't exactly the job Steven wanted, but he took it.

Of all the jobs in the circus he could have been offered, he ended up as a hawker of cheap ballpoint-and-pencil sets.

As the circus caravan crossed the state line heading west, Steven told Ralph, "The stars of Texas may be big and bright at night, but they won't be shining on me anymore. A kid like me can get shot in the Lone Star State."

***

51

Steven fitted smoothly into his new role as a carnie, manning a booth hawking ballpoint pens. The novelty was that these pens came in different colors—pink, purple, green, red, yellow, or turquoise—and no longer just blue or black. He was instructed to sell these pen-and-pencil sets for 25¢, but he actually asked $1.25 from customers. Most of them were willing to pay.

He also learned a new vocabulary, including "Lot Lizard," who was a female carnie who slept around, visiting the beds of various men at night. He told Ralph Porter, "In the houses where I worked, they were called whores." Ralph even had a name for the money that Steven was pocketing. Stolen money from a concession was called "oats."

Taking its name from ancient Rome, Circus Maximus traveled through the Southwest, including Arizona and New Mexico. It was three times as large as the previous circus that had employed Steven.

After his job as a roughneck, he welcomed and was even excited by the traveling company of performers who included clowns, acrobats, tightrope walkers, jugglers, unicyclists, trapeze acts, and hoopers. He was especially enthralled by the Bearded Lady and the Lion Tamer.

He also became enamored with a beautiful young woman named "Tiger Lily," who came from China. Both her Chinese mother and her Japanese father had been interred in camps in California during World War II. Tiger Lily dressed in a military uniform with a scarlet breast coat and traveled with a toothless leopard with which she performed nightly.

Steven had almost no affection for Tiger Lily and just used her for a release of his sexual tension. When they weren't in bed together, he spent no time with her, preferring to hang out with the other carnies instead.

Steve joined the circus in his new role as a carnie selling ball point pens. His attempt to save an elephant from cruelty led to the animal's death.

If anything horrified him about the circus, it was the brutal treatment of animals. To train them for animal acts, they were often beaten into submission. He would later remember seeing an Asian elephant being trained. Its trainer viciously attacked the hapless mammal, sinking a hook into its flesh until it howled in agony. The trainer, known only as "Frisco," because he was said to have come from San Francisco, struck the elephant in a sensitive spot behind its ears and used metal-tipped prods on the animal's legs.

Day after day Steven wanted to slug the trainer, but knew he'd be fired if he did. He came up with another plan. One night he unlocked the cage of the abused elephant and it escaped.

He hadn't thought out his plan too well. The elephant bolted but headed toward the main street of Laredo. Pedestrians and motorists were horrified. The police were called, and it took forty-three shots to bring down the elephant. The poor animal collapsed on the street, dying an agonizing death from his wounds. No one ever learned how the elephant had escaped.

It was in San Francisco that Steven's luck ran out. Always suspicious of Steven, the circus manager finally caught him. He found out that Steven had been selling the pens for $1.25 and pocketing the difference. Steven was fired on the spot.

That afternoon, Steven told Tiger Lily good-bye, packed up his clothes, and checked the three-hundred dollars in his pocket.

By six o'clock that evening, he was wandering the streets of San Francisco looking for a cheap hotel.

***

After a reunion that night in a seedy San Francisco tavern, Ralph Porter once again came to Steven's rescue. In the morning, the circus would be heading to Reno, and Steven wouldn't be traveling with it.

Ralph had no moral judgment about Steven stealing from the boss. "All of us carnies do that if we think we can get away with it," Ralph told him. "Some of us get caught. Some of us don't. I've been skimming for years. There's nothing like a little extra cash in my pocket."

After the third beer, Steven bluntly asked him, "Where in the fuck do I get a job in San Francisco? I don't want to have to hustle my dick to a lot of queens. The town is crawling with homos."

"Have you ever considered logging?" Ralph asked. "It's a dangerous profession but my brother loves it. Of course, another name for the logging profession is 'widowmaker.'"

Steven knew nothing about logging but it sounded like a high adventure. Later that night Ralph invited Steven to a seafood dinner at a waterfront tavern where he was meeting his brother, Don Porter.

Over a lot of beer and before the night ended, Steven had agreed to drive north to Oregon with Don where there was a job opening as a tree topper. Even though he wasn't exactly sure of what that job entailed. Steven was eager to sign on with the crew.

The next morning, after telling Ralph good-bye and wishing him luck,

Steven, with Don, headed north along the coastal highway to Oregon. Don drank most of the way there, so Steven did the driving. When the car broke down after crossing the California state line, Steven showed Don what an expert mechanic he was.

Don was the first logger Steven had ever met. He was a bruising powerhouse of a man, with a big neck and a thick set of muscles. He told Steven he'd once been a wrestler. Thick blond curls seemed to boil right out of his head. When Steven shared a latrine at a gasoline station with Don, he saw that he was not only massive up above, but down below too. "The girls scream when I plow this inside them. One woman told me it's like getting a man's arm shoved up inside her."

When Steven arrived in Oregon, he thought he was in "God's country." He learned the names of trees he'd never paid attention to before—sugar pine, silver spruce, tamarack. His favorite was the Douglas fir which almost looked blue in a certain light.

And then the rains came for eight whole days and nights. He'd never seen water come down like this. Along with Don, he joined his fellow loggers to see who could drink the most booze.

When the crew could go into the wet forest, Steven realized the first day that he'd been assigned the toughest and most dangerous job. He was also the smallest man and the lightest on his feet. He had to climb to the top of the tree's canopy, pruning it drastically before the tree could be felled.

After two days on the job, Steven suspected that his father must have been a monkey. He could scale the tree canopy with ease, in one case swinging from branch to branch like Tarzan. Don warned him not to take such dangerous chances.

At night he bunked with Don, discovering that Don had medical history's worst case of athlete's foot. Don and Steven always had drinks and dinner at the Lonesome Pine Café. One night when the plumbing got stuffed up, the men pissed off the back veranda overlooking a gorge.

There were always plenty of girls at the café, wanting to hook up with a logger for the night. Although Don urged him on, Steven told him he was going to wait until payday. Don always had plenty of money, and he bought what he wanted, never paying more than ten dollars a throw. On Friday night he staked Steven to a girl, and their double bed was creaking half the night as he did his prostitute on the left, with Don pounding away simultaneously on the right side of the bed. True to his boast, Don had his girl screaming in pain, not ecstasy.

Night after night Steven played poker with the loggers. Don taught him the game, and in a few weeks he became more skilled at the cards than his teacher. "I didn't learn much about logging in Oregon, but I sure learned about poker playing. I didn't realize how important poker would become in my future."

By the second week, Steven was getting too reckless. A tree branch was slippery after a recent rain, and he fell nearly thirty feet, catching a lower branch, which may have saved his life, or at least his spinal cord.

The next day, back at work, he wandered off into the woods at lunchtime, wanting some peace and quiet. Whether it was true or not, he told the crew about being chased by a hungry bear who wanted lunch.

One day, after a month on the job, Steven wasn't feeling well. He'd eaten a steak the previous night at the Lonesome Pine that may have been rancid. Don had told him that if he poured hot sauce over it, the meat would taste just fine.

Up in the tree tops, Steven felt dizzy but kept on working. He had determination. Suddenly, as he later reported, the world grew black. The last thing he remembered was falling through the branches. He tried in vain to hold on.

When he woke up, many hours had passed. He was in the hospital, and Don was with him. The doctors were amazed. Nothing was broken, especially his spinal cord.

Although badly scratched and bruised, he'd survived the fall. Perhaps the branches he met on the way down had broken the impact of the final plunge.

When his eyes opened and he realized where he was, he told Don, "This is the end of my logging career. There must be an easier way to make a living. I never want to see a tree again."

Don got him a ride when he was released from the hospital with an insurance salesman whose home was in Myrtle Beach, South Carolina. The insurance salesman wanted someone to share the ride, the gas money, and the driving. Steven volunteered.

He'd never been to the Carolinas, so he decided to give it a try. Once there, he'd figure out how to make a living.

As he'd later recall, "That was the most boring and the longest ride of my life. No man knows how big America is until he drives from Oregon to the Carolina coast. The asshole I was with—I don't know or care what his name was—slept and snored a lot. He ate greasy food at every pit stop and then farted it out later in the day. What a trip!"

"I never wanted to say good-bye to anyone more than I wanted to flip the bird to this creep I'd shared the ride with across country," Steven said. "At least he wasn't a faggot. When we did talk, which was rare, it was nothing but an endless boast of all the women he'd fucked. He said he had a wife and five kids in Myrtle Beach and another wife and three kids in Jacksonville, Florida."

"The geek let me out at the bus station," Steven recalled. "I didn't really plan to stay in Myrtle Beach. I decided I might press on to Charleston since I thought I'd have a better chance of finding work."

Since there wasn't a bus out for the next four hours, Steven was attracted to the jukebox across the street. A song by Peggy Lee was playing. With suitcase in hand, he crossed the street and entered the café. It was a typical hamburger and fries joint that touted a free Coke with every platter. He'd seen it all before.

What he hadn't seen before was one of the most beautiful girls he'd ever stared at in his whole life. She sat in the corner sipping Coke with three other girls.

Steven slipped into a booth near her so he could gaze upon her. Amazingly, when he placed his order, he looked at the girl and caught her spying on him. He smiled back but she hung her head in shame. Was that real or was she merely pretending? With all the brazen whores he'd known in his life, he wasn't used to modesty or shyness.

He would later tell friends in New York, "The moment my eyes fell on this gal, I knew she was going to become my wife. I couldn't imagine spending a day on this planet without her by my side."

"I was hopelessly in love," he said. "She was Scarlett O'Hara who'd just jumped from the pages of *Gone With the Wind*."

***

When the mystery girl in the café remained behind after her girlfriends left, Steven felt she'd done this just for his sake. Within minutes, he moved in on her and was sharing the booth so recently vacated.

Up close, she was even more beautiful than before, with long blonde hair and blue eyes like his own. Her name was Suellen Gordon, and he soon learned she was finishing her last year of high school. He guessed her age at sixteen, perhaps just turned seventeen.

He explained why he was in Myrtle Beach after having fallen out of that tree in Oregon.

"And now you've fallen into my life," she said in a heavily accented Southern voice. "Just like that."

"Perhaps you know where I might stay," he said. "Something cheap. I don't have much money."

"My aunt takes in boarders," she said. "She's got a place right on the beach."

"Will it cost me an arm and a leg?" he asked. "I don't have a job yet."

"Don't you worry your cute little head about that," she said. "If you're going to become my boyfriend, and I suspect you are, money will be the least of your worries. My daddy practically owns western South Carolina."

His earlier impression seemed wrong. This was no shy sixteen-year-old. She was surprisingly aggressive but masked it with a Southern belle façade. Perhaps she was Scarlett O'Hara after all. "By the way, were you named for Scarlett's sister, Suellen, in *Gone With the Wind*?"

"No," she said. "Margaret Mitchell wrote *Gone With the Wind* after I was born. I was named for a great aunt who's got a lot of money. I hope she leaves it to me when she croaks."

He was mildly shocked but amused by Suellen. Her words did not match her image. She seemed to be one determined teenager.

Leaving the café, he was surprised she had a license to drive a shiny new car. It was a Cadillac. "My first car," she told him. "Daddy bought it for me for my birthday."

Within the hour, he was installed in a beautiful room overlooking the beach at her aunt's luxurious B&B. There was no talk of money.

She came into his bedroom, shutting the door behind her. "I want you to come and have dinner with Daddy and me. Momma died last year. He has to approve before I can date a beau. But, first, do you have a good suit of clothes? My daddy always likes to see a well-dressed boy at table, including a jacket and tie."

"Then I strike out," he said. "I don't have a good suit of clothes."

"No problem," she said. "I'll talk over arrangements about your staying here with my aunt. Why don't you freshen up? We've got an errand to run."

Within the hour, he was in a men's clothing store selecting a dark blue suit. Suellen herself picked out his underwear and shoes. When they left, she told the clerk, "Just put it on Daddy's account."

Back in his room, she stood close to the door. "Dinner's at seven. I'll pick you up. Daddy's garage runneth over. I'm sure he'll give you some wheels tonight."

"Thanks for everything," he said. "You're swell."

"Why don't you walk over here and give your Sugar Momma a big sloppy wet one?"

He took her in his arms. As he'd later tell his friends in the future, "Suellen was one hell of a kisser. I don't know where she learned to kiss like that, but her tongue reached the back of my throat the moment our lips met."

Steven met his Sugar Momma and his Sugar Daddy at the Gordon manse near Myrtle Beach, SC.

Suellen's Daddy was the original "Big Mac." Everybody called him that. His full name was MacDonald Daniel Gordon, and he was a powerhouse of a man, vaguely resembling Orson Welles during his corpulent period.

At first Steven had feared meeting Big Mac. After all, he was just a hobo hitting town trying to scrounge for a living. He didn't think he was proper boyfriend material for a rich girl like Suellen.

Big Mac was all warmth and graciousness when welcoming Steven to his home. He couldn't have been more affirming or approving. "Suellen, it sure looks like you got yourself one good-looking motherfucker here. Thank God he's got blond hair and blue eyes, a member of the Aryan race. We men never know what our daughters are going to drag in these days. I have a friend, Custer Collingsworth. His daughter brought home a Puerto Rican she'd picked up in New York. She was pregnant. We speak English in this household."

"So do I," Steven said.

Over bourbon and branch water, Steven was trying to figure out Big Mac. In some ways, he was your typical Southern redneck racist, but he was different somehow. He seemed to take pride in Suellen and in her beauty and charm, but his attention and concern for Steven bordered on the obsessive. If Steven wanted another drink, Big Mac called to one of his "darkies." He seemed to have at least four servants working the household, including the cook, Bertha.

"You're a fine figure of a man," Big Mac told Steven, who had settled in comfortably after the first awkward half hour. "A man with your looks and Suellen's beauty would produce a lot of gorgeous white grandchildren for me. Until I met you, I hadn't approved of some of the boys Suellen brought home. You're the first one I've liked."

"I'm honored, sir," he said. "I think Suellen is a mighty fine girl, and I intend to respect her."

As Suellen summoned them to dinner, Big Mac heaved himself from the chair. On the way to the dining room, he felt the muscles in Steven's left arm. "You're a bit on the skinny side, but maybe you make up for it in another department." He laughed at his own comment. "Don't worry. Bertha's cooking will put some more meat on those bones. You may have missed a few meals bumming about the country, but those days are over. If there's one thing that even my enemies say about me, I've always been a good provider. Just ask Suellen."

After dinner, which Steven would refer to as "the best I ever had in my life," Big Mac took him out to his garage. "Suellen tells me you need something to drive around in. Take your pick, anything except my new Cadillac."

Not wanting to be greedy, Steven selected a new Ford. "Are all these cars in running order?"

"Some of them need work," Big Mac said. "There are at least three that haven't been driven since before the war."

Before the bourbon-soggy night ended, Steven had agreed to come over tomorrow morning and start work as Big Mac's new mechanic. He convinced Big Mac that he was an expert and would have all the cars running within a few weeks.

The idea seemed to thrill Big Mac. "You sure know how to pick 'em," he told his daughter. "At least in this case." After giving Steven a big bear hug, he retreated into the house, allowing Suellen to give Steven's mouth another of her tongue jobs.

Big Mac suddenly stuck his head out the front door. "Breakfast at eight and be on time. That's the one meal that can't wait. Wait 'til you see the spread that Bertha lays out in the morning."

"Can't wait," Steven called to Big Mac.

Behind the wheel of his newly acquired car, he floor-boarded it when he reached the coastal road. After ten minutes of this, a motorcycle policeman gave chase. Steven slowed down to face the ire of the patrolman.

"The car doesn't belong to me," Steven said when asked for the registration. "It's one of Big Mac's cars. I'm testing it for him. I'm Suellen's new boyfriend."

The patrolman stopped writing the ticket. "I see, Mr. McQueen," he said. "It's a fine little car, and I wish you good night." He turned, walked away, and got back on his motorcycle, roaring off into the night.

Fearing more trouble, Steven slowly drove back to his B&B. But before turning in, he took a nude midnight swim.

***

On his second visit to the Gordon manse, Steven was immediately accepted as a member of the family. His own mother might have rejected him, but in Myrtle Beach he'd never received such acceptance, although he found Big Mac's fondness for him a bit excessive.

Big Mac was even talking about Steven's future. He'd heard of Southern hospitality, but this was a bit much. He hadn't decided if he wanted to be a part of this family, but the decision was being made for him.

As for Suellen, he felt she could not wait until her wedding night to lose her virginity—that is, if she had it.

In his mechanic's overalls, Steven spent the rest of the morning tinkering with Big Mac's collection of cars, dreaming that one day he, too, might have such a medley. He broke for lunch with Big Mac and Suellen, served in a gazebo on their sprawling lawn. It was Big Bertha's special fried chicken and potato salad, followed by Southern pecan pie. If he stayed with the Gordons, Steven feared he'd be fat in a year.

It was while he was eating that Suellen noticed an odd habit of Steven's. Even while chewing on a chicken leg with one hand, he had a piece of pie in the other hand. It was as if he feared the kitchen would run out of food.

"You sure have a healthy appetite, boy," Big Mac said.

"And you eat like the food out here is all you'll ever get," Suellen said.

"That's because I've gone hungry for most of my life," he said.

Behind the wheel of Big Mac's Cadillac, Steven felt like King of the Road as he drove the car to Greenville, South Carolina, where Big Mac had a sprawling plantation style house he'd inherited from his mother on her side of the family. To him, the house evoked Tara in *Gone With the Wind*, except Big Mac's mother had long departed.

After wandering through the hallways, he learned that she must have been enchanted by her own image, as portraits of her, staring back at him, were hung everywhere. Steven felt like a hustler when he stared into the faces of those portraits. He bet that Big Mama would have spotted him as a hustler right away.

Before reaching Greenville, Steven had decided that this rich life was for him. As a former prostitute, he knew that Big Mac wanted more than grand-children from him, and he was prepared to give in at some point, providing Big Mac wasn't too demanding.

He couldn't wait to get Suellen in some lonely, dark spot. She'd already taken to feeling his erection while she tongue kissed him.

He was later to tell friends, "She was hot to trot morning, noon, and night-time too. I was looking forward to screwing Suellen but not looking forward to those blow-jobs that were going to come from Big Mac. The rewards seemed worth it, though. It'd beat hustling your ass on Santa Monica Boulevard to a bunch of queers."

Steven drove his newly acquired family to a cotton mill that Big Mac owned. It mostly employed girls and young women, Steven learned. Big Mac was excessively proud of his mill, explaining that he'd combined carding, spinning, weaving, even bleaching and printing all under one gigantic roof.

Even though the mill had shut down on a Sunday, the air was still thick with cotton dust. It was also hot and humid.

After a lunch of barbecued ribs, Steven drove Big Mac and Suellen to a sprawling farm that raised the largest, fattest hogs he'd ever seen. It dwarfed Uncle Claude's farm in Missouri. "Now hog farming, that's something I know something about," Steven said. "Hogs and cars."

"Good," Big Mac said. "I might just make you the overseer of this hog farm when you and Suellen get hitched."

Suddenly, the prospect of marrying into the Gordon family dimmed a bit.

Back in Greenville Monday morning, Big Mac was called to the cotton mill to settle a labor dispute between black and white workers. Pleading a headache, Steven remained behind in the family manse.

Suellen knew what he intended to do. He'd later recall, "She was no sweet sixteen. She was all over me. Wanted it three ways."

The following week Big Mac moved Steven into the west wing of his Myrtle Beach manse. He was now part of the family, and he suspected that Big Mac knew he was banging Suellen regularly but he never said anything.

After a month, Steven was asked to drive Big Mac down to Jacksonville, Florida, where he'd rented a yacht for some deep sea fishing with a full crew.

Steven welcomed the adventure and some relief from Suellen's sexual demands, although he feared an encounter with Big Mac. Both of them shared the stateroom. Big Mac suggested that since both of them were men, they might as well sleep nude.

Shortly after midnight, he woke up to feel Big Mac's suctioning mouth. He was an expert at what he did. Steven closed his eyes, imagining Big Mac was really Suellen.

During the whole act, Big Mac said nothing. Rising from the bed, he said, "Good rich cream. You'll make fine grandchildren for me."

Back in Myrtle Beach, it wasn't Big Mac's blow-job or Suellen's demands, it was something else. All his life he'd felt worthless and unwanted. Now everything was being handed to him, one of the main reasons being an appendage he had between his legs.

He began to feel, as he'd later tell his fellow Marines, that he didn't think he deserved all this rich life. The one thing he'd learned in Missouri was that you had to earn what you got in life.

On an impulse that he'd regret on and off for the next three years, he marched down to the nearest recruiting station and joined the U.S. Marine Corps.

If Steven had married his "Scarlett O'Hara," he might have ended up the owner of a cotton mill in western South Carolina.

***

It is through two of Steven's closest friends and confidants, Darron McDonald and Casey Perkins, that we know much about three years of his life from 1947 to 1950. A few others weighed in with incidents about what happened during that period as well. But Steven, in what he told his friends, remains the best source of information about what happened to him. Anyone with an intimate knowledge of his character will know that his own scenario has verisimilitude, although he may have embellished here or there.

The day he signed on as a Marine, Steven was about a month past his 17th birthday.

He was assigned to the 2nd Recruit Battalion of the Marine Corps Recruit Depot at Parris Island, South Carolina. Along with other recruits, he was sent to Camp Lejeune, North Carolina, for boot camp.

He claimed that after only one week in boot camp, "I'd made the worst mistake of my life." The regimentation and the sheer physical exhaustion were much tougher than anything he'd experienced in reformatory school. "To think I gave up the good life for this shit," he lamented.

During the closing months of reform school, he'd buckled down and had become an exemplary inmate. He hoped to apply that same discipline to the military, as he became Cadet McQueen, serial number 649015.

While still based at Camp Lejeune, he was assigned as a rifleman to C Company, 1st Battalion, FMF. By September 18, 1947, he was designated as Private First Class McQueen.

"I wasn't a Marine, I wasn't a tank driver, I was a fucking slave," Steven recalled to his friends. "I had to do such shit as make up officers' beds or run and get their clean underwear from the laundry."

Biographer Christopher Sandford commented on the only surviving picture of Steven in uniform, the photograph show-

Portrait of **Steven** as a marine.
"Submerged psychopathic tendencies."

ing "a teenager with a face so taut his garrison cap is sliding down it; scowling, thick through the shoulders and chest but cinched at the waist, Steve looked like a welterweight boxer with submerged psychopathic tendencies. Colleagues remember his legs were constantly restless and his feet 'gave nervous jerks.' Below shuffling energy; above, coolness and poise, a certain menacing handsomeness."

A fellow Marine made the claim "that look of Steven's bothered you until you got to know him, and then it bothered you some more. There was nobody better in the world to have on your side, and nobody worse to cross, than McQueen."

Even though Steven was a tiny guy when compared to most of his fellow colleagues, he knew how to deal with platoon bullies. If an enemy were too big and brawny to attack in open combat, he lay in wait for the man and deviously caught him with his pants down. That is a literal statement.

One of the biggest bullies who'd been harassing him for days was in the crapper relieving himself as he read a newspaper. Steven slipped into the latrine and attacked from behind, knocking him out cold with a baseball bat. "He didn't look like a bully no more," Steven said. "As he lay on the floor, one turd was only half way out of his fat ass."

"What those military recruitment posters don't tell you when you sign up is that you're committing yourself to the worst prison system this side of Alcatraz," Steven told his future comrades Darron and Casey. "The Marine Corps owns your balls. They tell you when to get up, when to go to bed, what to eat, even when you can take a shit. Believe it or not, you have to ask permission to go to the crapper. I was too independent for the Marines. I'm my own man. In a way, the Marine Corps tells you even when you can fuck. Unless you want to fuck one of your fellow Marines, you've got to wait until

A grinning **Steven** peers out of a tank at Camp Lejeune, NC
where he trained with his fellow marines.

the brass says you can take leave."

"Steven became known as the meanest poker player in C Company," said Private First Class Ralph Greenson. "He played for cold hard cash. He cleaned all of us out. When we went on leave, we didn't have enough money left to buy a whore. I've played cards all my life, and I've never seen a man as determined to win as Steven McQueen. He put even professional gamblers to shame."

"He always told me, 'To be a great card player, you've got to have balls. You can't let fear show on your face. Even with a bad hand, you've got to be steely cool. A lot of card playing is about bluff.'"

That rash decision to enter the Marine Corps would ultimately cost Steven his life. But it would take many a summer before he succumbed to cancer. His career as a movie star would come and almost go before he came down with mesothelioma, which is a deadly form of asbestos poisoning.

"Back at Camp Lejeune, and other places, you lived, breathed, and shit asbestos," Steven recalled. "The crap was even used to insulate our barracks. I once had to refit a troop ship's boiler room with the stuff. All of the pipes in that hellhole were lined with asbestos. You could see the fucking stuff you sucked into your lungs. That's how thick the air was with that poison."

"Steven was a bore," PFC Jack Wittaker said. "All he talked about was this gorgeous gal he'd left in Myrtle Beach, how rich her father was, and when he got out of the Marines, he was going back to marry the bitch and set himself up for life. The only reason I listened to his crap day after night was I wanted to get him out of his shorts and fuck that ass of his. Call me a pervert! Alas, my chance never came."

When Steven was granted his first weekend pass, he hitched a ride to Myrtle Beach, arriving on the doorstep of the Gordon mansion. Both Suellen and Big Mac received him like their beloved. At first Suellen had been furious when he joined the Marines, but she'd forgiven him.

Big Mac also accepted him. "A boy's got to serve his country. We'd have lost the war if all the service fellows stayed home with their gals."

Mac had arranged for Steven to move into Suellen's bedroom. He just assumed his daughter would marry Steven as soon as he was discharged from the corps.

While Suellen supervised the breakfast rituals downstairs, Big Mac, still the sexual opportunist, lingered in the bathroom upstairs. There he gave Steven the first of several blow-jobs. It was expertly administered while Steven shaved.

He was having such a good time with Suellen and Big Mac that he illegally extended his pass to two weeks. His commander reported him AWOL. It was at the beach while sunning with Suellen that Steven was picked up and transported across the state line back to the camp at Lejeune.

When brought before his superiors, Steven astonished the men by telling them, "I volunteered to join the Marines. I was not drafted. No one told me that I couldn't come and go as I wished."

The brass was not impressed with that defense. Steven was sentenced to forty-two days and nights in the brig. He had to survive for the first three weeks on bread and water.

"Those were the worst days of my life," he later recalled. "Before being hauled off, I'd been warned by some of my fellow Marines not to start jerking off. They told me, 'It'll fuck you up and good. Once you start, you'll be at it day and night. Your peter will fall off.'"

"Those days in the brig were the longest of my life," Steven said. "I played all sorts of mind games. I evoked every memory I could conjure up, the good and the bad. When I ran out of memories, I fantasized. At one point near the end, I even ran out of fantasies. I couldn't conjure up one God damn thing. All I could do was wait, wait, wait for my freedom train, which wouldn't even carry me to freedom but back to the restrictions of the barracks."

He later made the claim, "Before I was finally released, I considered holding my breath until I died."

***

After his release, Steven returned to barracks grub with gusto. He demanded and was given three helpings of everything. But after a few days, he complained of the rations. Fortunately, he was assigned to the unloading of supplies aimed for the officers' mess. The officers had far better food than the enlisted men.

Secretly, he stole cans of peaches, fruit cocktail, Spam, and canned chicken. Canned salmon from Alaska was his favorite. He ate this food cold right from the can. Soon he didn't even bother to go to the mess hall except for bacon and eggs in the morning.

Years later, he would admit to his close friends and confidants, Darron and Casey, that he experienced a "homosexual panic" while in the Marines. "I found I liked living in an all-male environment. I liked sharing shower stalls and polishing boots with other guys in the barracks. I watched their every move. The way they walked around in their skivvies or else stark naked. Sometimes we'd sit for hours shooting the bull. On occasion, we played grab ass. I was good at that."

"Some of the guys had real fuckable asses, but I didn't go there," he recalled. "At night after lights out you could hear some of the guys in their bunks beating their meat. The air was thick with the smell of semen. I was careful not to make any desire known. I didn't want to become a sissy-ass like some of the recruits. A few got their butts broken in by older guys in the service. One of my officers was pounding the butt of a good-looking guy who'd enlisted. Some of the bigger, beefier guys took advantage of the young recruits. Hell, they were kids just out of high school, meeting up with some of these tough veterans who had won World War II."

Steven finally got a pass to leave the base for the night. "I hooked up with some guys who went fag-bashing. I wanted to show them I wasn't a candy-ass. There was this city park where queers hung out hoping to score with servicemen. Since the guys thought I was sorta cute, I was used as queer bait to lure one of these suckers into the bushes. In about an hour, I found my victim. He was an older guy who made his intention pretty clear. He liked to suck off Marines. I lured him into the bushes. Instead of getting me, he met four husky Marines who beat the shit out of him. I heard on some occasions, one of these faggots got raped, but I wanted no part of that. Sounded too queer to me."

Sometimes a Marine would brazenly talk about his sexual exploits with homosexuals, always assuming the macho role. One Monday morning when Steven had had too much to drink the night before, he sat down with a Marine who was toying with his plate of bacon and eggs. "This bacon tastes like raw pork," the Marine said. "See that guy over there." He pointed to a young man at the grill who looked no more than sixteen. "He's the junior chef, believe it or not. He gives the best blow-job at camp but can't cook bacon and eggs. In fact, he can't even fry an egg. I think I'll have cornflakes this morning."

When Steven was granted his next weekend pass, he made "one of the most stupid mistakes of my life. Even now, I can't figure out why I did it."

With the pass, he hitched his way once again to Myrtle Beach and the Gordon mansion, where Suellen and Big Mac eagerly greeted him once again.

"Each of them still wanted a piece of my flesh," Steven later told his friends, "but they were willing to pay the piper, and I was willing to go along with their grand scheme for my life."

Once again, Steven's commander reported him AWOL. When the shore patrol picked him up at a seafront restaurant where he was dining with Suellen, the second arrest was different. Steven slugged one of the arresting patrolmen. That, he would learn, meant more time in the brig.

In recalling his life, Steven later claimed, "I don't remember one day I spent in that brig the second time around. I think I went crazy. You don't take a wild animal like me and cage it. I don't really know what I did to myself, but I remember I ended up in a hospital. I think I must have gone on a hunger strike, and you know how much I like to eat."

By November of 1947, he found himself in Quantico, Virginia, where he was assigned to the Amphibian Tractor Company, 22nd Marines, FMF. His job was as a crewman on a tank and amphibious tractor.

After leaving the South, Steven was transferred to San Diego where he was trained as a tank driver. "At last I'd found my calling in the Marines because I spent most of my days here doing work as a mechanic. I was a born mechanic. I loved all kinds of machinery, especially those that had wheels. It would become an abiding interest of mine for the rest of my life."

"I was just a wild and crazy kid," Steven told Casey and Darron. "Remember, I was only a teenager at the time."

That was his only explanation for the most impulsive stunt he ever pulled in the Marine Corps.

One morning, he went to a hardware store and spent all his money on pink paint. Back at the base, he painted his tank pink and drove it into downtown San Diego.

Of course, the police arrested him and called Marine Corps security to come and pick him up. Amazingly, Steven wasn't thrown in the brig this time, but he had to repaint the tank and pay for it out of his serviceman's pay.

One of his commanders, in recalling this bizarre incident, later said, "The guy I knew as Steven McQueen—now the actor Steve McQueen—was very similar in real life to the persona I saw in his movies. He kinda reminded me of the character he played in *The Great Escape*."

During his three years in the corps (1947-1950), Steven was busted from PFC back to private a total of seven times.

✦✦✦

From sunny California, Steven and his fellow Marines were shipped to Labrador for coldwater amphibious landing exercises. "I was miserable there," he recalled. "It was cold and bleak. Who in hell would want to live in a place like Labrador? It was the pits. To harden us for survival in northern climes, we were fed crappy K-rations—beef jerky, shit like that. We spent the night in sleeping bags that were never warm enough. I don't know how the Eskimos do it."

During one exercise, a transport vessel struck a sandbank, hurling five manned tanks into the Arctic waters, where submersion for just a few minutes meant instant death. Unable to escape from their tanks, eight Marines died that day. The other Marines escaped from their tanks into the icy waters to face inevitable death from hypothermia if not rescued immediately.

As the captain of an amphibious rescue craft, Steven heroically sprang into action. From a position onboard, he pulled four young Marines, dripping wet, to safety. A fifth seemed to be drowning. Steven jumped into the below-freezing waters and rescued a young teenage Marine, pulling him to safety aboard the craft.

As another Marine piloted the nearly drowned Marines to safety on shore, Steven noticed that one of the PFCs had turned blue. He lay on top of his body, giving him some body warmth while he performed mouth-to-mouth resuscitation. All the men reached shore where an ambulance waited to rush them to the hospital. Steven rode in the rear of the ambulance with the young Marine who was hardly breathing.

The next morning, Steven personally visited all the men he'd rescued, saving the fifth bedside visit for the young Marine in the most weakened condition. He learned that his name was Philip Buloff, and that he was from Indiana.

He weakly took Steven's hand and thanked him "for saving my life. I'll be in your debt forever!"

"You owe me nothing," Steven said.

When Philip was finally released from the hospital, he wanted to hang out with Steven all the time. At five feet five, weighing 130 pounds, he was even smaller than Steven.

"The kid followed Steven around like a lovesick puppy," said a fellow Marine, Warren Talbot. "He took his pay and bought cigarettes for Steven, even candy bars. The guys in the barracks thought the kid had fallen in love with his hero, and I think that was true."

"When their next leave came, Steven and this guy went off base together, and none of us saw them around town," Talbot said. "We thought they'd shacked up somewhere together. We laughed and joked about it. It wasn't hard to figure out who'd be top man in that relationship. At least this time Steven didn't go AWOL but showed up on time when he and Philip had to report to duty Monday morning at 6am. The kid looked a little worse for wear, but Steven was the bird who'd swallowed the canary."

Steven was hailed as a hero during amphibious tank landings in Arctic waters off the coast of Labrador

Back at base, Steven, the bad boy Leatherneck, was hailed as a hero. The brass took notice and Steven was given a soft job, a highly desirable one. He was assigned to the 1st Guard Company at the Naval Gun Factory in Washington, D.C. As such, he was made a member of the Honor Guard assigned to the USS *Sequoia,* the presidential yacht of Harry S Truman. Truman had successfully won the election of 1948, after having filled the last years of the presidency of Franklin D. Roosevelt after he'd died in office in April of 1945.

"Philip suffered for days after Steven left the base," Talbot recalled. "The kid took it real bad. He feared he'd never see Steven again. In some ways, puppy love hurts more than any other kind of love, I guess. I wouldn't know."

***

As part of the President's honor guard, Steven had just landed the easiest job in the Marine Corps. "Most of the time I stood around in full uniform looking pretty. When I joined the Marines, I thought it would be about charging ashore on Guadalcanal or up Pork Chop Hill. I ended up being a bartender, bringing bourbon and branch water to the Commander-in-Chief."

Steven quickly learned that the vessel had begun life as a private yacht, costing $200,000 in 1925. Before its purchase in 1931 by the government, it had belonged to William Dunning, president of the Sequoia Oil Company in Texas.

It was while assigned to the *Sequoia* that a fellow Marine guard introduced Steven to the glories of smoking marijuana. "It was a big mistake on my part," Steven later confessed. "I became addicted to pot. For me, a day without pot is a day going by when you can't take a crap."

Marijuana use aboard the President's yacht would make world headlines on May 25, 1973, when 28 marines and 18 sailors were reassigned because of pot smoking.

Steven had been assigned to the yacht for three weeks before Harry S Truman appeared late one afternoon in 1949 for a sail along the Potomac. Except for the Secret Service, he was alone.

As the new guard, Steven was introduced to the President, who immediately asked him where he was from. "Missouri," Steven said.

Truman looked mildly astonished. "Where all the best men come from," he said. "I should have figured you for a Missouri boy. Do you play poker, boy?"

"The best player east of the Rockies," Steven boasted.

"We'll see about that later tonight,"

Steven meets a fellow native of Missouri; he and **Harry S Truman** became poker-playing buddies aboard the presidential yacht.

Truman threatened.

That night marked the first of many that Steven got to spend with the President. Often he had officials aboard, and he always insisted that Steven serve the drinks. He quickly learned how much water to put in Truman's bourbon.

Sometimes when he had no VIPs aboard, Truman would sit and talk with Steven about growing up in Missouri.

The comments and stories Truman imparted to Steven would be remembered by him for the rest of his life.

He learned that the "S" in Truman's name didn't take a period because it stood for nothing since his parents couldn't agree on either Shippe or Solomon. Truman also told him that in 1945 he'd wanted to make a separate and unified country out of Bavaria, Austria, and Hungary.

"When I was told that Roosevelt had died, I was having a cocktail with Sam Rayburn," Truman said. "If you don't know your politics, he's the Speaker of the House. I said, 'Jesus Christ and General Jackson.'"

"Ol' Sam told me that when I became president, 'a lot of people are going to tell you you're the smartest man in the country, but, Harry, you and I know you ain't.'"

Truman's favorite expressions, or so Steven soon learned, were "Go to Hell!" and "That S.O.B.!"

Every time Steven played poker with the President, Truman won. "He was one hard-core poker player," Steven recalled. One night Steven decided he was going to win, and he did, although it involved cheating. For the first time he got a whiff of Truman's famous temper. The President stood up and scratched the dining table with a cigar cutter. Guests sailing on the *Sequoia* today can still see the scratch. After that, Steven learned never to beat Truman in poker.

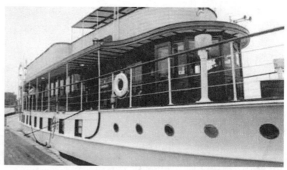

Steven joins the marine honor guard protecting
the presidential yacht, USS *Sequoia*. Presedental Seal at left.

When Steven was shipped out, Truman shook his hand. "Now stay out of trouble, boy, and don't trust the ladies. Keep in touch with me. If you do get into trouble, and as long as I'm president, I have the right to pardon you. But I hope I don't have to."

In May of 1949, Steven returned to the 2nd Amphibian Tractor Battalion at Camp Lejeune. There he would serve until his honorable discharge came on April 27, 1950.

After Steven had distinguished himself, his commander had urged him to re-enlist. "The Marine Corps needs men like you," he told Steven. The commander was deadly accurate. Steven's discharge came just three weeks before the outbreak of the Korean War. A few months went by before Steven read in the paper that his whole outfit had been wiped out in an ambush in North Korea.

In later life, Steven had mixed reactions about his service in the Marines. "In some ways, it made a man out of me. But it never really changed my character. I'm a bad boy, and I became a bad boy as soon as I got out of the service. I also did some good things in my life, but deep down I'm a rotter. Had I not gone into the Marines, I would probably have ended up as Suellen's husband, the owner of large landholdings, and maybe even the governor of South Carolina. Yes, that's it. I would have been a Republican governor."

It was springtime in the Carolinas in 1950 when Steven returned to Suellen and Big Mac in Myrtle Beach. All the flowers were in bloom. "It was a good time to be alive," Steven recalled. "I was full of piss and vinegar. Even though I was just twenty, I'd had a hard life. Now it was riding down Easy Street for the rest of my life, with an overly protective father-in-law, a hot-to-trot wife, and, perhaps, in my future, eight snot-nosed kids."

❦❦❦

Preparations moved forward at the Gordon mansion for the upcoming wedding of Steven and Suellen. Big Mac had even purchased a large silver set with the initials S&S entwined. "I'm gonna spare no expense," he told Steven. "You're the best-looking man in the county, and Suellen is the most beautiful gal, so I just know my grandchildren are gonna be the prettiest along the coast. I'm one proud man."

Two days before the wedding found Steven alone on a train headed north to Washington. D.C. Even to his closest friends in the future, he apparently never confided why he'd fled "the good life" and headed into an uncertain future.

There was only speculation. "All his life Steven had wanted love and protection, especially from his mother," Casey claimed. "In Myrtle Beach, he had

71

it, but I guess he decided he didn't want it all along. Maybe it was his future father-in-law hovering over him that helped him make the final decision to bolt. Maybe it was Suellen who was too clingy, too demanding. Maybe he wanted to take charge of his own future instead of having his life already charted for him. We'll never know, and Steven didn't want to talk about it, and when that guy clammed up, nothing could pry open his shell. Besides, it was nobody's business but his own."

Ever since he'd left Canada to serve in President Truman's honor guard, Steven had received letters from Philip Buloff, the young man he'd rescued from the icy waters off the coast of Labrador. For every ten letters Steven received, he'd perhaps answered one in his fairly illiterate prose.

After Philip had been discharged from the Marines, he'd headed for Washington, hoping to hook up with Steven there only to find he'd left for South Carolina after his own discharge from the Corps. Steven had virtually ordered Philip not to cross the Mason-Dixon line.

He took a low-paying government job in Washington and continued to write letters to Steven.

One night in Washington, Philip opened the door to his apartment and found Steven standing there, suitcase in hand. "In all my life, I've never experienced such joy." Philip, who had come down with the AIDS virus, recited these details to journalist Cliff Stevens in 1983, as part of an unpublished interview intended for *After Dark,* a gay-oriented New York City-based theatrical magazine.

"I couldn't believe it. The man of my dreams had come to me. I owed my very life to this man."

Philip claimed that the first three weeks of living with Steven "were sheer bliss even though I knew it wouldn't last forever. After spending all that time with me in close quarters, he got restless. I knew he was seeing girls on the side. It broke my heart, but I was willing to overlook it just to hold onto my man. He told me he could never be faithful to anyone. It wasn't his nature."

Steven got a job driving a taxicab. "I knew he sometimes met girls that way," Philip said. "Sometimes he wouldn't come home until ten o'clock in the morning, after I'd already left for work. Often when I rushed home at five o'clock, I'd find his dirty clothes thrown around the apartment. I'd always pick them up and wash them. I think he liked having a slave. It made him feel that he was somebody."

"He grew to hate the job of a cab driver," Philip said. "He was mugged twice. He wanted to pick and choose the passengers he let into his cab, and, of course, that wasn't allowed."

"Then one day the inevitable happened," Philip said. "I came home from work and found the apartment in disarray. Steven had checked out and taken his clothes with him. He left only a pair of dirty underwear which I have to this day. There was no note, nothing. I don't know where he went, but New York would be the obvious choice."

"This may sound strange considering our relationship, but Steven was not a homosexual," Philip claimed. "He was a man for the ladies as I painfully learned. Even though we were intimate, I made love to him. He never made love to me. During our time together, he never even kissed me. Sometimes when we were having sex, I think he was dreaming not of me, but of beautiful women with big breasts."

"Imagine my surprise when I went to see *Somebody Up There Likes Me* with Paul Newman," Philip said. "I sorta developed this crush on Newman since seeing him in *The Silver Chalice*. Suddenly, there was Steven on the screen. It was just a walk-on but I knew him at once. In all our time together, he never told me he wanted to be an actor."

"I watched in amazement when he became the biggest movie star in the world," Philip said. "I even saw *The Blob* eighteen times. I thought Steven looked more beautiful and sexier in this movie than in any other. I wrote many fan letters to him, sending them to various studios," he said. "I don't know if he got my letters or not. At any rate, he never answered. I think I was a memory and our time together in Washington was something he wanted to forget. At least I could go see him in the movies and watch as his face changed over the years. Even though our friendship was aborted, and he hurt me in many ways, I'd do the same thing all over again if given the chance. When I heard of Steven's death, I cried for days. I went on to other affairs, but never found a man to equal Steven. He was the pick of the litter, and then some."

***

Steven was twenty years old when he arrived to experience New York anew. After the war, it had taken on a new *joie de vivre*. Thousands of returning GIs had decided to remain in New York and desert their homes in the farmlands of the Middle West or in small Southern towns. The city brimmed with life and creativity, and these triumphant warriors of World War II wanted a slice of it.

After a night spent in a seedy hotel in the Times Square area, Steven headed for Greenwich Village, where he rented a coldwater flat that very day, priced at only nineteen dollars a month. He'd saved up some money as a Marine, but he knew it wouldn't go far, so he'd have to find work. His bill for beer and Mary Jane (his name for pot) would be even bigger than his rent, and he knew that.

"I spent my first week in New York getting wasted and getting laid,"

Steven said. "If a guy couldn't get fucked in Greenwich Village in 1950, he couldn't get laid anywhere. Newly arrived girls from everywhere were practically begging you for it. They wanted to experience the Bohemian life."

He had only one pair of shoes when he arrived, and the heel came off. In a storefront below his apartment house was an old-fashioned cobbler. Steven stopped in one afternoon and asked the man, who once lived in Poland, if he could repair his heel while he waited. The old man agreed.

Watching him work in leather fascinated Steven. Impulsively he asked the Pole if he needed an assistant. As it turned out, the man had lost his helper last week, and hired Steven on the spot for twenty-five dollars a week.

He was a fast learner and after one week he could repair shoes himself without the old man's advice. "I became really good at it," he said. "Sometimes I felt up a woman's ankle with a certain touch that turned her on," he recalled. "I got a lot of dates that way. Many of the women were married, but so what?"

"I quit because of the queers," Steven later claimed. "When they came into the shop, they were always making passes at me. I felt it was demeaning for me to get down in front of them and fit their shoes onto them. One asshole ran his fingers through my hair as I was on the floor servicing his stinking feet. I stood up and slugged him. Actually, I didn't really quit. The cobbler fired me. Violence against his customers, regardless of their sexual persuasion, just wasn't allowed."

"On the road to my horizon, I had a few odd jobs," Steven said. "I had to haul radiators out of condemned buildings to a junkyard in the Bronx. I even sold ballpoint pens like I did in the circus. I also sold encyclopedias to families who couldn't afford them. I later learned my competition, Paul Newman, got his start that way. I felt like a shark taking money from some of these families. I found that Puerto Ricans, in particular, wanted to better themselves, and they thought buying encyclopedias would give them the equivalent of a college education."

"I had some other jobs too while I was scammin' for dough," he recalled. "I even collected bets for a local bookie, and I worked nearly a month as a bag loader in the Post Office near 34th Street. I tried to become a boxer like Rocky Graziano, but I was knocked on my ass so many times during my week spent in a Brooklyn gym that I decided to leave the boxing game to Rocky himself."

At one point he drove a truck transporting fresh vegetables and other produce from the farm belt of New Jersey into the New York markets.

"At one desperate point, I took to rolling sleeping drunks down in the Bowery," Steven said. "Some of those bums had as much as five or ten dollars in their pockets, which they'd gotten from begging."

Like he'd done in the Middle West, he was so hungry one evening he went to the back of a Village diner named Louie's. He hoped to scrounge through the garage cans to find a half-finished steak. He did.

It was while he was chowing down that Louie himself emerged from the kitchen. Seeing this starving young man, he invited him in for a spaghetti dinner, with a veal steak.

That night Louie nicknamed Steven "Desperado," and made a deal with Steven. He'd let him run up a tab which Steven promised to pay when he got a job. He was a man of his word and paid Louie when he rolled some more drunks. "After meeting Louie, I knew I'd have food in my gut."

"I ate every night at Louie's," Steven said. "When my bill ran over twenty-five dollars, he'd cut off my credit until I settled it. On those lean days I could usually pick up a bitch in the Village who would take me back to her apartment. I'd fuck her in exchange for a home-cooked meal."

Years later, Steven recalled one of his greatest triumphs, when he walked into Louie's with Peter Lawford on one side, Frank Sinatra on the other. "Desperado!" Louie called out, welcoming him. "You're back and a big movie star at that." That night Steven left a hundred dollar tip.

"One day I figured out how to make easy money—and not by rolling drunks either," Steven said. "I went into this drugstore at 8th Street and 7th Avenue. I needed a nozzle for my shower. I picked one up to examine it. When a salesman walked up, he asked me if I was returning it. I claimed I was. 'It's defective,' I said. 'I want my money back.' He gave me six dollars in cash for the store's own nozzle. He did ask for a receipt, so I told him I'd lost it."

He tried this trick time and time again when he wanted money. Sometimes he didn't get away with it, but often he did. "The world was much more trusting back in those days," he said.

Wanting to buy a motorcycle, he hung out with gamblers in the Village. "A rough asshole crowd that would cut off your left nut if you crossed them," he later said. "But sometimes I made as much as $250 a week playing poker. President Truman taught me well."

With his new-found money, he purchased his first racing cycle, a much-used and rather battered K-Model Harley.

With his Harley, he competed in cycle runs on Saturday afternoon at Long Island City. Often he came back to the Village with prize money, usually around fifty dollars but on rare occasions, one hundred bucks.

Sometimes he'd be seen roaring around the Village shirtless on his Harley. Many gay boys whistled at him. One girlfriend remembered that he always complained about the attention his body received from homosexuals, but he never stopped riding that motorcycle and he never wore a shirt unless the weather was cold. "Frankly, I think he liked the attention he got from men. Somehow, it made him feel manly."

One night when he'd spent all his money, he wandered into the Candy Box, a bar on the fringe of the Village where he'd heard that a good-looking guy could "turn a quick buck from a queer," as he so colorfully put it to his friends, Darron and Casey, years later. Since gay bars were often raided, the Candy Box also allowed female hookers to work their trade. That way, the bar could conceal its gayness and appear heterosexual.

As he sat at the bar having a beer, a middle-aged man approached him. He offered to buy Steven another beer, and he accepted. The man identified himself as a salesman from Akron, Ohio, who was in New York on a business trip.

Steven decided to hit him up for twenty-five dollars since he was an out-of-towner and didn't know the going rate. The salesman didn't seem to find that too steep.

As he was negotiating with the man, Steven noticed a woman sitting on the other side of the bar. By the way she was dressed, he could tell she was a hooker, trying to pick up a trick, a heavyset man who sat across from her.

All of a sudden, he realized that he was staring at Jullian. He later told Darron and Casey, "It dawned on me. It was the lowest point of my life. No, that would come later. Here I was looking at my mother, the whore, trying to turn a trick. And here was the son of a whore. Both of us trying to pick up johns for the night. I wanted to die."

Steven's pride and joy was his K-model Harley.
He got whistled at by gay men whenever he rode
shirtless through the streets of Greenwich Village.

Chapter Three
The Making of a Tough Screen Guy

That was not the last time Steven encountered his mother. He continued to visit the Candy Box every time he needed money, and sometimes when he didn't. It could be speculated that he wanted to encounter his mother again. Greenwich Village was a much smaller place in those days, and nearly two months later he saw Jullian. She was sitting alone in a corner of the bar.

She'd put on weight, and her hair looked unwashed and matted. He told friends that he doubted if any man would want to pick up his mother and go to bed with her in her drunken condition. She was well past her prime, and her days as a workaday hooker were obviously coming to an end.

"She looked like she'd spent forty nights in a bar, as she got up and staggered past me in the barroom," Steven recalled. "She stopped and looked back at me. "Don't I know you from somewhere?" she asked.

"Get lost!" he told her.

"For Christ's sake, take my arm and get me to a cab," she said. "You owe me that much for giving birth to you."

Out on the sidewalk, he hailed a cab. Before she got in, she handed him a card which contained her phone number. "If you're ever to the Village again, give me a call sometime."

He watched as the taxi pulled out with her slumped over in the back seat. He didn't really plan to call, but, even so, he slipped the phone number in his pocket and headed for the Peacock Café. He needed "a bolt of java," as he put it. Seeing his mother was too painful.

He wanted to meet someone to take his mind off Jullian, and she appeared in the form of a rather beautiful, fresh-faced struggling actress named Betty Kaiser.

When he asked to join her table, she smiled and said, "It's a public place."

"I didn't want to intrude on your privacy," he said.

"What a line," she said. "Straight from an 1890 play. I know lines. I'm an actress."

"I'm sure I've seen you in something," he said.

"You've seen me in nothing, because I've been in nothing."

This rather testy exchange was the beginning of a hot affair. Before the night was over, Betty had confessed that she wanted to be like another Betty, or, as she was better known, Lauren Bacall. She told Steven that after she'd made it big on Broadway, Hollywood was sure to come calling on her.

By midnight Betty had agreed that he could come home to her coldwater flat, which was even more dismal than the one he occupied.

Betty herself didn't look like Bacall, more like Ann Blyth as she appeared in the 1945 *Mildred Pierce* with Joan Crawford. "The girl had the loveliest skin I'd ever seen on a white woman," Steven later recalled. "And she'd do everything I wanted."

"She wasn't much of a cook, but she made the world's greatest omelets," he remembered. "She had some secret, I didn't know what. She could make them with any ingredient. One day I asked for caviar. The poor thing went out and spent half of her paycheck buying me some caviar, but I didn't like the fishy taste."

"She was studying with Sanford Meisner, a famous acting coach back in those days," Steven said. "She begged me to come and take lessons with Meisner. He was almost as famous as Lee Strasberg of the Actors Studio. I kept resisting. Putting on makeup and playing make-believe didn't seem like a very macho thing to do."

For him to earn immediate money, she suggested that he join her brother, Peter Kaiser, in the emerging field of TV repair. It seemed that half of New Yorkers were buying TV sets to watch Milton Berle, and the number of breakdowns was enormous since these little boxes hadn't been perfected.

Sanford Meisner
was intrigued with Steve's
acting and also with his crotch

"With your knowledge of how things work, you'd be a genius at repairing these sets," Betty said.

The idea intrigued him, and he met with her brother, Peter, who hired him on the spot.

"I can't keep up with the demand for our services," Peter said. "Everybody in the city is buying a TV set, and half of them are fucking up."

Within a week, Steven had taken apart a TV set and figured exactly how it worked, or didn't work as the case might be.

He found that being a TV repairman provided an even better opportunity "to meet the chicks" than being a cobbler fitting sandals onto women in the Village. "It was the perfect setup.

Husband at work. Bored housewife at home, hot and horny, waiting for the fantasy repairman of her dreams. I was that man. I think in a few cases the women broke their sets just so I'd come calling again. The Mayor of New York should have given me a citation for services rendered to the public."

Betty had wanted Steven just for herself, but in those days, and throughout his life, he felt that he was too special to be selfishly shared with just one person. "I belong to the world," he once said. "Not me exactly, but my body. When God gives you an instrument like my body, he didn't mean for me to be selfish with it but to share it with others. I had at least a hundred affairs before Christmas of 1950 rolled around."

"I made pretty good money, at least by the standards of the early 50s, but I didn't spend it on women," he said. "They spent their money on me. I had other things to do with my dough. I wanted to save money to buy machines."

One day Betty came home to find Steven's mother, Jullian, passed out on her stoop. "She was completely drunk and wasted." Betty said. "I gave her ten dollars to make her go away. But she'd wait for hours and hours until Steven would come home so she could beg him for money to buy liquor. Sometimes he'd step right over her and shut the door in her face."

"He told me that he'd actually thought of killing 'the drunken slut,'" Betty said.

"If I ever hit it bigtime, and word got out that Jullian is my mother, it could destroy my career before it's even begun," he claimed.

Some nights, Steven showed up with money. "I've found a new scam," he said. "I go into restaurants and slip around very quickly and pick up the tips diners have left for the waiters."

***

Betty invited Steven to the movies to see *A Place in the Sun*, starring Montgomery Clift, the new acting sensation, the extraordinarily beautiful Elizabeth Taylor, then at her peak, and the rather dumpy Shelley Winters. Steven could hardly imagine at the time that one day he'd actually get to meet these screen images in the flesh.

He was overcome with the magnetic screen presence of Monty. Up to that moment, he never knew that

Montgomery Clift and **Elizabeth Taylor**
Doomed lovers, both on and off the screen

79

screen acting could be that realistic. He was so fascinated with Monty's acting that he returned the next day to see the film alone.

The following weekend Betty invited him to see *A Streetcar Named Desire* with Marlon Brando and Vivien Leigh. He'd never seen Brando act before, although he'd sat through Vivien Leigh's performance as Scarlett O'Hara in *Gone With the Wind*. Playing another Southern belle, Vivien was no Scarlett when she portrayed Blanche DuBois in *Streetcar*, a delicate, fluttering moth.

When Betty told Steven that Monty was going to address the students at the Sanford Meisner acting school, he was elated at the chance to meet his idol. After seeing Brando and Monty Clift on the screen, he took the subject of acting more seriously when Betty brought it up.

On the night Monty was to address the students, Steven sat with Betty in the third row, hoping to get a close-up look at the actor who had become his new idol. In many ways, he preferred Monty's acting to that of Brando's.

Monty did show up, but he was an hour late. The students had grown impatient, but no one left.

During his wait, Betty introduced Steven to Sanford Meisner. His reputation had already preceded him. He was one of the most respected and influential acting teachers of the 20th century, a rival of Stella Adler and Lee Strasberg.

Deep into a talk with Meisner, Steven was surprised when he attacked pure Method acting, claiming "actors are not guinea pigs to be manipulated." Steven was taken by Meisner's view of acting. "Keep it honest and simple," Meisner advised him. "Don't lay on complications, no frills. Just live truthfully under imaginary circumstances."

The teacher practically signed Steven on the spot. When Miesner went backstage to check on Monty, Betty told Steven "how lucky you are. He doesn't give many actors the time of day."

"But I'm not a fucking actor," he said. "I repair TVs. Besides, I'd never study under him."

"Why not?" she asked. "He's the best in the business."

"Didn't you notice?" he asked. "He hardly looked at my face. Kept staring all the time at my crotch. Maybe my jeans are too tight."

When Monty finally did come onstage, he was obviously drunk or drugged, but managed to pull himself together to share some insights into acting in the theater and how difficult it was to get a decent part.

At the end of the session, most of the actors filed out but Betty and Steven, along with a few others, lagged behind hoping to have a few words with Monty.

Monty virtually ignored Betty but paid close attention to Steven and seemed fascinated by him. He was extremely flattered to get such notice from a world-famous actor. He'd heard that every major producer in Hollywood wanted to star Monty in some script.

"What's your job in life?" Monty asked Steven.

For some reason, he blurted out, "I'm an actor too."

"Actually, he's a TV repairman," said Betty, bringing a moment of reality.

"That's great," Monty said. "My TV's on the blink. Could you come by tonight and fix it for me?"

"I sure could," Steven said.

Impulsively Monty invited Betty and Steven to dinner at this little Italian restaurant in the Village. Before dessert was served, Betty had excused herself, because Monty and Steven had talked to each other as if she didn't exist.

Monty could drink more than any man he'd ever known. He must have had an amazing tolerance for alcohol. Not only was he drinking, he was taking opiate-based "downs" with his vodka. He urged Steven to try some. Before midnight, when the waiter virtually kicked them out of the restaurant, Steven was experiencing the biggest high of his life.

On wobbly legs outside, Monty fell prostrate onto the sidewalk. Fumbling for Monty's wallet, Steven found his New York address printed on his license. Picking Monty up, he hailed a cab and almost had to pour the actor into the back seat.

At Monty's townhouse, he could not make it up the short steps, so Steven carried him. At the door, he searched into Monty's pockets until he located his keys. Finally, he managed to get him into the townhouse and into the living room where Monty collapsed on the sofa.

After checking out the living quarters, Steven carried Monty into his bedroom and stripped him down. At first Steven decided he should let Monty sleep it off, but then feared he might need medical attention during the night.

He pulled off his own clothes and crawled into bed with Monty. Shortly before dawn, he felt a movement and gradually woke up. He suddenly became aware that Monty was going down on him. At first he wanted to resist, but then rejected that idea. He closed his eyes and imagined that he was being serviced by the same lips that had kissed the stunning Elizabeth Taylor in *A Place in the Sun*. When his climax came, as he'd later tell his friends, he was thinking of

Monty Clift
"My television needs repairing."

Elizabeth and not Monty.

Somehow, after he'd climaxed, he fell asleep. When he woke up, the clock on the nightstand said two o'clock. It was in the afternoon. Monty was already up and in the kitchen walking around in his underwear preparing coffee.

Neither one mentioned the previous night. After breakfast, Monty told him he had an appointment but would be back around seven o'clock if Steven wanted to drop in. In the meantime, Steven could repair that TV set for him.

It took about an hour, but Steven got the set working again. Since he had time before meeting Monty again, he took a taxi to Greenwich Village where he was hours late for work. Betty had already called her brother Peter.

Steven encountered a very angry boss. Peter fired him on the spot. He also told him that Betty never wanted to see him again.

Out on the street, he seemed to comprehend what had happened to him. He'd lost his job and his girlfriend all in one afternoon.

Not knowing what to do, Steven didn't want to return to his apartment. He'd heard that for a man who wanted to work, jobs were plentiful. He headed east where he cut north along Third Avenue. After going twenty blocks, he saw a help wanted sign.

He went downstairs where an aging Hungarian man told him he wanted a boy who could assemble artificial flowers. The pay in this smelly little dark cellar was twenty-five dollars a week. Steven said he'd take it. He hated artificial flowers, but within an hour or so he learned to assemble them. He decided to stay on in this dump until he found something better.

That something better came within a week when Monty got him a job as a bartender in a dive on 10th Avenue where the actor went to get "wasted" once or twice a week.

Within a week, Steven had learned to mix most cocktails, and he was skilled at his work. Blake McQuire remembered hiring Steven. "I was a friend of Monty's and would do anything for him," McQuire recalled. "Even though McQueen had never tended bar, I hired him on the spot. He was a fast learner. He bragged to me that he could learn any manual job within two weeks, and I believe that was true."

"He not only was a great bartender, he was a hit with the ladies and nearly all the gay guys who dropped in," McQuire said. "In those days we catered mostly to out-of-work actors and actresses. Even though McQueen was Monty's boy, or so I thought at the time, I think he accepted an invitation or two to boogie. We got a lot of homos in those days, and Steven told me he hated queers, but I saw him go home with a few. But mostly he was a man for the ladies. I think he had his pick during the time he worked for me."

For the first time in his life, Steven felt he was somebody, and that he was going to become even more of a somebody as his life progressed. His mother may not have wanted him, but the rest of the world seemed to. After all, as a marine guard he'd played a wicked game of poker with the President of the United States, the man who'd ushered in the atomic age by ordering the dropping of two bombs on Japan.

And now through a chance meeting with the most sought-after movie star in Hollywood, Montgomery Clift had virtually adopted him.

His next goal was very clear, and he planned to keep it to himself. After seeing *A Place in the Sun*, he thought Elizabeth Taylor was the most desirable woman on the planet. He knew she visited regularly at Monty's, and he wanted to meet her. Because of close and personal encounters with the film actor, Steven knew that Monty didn't have what it took to satisfy a woman. But Steven knew *he* did.

His opportunity came when Monty told him he was hosting a party for about twenty-five friends and acquaintances. The guest of honor would be Elizabeth herself. Steven eagerly volunteered to tend bar for free, and Monty gladly accepted.

He was convinced of one thing as he told his buddies on 10th Avenue, "When that party takes place, and before the rooster crows, Steven McQueen, hometown boy from Slater, Missouri, will be plowing into Miss Taylor and showing her how a real man makes love."

***

In the Broadway play, *The Boy from Oz*, Hugh Jackman told audiences that whenever he read the biography of a movie star, he always skipped the first two chapters and shot to Chapter 3 when the subject of the biography meets Elizabeth Taylor.

It is now Chapter 3, and Steven had his eagerly anticipated meeting with Elizabeth Taylor herself, and, to him, she looked even lovelier than she did on screen.

Elizabeth stepped up to the bar and ordered a drink from him, without ever making eye contact. Monty was with her, and they were having an intense argument.

Monty didn't even bother to introduce him to Elizabeth. After Steven had made their drinks, both of them walked away without even thanking him. They continued their intense argument, and from what he gathered it was about why Monty didn't want to marry her.

"I'd marry the bitch," Steven later told his friends. "But she's so fucking stuck up she didn't think I was worthy of even a hello. I'll show her. Someday I'll be a much bigger movie star than she ever was."

***

Still sulking from Elizabeth's insult, Steven woke up one morning and realized that if he ever decided to become a big-time movie star, he'd have to learn how to act.

On an impulse, on June 25, 1951, he arrived at Sanford Meisner's ivy-covered studio, called The Neighborhood Playhouse. The cost of enrollment was steep for him, but he got some of the money from the G.I. Bill. "The rest I got from poker games and rolling drunks. A guy has to do what he has to do to raise tuition. Sometimes I raise my rent money by letting queers in the Village suck my dick for five or ten dollars. One pervert from uptown actually gave me a twenty, and I didn't even come."

"He had shaggy dog eyes," Meisner recalled. "He won me over from the moment I laid eyes on him. He was sexy but not in the menacing way Brando was or in the deep-hearted sensitive way Monty was. Steven was a jungle cat moving across the stage with panther-like grace."

Dripping wet, **Marlon Brando** appeared in *Truckline Cafe*. Steve eventually inherited the role.

As a student, Steven quickly became Meisner's favorite. When the acting teacher planned to stage a production of *Hamlet*, he wanted Steven for the lead. "I would have done it," Steven later said, "but there was no way in hell I was going to get in those green tights and show the outline of my dick to every faggot in Greenwich Village. It was bad enough that I was having to let Meisner suck me off at least once a week. I didn't want to go queer all the way."

When he turned down the role of *Hamlet*, he confessed to Meisner, "I think acting is for candy-assed guys, not a real man."

He told his acting coach that instead of acting, he was seriously considering learning how to lay tiles at $3.50 an hour.

Meisner planned a Christmas production of *Truckline Café*, which had starred Marlon Brando. Some critics even turned out when news spread that a "dynamite" actor was performing even better than Brando had himself, although clearly imitating the original.

Steven had learned to imitate Brando's voice to perfection. He stole both his style and his voice, but, to the astonishment of critic Mark Redcliffe, who'd seen both Brando and Steven in the same part, "McQueen did it better than Brando. I couldn't believe my eyes."

Word soon reached Brando himself, who showed up one night unannounced, finding a seat in the auditorium after the lights went out.

Backstage, Steven learned that Brando was in the audience. The ticket salesman in front had spotted him and sent word to the other actors. Steven later recalled, "I heard that Brando was in the house only minutes before curtain time. My first reaction was to throw up. I practically made my entrance that night with vomit on my mouth. My knees were shaking, but I gave the performance of my life. I wanted to show that fucker Brando that his competition had arrived in New York. Before the night was over, the conceited ass had to face reality—I was gonna become a bigger star than he ever was."

After the curtain went down, Brando came backstage to congratulate the actors, paying particular attention to Steven. "It's true what they say," Brando said. "You're better in the role than I was, and I was the best."

"That's bullshit, and you know it, but I love hearing it," Steven said.

Brando invited him to a neighborhood bar for a beer. Steven's initial resentment and hostility toward Brando—call it jealousy—faded under the star's mesmerizing charm.

Dominating the conversation, Brando brought up the subject of Jewish girls. "The town is crawling with them. They're better educated than I am, and most of them have apartments of their own. They're living in New York having a bohemian fling before retiring somewhere in Westchester to a sedate, rich life as some man's toy. In a few years their natural brunette coloring will be blonde, and you'll see them walking down Fifth Avenue in a mink coat. My suggestion to you is to specialize in Jewish girls. I can tell you're a Gentile like me. We're exotic specimens to these bitches. They'll treat us right and feed us well. In fact, it is a Jewish gal that taught me all I know about making love."

Steven promised he'd take that advice. He quickly switched the conversation to motorcycles, which occupied at least the following hour.

Before the bar closed down, Brando gave Steven some more advice. "After *Streetcar*, every actor on the stage is imitating Brando." He spoke of himself in the third person. "I have more imitators than Marilyn Monroe has lovers. One guy I know said I deliver something 'uncomfortable and dangerous' on the stage. Everybody's trying to get in my act."

Brando's advice to Steve: Target Jewish girls.

"You were good tonight but too close to the original," Brando claimed. "You've got to forget about me and find your own style. You have real sex appeal. I suspected every homo in the audience wanted to fuck your ass. I suspect you're a top. Am I right about that?"

"Does a bear shit in the woods?"

"I've got an idea," Brando said, standing up. "Let's ride our motorcycles all over New York City. The Bronx. Manhattan. Brooklyn, of course. Even Staten Island. Let's watch the dawn come up together."

When Steven told of meeting Brando to Casey and Darron, both men wanted to know what happened after the motorcycle ride. Steven suddenly clammed up. "If you guys don't mind, I prefer to keep that to myself. I tell you voyeurs too much anyway. There are some things that are sacred. Let's put it this way: After that night, Brando and I became secret buddies. Let's leave it at that."

***

Steven's next serious relationship came in the form of a raven-haired, brown-eyed dancer and actress who looked much like Steven's future wife, Neile Adams. She would later marry John Gilmore, the handsome actor and writer, who was a close buddy of James Dean and a future rival of Steven.

Nothing is known of Gena's background or even her maiden name. Eventually, after her breakup from Steven, she would marry John and become Gena Gilmore.

She lived with Steven for only a few short weeks, but quickly became his confidante, although much of what he discussed during pillow talk she found shocking.

John Gilmore:
Lover to James Dean,
rival to Steve McQueen

He was like no other man she'd ever met. Some of her revelations about Steven appeared in Gilmore's provocative, controversial memoirs, *Laid Bare*. She claimed that Steven stole food from markets, even if he had money to pay for his groceries. "He also borrowed money from anyone foolish enough to lend it to him, and he carted off anything that wasn't nailed down."

When Gena wanted Steven to become friends with Gilmore and introduced them, they became rival roosters instead of friends. Gilmore noticed the bitterness in Steven, who told him "he hated Jews, niggers, and wops."

"He said he hated me because I had blond hair and blue eyes, and chances were good that we'd both show up to audition for the same part," Gilmore said. "He really hated me when Gena left him and took up with me. I eventually married her."

But while Gena was still Steven's live-in mistress, he made one of his most shocking confessions to her, as exposed in Gilmore's memoirs.

"I'd suck anyone's cock, Jew or nigger—and I'd get fucked or fuck anyone to get a part in a show," Steven allegedly told Gena.

While he lived with her in the Village, she paid his bills. Partly because he insisted on unprotected sex, she eventually became pregnant with his child. He urged not marriage, but an abortion upon her. Regrettably, she had to pay for it herself. "It's your problem," he told her. "You take care of it."

She took a long time recovering from the abortion. Still bleeding, she went back to work as a waitress. "Chunks of coagulated blood and tissue fell out of me," she claimed.

The relationship came to an end when she caught Steven in bed with another actress he'd picked up. She kicked him out of her life, but he came back on occasion for sexual liaisons with her after he'd married Niele and Gena had married Gilmore.

***

After vowing he'd never call her, Steven reached into his wallet one night and dialed Jullian's number in the Village. He wanted her to be proud of him. When she came to the phone, she sounded drunk and hostile. That was not unusual for her.

He eagerly told her that he'd not only enrolled in Sanford Meisner's acting class, but had been given a key role in *Truckline Café*. "Brando did the part years before me. He came to see me act. He told me I was terrific. I'm gonna be a movie star one day. A big movie star. You've gotta come and see me in *Truckline Café*. I'll leave you a ticket at the box office tonight."

"Shit, kid, you couldn't act your way out of a paper bag," she said. "What are you trying to do? Become a full-time limp-wristed faggot?" She slammed down the phone.

As he would later tell Casey and Darron, "I don't think I've been so fucking enraged in my whole life. For the first time, I was convinced she hated me. She wanted me to fail. I could go to Hollywood and win nine Oscars, and still the bitch wouldn't be impressed."

He later told his friends something he claimed he'd never confided to anybody else on the planet. "There's something in every man's life he's ashamed of. Some dark deed we don't even want the Devil to know about. That dark deed was committed by me the night she slammed down the phone."

"I showed up at her apartment," he claimed. "She was in her robe. All my life she'd robbed me of my manhood. Her fucking boyfriend in Hollywood had turned me into a child whore. I wanted to show her I was a man. I wanted her to suffer from the abuse she'd dished out to me all my life. I went temporarily insane. I attacked my own mother."

Before his night with Casey and Darron ended, Steven provided no more details.

The next morning, he told his buddies, "Let's never speak about what I told you last night. Never again. We will never speak of it again. *Entiendo?*"

* * *

After *Truckline Café*, Steven decided to become a professional actor. "You have the whole day to yourself," he said. "All you have to do is show up at night, deliver a few lines, and collect a paycheck at the end of the week. Meisner got him a small role in a repertory company stage production on Second Avenue. The play was all in Yiddish, and he didn't even know what it was about.

The star was Molly Picon, the most famous female performer of Yiddish theater in her day. She had appeared in many films, including silent films. When she discovered that Steven didn't speak Yiddish and, therefore, gave his line no meaning, she demanded that the director fire him and "cast a nice Jewish boy instead."

"When the director translated my line for me—'nothing will help'—I decided that was true," Steven said. "The Picon bitch got me canned after only four nights. So, the shits didn't like the way I spoke Yiddish. Fuck 'em. The pay was only forty dollars a week. I could earn more than that tricking in just one night."

Molly Picon
"McQueen doesn't even speak Yiddish. Get a nice Jewish boy instead."

After his attack on Jullian, he never went back to the Candy Box. He'd discovered another bar in which to hang out. It was The White Horse Tavern.

Steven later recalled "that former longshoremen's bar became a place where I liked to hang my hat, except I didn't wear a hat," he said.

Anaïs Nin, the diarist, sitting at a table with James Baldwin, claimed that she remembered seeing Monty Clift come in one night with

88

Steve. "Baldwin was quite taken with McQueen," Nin remembered. "I didn't know who he was at the time. Baldwin even followed him to the men's room but was rebuffed, rather viciously I gathered."

"We were joined later that night by Jack Kerouac, who had entered the circle of my loved ones," Nin said. "Jack's eyes kept glancing at McQueen. He became so distracted by the young man's presence I felt jealous. Baldwin warned Jack, 'I think the guy is hopelessly straight or else he doesn't like black men.'"

"If blond beauty is so fucking straight, what in hell is he doing with Monty Clift?" Kerouac asked.

"I was in there on another night talking with some of the editors of *The Village Voice*," Nin recalled. "Their offices were nearby. I was told who McQueen was: a struggling out-of-work actor. New York was filled with such creatures in those days. That was the night Monty Clift introduced himself to Dylan Thomas, who had had more than his share of whisky. If I had been privy to the talk Monty and McQueen had with Dylan Thomas, I would have recorded every word in my diary. What a strange trio."

In later years, movie star Steve McQueen would claim a "great friendship" with the Welsh poet.

"He may have had only one drink with Dylan, although I'm not certain of that," Nin said.

Welsh poet **Dylan Thomas** drinking himself to death at the White Horse Tavern

New York's literati, left to right:
James Baldwin, Anaïs Nin, and **Jack Kerouac**
"If McQueen is straight, why's he with Monty?"

The poet tragically died in New York in 1953 at the age of thirty-nine. He literally drank himself to death at the White Horse Tavern.

"There is a footnote to my experiences at the White Horse Tavern," Nin said. "I wasn't there that night, but my friend, Jack Kerouac, was. Jack drank too much and got out of control that night, or so I heard. The manager kicked him out. Can you imagine my surprise when I learned who was with Jack that night? None other than Steven McQueen. At least McQueen and I have something in common. We both had Jack Kerouac for a lover. Perhaps I should meet with McQueen some night and compare notes."

The travel writer, Stanley Mills Haggart, who was a close friend of Gore Vidal at the time, remembered seeing Jack Kerouac talking with William Burroughs one night at the San Remo Restaurant in Greenwich Village.

"I was with an artist, Woody Parrish-Martin, at the time," Stanley said. "Kerouac was with a rather cute blond-haired boy who looked uncomfortable in this literary crowd. Woody told me that he was a young actor, Steven McQueen, and that he was the trick of Sanford Meisner."

"It seemed to me that McQueen was the trick of Kerouac that night," Stanley said. "Woody and I could hear the conversation going on. They were talking about non-virgin clubs opening throughout the Middle West. Boys were forming these clubs to deflower young virgins, and young virgins were joining to get deflowered. These clubs even extended as far south as Miami."

"I don't know what happened, but McQueen and Kerouac had a fight that night," Stanley said. "Gore came into the bar later. Jack was getting really drunk. Jack and Gore left the San Remo together heading for the Chelsea Hotel. Later I asked and got a blow-by-blow description from Gore about

The gossipy *avant-garde* evaluates Steve. Left to right:

Gore Vidal, **Woody Parrish-Martin**, and **Stanley Mills Haggart**

what happened that night. Kerouac was definitely bisexual."

Except for some random sightings, no source seems to know how Steven met Kerouac and exactly what was the nature of their relationship. Anaïs Nin claimed that Kerouac told her that he and McQueen had become lovers. According to Kerouac, McQueen was almost psychotic about anyone finding out. He said that one night in a bar he'd possessively put his arm around McQueen, and the young man stormed out of the bar in a rage. This rather harmless display of affection in public was more than McQueen could tolerate.

Contrary to Nin's impressions, other friends, enemies, or lovers have noted that Steven could be quite aggressive in his pursuit of both male and female companions for the night.

"He could talk big and come on strong, particularly with guys like Paul Newman, George Peppard, and Chuck Connors, all of whom he was soon to meet," said Sal Mineo. "But if anyone dared suggest he might have a gay streak in him, he'd beat the shit out of them. I'm speaking from personal experience."

***

When classes let out for spring break, Steven impulsively headed for the sun and sea of Miami Beach. He was accompanied by Fulton Bryant, a former Marine. He hated the name Fulton, so all his friends called him "Red," because of his thick carrot-colored hair. "I must have inspired Lucille Ball," he told his friends.

At first Steven had been somewhat reluctant to travel with him, claiming, "You're too fucking good looking. What gal is gonna go for me if she can get you?"

Red and Steven went to the outskirts of New York on the highway heading south. "My momma always told me, 'a pretty boy doesn't have to go hungry,'" Steven said. He then informed Red that he planned to hitchhike all the way to Florida. "Free gas. Free eats. Free motels. All you have to do is let some faggot suck on your dick at night."

History does not record Red's reaction to that plan. All we know is that he was spotted on Miami Beach hanging out with Steven at the Five O'Clock Club until their money ran out. For a place to stay, they slept with whatever girls they could pick up for the night.

All was going well until a minor tragedy struck. Red and Steven decided to go scuba diving in Biscayne Bay. Both of them had been trained in diving by the Marines. Reportedly, Steven gave chase to an exotic fish which eluded him. Resurfacing dangerously fast, he injured his left eardrum, which had already been badly damaged when he was a child.

Back in Miami, Steven went to a doctor to have his hearing tested. There he learned the bad news. In coming to the surface of the ocean that quickly, he'd punctured his left eardrum. Much to his dismay, the hearing in his left ear would be impaired for the rest of his life.

The doctor bill took all the cash both Steven and Red had. The next morning, both of the men went to a big hotel on the beach and applied for jobs as beach boys. The manager seemed quite impressed with them. He took them to his office in the rear and asked them to strip down and try on two tight-fitting bathing suits in red, white, and blue with stars.

"We put on quite a show for the faggot," Steven later claimed. "He must have liked the way we were hung because we both got the job. As I told Red when we set out on this fucking trip, 'a pretty boy doesn't have to go hungry.'"

"Both Red and I were busy all night after the sun went down," Steven said. "I think the manager hired us just to service all the horny broads in the hotel. We were given so many keys to so many rooms I thought we were going to wear out our peckers. I'd never plugged so many empty holes in my life."

One late afternoon the manager approached Steven and Red with a proposition. Steven later said, "I thought, 'Oh, shit, here it comes, the little queer wants us to sing for our supper.' It wasn't like that at all. He had something else in mind."

He asked Steven and Red if they'd like to participate in a male auction on a private island. A dozen well-built young men were going to be auctioned off at a private mansion to rich women who wanted their stud services for the weekend. If Steven and Red would participate, the manager claimed each of them would come off with one-thousand dollars by Monday morning.

A handsome and very young Steve in his secondhand British sports car, an MG-TC

"Sign us up," Steven said, volunteering without even asking Red if he wanted to sell his body. Apparently, Steven had figured out from their traveling together that Red had no objection to that.

"I got one over-the-hill Jewish broad that looked like Sophie Tucker on a bad night," Steven recalled. "Red fared much better. It wasn't so bad. Throughout my entire life, I had an occasional taste for old pussy. I never figured it out, but I did. In some ways the rich bitch I got reminded me of Jullian. She didn't let go of my pecker all weekend. But I wanted that thousand dollars real bad. And I got it too."

By Monday morning Steven and Red had their money, which was enough cash to buy a Greyhound bus ticket back to New York.

These secret male auctions were later exposed by *The Miami Herald*, the scandal even attracting nationwide press attention.

Steven knew exactly what he was going to do with his leftover cash. He had his eye on a British sports car, an MG-TC which carried a price tag of $750. He'd later tell biographers he earned the money by saving his salary from road shows and from poker winnings.

He preferred this myth to the truth.

***

On the streets of New York, Steven had three axles break on his MG-TC, and the spokes kept shredding out of his wheels. He didn't have money for repairs, so he agreed to work at a mechanic's shop on West 69th Street to earn extra money and also to repair his car. The shop repaired cars, but it specialized in working on motorcycles.

His newly acquired friends, Montgomery Clift and Marlon Brando, were out of New York making movies, so Steven fended for himself. He began to feel sorry for himself, feeling everybody else but him was enjoying spectacular success in the theater or the movies.

A stroke of luck and an opportunity emerged unexpectedly when he won an acting scholarship at the HB Studio. Uta Hagen, a respected member of the faculty there, had spotted Steven during an audition and became instrumental in getting him a scholarship to the prestigious school. He enrolled in 1952 and stayed there for two years, although he was rarely in class and often was gone for weeks at a time.

A student of Max Reinhardt, Herbert Berghof, a director and writer, had fled Nazi Germany in 1939, arriving in New York City. He'd founded the HB Studio in 1945 as a "home for artists" and a school for the dissem-

In love, **Herbert Berghof** became Steve's unexpected rival.

High priestess **Uta Hagen** taught Steve more than how to act

ination of his acting techniques. The location was in a loft at 23rd Street and 6th Avenue. Sometimes Berghof had difficulty in raising the modest rent. His former students had included such stars as Lee Grant, Eli Wallach, E.G. Marshall, and Jo Van Fleet.

Steven was mesmerized by Uta Hagen, who was eleven years his senior. From 1938 to 1948 she'd been married to the distinguished actor, José Ferrer. She would later marry Berghof himself.

When Steven first met Hagen, she'd won a Tony for her stage role in *The Country Girl*. In the same part, Grace Kelly would win an Oscar for her portrayal in the film version.

Maureen Stapleton, a friend of the author's, used to visit the HB Studio frequently to watch student productions. She'd been a student there herself. Steven told her he'd been "awed" by her performance as the Italian heroine in Tennessee Williams' *The Rose Tattoo*, which had brought her a Tony Award.

"Steve and I were drinking buddies for a while at the White Horse Tavern," Maureen said. "We talked about acting, and he shared his dreams with me. He called me a smokestack. I was always lighting up."

Maureen could consume almost a quart of vodka in a night, and she was a heavy smoker, dying of chronic obstructive pulmonary disease at the age of eighty.

Years later, Maureen claimed that Hagen fell for Steven. "Older woman. Cute young guy. Uta was one smart cookie, and she knew from the beginning the affair was doomed. Steven had a wandering eye. He even came on to dumpy me."

Actress **Maureen Stapleton**
"He was a cute young guy who came on to me."

A discreet woman, Hagen masked her affair, keeping it from Berghof, who was already falling in love with her. She also didn't want the studio's students to know that she was "mad about the boy."

"Uta told me that she and Steven had a glorious fling," Maureen claimed. "She found Steven's lovemaking genuine and from the heart. I can remember her exact words."

"He was loving and giving, even though somewhat inexperienced in the finer points of lovemaking," Hagen reportedly told Maureen. "He was not the skilled seducer that José Ferrer was, but I loved Steven's boyish awkwardness. He was my first experience with a boy with cornflower hair from the Middle West. His seduction of me put me more in touch with the spirit of the

American male, which I had never understood. American men are so different from Europeans."

There is something suspicious about this declaration. Although born in Germany, Hagen had actually been raised in Madison, Wisconsin, so she was already familiar with the American heartland before coming to New York. Later in life, she'd give acting lessons to both Al Pacino and Robert De Niro, whom movie star Steve came to regard as his rivals.

Steven never went on record about his romantic involvement with Hagen, so we don't know how he interpreted the experience. He did tell Maureen that, "Uta is the greatest actress in the world. Not only that, she's the world's best cook. Until I met her, I thought only men made great chefs." Hagen would one day write a book called *Love for Cooking*.

While a student of Hagen's, Steven carried around a little red notebook, in which he wrote down quotes by her he wanted to remember. His favorite was, "Nobody ever learns how to act. The search for human behavior is infinite. You'll never understand it all. I think that's wonderful."

Long after he'd gone to Hollywood, Steve the movie star read in the newspapers that Hagen had married Berghof in 1957. He sent her one hundred yellow roses, her favorite flower. He also sent her another hundred yellow roses when she opened on Broadway in *Who's Afraid of Virginia Woolf?* in 1963.

He would not be around when she reprised her signature role of Martha in *Who's Afraid of Virginia Woolf?* at the age of eighty, receiving wonderful reviews.

When Steve ran into Maureen in 1973, he made a final confession. "I should have married Uta. She once proposed marriage to me, but I was too hell set on playing the field. If I'd married her, I would have turned my career over to her. Let her select all my film properties. I would have become the greatest film actor of the 20th century and might never have made *The Blob*."

But Steven later dumped Hagen, and she was dismissive of him in the years ahead. "He had unrealistic goals. His range as an actor— if that's what he could be called—was very limited. He and Marilyn Monroe wanted to be known for their brains. What a difficult pursuit. I am not certain that either of them had the patience to read through a book, or even a play, in its entirety. On a personal note, I've had better lovers. In bed, Steven was just like he was on stage. Lacking technique." She sounded bitter.

She gave this appraisal to Shelley Winters, who dismissed her comments. Shelley herself was always jealous of Hagen's acting skills. "I think the bitch lied to me. What she didn't tell was that she'd fallen big time for Steven."

***

In David Dalton's book, *James Dean The Mutant King*, the author describes when Steve McQueen, then a star, encountered Martin Landau at a Hollywood party. According to the account, when McQueen met Landau, he said, "Oh, sure, we've met before. I remember the first time I saw you, though you may not remember me. You came into a garage on West 69th Street on the back of a motorcycle Jimmy Dean was driving. I was the mechanic."

Landau, on the Larry King Show, once maintained that his friend, James Dean, was not gay, as if anybody would really know about a person's sexual preferences unless you followed someone around for 24 hours a day with a video camera.

Rogers Brackett, who was Dean's mentor, sugar daddy, confidant, father figure, and lover, told a very different story. Even though it made Brackett jealous, Dean insisted on describing his other love affairs to him during pillow talk.

"Jimmy was immediately intrigued by McQueen," Brackett claimed. "Sometime during that afternoon, Dean slipped McQueen a piece of paper. It merely said CALL ME and listed his phone number, which was actually my number because Jimmy was living with me at the time."

"Jimmy was very gay, but I gathered that McQueen was not," Brackett said. "From what I heard, he was crazy for the girls but liked to sleep with a man on occasion. I wouldn't call McQueen gay, perhaps bisexual, but if such

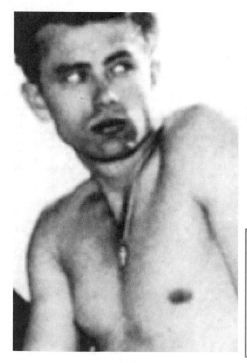

Left to right:
James Dean bares it all for TV producer
Rogers Brackett.

"It was a father/son incest thing."

stars as Monty Clift or Marlon Brando rang him up, McQueen seemed ready, willing, and able to oblige."

"Amazingly, Dean was carrying on affairs with both Paul Newman and McQueen around the same time," Brackett claimed, "and neither of them knew it, although I think they wised up pretty soon. Both Newman and Jimmy were hip about closet relationships in those days."

Paul Darlow, a friend of Dean's, told author Christopher Sandford about an encounter he'd witnessed at Jerry's Bar in New York in 1954.

Dean asked Steven "to do my hair," and Steven obliged. "He patiently back-combed the famous coif, thick and shiny as a mink's, breathing or perhaps lightly chuckling down the back of Dean's neck," Darlow claimed. An oddity about that story is that Dean carried a hairbrush into the bar.

Uta Hagen once invited actor Karl Malden to see a student performance at the HB Studio and give the actors a critique.

"I arrived late and sat in the rear," Malden told the author. "I had already met McQueen and Dean, and I suspected both of them were involved with Marlon. Dean and McQueen weren't interested in watching the play—Ibsen, if I remember—but in each other. They engaged in old-fashioned necking throughout the production. Dean giggled, McQueen was a silent lover. A lot of actors back in those days referred to Dean and McQueen as swishes. I didn't condemn their behavior at all except in one regard. They were invited to watch a play and take it seriously. Those commando tactics they were engaged in could wait for later. At the end of the play, I stood up and advised those boys to 'get a room.'"

Brackett claimed that Dean's seduction of Steven began when he had to fly to Chicago to shoot a commercial for one of his advertising accounts. "While I was away, they used my bed, and Jimmy later told me all about it. Jimmy told me that McQueen wasn't such a great lay but expected him to 'do all the work.' I would have suspected that. If McQueen had been a hustler, and I think he'd done some of that in his life, I'd call him 'gay for pay.'"

Nonetheless, Steven came to idolize Dean and told many of his friends that "James Dean is the greatest actor on the planet, even better than Monty Clift and Marlon Brando." As an homage to Dean, Steven practically stole the actor's persona for his appearance in the film, *The Blob*.

At the Blue Ribbon Café, an actors' hangout, Mildred Sacker came there every day to sip coffee and catch up on information about any auditions that might be occurring on Broadway. "I remember James Dean and the guy who became Steve McQueen coming in often. They never talked to anyone else but sat in the corner with eyes only for each other. McQueen hung onto Dean's every pronouncement. It was clear that McQueen idolized Dean. All the girls back then—mostly out-of-work actresses—thought both Dean and McQueen were gorgeous. But we never flirted with them. We just assumed they were two homos with eyes only for each other."

Many older men still talk about spotting Steven and Dean, both shirtless, roaring their motorcycles through the streets of Greenwich Village, weaving in and out of traffic. "They were hell raisers, wild kids," said Samuel Miller, who lived in an apartment building near Steven's. "On those motorcycles, they were speeding. I don't know how fast they were going. To me, both of them seemed to defy death. They liked to take chances. But they were a sight to be seen. I only wish the two of them on their motorcycles could have been caught on camera. Such scrumptious testosterone."

Biographer Penina Spiegel explained why Steven was called "The Shadow," because of his stalking of Dean. "They shared a certain sulky arrogance, a self-absorbed moodiness, and an intense sexual appeal. Yet, while Jimmy collected jobs and awards, Steve was still struggling, going nowhere," she said.

Not just Spiegel, but others noted how Steven followed Dean around like a puppy dog trailing its master. Steven tried to emulate Dean in almost anything he did. At the café they frequented, he would order what Dean ordered. Steven used to drink his coffee with cream. He took to drinking it black like Dean. "Steven would copy Dean's reading of a paper, how he held the paper, how he turned the pages," Spiegel claimed.

Arthur Kennedy starred with Dean in his Broadway debut in the play, *See the Jaguar*. Dean appeared on stage locked in a cage. The play ran for only five performances, and Steven was there every night.

"Dean was a real hothead," Kennedy said. "When he got into a fight with another actor, he pulled a knife on him. I intervened before Dean seriously injured the poor guy. I took Dean for a walk and told him that violence would not be tolerated."

Actor **Arthur Kennedy**: Privy to details about Steve's relationship with James Dean

"In a nearby park, he practically broke down and cried," Kennedy said. "He talked very openly to me about his homosexuality and the fear of exposure and what it might do to his career. He also claimed he was frustrated in his relationship with McQueen. He said that McQueen refused to let him fuck him, and that was driving him crazy. He confessed that he was considering getting McQueen high one day, tying him up, and then raping him. Of course, I don't know if he carried through on that threat or not."

"I hardly knew McQueen but found him very hostile," Kennedy said. "He reminded me of an aging juvenile delinquent. I'd heard awful stories about him—reform school, rolling drunks, even stealing. I thought he was a very unsavory character and could only do Dean harm. I once told Dean to drop McQueen. 'Nothing good will come out of this friendship,' I warned. Dean was defiant. 'I don't drop my acolytes until I'm finished with them. When I accomplish what I want with Steven, I'll drop him, but not before.'"

Kennedy said he asked Dean, "What do you possibly want from McQueen? He's a bit rough around the edges. Must have made it at least to the eighth grade."

"Don't put him down," Dean said. "He's got some good points. He's like a wild stallion. He needs to be broken in. I'm the man for the job."

"Dean never explained to me what 'breaking in' meant, but I had my own idea what that involved. After that talk, I began to feel that McQueen had more to fear from Dean than vice versa."

"Amazingly I got to know McQueen a lot better many years later when we both starred in *Nevada Smith*," Kennedy said. "He was the biggest star in the world then. At the peak of his career. I had totally misjudged this juvenile delinquent. It's incredible how far you can climb in America if you get the breaks. I ended up with the greatest respect for him. Of course, he had the morals of an alley cat but this was part of his macho charm."

***

Even though Steven worked on his British sports car, the upkeep proved too costly, and he was forced to sell it. He purchased a used motorcycle from the garage itself, deducting the payments from his paycheck at the end of every week.

With the coming of summer, Steven, through the intervention of Uta Hagen, landed a summer stock role in *Peg O' My Heart*, starring Margaret O'Brien, the former child star at MGM.

Margaret was seven years younger than Steven, but she was fairly grown up. He had seen her play "Tootie" in *Meet Me in St. Louis* opposite Judy Garland. Her short heyday was the 1940s, especially the war years. Roles for "America's favorite sweetheart" had dried up, and she was now taking road work.

Former child star
Margaret O'Brien
Steve never got around to her deflowering.

"My attempt to play adolescent roles was a bit brief," she said to Steven. "Did you see *Her First Romance*"?

99

Steven admitted that he hadn't.

"Neither did anybody else," she said.

"During the run of the play, I planned to get around to fucking her, but I never did," Steven later said. "Too bad. She missed out on the best."

He played his minor role in a small theater company formed by Paul Crabtree in Fayetteville, New York.

"I didn't attract raves in this turkey," Steven said. "When one of the jealous actors in the cast told me I stunk, he lost two front teeth for his theatrical critique."

"The actor didn't deserve my fist," Steven said. "He was right. I forgot my lines. I was shaking like a leaf in the wind." His self-assessment was odd for a star who one day would be called "the King of Cool."

In spite of his lackluster performance with Margaret O'Brien, Steven was hired to perform in the Rochester Stock Company's production of *The Member of the Wedding*. This play by Carson McCullers, with a little help from Tennessee Williams, had been the hit of Broadway.

The play's big draw on the road was Ethel Waters, who was hailed as "The Blackbird of the Blues." She was also known for her acting talent.

"She was my kind of woman," Steven said, "and I don't mean sexually. She'd forgotten more about acting than I would ever learn."

Waters, of course, was the first black superstar, opening theatrical doors for other performers. Married at thirteen, she escaped her abusive husband and worked as a chambermaid for $4.75 a week.

In the play on Broadway, Waters had won the New York Drama Critics Award for her performance in *The Member of the Wedding*.

When Steven met her, her brilliant career was fading. She told him that her paycheck was being "grabbed up" by the IRS. She also complained that her health was declining. "But she gave it her all every night," he said. "I often hung out with her and listened to her fabulous stories. One night at this seedy bar, she sang 'Stormy Weather' just for me. She'd been a sensation when she'd sung that in Harlem back in '33."

Ethel Waters
She taught Steve the
hip shimmy shake.

As surprising as it seemed, Steven had a lot in common with Waters, and not just the childhood rape both of them had endured. She once told him, 'No one raised me; I just ran wild.'"

"My life story, too." he said.

She always called Steven "Sugar," and even taught him the "hip shimmy shake."

"She was my Sweet Mama Stringbean, and I loved her dearly," he said. "When we had to say good-bye, I gave her a big, gooey wet one."

Waters backed away in surprise but was obviously thrilled at the kiss. "Listen, white boy, if it was still 1910 I'd have those blue jeans off you before you could say Possum Rag."

Waters and Steven departed the play as friends, and he kept in touch with her over the years, even when she spent her last months touring with the evangelist Billy Graham.

Waters died in 1977 but when Steven faced death himself only three years later, he remembered all the fine praise Waters had heaped upon the evangelist and sent for Graham in his darkest hour.

***

Upon Steven's return to New York, a reunion of sorts occurred between Jullian and him. The violence that had taken place between them was never to be spoken of again.

After she finally reached him, he went to Bellevue Hospital where he helped to discharge her from the ward where she had been treated for acute alcoholism. No words passed between them as he took her arm and guided her through Gramercy Park and along Irving Place. He shuddered when she asked to stop in at the landmark Pete's Tavern where she ordered a beer. He had one with her. A stony silence had emerged between them.

Back in her small apartment, she told him that her rent was three months in arrears and asked him to pay it. Since he'd saved some money from his $175-a-week paycheck on the road, he agreed to do it.

As he'd later tell his close friends, "She looked up at me with the most mournful expression on her face. It was pathetic, really. With tears falling down, she told me that, 'I'm too old to work any more. Men no longer find me desirable. On a few occasions, I've been able to find a black man wanting a blond. But I haven't had a white boyfriend in months.'"

He wanted to blot out her words. After he went grocery shopping for her, he returned to the apartment and put the perishables in the refrigerator. "I checked on her in the bedroom. She was snoring, her mouth open like some gaping hole. She looked grotesque. The story was all but written for Jullian. I expected her to die that winter."

"Amazingly, she lived for years to come, but from then on, it was all downhill," he said. "In the future, I would pay her bills, but I didn't want to see her. It was too painful. All my life, especially as a kid, I'd wanted her to love me. All of a sudden, I realized I'd changed. I didn't really need or want her love anymore."

"I was ashamed of my own mother," he said. "I was determined to make something out of myself. Jullian used to tell people that I'd end up in prison serving a life sentence. I left that stinking apartment that day determined to show the bitch."

With winter coming on and in need of money, Steven took one of the worst jobs of his life. He worked the docks in Hoboken, New Jersey, for three long months. His job was to unload freight from cargo ships along the Hudson.

"The wind off the Hudson just cut through my body like a knife," he later said. "There was also this foreman who found out I was an actor."

When the foreman learned that, he seemed determined to give Steven no peace. He taunted him daily. "You fucking pansy actor," he shouted at Steven one day. "What makes a sissy boy like you think you can handle freight like a tough bastard of a longshoreman? I thought all you actors do all night is suck some producer's dick."

The taunts were unrelenting, but Steven needed the job, and he stuck it out until he could take it no more. One afternoon that foreman grabbed his crotch. "Get your ass over here McQueen and suck my dick. I know you've been panting for it. C'mon, you fucking bitch. You can't load freight. You must be good for something, you stinking queer."

Steven always had a low boiling point. That day he could take it no more. With all the power in his body, he slugged the foreman. He walked off the job and out the gates, never to return to Hoboken again.

***

He'd fully decided that there were ways to make money in this world other than cleaning out latrines on rusty tankers, hustling condoms and towels to the patrons of whorehouses, lugging cargo at a waterfront, and hauling out antique radiators from condemned buildings.

The next morning Steven woke up and counted the money in his battered old wallet that he had left over from his days of rolling drunks. He counted out exactly eight dollars, all the money he had left in the world. It was plenty of money to have a spaghetti dinner at Downey's, but he had to make some real dough and soon.

That night Steven found a substitute lover/mother when he dropped in to

Downey's Restaurant, an actors' hangout called the poor man's Sardi's. He'd been there several times before, always ordering the same dish, a plate of spaghetti and meatballs.

"It was the cheapest thing on the menu, and one of the waitresses thought I was cute," he said. "She always slipped me a second helping. In those days the kitchen turned out this awful salad of iceberg lettuce and grated carrots with some pussy pink bottled dressing. Many customers left their salad ungrazed. I was pretty brazen. I'd go over to a table and asked if they were going to eat that salad. Most of the time they said no and gave it to me. I think they were so shocked they gave it to me even if they wanted it. I'm sure they figured I was an out-of-work actor starving to death. A table one night even sent me a free bottle of wine."

Momentarily between boyfriends, Shelley Winters arrived alone at Downey's one night. She made quite an entrance in a fake fur. Steven looked up but didn't recognize her at first. He'd seen only one of her movies, *A Place in the Sun*, playing a dumpy girlfriend that Monty Clift drowns to get to the very glamorous Elizabeth Taylor.

On this night, Shelley had applied the makeup and had her blonde hair styled. She was clearly the most glamorous actress in the room— not the most beautiful, but the most ostentatious. She was on a manhunt.

Seeing every table full, she walked over to Steven's table where he sat eating that second helping of spaghetti. "Mind if I join you?"

"Miss Winters," he said, standing up. "I'd be honored."

She looked him over carefully. "I think I've heard of you. You're Steven McQueen. Marlon told me about you. Said you had a most respectable dick and knew how to use it."

He felt mortified—first, because Marlon Brando was going around town revealing his secrets, and, second, because he'd never known a woman who talked in such a brazen fashion, even though he was the son of a prostitute.

Steven had never met a woman like Shelley before, and he didn't know they made movie stars like her. She was wise cracking and zany one minute, suddenly seri-

Shelley Winters
during her bombshell period.

"I came to New York to get fucked."

103

ous the next moment, especially when she almost cried telling him that "no one loves me any more."

"I've just come from California," she said. "Christ, I have to go to New York to get fucked. All the cute fellows out there on the coast are fucking each other."

"Did you know when I was a teen, I worked at the five-and-dime," she said. "Now, look at me. Big-time movie star. The press calls me a blonde bombshell."

When she brought up Brando again, Steven became defensive. "I hope he didn't give you the wrong idea. I'm a pussy man myself. I don't go in for that queer stuff."

"Oh, honey," she said, leaning over the table and giving him a soft kiss on the lips. "There doesn't have to be any pretense with us. You're an actor, darling. All actors, at least at some point in their lives, do it with each other. It's written in the book."

"What fucking book are you talking about?" he asked.

"Oh, I don't know," she said. "There must be a book somewhere with someone writing shit down."

It was at this point that he came to realize she might possibly be "a nut job," as he'd later put it, but he adored this woman. He wanted to be with her. He'd known more beautiful women in his past, and would know some of Hollywood's most spectacular bombshells, blonde or otherwise, in the future. But in Shelley he found he didn't have to indulge in macho posturing. He liked the way she didn't judge men and seemed to understand them.

Burt Lancaster:
In and out of the boudoir, as spied upon through the keyhole

That the night was going to end with his seduction of Shelley seemed an inevitable conclusion. Or, he wondered, would it be her seduction of him?

The evening did not go as planned. "It was like a Max Sennett comedy," he said.

Shelley wasted no time getting out of her clothes after taking him back to her hotel suite. He was soon out of his shirt and blue jeans and was mounting her when there came a loud pounding on the door. A man's voice was yelling, "SHELLEY! SHELLEY! OPEN UP!"

"Oh, my God," she said, shoving him aside and grabbing her nightgown. "It's Burt. The bastard's back. Hide in the closet."

She promised him she'd slip him a bottle of wine, and he could oversee the action. "We'll take up where we left off when Burt leaves. He never stays long. I'll keep the music loud."

True to her word, she slipped him that bottle of wine when Burt was in the bathroom. Through the louvered panels, he got to see the show of his young life: Burt Lancaster stripping down and mounting Shelley as he'd so recently done. The world-famous movie star had a great body but looked rather small where it counted.

Steven produced an erection while overseeing the action. As Shelley had predicted, Burt couldn't stay long. Putting on his pants, he made excuses and mumbled something about calling Shelley when he got back to the coast.

After he'd gone, she opened the closet door. "If you don't mind sloppy seconds, let's finish where we left off."

"I love sloppy seconds," he said, emerging nude and fully erect from the closet.

That evening with Shelley marked the beginning of many a night with her. She became his Mother Confessor. For different reasons of their own, they agreed to keep their relationship a secret. He would come to like his clandestine involvement with her. It made the friendship more exciting.

The next morning, as she made coffee for him, she seemed to take charge of his life. "You can forget all this Sandy Meisner crap. And, after me, I'm sure you're tired of fucking Uta Hagen. I want to take you to the Actors Studio this morning. You've got to meet Lee Strasberg. If you listen to him, he can make a big star out of you. Maybe even bigger than Brando."

"No one can be bigger than Brando," he said.

Actually Shelley had hit upon his secret dream. He did indeed want to be bigger than Brando.

"As you well know, sugar," she said. "Your dick's bigger than Marlon's, and certainly bigger than Burt's. So you're halfway there. You'll go over big in Hollywood if you fuck the right people. I did."

Later that day, Shelley not only introduced him to Lee Strasberg, but got him an audition. She selected a scene from the play (later a movie) called *Golden Boy*. Out of two thousand aspirant actors, he was one of the five selected to join the Actors Studio.

Strasberg told him, "You're a natural. You have potential."

Steven later told Shelley that "potential doesn't pay my bills."

Knowing he needed work, she intervened through

Lee Strasberg
"Potential doesn't pay the rent."

some unknown friend of hers and secured Steven his first major recognition as an actor. He appeared in a Studio One hour-long drama, *The Chivington Raid*, which aired on March 27, 1955. One TV reviewer called him, "A future Marlon Brando in the making." That same reviewer had used the exact appraisal to describe Paul Newman in another teleplay.

Other Studio One productions would follow in 1957 and 1958 in dramas called everything from *West Point* to *Deep Water*.

Steven felt that he was on his way to stardom, except that it would take much longer than he'd ever dreamed.

***

When Monty returned to New York, he contacted Steven and asked him for dinner. He was returning to the stage in *The Sea Gull* and claimed that he was going to take a long sabbatical from the screen. For a major star like he was at the time, this was almost unheard of.

Although he'd been pleased with his performance in *From Here to Eternity*, with Burt Lancaster and Frank Sinatra, he said he absolutely hated watching himself perform with Jennifer Jones in Vittorio de Sica's *Indiscretion of an American Wife*. "It's little more than an extended dialogue between Jones and me at a rail terminal," he said.

Monty seemed to have moved even deeper into drugs and drink. He was still wallowing in his depression over the loss of the 1953 Oscar to William Holden who won it for his performance in *Stalag 17*. "Everybody claimed I was the leading candidate for my role as Prewitt in *From Here to Eternity*," he said. "But since Burt Lancaster was also nominated for Best Actor in the same

Greta Garbo:
enigmatic, as always,
but this time
praising bartenders

picture, we gave the fucking Oscar to Holden. The goddamn thing belonged to me. It was my turn." He seemed very bitter.

That night in his bedroom, Monty didn't want sex. He wanted to be held. "The furies are riding high on me tonight," he confided to Steven. "They're gonna get me sooner than later—I just know it."

Heavily drugged, he slept throughout most of the night.

Around noon of the following morning, Monty came into his kitchen where Steven very slowly and methodically was reading a script which a friend had sent him.

Unlike the previous evening, Monty seemed high-strung and nervous. He'd obviously popped some pills. Impulsively he announced that he'd decided to throw a party that night, and he wanted Steven to be bartender once again. He agreed, hoping he'd have another encounter with Elizabeth Taylor.

"This time just for the hell of it, I'm going to invite the *demimonde*," Monty said.

Steven didn't know what that meant, but he learned fast when the guests started to pour through the door. He was surprised that so many famous people had nowhere else to go that night and were willing to accept an invitation on a moment's notice. Monty later explained that many of the guests cancelled other plans just to attend his party. "I'm hot," Monty told him. "The hottest property in Hollywood."

Instead of Elizabeth Taylor, Monty spent most of the evening walking around with Mira Rostova at his side. Steven was told that she was his acting coach. "You have Uta Hagen, I have Mira," Monty told him.

Steven had a hard time mixing drinks, as he spent most of the evening figuring out how many famous faces he could recognize. Even Frank Sinatra put in a brief appearance with some blonde showgirl, but had to leave early.

Rock Hudson arrived unaccompanied, and spent more time talking with Steven than anybody else.

Steven definitely felt that Rock was coming on to him. Even so, he exchanged phone numbers with Rock. After all, he was a big star. Rock virtually made him promise to call when he got to Hollywood. "I might get you a part in my next picture," he promised.

The appearance of the mysterious Greta Garbo caused a hush to fall over the party, as all heads turned in her direction. Like Rock, she too had arrived

at the party unaccompanied. At the time, Steven was not aware that she was a close friend of Monty's.

She did stop by for a glass of white wine. "What do you do, young man?" she asked him. "Other than pour drinks. An actor, no doubt."

"No, I'm just a lowly bartender," he said, not willing

The most famous transsexual of the 1950s, **Christine Jorgensen** (left), is escorted by *enfant terrible* **Truman Capote.**

It was a set-up for Steve.

107

to admit he was an out-of-work actor.

"Bartenders are not lowly creatures," she said. "Some people consider them God's chosen." After that pronouncement she walked away.

Among the last guests to arrive were Truman Capote and a blonde. He didn't know who the woman was until Capote introduced her. She was the notorious Christine Jorgensen, among the most famous women in the world and America's No. 1 topic of speculation. She'd once been a G.I. named George until she'd had a sex change in Denmark.

Obviously very drunk, Capote was very flirtatious with Steven, who gave him no encouragement. He was much too effeminate for Steven to be seen in his company.

But Capote, years later, would remember this chance encounter with the young actor. When he sold his best-selling novel, *Breakfast at Tiffany's*, to the movies, he requested that the lead roles go to Marilyn Monroe and the emerging actor Steve McQueen.

As midnight neared, nearly all the guests had left except Mira who sat possessively with a drunk Monty. Rock Hudson was still there too, having spent the rest of the night talking to Capote.

At one point Capote approached Steven. "Rock has agreed to let me go back to his hotel tonight to suck his cock," Capote confided to Steven. "He was hard to convince to throw me a mercy fuck. But when I told him that Errol Flynn had let me do that to him, he agreed. Which brings up a final point. Would you escort Christine back to her hotel?"

"If you wish, and if she agrees, it would be an honor," Steven said. "That is, if escort her back is all that's involved."

Capote smiled lasciviously. "That's up to the two of you." He looked Steven up and down. "Out of the corner of my eye, I've been studying you all evening. Please give me your phone number. It's not what you think. Although that would be a wish fulfillment of mine. It's strictly professional. I have a friend who's casting a play. There's a part in it that would be ideal for you. Melvyn Douglas is the star."

"I don't know who that is."

"Oh, you young kids," Capote said. "He was Garbo's leading man."

"What's the play called?" Steven asked.

"*Time Out for Ginger,*" Capote said.

"It's a Broadway comedy, sort of."

Steven scribbled his number down on a piece of paper. "I'll call you tomorrow," Capote promised. He tottered over to Christine and said something to her. She looked over at Steven and smiled.

After everybody except Christine and Mira had departed, Monty slipped Steven a hundred dollar bill, gave him a kiss on the mouth, and promised that he'd call.

Suddenly Christine was by Steven's side. She linked her arm with his. "That darling Truman has told me that you are to be my escort for tonight. I'm thrilled."

He found her strangely attractive and immaculately groomed. She was more lady than many he'd dated. He wanted to know so many things about her and had so many questions to ask, but he didn't know how to go about it.

Out on the sidewalk, he hailed a taxi for them. Before she stepped into the back seat, she turned to him and took his hand. "To get that bewildered look off your face, I'll answer the question that's foremost on your mind. Yes, I'm a real woman."

***

Despite the presence of other movie stars dining that night at the Russian Tea Room, Christine Jorgensen was the cause of the greatest number of turned heads.

The coat check girl had to lend Steven a jacket for the evening. Over caviar, which he tasted and didn't like, Christine confessed that she was tired of hearing all those Christine Jorgensen jokes.

In spite of the harassment, it was evident to Steven that she was clearly basking in her new-found celebrity. It also meant professional bookings in night clubs and guest appearances on TV.

"Not just Truman Capote, but everybody is inviting me to their parties, even Samuel Goldwyn. Of course, Milton Berle invited me, and even put my hand down there to feel the mammoth size of it. Danny Kaye invited me to meet Laurence Olivier. I was seen lunching with Elsa Maxwell. But an invitation from Dr. and Mrs. Ralph Bunche—I couldn't believe it."

"It seems they're treating you like some freak," he told her. "I don't like that. Not at all. I'll never treat you like that."

One obnoxious drunk stopped at their table. "By George," he said. "It's Christine!"

"I get that all the time," she said when he staggered off. "G.I. George becomes Christine. I should be used to it by now."

"If one ever gets used to such crap," he said.

"You seem very *simpatico*," she said. "I don't find that in many men I meet. Most men are only thinking of what I gave up in Copenhagen, not what I have now. Not the woman I've become."

"You're a fine and brave woman as far as I'm concerned," he said. "And let's leave it at that, and talk about something else."

At this point Steven looked up and was astonished to see Porfirio Rubirosa standing beside their table. He hadn't seen his benefactor since he'd left Ciudad Trujillo. With him was a fading movie star Steven recognized at once. It was Veronica Lake, the famous peek-a-boo blonde of World War II movies. Steven had seen her appear opposite Claudette Colbert in *So Proudly We Hail*. Thanks partly to his suave manners and continental charm, Rubi was invited by Christine to join them at table. Nothing embarrassing or untoward popped up in their conversation. But Broadway gossip columnist Leonard Lyons spotted the table and wrote in his morning column that Rubi, the famous playboy of the Western World, was dating Christine Jorgensen.

"Serving as chaperone was Rubi's old flame, Veronica Lake, who was accompanied by some unknown actor," Lyons wrote. Steven wasn't that concerned that the columnist got their dates mixed up, but he asked his friends, "How did the shithead know I was an actor?"

Before Rubi departed, he invited Christine and Steven to join him at a party he was throwing the following evening. "It's formal," Rubi said.

When he had to go to the men's room, Rubi asked Steven to accompany him. "Stand next to me and shield me from the voyeurs. Every time I try to use the urinal, there's practically a stampede of men wanting to get a look at it."

In the men's room, as Steven shielded Rubi from view, he said, "I don't have a dinner jacket."

"No problem," Rubi said. "Drop by my suite at the Plaza around three o'clock tomorrow afternoon. I'll have my tailor fit you into one of my tuxedos."

Back at the table, Rubi kissed Christine and Steven on both of their cheeks, before disappearing into the night to pound Veronica. At the conclusion of the meal, Christine attempted to pay for the dinner, only to discover to her delight that Rubi had generously taken care of it. Feeling romantic and making it evident, she invited Steven back to her hotel suite. At first he was tempted to run, but his curiosity won out.

He would later give Shelley Winters, his newly minted friend, only the barest details of how that evening concluded.

"What was it like fucking her?" Shelley bluntly demanded to know. "What did it look like?"

"I'm no gynecologist," he said. "The room was dark. It was a hole like any

110

other. The sensation was exactly the same. My pecker could tell no difference between the real thing and what she had had surgically created."

"Sounds to me like a fake pussy, though," Shelley said. "There couldn't be that much sensation for her. Not like the real thing."

"I like her," he said. "I really do. I'm sort of looking forward to taking her out tonight."

***

Paid for by the Dominican Republic, Rubi's party was Steven's first big social event. He sort of liked the look of being in a tuxedo, a first for him. Rubi's tailors had hastily made it a perfect fit. Even Rubi himself approved. "You're so handsome in my tux that I'm tempted to fuck you myself."

"Don't even think about it," Steven said. "I'd be in a wheelchair for the rest of my life."

Before he left Steven's suite to pick up Veronica, the entrepreneurial Rubi proposed a business scheme, a clever way for Steven to make money between acting jobs.

He asked Steven to come into his bedroom where he produced a black-and-white eight-by-ten photograph of himself posing in a mammoth jockstrap.

"Mighty impressive," Steven said.

"I have the negative of this picture," he told Steven. "Before I leave New York, I'm going to have a hundred copies made and give them to you. I'm also going to have a hundred of my jockstraps duplicated and give them to you."

"Just what in hell am I going to do with all those jockstraps?" Steven asked in astonishment. "Surely not wear them. They wouldn't fit me."

"You're going to sell them for a hundred dollars each," Rubi said. "Women, but mostly queers, write and ask me for my jockstraps or even my dirty underwear all the time. There's good money to be made. When you run out, I'll see you and give you some more."

"Queers will pay good money for this?" Steven asked in astonishment.

"Welcome to the world, my boy," Rubi said. "You've got a lot to learn. There's more. Instead of those crappy jobs you've been taking, there's easy money to be made. I have a friend who runs a male escort agency. It's called Gentlemen for Rent. Seeing you in that tux gave me an idea. I can get him to hire you. All you have to do is take a lady out to some big event, perhaps a charity dance or something. You get a hundred dollars and that's it."

"That sounds like easy money," he said. "But will I have to fuck these old broads?"

"That's another arrangement," he said. "That's between you and the lady. Fucking would cost more."

"I'm intrigued."

Rubi hastily scribbled down the phone number of his friend. "Tell him you come with the highest recommendation from Porfirio himself."

"I'll think about it," Steven said, not wanting to commit himself right away.

With business offers coming in, Steven woke up the next day, his mind a blur of confusion. Regardless of the outcome of his next maneuvers, he decided that if he played the game right, he would never have to be unloading cargo at the harbor in Hoboken ever again.

The way he saw it, money was not just about being rich, it was about being free. Freedom was precious to him, and he was willing to walk down any road, regardless of how shady, to achieve it.

His day's agenda was finalized when he heard the wispy voice of Truman Capote on the phone, inviting him to lunch. Melvyn Douglas would drop in, Capote promised. Allegedly, the actor had expressed an interest "in working with young Steven" on the road in *Time Out for Ginger*.

Steven dressed and went to the library and looked up the name of Melvyn Douglas in a theater book. "I found out he was a big shit and had played in a hit film, *Ninotchka*, with Garbo. But his last film with Garbo ended her career. It was *Two-Faced Woman* in 1941."

In person that day at lunch, Douglas was suave and charming, as he explained the play to Steven and his role in it as Eddie Davis. It didn't sound like Steven's thing, but he listened politely. If it was offered, he knew he'd accept.

Helen Gahagan Douglas
"Pink right down to her underwear."

Capote wasn't particularly impressed with "the silly little play," even suggesting that "you guys should be starring in a play written by me if I had one to offer, of course." The author was far more interested in hearing gossip about Richard Nixon.

Douglas' wife, Helen Gahagan Douglas, had run for a Senate seat in California in 1950 in the nation's most controversial political race. Her opponent was a small-time, Red-baiting Congressman from Whittier named Richard Nixon. He tarred her with the accusation that she was a "pinko, pink right down to her underwear."

Nixon, of course, won and went on to greater infamy. Helen, however, forever nicknamed him "Tricky Dicky" because of his unethical

112

behavior and dirty campaign tricks.

"As a result of all this, I've been more or less gray-listed," Douglas told them. "Gray for my alleged Communist activities. My enemies forget I was one of the leading lights of the anti-Communist movement in the 30s."

"Just what is gray-listed?" Steven asked.

"It's not exactly blacklisted," Douglas said. "It means you just aren't offered work. And it is for that reason, dear boy, that we're doing the road show of *No Time for Ginger*."

With that remark, Steven knew he had the summer job. It was just a matter of signing the contract.

After Douglas departed, Capote quizzed Steven for anatomical details about Christine Jorgensen before telling him about his latest plan involving Rubi.

"I've hired the three most beautiful hookers in New York to service Rubi," Capote said. "And he's agreed to perform. There's a catch. I told him I wanted to oversee all the action. Without a blink of the eye, he agreed. After all, he has nothing to be ashamed of."

With a kiss on the cheek, Capote told him good-bye, promising he'd encounter Christine and him at Rubi's party that night at the Plaza.

Later, Steven confessed that the glittering party for what remained of New York café society passed like a blur before his eyes. "With Christine at my side, I was stoned out of my mind. I remember talking with Gene Tierney at one point. Doris Duke was there. She'd married and divorced Rubi, but I gathered they were still friends. I remember meeting Oleg Cassini. Marlene Dietrich was there and spent a good part of the evening talking to Frank Sinatra."

"It was one hell of a party," Steven said. "I even had a conversation with the Ambassador from Argentina. I think we talked about Evita Perón, but I really can't be sure."

"In the men's room, a guy named Jimmy Donahue cruised me and propositioned me for sex," Steven said. "When I asked her about it later, Christine knew all the gossip about Jimmy. He was the kissin' cousin of Barbara Hutton, the second richest woman in the world after Doris Duke herself. Rubi had also married Hutton but they divorced soon after. Christine knew all the real dirt. She claimed this Donahue creep was fucking both

Doris Duke,
the world's richest woman, dumps Steve for a naked black drummer

the Duke and Duchess of Windsor. Heady stuff, wouldn't you say?"

Steven accompanied Christine back to her hotel suite and spent the night. He'd later tell friends he had sex with her once again. Reportedly, she'd told him, "It was to spend a night with men such as yourself that I had the operation." By two o'clock that morning, she was proposing that he accompany her on a singing engagement to Miami Beach.

Before she fell asleep, she told him, "I think I'm falling in love with you," Steven claimed.

That was it. He didn't sleep for most of the night. By five o'clock the following morning, he wrote her a brief note, leaving it in her living room. It said: "Thanks for the ride, but it can never be." After he quietly left the hotel, he never saw her again.

***

More than being the traveling companion of the world's most famous transsexual, Steven wanted a new sports car, and he didn't have the money to buy one. Back in his apartment, he took out the phone number of the Gentlemen for Rent escort agency that Rubi had given him.

He looked at himself in the mirror and discovered that he was too wasted from a sleepless night to call on the agency today. He'd have to catch up on his beauty sleep before doing that.

Between escorting rich women around town in Rubi's tux and selling the stud's jockstraps, he fully expected to have a new sports car in just a few weeks before he went on the road with *Time Out for Ginger*.

When entrepreneur Floyd Wilson failed to become a Broadway star, he turned to another form of employment. Handsome, intelligent, and "with oodles of charm"—his own appraisal—he began escorting rich, lonely women around New York and the Hamptons. There was no age limit to the ladies he was willing to take out. The companionship came at a price. After midnight, the meter for his services went into overtime.

When the demand for his escorting became too much for him to fulfill himself, he began to hire out-of-work actors to take his castoffs. Soon he retired from the business of being an actual escort and became head of the successful agency Gentlemen for Rent.

A friend of Rubi's, Floyd gladly received Steven at his office, immediately informing him, "You're cute in an offbeat kind of way. I think rich women will really go for you." Steven was too hip not to know that his interview with Floyd would involve an "audition." That pitch came when Steven was invited for dinner that night at Floyd's apartment.

"He settled for a blow job," Steven later told Shelley Winters. "He told me he wasn't really queer, but had to audition me this way to test my sexual prowess in case some of his rich lady clients wanted to carry things a bit far. It was easy for me. All I had to do was lie on his sofa and dream about Marilyn Monroe while he did all the work."

"You like Marilyn a lot?" Shelley asked. "She's my friend. A former roommate. Perhaps I'll introduce you sometimes. But, frankly, I'm jealous."

Realizing he'd made a mistake, Steven quickly corrected himself. "I don't have to dream about you. I've got reality with you, which, I guess, makes me the luckiest man on God's green earth."

"Bullshit!" she said. "But go on. I like the sound of it."

Steven had time to take four escort jobs before going on the road with Melvyn Douglas. Each experience was completely different. The first call that came in involved Steven joining ten or twelve other young men to accompany women without dates to a gala charity event in Southampton.

Escorting was all that was involved in that first gig, and Steven had the rather elderly *grande dame* delivered back to her mansion by midnight. "She slipped me a hundred dollar bill as a tip," Steven later claimed. "It was boring, but about the easiest job I've ever had in my life."

The second escort gig was even stranger, and he was specifically requested to wear old clothes, preferably jeans. When he arrived at the Park Avenue residence, he was greeted by a woman who looked to be well past eighty. He wondered what she had in mind.

To his astonishment, she wanted him to rearrange the furniture in her living room. "These antiques belonged to my mother, and they are very precious to me. Moving men today are notoriously bad. Sometimes they've even sent a Negro to my house. I know all of Floyd's men are well educated and have good manners. You look like a nice boy. I know you'll take good care of my antiques."

He spent the afternoon moving furniture around. The old lady was very pleased with his services, and even wrote Floyd what a nice young man Steven was.

Amazingly, his early gigs as an escort did not lead to sexual adventures, although he had a near miss in one case. Through Rubi's intervention, Floyd arranged for Steven to escort Doris Duke, his former wife, to an event.

Doris wanted him to escort her to a formal pre-dinner cocktail party at a Fifth Avenue penthouse. He never talked much about that evening, but said he had absolutely nothing to say to any of the guests. "I didn't even know what they were talking about."

Steven found himself rubbing shoulders with five cast-off mistresses of deposed kings who ruled before the advent of World War II. There were at least six ambassadors at the party, plus a British heiress who'd married an

American millionaire, only to have him die and leave her everything after only three months of marriage.

One woman was said to be a Rockefeller. Two people he met carried royal titles. Another woman, who was said to be the ruling duenna of international society—Steven never got her name—was a stunning, fascinating personality. Her hair was lavender colored, and her outfit, something that Gloria Swanson in her silent screen vamp movies might have worn, gave her the exoticism of a rare swamp bird on the endangered species list.

After the gathering, Doris in a chauffeured limousine took him to what he remembered as "this fancy French restaurant on the Upper East Side. I didn't like the food at all. It didn't stick to my ribs. But Doris seemed to enjoy it."

"What I did remember was her ordering a ten thousand dollar bottle of wine. I drank it and liked it, but all I kept thinking about was the money. I felt I was drinking liquid gold. Those were the days when the average family had five-thousand dollars a year to live on, and here Miss Duke and I were drinking a ten thousand dollar bottle of wine."

"Later she brought me back to this elegant apartment," he recalled, and he just assumed they were going to have sex. But it didn't work out that way. When a servant let them in, Steven heard the sound of drums coming from her living room.

When he entered the room with her, he was shocked to see a large black man completely naked playing his drums. "He was wasted," Steven said. "Drugs, drink, whatever."

Doris told Steven that he was a friend of hers, Count Basie's drummer.

"After paying me off, she dismissed me, telling me I'd been a doll," Steven said. "I called Rubi the following day, and he told me that his former wife liked, among others, black musicians."

"I had told Doris that I was leaving to be part of a national road company tour," Steven said. "She wished me luck and told me she'd arrange with Floyd to send me over to her again when I came back into town. As she put it, 'We have some unfinished business.'"

***

Initially, Melvyn Douglas had liked Steven, but that first impression didn't last long on the road. When *Time Out for Ginger* reached Chicago, the veteran actor had had it with Steven. On several nights he appeared high on marijuana. One night he missed his cue by five minutes. Following in the steps of Molly Picon, Douglas went to the director and demanded that he fire Steven.

In New York, Peter Witt, who was Steven's agent, heard of this and pleaded with the director to let Steven resign. If word that he was fired got back to

New York, it could seriously damage Steven's hopes of becoming an actor. No other director might want to hire him.

Dejected and broke, he returned to New York and his shabby Greenwich Village apartment. James Dean had gone to Hollywood, where he was the toast of the town, appearing in *East of Eden*, and preparing for his upcoming role in *Rebel Without a Cause*. He called Steven on occasion, inviting him to Hollywood. But without any prospects there, Steven turned down the offer. The way he figured it that summer, he'd be better off competing in the Broadway theater before he fell on the mightier sword that was Hollywood.

He didn't really want to return to the escort business, but needed money for the summer. He found escorting women for pay demeaning, and he feared if word of that got out, he could be ridiculed as a gigolo. He made an attempt to contact Doris Duke but she was in Hawaii. As for Rubi, he was in Paris.

But Shelley Winters breezed into town, and he resumed his brief on-again, off-again fling with this dynamo. When he didn't hang out with her, he escorted older women to events and got them home by midnight, according to the terms of their agreement with Floyd.

There was no sex involved. He had Shelley for that plus a young dancer at the Latin Quarter. Even though they had what he'd later describe as a "torrid affair," in the years ahead, he could no longer remember her name.

He did find many aspiring actresses from the Actors Studio who were willing to go to bed with him for the night. Sometimes he picked up young women from the coffeehouses of Greenwich Village, particularly along Bleeker Street, which turned out to be the best hunting grounds for something on the hoof.

Allegedly, he had two or three discreet affairs with some actors as well, as they would later claim when Steven became a movie star.

Assessing Steven's allure, author Penina Spiegel claimed that he "was catnip for women. Women who from others would require courtship—dinners, roses, compliments—fell instantly into Steven's bed like ripe fruit dropping from the vine. He had a wonderful vitality, a soaring, wild energy, combined with his striking blue eyes, hard-muscled body, and his little-boy vulnerability, had a powerful appeal for women. Some of them were as surprised to find themselves in Steven's bed as Lady Chatterley was to be in her gamekeeper's."

Rod Steiger
Comparing Steve unfavorably to Brando, James Dean, and Newman

Rod Steiger, who'd met Steven at the Actors Studio, said he just didn't get Steven's appeal. "I knew Brando. I knew James Dean. I knew Paul Newman. I understand why they made women—or men in their cases—turn hot under the collar. To me, McQueen looked like a grease monkey. From working on those cars all day, he always seemed covered in grease and grime. He was illiterate. He couldn't converse on anything except cars or motorcycles. He was just as mute as Dean was on most occasions. There seemed to be some bubble around his head. He was completely self-centered. He was a narcissist, even though I don't think he knew what the word meant. But when he told a gal, 'Come here, baby,' the bitch came running to his side."

A financial reprieve came when Truman Capote called once again and invited Steven to lunch. Capote reiterated his desire to write a film script to star Steven one day, but he dismissed that as merely a seduction tool.

When Capote learned of Steven's cache of jockstraps, a gift from Rubi, he was utterly fascinated. Weeks later, he and many of his homosexual friends would purchase Steven's entire inventory. These gay fellows wanted to send the photograph of Rubi, along with one of his jockstraps, as a Christmas gift to their friends.

With this unexpected windfall, Steven purchased a used red convertible MG-TC, a tiny two-seater with well-worn red leather upholstery. He frequently tinkered with its engine to make it go faster, and he installed "the loudest horn in New York City," or so his friends claimed.

Steven took five-hundred dollars of the Capote money and went to the Greenwich Village apartment of Jullian. "The bitch just stood at the door in her slip with her tits hanging out. It was clear to me that she was in bed with some creep she didn't want me to see. Probably some bum she picked up on Skid Row. She just accepted the money and closed the door on me. She didn't slam it—just closed it. Not even a 'fuck you.' She just knew I'd be back to give her more dough when I had my next windfall."

Back in his new but old car, Steven decided to go for a long drive along the New Jersey coastline, planning to pick up some chick along the way, anything he could think of to clear his head of memories of Jullian.

He often roared up and down the streets of New York and through its canyons. He remembered that he received a lot of speeding tickets in those days. But he always tore them up. "It's a free country, and I'm a free man. No God damn cop is gonna tell me how fast I can go. The fucker doesn't know that I'm racing against time and in a hurry to get where I'm going."

***

Through Shelley he met a very handsome young actor named George

Peppard, who was to become a friend "bonded at the hip"—Steven's words—for life.

He was two years older than Steven but had the same blond hair and blue eyes. Like Steven, he'd enlisted in the Marines after he'd graduated from high school in Detroit in 1946. They'd both done boot camp at Parris Island before being stationed at Camp Lejeune.

Studying at the Actors Studio, George and his wife, Helen Davies, lived on Bleeker Street in the Village in a coldwater flat that cost ten dollars a week. To pay for his living, George drove a taxi during the day.

The exact nature of Steven's personal relationship with George may never be known. Although Steven discussed his affairs with some of his closest confidants, he was always silent about George, perhaps wanting to protect his new friend's privacy and macho image.

The more outspoken Shelley always made the claim that the two men became lovers. "I hung out with them and drank both of them under the table on some nights," she said. "They had this secret code between them that I was not a part of. It was more than two men liking each other. They were soul mates, occupying a place in each other's hearts where no woman could ever go."

Shelley claimed that Steven was quite open when he talked about some other aspects of his life during the evenings she spent with George and him. "Steven said he wanted to become a star because it meant he could be secure," she said.

"All my life I've been poor," Steven said. "I had nothing, and sometimes even nothing would be taken from me, including the roof over my head. There were many nights I didn't know where I was going to sleep. George here has a lot more education than I do. I can't read or write very well. George has promised to read all the scripts I'm offered. Trouble with that, I ain't been offered no scripts to read."

Lee Strasberg of the Actors Studio noted the growing attraction between the two men. "Most of us at the studio thought they were lovers, but very secretive, very closeted ones. They both were careful to protect their masculine images. Steven one time, in an unguarded moment, told me that he felt George looked like a Greek god."

Handsome **George Peppard:** "Treated like a piece of meat."

"In the years to come, George will get cast in romantic Rhett Butler parts," Steven said. "I

119

don't know if I can make it as a leading man. I'm a little on the short side. I have a wiry body, and I'm not ashamed to take my shirt off anywhere, but I know I don't look like Steve Reeves playing Hercules. I don't think I'm gonna win any Mr. America contests."

"'Young man,' I told him, Strasberg said. "'Many people in an audience prefer talent over pecs.'"

Although Shelley failed to get Steven to open up about his intimacy with George, she tried to get George to talk one night when they were alone together. "He was pretty closed-mouthed too," she said. "All I got out of him was that they went on a date together to hear a Judy Garland concert."

"One night when George had had too much to drink, he told me that he and Steven didn't really like actresses, except for *moi*, of course," Shelley said. "He claimed that both of them felt actresses were sick, fucked-up people who could see nothing but what was in the mirror."

One time George complained to her, "Ever since I arrived in New York, everybody treats me like a piece of meat, present company excepted. I'm not a piece of meat. I'm a human being, and I want to be respected as a man. Steven's my best friend because he never goes too far with me, and he never loses respect for my manhood. When I'm with him, I feel I'm an equal. We're going motorcycle riding this weekend on Long Island. By the way, my marriage is beginning to unravel."

"Who's isn't?" Shelley said.

George was known as the straight, conservative type," Shelley said, "but with Steven he could be a kid again. If those two let their hair down and had enough to drink, they could giggle with each other like two school girls. George and Steven were so different. George was a Republican, Steven God knows what. I'm not even sure Steven knew who the President of the United States was. But it was their very opposites that attracted one to the other. Steven would get wild and stoned out of his head on MJ at times. George preferred to get his high from the bottle."

"The most telling line about the relationship was told to me by George one night at Downey's when Steven got up to take a piss," Shelley claimed.

A drunken George leaned over to Shelley and said, "I don't feel alive— *really* alive—unless I'm paling around with Steven. We're like twins. I know what he's thinking. Sometimes we're thinking the same thing. It's crazy, I know. We once thought that we'd make the perfect man if we could combine what he was with what I have into one incredible human being."

***

Over the phone, Floyd Wilson told Steven, "you did so well with Doris

120

Duke, I've arranged the escort job of a lifetime for you—the date of dates."

"Another antique pussy," Steven said skeptically. "As you know, I'm not opposed to old pussy from time to time, providing it's not a steady diet of it."

"This is one *grande dame*," Floyd told him. "La Dietrich herself."

"I can hardly believe that a woman like that needs to pay for a date," Steven said.

You'd be surprised," Floyd said. "A friend of mine runs a similar escort agency in Hollywood. You can't believe the living legends sitting home at night waiting for a date. Most men assume, like you did, that they are fully booked or else they're too intimidated to call."

"I've always wanted to meet Dietrich, Mae West, Joan Crawford, Bette Davis," Steven said. "Might as well start with the Kraut herself."

"I'll call later with the details," Floyd promised. "For god's sake, don't call her a Kraut."

Later that evening a black maid ushered Steven into the living room of Marlene Dietrich in her suite at the Plaza. He was stunned to see photographs of her from movie stills lining the room. Dietrich came into the room and said, "Hello," in a voice that was instantly recognizable to him. Her gold gown was form fitting.

She sat across from him, revealing her world-famous gams when she crossed her legs. A strand of black pearls encased her throat, and she wore emeralds to set off her beauty and the dress.

Before her, she had some movie stills on a coffee table. She picked them up and began to examine them one by one. "Quite lovely, don't you think?" she said. "What am I saying? You haven't had a chance to enjoy them yet."

She hadn't even introduced herself or asked his name. He thumbed through the stills and looked over at her with a smirk. "God sure did know how to create some exceptional women. Trouble is, except for you and a few others, he didn't create enough of them."

With that remark, her carefully arranged face broke into a mild laughter. When she laughed, her wrinkles, in spite of the artful makeup, became more pronounced. Even so, as he was to tell his friends, "she was one gorgeous dame—

Smoke gets in your eyes.
Marlene Dietrich
"The Kraut knows her business."

121

nothing natural about her, though. It was all a carefully orchestrated creation."

Like General Dwight Eisenhower planning the D-Day landings, she outlined to him her plan for the night. They would be joining Joseph F. Kennedy and his wife, Rose, at a charity event in the Plaza ballroom. The former ambassador and his wife would also be joined by John F. Kennedy and his bride, Jacqueline.

"At some point in the evening, the ambassador will excuse himself," Dietrich said. "Your job will be to distract Rose Kennedy at this time. I will also excuse myself to repair my face. We'll be gone for no more than twenty minutes. Joe is quick on the draw. We will re-enter the ballroom at separate times. Again, make sure Rose Kennedy is distracted."

"When I entered the ballroom, I was quaking in my boots," Steven later confided to Shelley Winters. "I met the Kennedys, although I wasn't sure who they were until it was explained to me later. Jackie was beautiful, in spite of some bad skin which she'd tried to cover up with makeup. Rose was a bit dowdy. John was rather dashing, but old Joe was an asshole. Somehow I got through the evening—don't ask me how."

At the agreed upon time, Marlene departed the ballroom. In a few minutes, Joe Kennedy excused himself to go to the men's room.

"I sat in a plush chair talking to Rose, who immediately asked me what my religion was. I told her I didn't have one. Would you believe she tried to convert me to Catholicism right there in the ballroom?"

When the music started, Steven asked Rose to dance. She was short but skilled on the dance floor. Within minutes her son, John, cut in.

The Kennedys (left to right):
Rose & Joseph and **Jacqueline & Jack**
Adultery, subterfuge, and a question
of size

"I found myself dancing with his beautiful bride," Steven said. "She smelled wonderful, but not in any artificial way. It was a sort of natural smell, like dew on the grass at dawn. I thought Jacqueline was lovely in spite of the bad skin."

With Dietrich and Joe Kennedy still out of the room, Rose ordered drinks for the table. "Only Irish whiskey would do," Steven said.

Rose told Steven that her husband was always inviting unexpected dinner guests. "I long ago learned how to keep my food budget intact," she said. "I buy a lot of hot dogs. I serve his cronies hot dogs while I, at table, devour a juicy steak."

Joe was the first to come back into the room. "I knew he'd visited the Garden of Delights, and I also felt that Rose knew where he'd been, but she didn't say anything," Steven said.

"Joe asked Rose to dance, and I excused myself to go to the men's room," Steven said. "To my surprise John—he said I could call him Jack—decided to go with me. We stood side by side at the urinal, and I noticed he was checking me out. Christ, God, and Holy Mary, was he also a faggot?"

"I see that you have more than I do," he said, "but I bet before it's all said and done, I will have fucked more movie stars than you."

"It's a bet," Steven said.

After shaking the urine from his penis, he shook Steven's hand at the urinal.

"We'll meet in a few years, compare notes, and see who's the best man," John said. "Size isn't everything, you know."

Back in the ballroom, Rose and Joe had departed for the evening. Dietrich sat talking with Jacqueline. When her husband returned, Jacqueline quickly excused herself, and she soon left with her husband.

Smoking a cigarette, Dietrich watched them go. "I'm sure she's already heard the story on the Riviera when Joe passed me along to his seventeen-year-old son, John," Dietrich said. "As a lover, I found him weak lemonade."

"You gotta give the kid a break," Steven said. "After all, he was only seventeen."

"Yes, we have to go through life making excuses for the young."

Back in her hotel suite, she began to remove some of her jewelry and part of her wardrobe. "You men," she said, appraising him, "you always demand *numero segundo*. Why is it none of you will settle for *numero uno*?"

"I'll settle and happily," Steven said.

He'd later tell Shelley Winters that "Dietrich gave me the blow job of my life. That Kraut knows her business. Such technique."

"No wonder," Shelley said, "she's sucked off everybody from George Bernard Shaw to Gary Cooper, even Howard Hughes."

"From all I know, even Hitler himself," Steven said.

After all the glitz and glamour of the Plaza, he took a taxi home to his fifth floor tenement walk-up on Tenth Street in the East Village. The toilet was in the hallway. The bathtub, thanks to a piece of plywood laid on top of it, doubled as a countertop. Whenever he wanted to take a bath, he had to remove it and crawl in.

At three o'clock that morning he woke up to the sound of heavy rain.

On an impulse, he jumped out of bed and slipped into his jeans. Barefoot and shirtless, he descended into the street for a walk around the block.

As he would confide to Shelley, "I held my face up to the rain and let it pepper me. "Everybody I'd met that night was someone important. I was nothing. I couldn't really call myself an actor. A hustler, perhaps. Like Scarlett O'Hara in *Gone With the Wind*, and 'with God as my witness,' I decided right there that I was gonna be something. I mean something really big. Like the biggest box office attraction in the world. Shit like that. Nothing was gonna stop me either, and if somebody tries to, I'll knock them down and keep going without looking back."

Chapter Four
"Cute as Hell" and Ready to Rock

"Who do I have to fuck to get a job in summer stock?" Steve asked his surrogate mother and lover, Shelley Winters. If there was an acting job available, she seemed to have her radar tuned to whatever was being offered.

After a weekend with Steven—he referred to it as "a shack-up"—Shelley came through for him. "Reliable in bed, reliable as a job opportunity bureau," Steve later said of this bombastic bombshell.

In 1952, she had appeared onscreen with a married couple, Bette Davis and Gary Merrill, in *Phone Call from a Stranger.* Shelley had learned from Gary that his friend, the director, Jack Garfein, was casting a 1955 summer stock production of *Two Fingers of Pride.* Written by Jim Longhi, it was to be staged at a theater in Ogunquit, Maine. Garfein hoped that Broadway producers would visit and option it for an autumn production in New York.

Shelley had read the play and thought that there was a part in it for Steve as Gary Merrill's younger brother, Nino. The role called for a twenty-two year old. "So, you're twenty-five," Shelley said. "Just take three years off your age. Oh, and you're supposed to be Italian. I realize you know Garfein, but he doesn't know much about you. Tell him your mother is Italian."

Shelley arranged for an audition for Steven with Garfein. The night before the audition, he laboriously rehearsed the role of Nino. It was one of those pro-labor dockyard dramas eerily evocative of Marlon Brando's recent success in *On the Waterfront* (1954). For Steven, the drama evoked his own disastrous experience working as a longshoreman on the docks of Hoboken. "I've lived the part," Steven told Garfein when they renewed their brief acquaintance.

Unfortunately, Steven was not a member of Actors Equity. Garfein agreed to give him the thirty-five dollars needed for membership, although, he recalled years later, "the fucker never paid me back."

When Steven met his fellow cast members, not just Merrill, but Sam Jaffe, Peggy Feury, and Olga Bellin, he later said, "I was the only greenhorn in the cast. They'll make mince meat of me."

He buckled down and worked hard with Garfein who became his mentor, even though he was a few months younger than Steven.

Steven found Garfein a good drinking buddy. He'd survived the concentration camp of Auschwitz and had seen his mother and father gassed. At the end of the war, he was held in a refugee camp in Sweden for displaced persons.

As a director, Garfein had brought stardom to a young actor, Ben Gazzara, when he'd cast him in the Broadway production of Calder Willingham's *End as a Man*.

Garfein laughed about "what a pest you were." He was referring to Steven showing up every night backstage at the production of *End as a Man*. "You begged me every night to fire Ben Gazzara and give you the part."

Garfein had married the beautiful blonde-haired actress, Carroll Baker, whom Steven had seen at the Actors Studio but had never met.

When Steven was finally introduced to Garfein's wife, Carroll, it was love at first sight. Regrettably for him, she was in love with her husband.

After Steven met Carroll, she remembered running into him "somewhere on Broadway almost every day." Unknown to her, Steven was actually stalking her, determined to seduce her.

Bette Davis and **Gary Merrill** met on the set of the legendary film *All About Eve* (1950) and became lovers, and later, man and wife. Gary's mistake involved asking Steve to drive Bette to get her hair done.

"I thought he was a super guy," Carroll later recalled. "We used to stand and gab, laugh and giggle, make silly gestures, and gossip about the other kids at Actors Studio. It was fun to know him because there was nothing introverted or brooding about him. As warm and close as our relationship was and remained, we never became lovers."

One day in Maine, Gary Merrill asked Steven if he'd drive his wife into town to get her hair done. He gladly accepted. Bette Davis was one of those "antique pussies" he claimed he'd always wanted to seduce, along with her nemesis, Joan Crawford. "How else can I compare which of the two is the more talented?" he facetiously asked his buddies.

He'd later tell Shelley, "I fucked Davis in the dunes when I lured her to stop along the coast for a swim. When that swim was over, she really did need to get her hair done. The old girl was a minx. She even gave me a blow-job. She told me her blow-jobs drove Howard Hughes wild."

"With Steven, you never knew," Shelley said. "I knew Bette, and she knocked off a piece here and there, sometimes with a grip. It was entirely possible she'd succumbed to Steven's charm. If she were attracted to Marlon Brando, and she was, I guess she could also have been attracted to Steven. Frankly, he gave me such a blow-by-blow description of his seduction of Bette that I believe the little rat. I've been around show business people long enough to know that shit like that happens. If I'd been riding in Steven's red convertible MG, I would have easily given in to him, too. He was one cute guy."

Steven's hard work paid off. In spite of his being surrounded with some of the most veteran actors in the theater, he garnered the best reviews.

Although Broadway producers journeyed to The Ogunquit Playhouse in Maine to watch the summer tryout, the show found no backers and died at the end of its run.

At the close of the play, Steven asked Garfein, "Any more work?"

"I don't have anything but I think I can get you an appointment with MCA," Garfein said. "They might handle you. Those guys know where all the jobs are."

After his summer stock adventure in Maine, which had been highlighted by his introduction to the awesome Bette Davis, Steven returned to New York with high hopes, hoping to make a dramatic entrance into the Madison Avenue offices of MCA, the talent agency. He rode into the lobby on his Harley and even navigated it onto the elevator for a ride to the eleventh floor. Security guards could have kicked both him and his machine out of the building, but his audacity so shocked and impressed MCA's talent scouts that he was signed on as one of the agency's clients.

Agent John Foreman remembered Steven's spectacular entrance, claiming he thought Steven "was cute as hell." But he had another "cute as hell actor to promote" whose name was Paul Newman.

Back in New York, Steven developed a deep and abiding friendship with Peggy Feury after acting with her that summer.

Director **Jack Garfein** and his wife **Carroll Baker,** who claimed a close but non-sexual bond with Steve.

127

Closely associated with Method acting, blonde-haired Peggy became another mentor. Steven compared her to the actress/dancer Mitzi Gaynor, who was popular in the 1950s. "Peggy taught me more about acting than anybody," he later said.

"He loved my angel food cake, and I think he sort of fell in love with me, but nothing ever came of it," she said. "Sometimes the success of other actors, such as Tony Franciosa and Ben Gazzara, would make him furious."

"Everybody thought Steven and I were having an affair," she said. "But I think at that time he was more interested in George Peppard than he was in me. One time during a scene we were performing together, he kept scratching himself. I asked him if he had crabs. 'No,' he said, 'I borrowed George Peppard's jockstrap last night, and it doesn't fit me.'"

"Our relationship ended when he accused me of sleeping around with other men," Peggy said. "That was strange. I wasn't his girlfriend. We weren't having an affair. Even so, he was furious when he caught me out one night in the Village with another guy."

Years later, Steven forgave Peggy, not that she'd done anything to forgive. When she opened her own acting school, The Loft Studio, he contributed $10,000 to its operational costs. In time, Peggy's students would include Lily Tomlin, Sean Penn, Angelica Huston, and Michelle Pfeiffer. Peggy always bragged that, "Steve McQueen was my first—and best—pupil. I love him dearly."

For years Peggy suffered from narcolepsy, which was the cause of the car accident that took her life in 1985.

***

Late one night in New York, Steven picked up the phone after its fifth ring. "Hi," came a voice on the phone. "I'm in town and ready to fuck."

"Who in hell is this?" Steven asked sleepily.

"It's Jimmy," came the voice. "The toast of Hollywood. Your *Rebel Without a Cause*. I'm calling you because you're the only guy in New York who knows how to use your pecker."

"Well, I'll be a rat's ass," Steven said, sitting up in bed. "Get that much used ass of yours over here."

The next morning over breakfast, Dean tantalized Steven with stories of his adventures in Hollywood. He seemed wryly amused by his growing reputation and the speculation about himself and his preferences. "The word is," Dean said, "that I'd fuck a snake to get ahead. Whoever said that is right on the mark."

He told Steven of a wild affair he'd had with young Sal Mineo, who'd played Plato in *Rebel Without a Cause.* "Sal plays the first gay teenager in movies. Nicholas Ray filmed a scene in which we kiss, but I'm sure that will end up on the cutting room floor."

"Some people in the press are writing that my personality is androgynous," Dean told him.

"I don't know what that means," Steven said.

"Neither do I."

During the course of the day, Steven began to realize how Dean had changed after two movies in Hollywood. He filled him in on stories of his visits to The Club in Hollywood, an S&M bar and hangout for the leather set. He claimed he'd discovered the pleasure of having guys stub out their cigarettes on his chest or ass, and even showed Steven some of the burns. When Dean died, a coroner's report noted the "constellation of keratoid scars" on his chest.

"Don't try to pull any of that shit with me," Steven warned.

"I won't," Dean said. "You're not the type to enjoy the pleasure of pain, only the infliction of pain on others."

"Now you're talking my language," Steven said.

Before mid-afternoon, Dean revealed his secret career moves. "Offers are pouring in even from fuckers who haven't seen my films. I may be offered a part in Edna Ferber's *Giant,* which is set in Texas. There's talk I'll star opposite William Holden. Ben Gazzara wants to do *End As a Man* as a movie. It's been retitled *The Strange One.* I want to steal that part from Gazzara. I know I can play the role better than he can."

"That's crazy, man," Steven said. "What a coincidence. I used to show up every night at the theater where *End As a Man* was playing. I begged the director to give me Gazzara's part."

"So we both know what a great role it is," Dean said, seemingly not interpreting Steven as future competition.

"I'm also after another role," Dean said. "Robert Wise is talking to me about playing Rocky Graziano in a movie called *Somebody Up There Likes Me.* That's my lead-in for us to go to the gym today. I want to practice my boxing."

"That's not for me," Steven said. "I tried boxing. I'm no good at it."

Dean could be very persuasive, and soon Steven found himself in a Brooklyn gym boxing with the actor.

Unknown to either of them that day, there would in the near future appear two additional contenders for the role of Rocky Graziano, such formidable talents as Marlon Brando and Paul Newman.

***

Dean disappeared abruptly for a few days to do whatever he was doing in the precious few months that remained for him on this Earth. To his surprise, Steven received another call from a Hollywood star, Rock himself, who reminded Steven that they had met while he was bartending at Monty Clift's party.

"I know who you are," Steven told him, "and I don't need to be reminded of where I met you. How can a guy forget meeting Rock Hudson?"

"I'll take that as flattery," Rock said. He invited Steven for dinner that night in his hotel suite and held out a tantalizing proposal. "I think I've found the ideal role for your movie debut."

In his hotel suite over a steak dinner ordered from room service, Rock was gracious and charming and filled with anecdotes about Hollywood. He also had a sense of self-deprecation said with good humor. "A friend working with John Wayne told me the Duke, referring to me, said, 'What a waste of a face on a queer. You know what I could have done with that face?'"

"I have this great friend, Mark Miller," Rock said. "Before coming to New York, he warned me, 'Just because it wiggles, you don't have to fuck it.'"

Eventually, Rock got down to business. He told Steven that all of Hollywood was talking about the casting of *Giant*, based on the Edna Ferber novel and set in Texas. "William Holden wants it. Alan Ladd wants it. Gary Cooper wants it. Clark Gable wants it. But right before flying to New York, George Stevens, the director, called me. The role of Jordan Benedict belongs to me. Those other golden oldies can sit around their dens looking at old movie stills of themselves. The Hollywood of the late 50s will belong to guys like us. Incidentally, I'll be appearing opposite Elizabeth Taylor. I know you know her. I saw her at your bar at Monty's party."

Heartthrob **Rock Hudson** plotted to eliminate James Dean from *Giant* and maneuver Steve into the coveted role instead

"Miss Taylor doesn't have a clue as to who Steven McQueen is," he said. "But she'll get the idea one night when I'm fucking her."

Rock appeared only mildly startled at that statement. "Here's how you fit in. Stevens is considering James Dean for the role of Jett Rink. I don't like Dean. I don't want him in the role. I'm trying to persuade Stevens to cast you instead."

"Hey, pal, that sounds great, but I don't know if I'm up to such a big break," Steven said.

"Do you think I was up for my big breaks?" Rock said. "I was thrown into a part and ran with it. There I was appearing opposite Oscar winner Jane Wyman, and I didn't have the experience. Sometimes Hollywood throws you into the big time whether you're ready or not."

"Let's go for it," Steven said. "I'm a fast learner."

"It's not definite, and Stevens is a hard man to convince, but I wanted your permission before I begin my big push of you," Rock said. "There's no way I want to work with this Dean creature."

Years later it was revealed that Steven was just one of many young actors that Rock pushed forward for the role of Jett Rink. The speculation was that he feared that Dean, based on the favorable reviews of his previous films, would steal the movie from him.

Ever the opportunist, Rock also used the lure of the role of Jett Rink as a seduction tool, even though he had only the power of recommendation and didn't make the final decisions.

Steven had very little to say about his relationship with Rock, although they would continue to see each other privately when Steven went to California. A room service waiter reported that he found both men in bed together and presumably nude when he delivered their breakfast the subsequent morning in New York.

Only bits and scattered pieces of what went on in the friendship between the two actors have been revealed. Steven told Shelley Winters that Rock had said, "I've done my share of mercy fucks with the old stars—Joan Crawford, Jane Wyman, Errol Flynn, Tyrone Power. I even fucked Liberace one night, and, dare I confess, Tallulah Bankhead in Las Vegas."

Before leaving New York, Rock promised that he'd hang out with Steven when he made it to the coast, regardless of the outcome of the casting of *Giant*.

"I have this gut instinct that we're going to work together one day, and that each of us, in our own separate ways, is going to become the biggest box office attraction in the

Privately, Steve was devastated at the news of James Dean's death in a car crash, but he covered his emotions, claiming, "I'm glad Dean is dead. That eliminates my main competition."

131

country."

As it turned out, Rock was only half a prophet. But Rock Hudson and Steve McQueen would each reign for a short while as the nation's number one male box office star. They would never work together, of course, and the role of Jett Rink eventually went to James Dean.

During a final meeting with Dean before he returned to California, Steven was discreet and didn't admit that he'd become intimate with his rival, Rock.

"It didn't work out for me to be in *The Strange One*," Dean told him when Steven drove him to the airport. "Gazzara is gonna do it after all. But after *Giant*, I've agreed to play Rocky Graziano. I told Robert Wise that if something happens to me, I want the role to go to you."

"Nothing's gonna happen to you," Steven assured him, "except growing so old one day your pecker won't rise to do its duty."

Dean kissed Steven good-bye.

That was the last he ever saw of his friend. On September 30, 1955, a news bulletin announced that James Dean was dead.

His Porsche had become his coffin.

"I'll probably die in a machine, just like Jimmy," Steven told George Peppard. "I can see it now. Some lonely stretch of highway along some back road somewhere. Death will be instant. I'm sure my head will be severed like Jimmy's. But what a way to go. Floor-boarding it and rushing head-on to meet death. If cars weren't meant to go fast, they wouldn't have been made to do so. Man craves speed. The only time I feel really alive is when I'm speeding and defying death. I understand Jimmy's need."

***

Another of Steven's mysterious bouts of male bonding occurred with the actor George Maharis.

Presumably, Maharis (a Greek-American, New York-born actor) met Steven at the Actors Studio when he was appearing in off-Broadway productions which included Edward Albee's *The Zoo Story*, and in teleplays for Studio One or the Goodyear Television Playhouse.

In 1960 Maharis would shoot to stardom thanks to his role as Buz Murdock on the popular TV series, *Route 66*, which co-starred Martin Milner. After the series, a number of unsuccessful films followed. Despite the failure of those films, Maharis remained a sex symbol, posing nude in 1973 for history's second issue of *Playgirl*.

Two arrests in men's rooms, one in 1967 and another in 1974, would seriously damage his career and macho image.

Maharis and Steven, or so it is speculated, shared their hopes and dreams with each other. What else they shared with each other is not known. Maharis did confess to Steven that he'd wanted to be a professional singer, but had injured his vocal cords through overuse, which led him to switch to acting.

"I don't know what they were doing together," said Shelley Winters, "but I had my own ideas. They certainly made a handsome couple. I think they rode motorcycles together and spent evenings listening to several LPs Maharis recorded for Epic Records. Steven told me that his friend was a better singer than Frank Sinatra. Perhaps he was exaggerating. I think Steven went to some nightclubs that featured Maharis. I know he was thrilled when Maharis gave him an Impressionistic painting he had done. 'The guy can sing, he can act, and he can paint,' Steven told me. 'What a guy.'"

Years later, he told Shelley that he was "mighty impressed when George agreed to pose nude. Imagine daring to do that alongside a horse. He sure had confidence."

***

Through the Actors Studio, Veronica Lake had called Steven and asked that he get in touch with her. He was surprised that she was trying to reach him, as he'd met her only briefly when she was escorted by Porfirio Rubirosa.

When he returned her call, he learned that she was occupying a house, presumably one belonging to Howard Hughes, with whom she'd been linked romantically, in a remote area of Long Island.

She extended an invitation to a private party at that manse for the upcom-

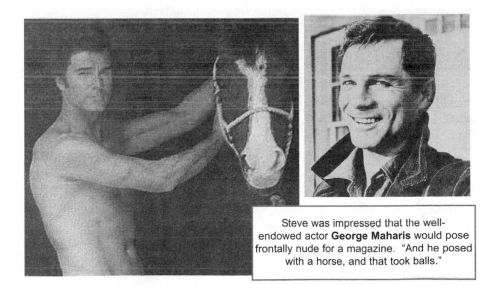

Steve was impressed that the well-endowed actor **George Maharis** would pose frontally nude for a magazine. "And he posed with a horse, and that took balls."

133

ing Saturday night. "Bring along some of your biker friends," Veronica instructed him. "But no gals. We'll have enough of those here already."

What Steven knew about this fading star had derived mainly from gossip he'd heard at Downey's and the Actors Studio.

As a teenager, she'd been diagnosed as a schizophrenic. Her mother refused to have her committed or treated for her illness. As Veronica grew older, the schizophrenia deepened. Her sex and booze orgies, which became notorious in Hollywood, were a manifestation of her deeply rooted psychological problems.

At one time, she'd called Hollywood "one giant, self-contained orgy farm, its inhabitants dedicated to crawling into every pair of pants they can find." She also had been known for picking up strange men randomly encountered. Sometimes she pulled her car up to a curb when she saw a man she liked. "Hi, I'm Veronica Lake," she'd say. "Get in if you'd like to fuck a movie star. I'll let you play with my peek-a-boo if you'll let me play with yours."

That Saturday afternoon, Steven rounded up five of his biker buddies and roared along the highway to almost the end of Long Island where an ancient old manse stood surrounded by walls and fences. A security guard blocked their entrance until he confirmed that Steven McQueen and "his guests" should be allowed inside.

Over the years, Steven provided only sketchy details about that orgy. "Frankly, I was so high by the time I got there, I was already gone. There were a lot of bodies, a lot of candles, and not much light," he recalled. Veronica was in her bedroom, receiving gentlemen callers one at a time."

Veronica Lake was the fabled peek-a-boo girl of World War II. "Wanna fuck a movie star?" she'd ask strange men who attracted her.

He did later brag that he'd sampled eight different women of various ages and figures that evening, although most of them seemed young and beautiful to him. When one of Veronica's security guards summoned Steven up to her bedroom, he said he did at last get a chance to "sample her charms—talk about sloppy seconds."

He heard that actor Zachary Scott was there at the party, receiving men one at a time into one of the spare bedrooms for blow-jobs. He'd seen Scott in *Mildred Pierce* when he'd played Joan Crawford's effete husband. He knew that Scott and Veronica had recently made a low-budget film called *Stronghold* together. "So what if Zachary Scott is gay?" Steven later said. "Who isn't, out there on the coast?"

Another rumor circulated that Victor Mature was also upstairs within one of the upstairs bedrooms, but Steven never got to see him. "If stories of that appendage of his are true," Steven said, "he must have been busy all night. All the girls at the orgy wanted to try Mature for size, although they probably ended up walking bow-legged for a month."

After that night, he never saw Veronica again. Nor was he ever again invited to another of her orgies.

***

Shelley Winters called Steven and invited him on a blind date. Her escort for the evening was Marlon Brando. Normally, Steven didn't like to be fixed up on a date, as he preferred to do his own hunting. But Shelley promised that his date would be "something special, real dreamy, and she kisses on the first date but doesn't tell."

Shelley even let Steven pick the restaurant, and he chose Louie's, claiming, "Let's face it, it serves the best Italian food in the Village."

Steven arrived alone at Louie's and had to wait almost an hour for his party to arrive. An impatient kind of man, he at first considered getting up and leaving, but only after devouring a plate of spaghetti and his succulent veal cutlet. He always ordered the same dishes at Louie's.

Suddenly, as he looked up, he noticed all diners had stopped eating and had trained their eyes on the entrance.

No wonder. Marilyn Monroe in a low-cut white dress had made a spectacular entrance. Even from a distance, he was mesmerized by her beauty. He suspected she glowed in the dark. He'd really owe one to Shelley for fixing him up with this goddess.

"Hello, Stevie," she said in a baby girl voice as she stood before him. At times she seemed to coo or even whisper. But when everyone had resumed eating and had become accustomed to her unexpected presence, if such a thing were possible, she settled down and talked in a soft but fairly normal voice.

It was obvious that with Shelley and Marlon, she was among old friends and could speak unguardedly. Steven was

Shelley Winters fixed Steve up on a blind date with the reigning screen goddess, **Marilyn Monroe,** seen here performing "Diamonds Are a Girl's Best Friend."

flattered that she included him in her confidence.

As Marilyn talked, he studied her face. She'd painted her mouth a brilliant red, although she didn't seem to wear any other makeup. Her eyes, blue as Delft tiles, reminded him he'd once wanted to install tiles for a living. Every now and then, she would reach out for his hand, squeeze it tightly, then release it like a bird set free.

Except for smiles, she hadn't paid much attention to Steven. At one point she trained her eyes on him. "What's your favorite color, Stevie?"

"I never thought about it," he said. "I guess I don't have a favorite color."

"My favorite color is blue," she said.

"Looking into those eyes of yours, I guess my favorite color is blue, too," he said.

"Let's leave these two lovebirds alone," Shelley said, rising after she'd finished two desserts. "Besides, before Marlon gets too tired tonight, I need a really good fuck."

Marlon and Shelley kissed both Marilyn and Steven on the lips, then departed.

"Did Shelley tell you, I'm descended from James Monroe," she said, sitting down again. "He was America's fifth president."

"I always thought Abraham Lincoln was the fifth president," he said.

"No, I think he was the seventh president, but I get mixed up about these things."

Her face suddenly acquired an expression like it'd been hit with an electric shock. A strange smile came across her face. "Shelley tells me you want to make love to me. That I'm your dream girl. Is that true?"

"I may not be the greatest lover in the world, but I'm sincere," he said.

"I'll let you fuck me but you have to stay on top of me and all during the act keep looking down in my face with those baby blues of yours," she said. "There's nothing I'd like better than that."

An hour later, when he was standing in Marilyn's bedroom, looking down at her body as he himself stripped down for action, he took in her figure. He'd seen girls with longer and more beautiful legs. Marilyn was a bit short, and her thighs were rather thick for a film goddess's. And as he lay down on top of her, he realized that her stomach was anything but flat. In fact, she was a bit pudgy. As he licked and sucked her breasts, he felt they weren't as firm as some he'd known.

Yet, in spite of these flaws, she gave him the most genuine erotic thrill of his life. He didn't know if he was seducing a real girl or an image, and that image fired his erotic imagination. He wanted to perform every act he'd ever known.

And so he did.

In her robe, she escorted him to the door of her apartment at four o'clock that morning. At the door, she said, "I'm always singing that diamonds are a girl's best friend. But what if they aren't? I'll have to think about that."

She gave him three rapid kisses on the mouth. "You showed me a good time, Stevie. She leaned in close and whispered in his ear. "I didn't get enough of you. I want more."

"And I want more of you."

"See you here at six o'clock this evening," she said, making it sound like a command.

All day he could think of nothing else but Marilyn. He was falling in love with her, and he was convinced she was falling in love with him.

Exactly at six o'clock he rapped on her door. It was opened by a maid who looked as if he were the last person on earth she wanted to see.

"I'm here to see Miss Monroe," he said. He'd even brought roses.

"Miss Monroe had to leave unexpectedly this afternoon for Los Angeles," the maid said before firmly shutting the door in his face.

He stood in the hallway bewildered and lost. For a moment, he didn't know where to go. Out on the sidewalk again, he tossed the roses in the first trash can he spotted.

A light rain had begun to fall.

That night he lay nude in bed imagining her smell. Her fragrance had lingered with him. It carried with it a tinge of absinthe.

***

Steven was vastly disappointed when the papers announced that Paul Newman had been cast as Rocky Graziano in *Somebody Up There Likes Me*, to be directed by Robert Wise. "The fucking part belonged to me," he told anybody at Downey's willing to listen. "At least Newman is getting sloppy seconds."

Steven was obviously referring to the fact that both Monty Clift and Marlon Brando had turned down the role.

Even if he couldn't be the star, Steven still wanted to appear in the film. When he heard that Wise was auditioning actors to play street gang hoods, Steven said, "For me, that's type casting. I know all about

Paul Newman as Rocky Graziano in the film *Somebody Up There Likes Me*. The memorable role helped propel him into stardom.

137

street gangs. I was a member of more than one gang."

"He came in for the audition," Robert Wise recalled. "He wore this five dollar, very loud sports jacket. He had on a silly little beanie, and he looked sort of gangly. He seemed real cocky, sure of himself. I had a small role available, a guy called Fido. It paid $19 a day. If he appeared in a close-up, the fee rose to $50 a day."

"One day during a shoot, I noticed Steven standing on the sidelines, staring intently at Paul Newman," Wise said. "The kid had a strange look on his face. It was jealousy, but more than that. I suddenly realized that Steven McQueen wanted to be Paul Newman. We were building Paul up to be a big star, but Steven felt that effort should go toward building him up instead."

"As I got to know the movie star, Steve McQueen, I realized that Paul had become his measuring stick for success," Wise said. "On that long ago morning, it never occurred to me—not in the remotest brain cell—that I would be directing Steve in his only Oscar-nominated role, *The Sand Pebbles*. Only in Hollywood, kids, can things like this happen."

The street scenes were shot on location in Brooklyn. Steve McQueen, future star, was introduced to the world as Paul, in a pool hall with a cigarette hanging out of his mouth. Critic Casey St. Charnez called it "a shot, a slash, a scowl, a stare, a shrug, a smile." Later scenes called for him to appear as a punk in a beret stealing a hubcap, as Rocky fights off the owner of the vehicle.

The panther-like crouch Steven displayed in this movie would become a hallmark of his films. In one scene in *Somebody*, Steven's appearance is the most vivid. He stands next to Sal Mineo waiting to learn the value of his share of the spoils from a fencing operation.

Steve as a punk, a $19-a-day extra on the set of *Somebody Up There Likes Me.* Even his first wife, Neile Adams, admitted that Steve was "awful" in his small role.

In the film's staged rumble, Steven showed that he was handy with a switchblade. He was also good at ripping off clothing from a rack of garments, or fishing from rooftops through open windows to bag a radio.

Later, when he saw the completed film, Steven claimed, "I'm terrific, the best thing in that film." Some of the brass at MGM asked Wise, "Where in the fuck did you find this punk? Don't ever use him again."

"The first day I ran into Steve—or Steven as he was known back then—I admit I made a play for him," Sal Mineo told the author. "I was crazy in the head back then. I was still mourning Jimmy's death. Somehow I got it in my mind that I could be closer to Jimmy by seducing some of the same guys Jimmy had fucked. I'd heard rumors that Steven and Jimmy were seen hanging out at a lot of places in New York together, and that Steven had a sort of puppy-dog crush on Jimmy, the same one I developed in *Rebel Without a Cause*. I also heard that Steven could be had."

"It happened after a late-night shoot, when I asked Steven if I could hitch a ride on his motorcycle," Sal said. "He agreed to take me home. He told me to hold on tight. I took him up on that offer. By the time I got home, I'd felt up his body in so many ways that he was hot as a firecracker. I was one little hot number in those days, and on occasion, I could even get a straight man to fuck me. When I invited Steven up to my apartment, he didn't make one protest. He was mine for the night, and I wanted to make it so good for him that he would keep coming back again and again."

"Somewhere during the course of our time together on *Somebody*, I let slip that the star of the picture, Mr. Paul Newman and myself, were having a fling," Sal said. "This fascinated Steven. At that point, he didn't know that Paul kept himself locked in the deepest closet in Hollywood but the door could be blasted off by the right person."

"Somehow Steven got the idea—not from me, perhaps from Brando—that one way to vanquish the competition is to seduce them," Sal said. "Brando had pulled some shit like that when Burt Lancaster was up for the stage role of Stanley Kowalski."

"One night Steven asked me how he could seduce Paul, and I told him the only way was to be very aggressive," Sal said. "I told Steven he had to come on real strong and break down Paul's defenses like I did. Deep down I always felt that Steven was never really that attracted to Paul, but he wanted to seduce him to subdue him. It was like one of those Roman soldiers I'd read about. Once they'd conquered an enemy, they liked to haul them back to their tent to screw them. Steven desperately wanted to bring Paul down to size, and to do that he sort of wanted to turn Paul into his bitch. I don't think that ever happened, but I know for a fact he did seduce Paul because he told me all about it. It took a little doing but Steven eventually melted the guy I used to call Mr. Ice Cube, because he tended to freeze the first time a guy put the make on him."

"I thought Newman was arrogant," Steven once said, "and I always thought I was the better man, even though he was getting all the acclaim. When I finally got him into bed, I taught him who the man was."

***

"Marlon also told me that to capture Paul's attention, I had to come on strong and be very provocative," Steven said. "It was a big chance I was taking. If I had misread Paul's signals, I could have been fired from the picture."

Seeing Paul relaxing with a beer on the set, Steven walked right up to him. "Hi, I'm Steven McQueen. Can I talk to you or have you gone Hollywood?"

"I'm the last person in Tinseltown who will ever go Hollywood," Paul said, reaching for the extended hand.

"I think Paul at first, to judge from the look on this face, thought I was some greaser from the streets of Brooklyn, a fan perhaps. He soon realized I was in disguise as a blade-wielding punk from Graziano's street gang."

"So, how does it feel starring in another of these Hollywood fairy tales?" Steven asked him.

"This isn't Walt Disney," Paul said. "This is gritty *film noir*."

"Bullshit!" Steven said. "Poor kid grows up on the East Side. Shithead father. Weak mother. Joins a gang. Becomes The Thief of Brooklyn. Gets sent up. Trouble in the military. Crawls out of a gutter using his fists—not his brain. Turns out a winner. Rags to riches. Meets a girl. Happy ending.

"Maybe it's a fairy tale after all," Paul said. "I never thought of it that way, kid."

"Don't call me a kid," Steven said defensively. "I'm just as much of a man as you are. Maybe more so."

"I wouldn't be so sure about that," Paul said.

"You want to check into some seedy motel with me, so I can prove it?" Steven said.

The two men seemed to circle each other for a silent moment, like two roosters sizing each other up before combat. "I don't go that route. You have nothing you need to prove to me."

"Don't kid a kidder," Steven said. "I know you want it. Everybody on the set knows you're pounding pretty boy Mineo every night. Why not take on someone more experienced?"

"So what if I am?" Paul asked. "That's none of your God damn business. And if I'm so satisfied with Mineo, that would leave nothing left over for you."

"That's not a problem," Steven said. "Even if you're worn out, we still could get it on. You see, I'm the pounder, not the poundee."

"My ass is strictly off limits," Paul said. "Don't even dream about it."

Steven grabbed his crotch. "Within a week, I'll have you begging for it."

"Not bloody likely," Paul said. "With every hole in Hollywood spread before me, what makes you think I need to hook up with a cocky bastard like

140

you?"

"There's a chemistry between us," Steven said. "I could feel it the first time I saw you on the set. It's strange. I'm a man for the ladies, but when I saw you I said to myself, 'Self, I'm gonna fuck that handsome boy one day. Sooner than later."

"That will never happen, but I must tell you, I admire your approach," Paul said. "I've been hit on by any number of guys, but your way of propositioning me is completely original. Believe it or not, I like you, in spite of your crude technique."

"Believe it or not, we're gonna be friends," Steven said. "It'll be more than liking me. You'll end up loving me."

"You know, I would like to hang out with you," Paul said, "and I can't believe I'm saying this. You're one of the most interesting characters I've ever met. Maybe if I get to know you, I'll find out if you're real or not."

"I'm all flesh and blood, red blood, that is," Steven said. "You'll find out just how real I am, man. One night when I'm plowing into your ass, and you're begging for me to stick in the final two inches, you'll know how real I am."

"To repeat myself, that will never happen," Paul said.

"I've got to go," Steven said. "I'm due on the set. Now gimme a kiss until we meet again."

"A peck on the cheek is all you're gonna get from me," Paul said.

Steven leaned into him. Before Paul realized what was happening, Steven's lips seemed locked onto his, and his tongue explored Paul's mouth. Breaking away, and within an inch of Paul's ear, he said, "I just pretend to be a tough guy. After midnight, I'm an adorable, cuddly love machine."

Without saying another word, Steven sauntered off.

***

The inevitable happened the fourth time Paul went out with Steven. In spite of his initial aggression, nothing really intimate had yet transpired between these two hot young men. Meeting Steven at Pete's, his favorite hangout, Paul settled into a booth opposite Steven.

He found that he could talk and drink with Steven for hours, during which he had no sense of time. They were forming a friendship that would always be tinged with rivalry. Their mutual competition would dominate their careers for years, as future directors would often propose both of their names for the same leading role. Yet in spite of a slight jealousy, Paul found himself attracted to Steven and wanted to spend as much time with him as he could.

Although James Dean had vaguely suggested that Steven might fill in for the role of Rocky Graziano if something ever happened to him, Steven altered the story. He claimed to Paul that Robert Wise had originally promised the role of Rocky to him. Paul didn't believe that. He told his friend and confidant, the actress Janice Rule, that "he just made that up."

Steven didn't stop with the lie about Wise. He also maintained that during the course of his affair with James Dean, the actor had promised to maneuver Steven into each of the many roles being offered to him at the time. According to Steven, Dean planned to retire from the film industry after the completion of *Giant*. Steven, or so it appeared, had almost convinced himself that this was Dean's wish.

There is nothing on record to suggest that Dean either planned to retire or else make Steven his heir apparent in the film industry.

On most nights it would take eight to ten beers before Steven lost his tough guy image and became a vulnerable human being. He confessed to Paul that, "Just like the next guy, I'm looking for a little love and understanding. Hollywood is a cold place. Sometimes, I need to hold someone by a fire. Someone who can turn a tough street kid like me into a lover. Someone like you."

"You're barking up the wrong tree, kid," Paul said. "I'll be your friend. But let's keep it at that. I don't want to venture beyond that."

Somehow, however, that night at Pete's was different from the others. Paul would later confide in Janice Rule that "you could cut the sexual tension between us with a knife. I was too drunk even to think straight, much less act straight. As the night wore on, he kept looking better and better."

"With my defenses down—blame it on the *cerveza*—I agreed to go back to his place," Paul said. "I knew what was going to happen. I can't pretend to be some college boy who wakes up the next morning and claims, 'I was so drunk he took advantage of me.' Back at his place, a smelly hole, we had a little fun, but we were pretty wasted. It was ten o'clock the next morning before we really got it on."

After that night, Paul confided in Janice that he was going to continue to see Steven. "He's got this fabulous technique. He licks you all over until you're hotter than a firecracker. Then while he's got you all worked up and panting, he comes on like gangbusters. Sexually we're pretty evenly matched. Even our dicks are about the same. We could be brothers."

***

In the weeks following Shelley Winters' Broadway opening in *A Hatful of Rain* on November 9, 1955, Steven was backstage practically every night, hanging out with Shelley and the new love of her life, Anthony Franciosa, who had the third lead in the play.

Steven badgered the writer, Michael Gazzo, and the director, Frank Corsaro, to let him understudy for the star, Ben Gazzara, who was riding high from his success in the Tennessee Williams' play, *Cat on a Hot Tin Roof.*

At one point, not willing to settle for a role as understudy, Steven begged Corsaro to fire Gazzara and let him star instead. "I can play the part of Johnny Pope a hell of a lot better than Gazzara," Steven told Corsaro.

There was absolutely no reason to fire Gazzara, who was superb in the role, and even less reason to hire the much less talented Steven McQueen. Still, he was persistent, and seemed immune to rejection.

He desperately wanted to play Johnny Pope, a soldier returning from the Korean War. After time in a military hospital, he'd become addicted to morphine. The play was the first major drama on Broadway to deal with the impact of drug addiction. "If there's anything I know about, it's drug addiction," Steven told the director, referring to his constant intake of marijuana.

The rumor backstage was that Steven, Shelley, and Tony Franciosa were having a three-way. The couple, who had recently entered into a tempestuous marriage, liked, on occasion, to invite a man into their bed. Privately, Shelley told Steven, "It livens things up. Tony is quite a swordsman and an Italian stallion, but—let's face it—everybody male or female, likes to handle a cock from time to time."

Shelley confessed to George Peppard that Steven seemed "only too willing to join Tony and me in bed. If only it could have been filmed. What a shocker that would be."

Steven's future rival, Paul Newman, would turn down a similar invitation from Shelley and Tony.

* * *

Only the night before, Steven had told a friend, "I live for myself. Fuck 'em and leave them. There's no woman on this earth I'd marry and be hog-tied, regardless of how gorgeous she looks."

The following night, an actress-dancer, Neile Adams, walked through the door of Downey's with her date. Legend has it that Steven was so startled by her beauty that he dropped his plate of spaghetti in his lap, although that tale could be apocryphal.

Starring in her second musical on Broadway, *The Pajama Game*, Neile was twenty-three years old—three years younger than Steven—and had a pixie-like quality to her aura. She was an *ingénue* with raven dark hair cut short like a gamine. She flashed her chiclet white teeth in a smile at Steven. Actually he'd seen her before when he was walking with a group of actors along 6th Avenue. His only words to her at that time was "Hi, you're pretty."

"You're pretty too," she shot back before he was called away.

On that unseasonably hot night in June of 1956, Neile had entered Downey's with actor Mark Rydell.

Four years younger than Steven, Rydell later became a major player in Hollywood, directing eight actors to Oscar nominations including Katharine Hepburn in *On Golden Pond* (1981).

Steven was sitting with Ben Gazzara and director Frank Corsaro, as he was getting ready to replace Gazzara at the end of his contract in the Broadway play *A Hatful of Rain*.

In Homage to Neile Adams

After her release from a Japanese P.O.W. camp, **Neile Adams** made it to Broadway. This actress/dancer was a petite bundle of talent headed for bigtime stardom until one night she walked into a New York City restaurant and met a young actor named "Steven McQueen," who derailed a promising career.

Neile was on her way to stardom, not only on Broadway but perhaps in Hollywood. She was playing a star part, a secretary named Gladys, in *The Pajama Game*. To some degree, the role had already become a Broadway legend. On opening night, Carol Haney had sprained her ankle, and she was replaced with Shirley MacLaine, who in this role would propel herself into Hollywood stardom. When MacLaine left the show, Neile took over her role.

Had it been a year earlier, Neile might have shown up at Downey's that evening with a young actor named James Dean. All of her friends kept trying to arrange a blind date between the two. When Shelley Winters heard of this, she said, "What irony. Steven McQueen and his Lady Love might have ended up dating the same stud muffin."

At Downey's, Steven was only vaguely aware of who Neile Adams was. A half-caste—called a *mestiza* in her native Philippines—Neile was of uncertain origins, never knowing her father, something she had in common with Steven. Her Spanish mother, Carmen Salvador, was a noted performer, dancing under the name of "Miami."

While growing up in Manila, Neile met General Douglas MacArthur, who came on occasion to call on Miami. The famous general gave Neile candy bars and told her to "go out and play."

War came suddenly with the Japanese attack on Pearl Harbor. By January of 1942, Neile's world had come to an end, as arrogant Japanese soldiers marched throughout the streets of Manila.

Miami's involvement in the guerilla movement landed her in a Japanese concentration camp. She was granted permission to take Neile with her. Their nightmare lasted three years, and it has long been rumored that Miami and her five-year-old daughter Neile were "used" by Japanese soldiers, although this has never been confirmed.

At the end of the war, eight-year-old Neile, weighing only forty-two pounds, was released from the concentration camp. No longer a performer, her mother launched a business with her newly acquired lover, Victor Rodgers, an attorney in New York City. Soon they were profiteering from war surplus commodities, including Jeeps and guns.

By 1948 Miami had enough money to ship Neile to a boarding school, Rosemary Hall, in Greenwich, Connecticut. Ironically, Ali MacGraw would attend the same school.

After seeing *The King and I* on Broadway, Neile decided she wanted to be a dancer, although her mother insisted she go to secretarial school. Neile was determined and managed to win acceptance in the school of the black dancer Katherine Dunham.

To pay expenses, she modeled for crime magazines. In one shoot, she posed as a prostitute in panties and brasserie being hauled away by a cop. In a bit of irony, Steven also earned extra bucks this way by working for some of the same magazines, although their paths never crossed.

In one shoot, he portrayed a rapist about to violate a large breasted young girl in the hayloft of a barn, a photograph eerily evocative of Jane Russell in Howard Hughes' *The Outlaw* (1943).

Neile studiously applied herself and eventually got cast in *Kismet*, starring Alfred Drake, which opened on December 3, 1953. In time she would take over the role of the secretary in *The Pajama Game*, which got her a spread in *Life* magazine.

That June night at Downey's, Steven excused himself and walked over to the table where Rydell sat with Neile. Using the pretense of saying hello to Rydell, whom he knew casually, Steven at last was introduced to the girl of his dreams. "At first my only intention was to fuck her," he later admitted. "But somehow things got out of control."

When Neile excused herself to go to the women's room, Steven warned Rydell that, "I'm moving in on your gal. All's fair in love and war."

When Neile returned and Rydell went to the men's toilet, Steven asked Neile out on a date. "I know I shouldn't have, but I accepted. He was one cute guy."

The next day, Neile's friends, the "gypsies" along Broadway, warned her about Steven, claiming "he fucks anything that moves." Even so, she was intrigued. He didn't call her for a date, but showed up unannounced at her stage door in the St. James Theater alley.

He was in jeans and a T-shirt, and she wore a fancy dress, but she rode sidesaddle on his motorcycle downtown to Greenwich Village. Once there, he took her on a tour of the coffeehouses along Bleeker Street. By four o'clock that morning he was sleeping in her bed. He'd later confide to George Peppard, "That was the best piece of pussy I've ever had in my life."

After only a week of knowing her, he moved into her small studio apartment on West 55th Street.

He showed up at her apartment door carrying a battered suitcase, his cycle drag, and a bus stop sign that doubled as a barbell. It is known that he still owned that tuxedo, a gift from Porfirio Rubirosa, but he didn't bring it with him. He would also appear with it in Las Vegas and in Los Angeles. He explained to Neile that he insisted on keeping his wiry body in shape—hence, the bus sign barbell. He'd sold his MG sports car and was riding around Manhattan on a BSA motorcycle.

Steven wasn't an easy roommate to live with. He was sloppy, tossing his meager clothes around the small studio and not cleaning up after himself. He left soap stains on the bathtub. His moods would undergo wild fluctuations, especially when he was influenced by the marijuana he constantly smoked. He imagined that men were coming on to Neile when they were being merely friendly. He was often depressed, especially if his past was brought up. Quick to take offense, he often punched out his adversary even if the guy was twice his size.

Whereas Neile was open, honest, and upfront with people, Steven lived in a world of doubt, suspicion, and shadows, trusting no one. She made friends easily. But no one, certainly not his three wives, would ever really get to know Steven. He tried to keep the various worlds he lived in from colliding. For example, he didn't want his straight friends to meet any of his gay pals. To disguise his adventures into homosexuality, he attacked "queers" whenever the opportunity rose. "Faggot!" was one of his favorite put-downs.

The actors whom both Steven and Neile knew didn't give their sudden romance "the chance of a rat fart in a hurricane," as Shelley Winters so colorfully put it.

"I thought the relationship would last three long, dreadful weeks," said Lee Strasberg. "After all, Steven was known as the King of the One Night Stand."

***

Steven was nervous and jittery when he finally was awarded the role of Johnny Pope in *A Hatful of Rain*. "I had big shoes to fill. After all, Gazzara was getting standing ovations, and the critics were calling his performance 'titanic.'"

At the end of his contract, Gazzara left to film *End as a Man*, which he'd already played on the stage. The film had been retitled *The Strange One*.

Shelley and Tony Franciosa also left for greener pastures. Steven felt alone and deserted in the role, with actors he didn't really know. It was only after the show had run for a week that he learned that Corsaro had originally wanted his closest male friend, George Peppard, for the role. The director finally decided that Steven would be more convincing as an addict.

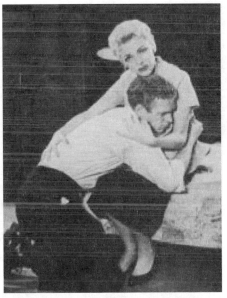

Vivian Blaine immortalized herself as Miss Adelaide ("A Person Could Develop a Cold") in *Guys and Dolls*. In *A Hatful of Rain,* she played Steve's wife. Critics thought she looked more like his mother.

147

"George did not speak to Steven for a month, and I don't blame him," Shelley later said. "It would have been a big break for George on Broadway, but Steven beat him out. Conflicts like this often arise in the theater, even among two guys who call themselves asshole buddies."

Although nearly a decade older than Steven, Vivian Blaine was cast as his wife to fill in for Shelley. She was fresh from her hilarious success as the inimitable Miss Adelaide ("a person could develop a cold") in Frank Loesser's smash hit, *Guys and Dolls*, with Frank Sinatra and Marlon Brando.

Although she delivered a first-rate performance, the critics were cruel, suggesting she'd be better cast as Steven's mother, not his wife.

Steven later claimed to Shelley Winters and George Peppard that he seduced his stage wife during his appearance in *Hatful*. "It made me determined," he said, "to seduce all of my leading ladies in the future. I don't know what it is about me, but every woman I meet undresses me with her eyes."

"From what I hear, they do more than that," Shelley cracked.

Neile was an exotic beauty with a show-stopping talent, but director Corsaro dismissed her as a "sawed-off Chita Rivera" and as "Rita Moreno on a bad hair day."

In spite of that put-down, Neile's career was soaring, with offers coming in from the Tropicana in Las Vegas and a studio contract from Hollywood.

In contrast, Steven's performance in *A Hatful of Rain* seemed to grow more dismal every night. Corsaro became increasingly alarmed, and was being urged by the producers to fire him and find a replacement at once.

Lee Strasberg, who saw both Ben Gazzara and Steven perform in *A Hatful of Rain*, later compared the two rival actors. "Gazzara is a great stage actor," Strasberg said. "In the movies he failed. Steven was one of the worst presences

Steve's rival, **Ben Gazzara,** was a triumph on the stage, a failure in movies. In contrast, Steve failed on stage, but soared to stardom on the screen.

I've ever seen on the Broadway stage. But in the years ahead, when a Hollywood camera was turned on him, something magic happened. The screen transformed him, electrified him, and brought him to life. It was amazing to watch."

Corsaro finally was forced to fire Steven from *A Hatful of Rain*. "He was stoned on most nights. He got worse and worse as Johnny Pope. A young Marlon Brando could have pulled it off. I made a mistake in telling Steven that. I had hoped to challenge him. But my attempt failed. He looked at me in a rage, like he was going to kill me. For a dreaded minute, I thought he might do that. I'll always remember him standing there and shouting at me, 'I'm gonna be the biggest fucking star in Hollywood.' The next day I fired the little fucker."

***

With Steven fired and Neile's show closing, he decided to go with her to Slater, Missouri, where he'd grown up. She was the only woman he ever took to meet his family. Neile had already met Jullian when Steven had checked her out of Bellevue for acute alcoholism.

In Slater, Steven found Uncle Claude looking far older than he could have imagined, sitting on his front porch, as if the world had passed him by. Eva, his wife, was still in charge, and perhaps a little too eager to inherit the hog farm. She, too, looked older than her years, and it was hard to imagine she'd ever been in show business.

Steven's visit was just in time, as Uncle Claude would soon die. On the farm, Neile felt like Eva Gabor in the sitcom, *Green Acres* ("Give me the city life").

Uncle Claude had some dying advice for Steve. "Don't become an actor. Actors are sissies, and I know you're a real man. If you stay in the theater, some queer director or producer is gonna make you his wife, and you won't be a man any more."

Back in New York, Marlon Brando contacted Steven and invited him for a candlelit dinner in Greenwich Village. He'd just heard that Steven had been fired from *A Hatful of Rain*. "I ran into Elia Kazan the other day. He's not my favorite person, as you know. We spoke about you. He claims you're washed up in the American theater. You fail in a big Broadway play and your name is shit. Broadway is about money and success, not failure."

"What do you think I should do?" Steven asked. "Deal in drugs?"

"No, break into the movies," Brando said. "You have to be a real actor to pull off stage work. Not so in the movies. Look at those boys. Rock Hudson, Tab Hunter, Robert Wagner, Tony Curtis, Paul Newman. Jimmy Dean couldn't act either. All he could do was imitate my style of two or three years ago."

"What kind of roles do you think I could play?" Steven asked.

"With your quirky looks, you could never be a romantic leading man," Brando said. "A villain—that's it. With that punk face of yours, you could play a villain. Bank robber, sex pervert, psycho, drug addict, rapist, child molester, an S&M type guy in a leather bar."

Steven looked startled. "I didn't know they were writing roles like that."

"Not so much right now," Brando admitted. "But stick around. In the not-so-distant future, the screens will be filled with roles like that. I think you could also make it big in westerns. If I come across a part that's right for you, I'll give you a call. Now let's stop talking about acting. I want you to come back to my place for some fun and games."

Brando kept his promise about calling Steven with that movie role, but it wouldn't happen until 1968. "I've just read this script. Right now they're calling it *The Sundance Kid and Butch Cassidy*. But I think *Butch Cassidy and the Sundance Kid* sounds better. I thought about playing it for a while but I've turned it down. It's got your name written all over it. If you sign on, you can play Paul Newman's bitch."

***

Although both Neile and Steven were out of work, she vaguely suggested marriage, but he let it be known that, "I'm not the marrying kind." In vain, other girls had tried to tempt him into marriage. He always told them, "I'm too young, too free, to settle down with just one broad."

Robert Wise, who had directed Steven in *Somebody Up There Likes Me*, wanted Neile to fly to Los Angeles for a screen test for an upcoming film, *This Could Be the Night*. She asked Steven to go with her. But he felt that his macho image would be threatened if he were some tag-along kept boy. He already knew that Hollywood was filled with young men like that, and he didn't want to join their ranks.

Instead, in 1956, during the dying months of the pre-Castro Batista regime, he impulsively decided to return to Havana to revisit some of his old haunts.

He planned to go there on his 650 BSA motorcycle, which he had maintained in good running order. He'd figured out the route, involving a ferry crossing to Cuba from a point near the southernmost tip of Florida.

He invited Neile but because of the political turmoil in Cuba at the time, she refused to go on what she viewed as a dangerous trip. That very afternoon Steven rounded up some biker buddies—an out-of-work actor, a writer who'd never written anything, and what Steven called a "kook." Each of these young men had a cycle, and was willing to roar down the Eastern seaboard all the way to the Florida Keys, where on Stock Island they could board a ferry to Havana.

Havana's heyday as a city of legendary sin and corruption was nearing its end. On the streets, Steven noticed dozens of young men in uniform. They were members of Batista's army recruited to battle Fidel Castro's guerilla fighters in the Sierra Maestra.

In the cafés of the city, Steven and his buddies heard lots of talk about the revolution, many residents expressing fear that Havana would soon be overrun with Castro's guerilla soldiers. Gambling and prostitution still flourished, as it had when Steven had worked as a towel boy here in a bordello.

He invited his buddies to the whorehouse where he'd worked, but encountered a whole new cast of characters. "We had a great time fucking all the *putas*," Steven recalled.

But the next day he realized he'd spent too much money. He needed cash real bad for food and gas for his cycle, because they were contemplating a long trip through the Cuban countryside to the city of Santiago.

In Key West, he'd purchased two cartons of Yankee cigarettes. While attempting to sell the illegal American contraband to two soldiers, a Havana policeman arrested Steven and tossed him in the *calabozo*.

Desperate for money, he wired Neile in New York.

I LOVE YOU, HONEY, SEND ME MONEY. LET ME KNOW WHAT'S HAPPENING. IN CARE OF WESTERN UNION.
CON AMOR, ESTEBAN

The cable arrived two days before Neile was to depart from New York for her screen test. After thinking it over, she decided that by sending him money it would only delay his return to New York. In a moment of tough love, she wired back:

I LOVE YOU TOO, HONEY. NO MONEY. HOME DAY AFTER TOMORROW.
NELLIE.

She'd signed the cable "Nellie" which was Steven's pet name for her.

In jail in Havana, Steven was furious with her response. He threatened never to return to her. "That fucking bitch," he told his buddies. "After all that loving and this is the way she treats me. Even if I go back to her, I'll cheat on her every chance I get. Call it pay back time."

Apparently, only one man in New York knew how Steven managed to return from Havana. It was Rod Steiger, who was a friend of both Brando and Paul Newman. On occasion, Steiger lived in the apartment above Neile and Steven on 55th Street.

After Neile refused to send money, Steven wired Steiger, who was a successful actor in those days. Unlike Neile, Steiger immediately wired five hundred dollars. "He never paid me back," Steiger later noted.

With three hundred dollars of this bonanza, Steven bribed his way out of the jail. "I took a twenty and visited another one of the whorehouses for old time's sake," Steven later told Steiger. "With the rest of the money, I paid for my gas and food on the way back."

"He admitted to Steiger that funds were low by the time he reached Jacksonville. "I went home with two *mariposas* I'd met in a bar. Instead of my dick, the queens got my fists. I beat the shit out of them and rolled them, making off with about two hundred dollars."

"Even so, I still ran short before I got to New York," Steven said. "Along the way, I met a chick or two in bars and went home with them. They fed me; I fucked them, and I made off the next morning with whatever they had in their purses."

Shortly after returning to New York, Neile was notified by Wise that he'd cast her as a stripper in *This Could Be the Night*, starring Jean Simmons. The stellar cast also included Paul Douglas, Joan Blondell, ZaSu Pitts, and Anthony Franciosa.

Franciosa had starred with Shelley Winters on Broadway in *A Hatful of Rain*. Steven could only hope that he was discreet and wouldn't tell Neile about the three-way he'd had with Steven and Shelley.

Outwardly, when Neile rushed back to New York and into Steven's arms, he pretended not to hold a grudge against her for not sending him the money. Inwardly, he seethed with resentment.

The next day he called Floyd Wilson and told him he was available as an escort again. "But, please, no pigs. If you get any visiting movie stars, that's my game."

"Well, I never got a bad report card on you, so you're on." It turned out that Wilson had been the custodian of Steven's tuxedo, keeping it dry cleaned and wrapped in plastic waiting for his return.

Steven shared his final adventures in the escort business with Rod Steiger, his benefactor. When Neile returned to the West Coast to shoot her film, Steven lived reasonably well off his earnings. Sometimes sex was involved, but often it wasn't.

Since Steven had last worked for Floyd, his agency had grown in prestige. His young escorts, often Harvard educated, were escorting only the finest of *grande dames*, as well as plenty of visiting celebrities from Hollywood. The washed-up film star, Kay Francis, used the service. Even the gangly, bean-pole-shaped comic, Charlotte Greenwood, occasionally needed one of Floyd's young men for the night.

Steven's big moment came when Wilson called to tell him that Joan Crawford was in town and needed someone "respectable looking" to escort her to 21 for dinner. The famous star presumably was between husbands and lovers. Actually, she was in New York having a reunion with her longtime lover and former co-star, Clark Gable, but she didn't want the press to see them out on a "date."

"I was shaking life a leaf in the wind when I got to the Waldorf-Astoria to call on Miss Crawford," Steven told Steiger. "I'd heard a lot of stories about her, none of them good. All I could think of in the elevator on the way up was that I was not only going to meet Miss Mildred Pierce but take her out to dinner. I just hoped she carried money in her purse to pay for the grub when the waiter presented the tab."

***

Joan Crawford, not her maid, opened the door herself to her suite at the Waldorf-Astoria. To him, she looked very much as she did in the 1949 *Flamingo Road* when she played Lane Bellamy after she'd moved to the right side of town.

"Miss Crawford," he said, "an honor to meet my dream gal of the movies. I'm Steven McQueen."

"You can call me Joan," she said, leading the way to the bar. "Joan, though, has become such an ordinary name. Thousands of baby girls across America are christened Joan every year in my honor."

As both of them drank, a secretary came in with letters for Joan to sign. She was not introduced. "I personally sign all my fan letters. A lot of stars don't, you know."

"I didn't know," he said, "but I could well imagine."

One letter particularly angered her. "They're having this Joan Crawford Festival in Seattle, and they want a print of *Our Dancing Daughters*. I don't have one. Back when I made that, the studio didn't give stars prints of their films. If they had, we'd preserved them. So many are lost."

"I thought they were all preserved in a film library somewhere."

"You darling child," she said, seemingly surprised at his naïveté. "I guess you have a lot to learn about Hollywood."

After making a grand star's entrance at 21, she was ushered to one of the best tables in the house. More drinks were ordered, she preferring vodka, he going for a beer.

"That darling Floyd tells me you are an actor," she said. "On Broadway, no less, in *A Hatful of Rain*. Sorry I didn't get to see

Joan Crawford to Steve McQueen: "You're not one of the boys, are you?"

it. We must know some actors in common."

"Melvyn Douglas for openers," Steven said. "I worked with him on tour. He got me fired."

"Consider it a compliment," she said. "I've worked with that asshole before. *The Gorgeous Hussy. A Woman's Face. They All Kissed the Bride.* My only memory of him is his bad breath in all those close-ups."

"Fortunately, he and I didn't have any love scenes."

She smiled and took a hefty swig of vodka. "Thank God, you've got a sense of humor. I like that in a man. Incidentally, you're not one of the boys?"

"I'm a ladies' man," he said.

"That's good news to know there are still some left in the acting community." She turned the same eyes on him that had appraised a thousand potential lovers in her past. "You're really quite handsome in an offbeat sort of way. Perhaps you and I will do a picture together one day. You don't have a problem appearing with an older woman."

"I love them, and they love me back," he said.

"I'm sure they do," she said. "I'd like to spend time with you tonight but I'm promised to Clark Gable. He and I go way back. I think I'll book you for tomorrow night."

"That is one occasion I can rise to," he said.

"I'll take that as a promise."

At that point Shelley Winters and Tony Franciosa walked by, stopping when they spotted Joan and Steven.

"What a lovely couple," Shelley said. "Wait till I alert Walter Winchell."

After pleasantries and kiss-kisses were exchanged, Shelley said to Steven, "Joan is my idea of a movie star. She can chew up two directors and three producers—all before lunch."

After Tony and Shelley left, Joan leaned back and said, "I saw Monty Clift with Elizabeth Taylor in *A Place in the Sun.* Shelley was in it too. Her acting surprised me. Sensitivity was never one of her virtues."

She ordered his dinner for him—a rare steak—without asking him what he wanted. When he started to eat, she was appalled at his table manners. Very slowly and patiently, she taught him how to cut and eat his meat. "You just might become a big star one day, and you'll get invited to all the A-list parties. You must learn, dear boy, how to use a knife and fork."

"Of course, you may be a part of that kitchen school of acting like Marlon Brando," she said. "What a shit he is. I asked him to appear opposite me in *Sudden Fear*—a big hit, incidentally—and he finally wrote back that he wasn't interested. He said, 'I'm not doing any mother-and-son pictures at the present time.'"

"Marlon can be a bit crude," he said. "I'll overtake him one day. Then you and I might star in pictures together, like you said."

"You are one cocky guy," she said, smiling to soften her words. "That can be sexually attractive in the male animal. Before I leave New York, I must find out just how cocky you are."

"I'm all for that," he said.

"I'm going to make a picture called *Autumn Leaves*," she said. "You might be suitable for the male lead. He's mentally disturbed, though."

"If the character is crazy, then I know I can play it," he said.

After kissing Joan good night at her suite, he made a date to escort her out the following evening.

When he related the story of his two-night involvement with Joan to Rod Steiger, the older actor pressed him for details.

"Just between us, I like sloppy seconds," Steven said. "I got my wish. Steve Cochran, Greg Bautzer, Yul Brynner, Kirk Douglas, Henry Fonda, Clark Gable, Cary Grant, Rock Hudson, Tyrone Power, John F. Kennedy, Spencer Tracy, Barbara Stanwyck, Martha Raye, John Wayne, Johnny Weissmuller. I could go on but we don't have all night."

"With Crawford, you're dealing with a very experienced woman," Steiger said.

"And just between us men, her ninny pies are still firm," Steven said.

"What in hell are ninny pies?" Steiger asked.

"What she calls her not altogether fallen breasts."

***

His other big moment as an escort came when he was asked to take Lana Turner to a private party for Frank Sinatra in a room at the Plaza Hotel. Joan Crawford had arranged this through Floyd Wilson. She'd known Lana since her days at MGM, when the younger and older actress took turns servicing Clark Gable.

Some men, among them Steven, liked natural women. But in some secret part of his heart he had a definite lust for all the superficial glitz that Lana had represented during the studio era.

Picking her up at her suite at the Plaza, all he had to do was escort her to a private room downstairs. In a form-fitting white gown with a ruby necklace, she looked as sexy to him as when he saw her in *The Postman Always Rings Twice*. Age had been kind to her, or else she was incredibly skillful at applying makeup.

"A blond," she said, appraising Steven when he was ushered into the living room of her suite. "Usually I don't date blonds. The agent, Henry Willson, always told me I should date men with raven-black hair to offset my own blondness. That's why he fixed me up with Rory Calhoun."

"If I'd have known, I would have dyed my hair black," he said. "That's what I did when I appeared in *A Hatful of Rain* on Broadway. I was playing an Italian, and I thought black hair would make me look more the part."

"Actually I like blond-haired men," she said. "You're adorable looking and will be just fine." She looked him up and down. "Of all my movies, which one did you like the best?"

"*The Merry Widow*," he said. "You were so beautiful. Incredible."

"It's true," she said. "I was. As for that Fernando Lamas, he can stick a dildo up his ass."

Over a pre-party drink, Lana told him she was furious over something that had been written in a Hollywood column. "I wasn't named, but everyone in Hollywood knew it was me. Some jerk claimed that if I saw a stagehand in tight pants with a muscular build, I'd invite him into my dressing room. That is simply not true. Gross libel."

"All I can say to that is some stagehand must have been out of luck," he said.

"I will take that as a compliment," she said, rising from the sofa. "We'd better go downstairs. All the gang will be there. Not just Frank, but Dean Martin, Sammy Davis Jr., Judy Garland, Peter Lawford."

The postman did indeed ring twice that night, and the package he delivered was the sultry blonde screen queen
Lana Turner

Accompanying her to the party, where she made a grand entrance, Steven met each of these legends and a lot more big stars. Months later, he'd tell Rod Steiger, "If someone told me I'd soon be co-starring in a big picture with Sinatra, I would have thought they were out of their mind. If someone told me that Sammy Davis Jr. would one day be teaching me how to shoot, I would have thought them crazy. The same if they told me I'd get an invitation from Judy Garland to fuck her. And I hardly knew at the time that Peter Lawford would get off sucking my dick."

Steven was particularly amused by Sammy Davis Jr. It was the beginning of a beautiful friendship. A band had been hired for the night, and Sinatra sang four songs to his friends. On the dance floor, Steven held Judy in his arms. To his astonishment, she unzipped his pants and "felt the family jewels," as Steven later reported to Rod Steiger.

"She does that to all her dance partners, so don't think you were singled out as anything special," Steiger said.

At the end of the evening, Steven's only surprise came when Sammy, in saying good-bye, lip-locked him with a wet kiss. Steven later reported it to Lana with a certain astonishment. "He does that to all his white friends. It's Sammy's way. It's so Hollywood. You'll get used to it."

"I hope he doesn't think I'm a fucking faggot," Steven said.

"Oh, darling, don't be so judgmental. Without so-called faggots, there would be no Hollywood, and I wouldn't have become a screen goddess."

He fully expected to escort her upstairs where he hoped she'd invite him to spend the night. Instead she asked for her sable and headed outside the Plaza. The doorman hailed her a cab.

"Come with me," she said. "I have an errand to run. We're going to the Carlyle."

Once inside this swanky hotel, she directed him into the bar. "I have to see a special friend upstairs. He never takes very long, so I'll be back down here within the hour. I want you to wait for me."

About thirty minutes later, a waiter tapped him on the shoulder. "You're wanted on the house phone." It was Lana calling from a suite upstairs.

"He says he knows you," Lana said.

"Who do you mean?" Steven asked.

"My friend," she said. "Come on up. He wants to have a drink with you."

To his astonishment, John F. Kennedy opened the door to the suite. He was in his underwear. Presumably Lana was in the bathroom, repairing her makeup.

"Come on in and have a drink," Kennedy said. "I'm still keeping our tally about seducing movie stars. I bet I got to Lana long before you did. We've been going at it on and off for years."

"I'm not opposed to sloppy seconds," Steven said, accepting a drink. "I'm sure you've got me beat, but I'm going to Hollywood, and I'm gonna catch up with you yet, you fucker."

"That's a good name for me," Kennedy said, smiling.

Standing beside him at the bar, Kennedy said, "I'll give you a tip about Lana. She claims she doesn't go in for the oral stuff. She wants her men to get right to the honeypot."

"Thanks for the advice," he said.

He whispered something else. "Now I want you to get her out of here and quick. I've got something else lined up, and she's due here soon."

"Care to tell me her name?" Steven asked.

"Jayne Mansfield," Kennedy said.

"You partial to blondes?" Steven asked.

"Blondes for bedtime, brunettes for marriage," Kennedy said. "Remember that."

"All throughout my life, I'll follow your advice."

And so he did.

***

Waking up in bed with Lana Turner, Steven decided to marry Neile, or so he told Rod Steiger before flying to Los Angeles. He'd borrowed money from some of his buddies, and some of them were on the verge of threatening him physically as an incentive for him to return it.

When he settled some emergency accounts, he had nothing left. He knew a jeweler who, for a $25 deposit, would give him a wedding band. As it turned out, Neile would have to make the other eight quarterly payments. For his one-way ticket, he hocked the gold watch his Uncle Claude had given him in Missouri.

When she learned of Steven's intentions about marriage, Neile had misgivings, a case of cold feet. She was on the dawn of what could be a major career in theater or in films, and although she was very much in love with Steven, her career concerns were also important. Her manager, Hilliard Elkins, even suggested that Steven might be marrying her for her money, since she was taking home a good paycheck.

She'd arranged for Steven to be admitted to her motel room in Culver City. Once there, he threw some of her possessions into the back of a rented Thunderbird and headed for MGM.

There, he almost swept Neile off her feet with the suddenness of what was happening. It was Friday afternoon, and she had the weekend off from filming.

In the car heading south, Steven informed her that he planned to marry her in San Juan Capistrano, famous for its swallows, but had made no arrangements. Once at the mission, a nun told him he couldn't get married in the chapel because banns had to be published first.

Speeding on his way to the next town, San Clemente, he was pulled over by a pair of highway patrolmen. Steven, using all his personal charm, claimed he was rushing to get married. The policemen were sympathetic and led him to the home of a Lutheran minister, who agreed to marry them in a church.

Shortly before midnight on November 2, 1956, Steven and Neile Adams were wed. "With two policeman standing by with guns, it looked like a shotgun wedding," he later said. Leaving the chapel, Steven and Neile launched a union of both happiness and sorrow that would last for nearly sixteen years.

For her wedding supper, Steven bought her a bag of potato chips and a cup of black coffee before they moved on to San Diego, arriving in the wee hours of the morning.

After a whirlwind weekend of T-bird racing along the beach, firecrackers, cherry bombs, and rockets, he had Neile back at Culver City in time for her to report to the studio that Monday morning.

Perhaps because of his experience with the escort agency, Steven took to being a kept man with gusto. At one point, Rod Steiger called him a gigolo. He figured that Neile was making good money, and she had a husband who knew how to spend it on new clothes for himself, on gambling, and even on advance payments for a Corvette.

If anyone asked, he claimed, "I'm married to a star—she's gonna be big—and I've got to help her keep up her star image."

Having no work, Steven went on a search of various neighborhoods, following blind clues in the hopes of finding of his father, William Terrence McQueen. No one had ever heard of him. Jullian was not particularly helpful, claiming he was "living somewhere in California."

Steven concluded that even the FBI would have a hard time tracing this mysterious figure. When not looking for his father, Steven practiced shooting, convinced as he was that he was about to be cast in a big Western TV series. Indeed, that would eventually be true.

When Steven visited the set where Neile was rehearsing, Paul Newman would often drop by. He too was making a movie that also starred Jean Simmons. It was called *Until They Sail*, and it featured Piper Laurie, Joan Fontaine, and a teenage Sandra Dee.

Neile would see Paul and Steven involved in deep conversation. In her autobiography, she remembered them as "two young gods." Sometimes they would disappear from the set and not come back for one or two hours.

Presumably, Neile didn't have a clue what was going on. Although she was smart enough not to trust Steven with other women, she apparently had no clue that he'd been introduced to the world of bisexuality.

***

Often, after a hard, strenuous day at the studio, Neile came home to find Steven bored and hungry. He demanded that she serve a home-cooked meal every evening. When she tried to buy food already prepared at a deli, he threw the plate with the food on the floor.

In his first venture into the theater, Steven had been criticized, even by

Neile, for following too closely the styles of James Dean or Marlon Brando. In Hollywood, he became fixated on the acting style of Paul Newman, and would often visit his friend on his MGM set.

Rod Steiger, Steven's confidant, later claimed that Steven wanted "to become the second Paul Newman. Paul was on his way toward becoming a big star, and Steven thought he was hot shit and wanted to trail after him to stardom."

Long before he took off as the commander of *Star Trek* for the exploration of unknown galaxies, **William Shatner** was a struggling actor like thousands of others.

"I think Paul was using Steven sexually," Steiger claimed. "Steven mostly liked girls, lots of girls, but he didn't know how to say no to a big movie star. I know that he was also slipping over and seeing Rock Hudson on the side."

Neile later said that Steven would come in drunk many a morning as she was getting up for an early call at the studio. What he didn't tell her was that he'd spent many of those nights at the home of Rock Hudson.

On other nights, he was out with a different woman. With time on his hands, he would go for long rides on his motorcycle. He told his buddies, "I can have any biker chick I set my eyes on." He found the Ballona Creek bars a good stamping ground for pick-ups.

What Neile got in her marriage was not a faithful husband, as she would so painfully learn.

Early in his Hollywood days, sexual rumors began to spread about Steven, as they would throughout his years on the West Coast. The word was out that "Steven McQueen would screw anything with a pulse." The talk around the studio was that he often shacked up with Paul Newman or Sal Mineo, along with countless women, some well beyond the age of forty.

Homosexuals also pursued him, mainly because he projected such a macho image, riding bare-chested on a cycle to which he'd fastened a bullwhip. Some gays speculated that he was a sadist, rather blatantly advertising for a masochist to use that bullwhip on. Sometimes, when approached by a homosexual in a bar, he would slug the man.

Early in his career, Steve worked on the road with fading stars like **Ralph Bellamy,** who, in movies, was always losing the girl to either Fred Astaire or Cary Grant.

160

Neile realized that Steven would soon bolt from the marriage if he continued his existence as a tumbling tumbleweed. She pleaded with her manager, Hilliard Elkins, as well as her agency, "the boys over at William Morris," to find work for her husband.

"Just what we need," said Stan Kamen, a William Morris agent. "Another blond, blue-eyed, out-of-work actor, and one who's not tall in the saddle at that."

Yet out of loyalty to Neile, the agency did snare a coveted role for Steven in *The Defenders*, a two-part teleplay, part of the popular Studio One series. He was cast as a young man who kills the wife of a psychologist.

His co-stars were the famed but fading movie star, Ralph Bellamy, and William Shatner, who would go on to glory in *Star Trek*. The director, Robert Mulligan, decided to take a chance on Steven. By 1962, Mulligan would direct Gregory Peck in his big Oscar win, *To Kill a Mockingbird*.

Unlike another veteran actor, Melvyn Douglas, Ralph Bellamy got along easily with Steven, who later recalled, "I liked the guy. I always remembered him as the poor sucker who loses the girl to Cary Grant in every picture, including my favorite, *His Girl Friday*."

Years later, when Steven encountered Shatner again in Los Angeles, before his great success as the square-jawed Captain James T. Kirk, commander of the starship USS *Enterprise*, Steven learned that the star was living in a truck bed camper, waiting for higher paying roles to come his way.

The director's gamble paid off. Steven's appearance on *The Defenders* produced numerous phone calls and letters to CBS. Many wrote in, "Who is this sexy man? We want to see more of him." Most of the letters were from young women, but many were from young men.

Elkins called Neile, telling her, "The kid's got something. Those eyes. There's a screen presence there. He might just go some place in this business after all."

Steven was particularly effective in a scene with the Philadelphia-born actress Vivian Nathan, who was nine years older than Steven and who was cast as his mother.

Neile had secretly directed him, advising him to warm up his on-screen personality with an occasional winning smile to make his role of the killer more sympathetic. Her advice worked.

With E.G. Marshall and Robert Reed heading the cast, *The Defenders* would go on to become television's seminal legal drama pioneer in New Frontier liberalism.

Trading in the Corvette, he purchased a red MG. "We're driving back to New York," he announced to Neile at the completion of her film. "I want to show you America. Besides, New York is the only place you can get a decent horsemeat burger these days."

As 1957 came to an end and Neile and Steven faced the year's tax implications, he was embarrassed to learn that he had earned only $4,000 for his year's work, whereas her income had totaled $50,000, a sizable sum in the late 1950s. She had to assure him that in spite of the disparity in their incomes, "One day you'll be a big star."

"What in hell are you talking about, woman?" he shouted at her. "I'm nearly thirty years old."

"So was Paul Newman when he finally made it in films," she pointed out.

In New York, rising star Neile Adams, now Mrs. Steven McQueen, appeared on television, guesting on *The Walter Winchell Show* and later on Pat Boone's television show. Steven called Boone a "candy ass," referring to Winchell as a "right wing jerk."

Neile was a hot property, and her manager, Elkins, had her fully booked, first with John Raitt in the Pittsburgh Civic Light Opera's production of *The Pajama Game* and then at the Kansas City Starlite Theatre. After that, she was scheduled to fly to Las Vegas for a $1,500-a-week gig at the Tropicana.

Amazingly, after being fired from the Broadway production where he played Johnny Pope in *A Hatful of Rain*, Steven was asked to repeat the role at the Fairmont Park Theatre in Philadelphia.

He was cast opposite Kim Hunter, who had scored such a big success as Stella Kowalski in *A Streetcar Named Desire*. Coming back to see her in her dressing room, Steven, as a joke, called out, "STELLA! STELLA!" doing a perfect imitation of Brando.

She was not amused. But by the second day of rehearsal, he had won Kim's heart with his winning smile. "He was tough on the outside, but tender on the inside," she said. "Somehow I reached that little boy that still dwelled inside him. I know that sounds corny. But he hadn't quite become a man yet."

On one drunken night with Kim, he grew almost violent. He told her, "I'm gonna go back to Hollywood and become an even bigger star than Brando."

Far from feeling threatened by this new competition, Brando was merely

Kim Hunter went from repeatedly falling into the arms of Marlon Brando in *A Streetcar Named Desire* to wet-nursing a drug-addicted Steve in the role he played in *A Hatful of Rain*

amused when Kim related the incident to him.

Kim and Steven would carry their summer theater tour throughout the East, with stopovers at such theaters as the Pocono or Westport Playhouses. Since the producers of the summer road show were different from those associated with the Broadway production, Steven bragged about what a success he'd been in *A Hatful of Rain* in Manhattan.

Kim knew that he'd been fired, but she didn't contradict him. "It's not all backstabbing in the theater," she later said. "Besides he was heating up every hotel bed I slept in. Frankly, I wanted to marry him myself had he been free. I don't take husbands away from other women. I only fuck 'em."

Steven later admitted to Rod Steiger that, "I fell in love with Kim Hunter that summer, since Neile was far away. Kim was a very talented actress, very intelligent, with no mannerisms or frills, just plain talent on the stage. Actually she'd wanted to be a concert pianist, and we hit several bars together on the tour. Even after performing all night on stage, Kim would entertain the boys in the bar. They loved her music. They loved her. She added a touch of class to the seediest tavern."

He was very impressed that she'd won the Oscar for Best Supporting Actress for her role in the film version of *A Streetcar Named Desire*. He was also impressed that she'd starred opposite Humphrey Bogart in *Deadline U.S.A.* (1952), which had also featured the great Ethel Barrymore.

Upon his return to New York, Steven bragged to Steiger that, "Kim thinks I'm gonna become Hollywood's next Bogart. Even today, if I meet up with Ingrid Bergman, regardless of what she looks like, I'm gonna throw her down and fuck her good. She really turned me on in *Casablanca*."

Steven was very sympathetic to Kim's plight, because film offers had dried up for her. She'd been blacklisted for her pro civil rights stance.

Years later, he'd remember Kim for her cooking. "It was so much better than that slop Neile served." On the road Kim carried a hot plate, which she would plug into a hotel room's electrical socket. Even with these limited facilities, Steven claimed she prepared "the best grub an actor on the road could ever ask for. Sometimes I didn't know if I loved her or her cooking more."

Kim would later write an "autobiographical cookbook" called *Loose in the Kitchen*.

Before the end of the run for the show, Steven got up enough nerve to ask Kim the question he'd been anxious to ask all summer.

"Am I better in bed than Marlon?"

"Of course, you are," she said to reassure him. "Regrettably, Marlon forgot he was Marlon with me. He played Stanley Kowalski on stage and in bed."

***

163

With Neile in Las Vegas, "I became a slut in New York looking for sluts," Steven admitted to Rod Steiger. The actor said that Steven had a string of women coming back to 55th Street, and some of them looked like they didn't go near the water.

"Seeing me with all these hussies caused the guys at Louie's to start calling me Desperado again," Steven said. "Most people, especially my sluts who I picked up and dumped the following morning, called me a shit. I loved it when the bitches did that. I don't know what it is with women, but every time I go to bed with one of the *putas*, they fall madly in love with me. Is it my pecker or something else?"

TV spots were few and far between, but occasionally something would pop up. Something that did was a brief stint in the teleplay *Four Hours in White*.

At long last, the "mad Hungarian," Peter Witt, who had been Steven's on-again, off-again agent, came up with a starring role in a legitimate movie. "You've paid your dues," Peter told him. "Your time has come. This picture is going to make you a star."

Studio photographers didn't quite know what
to do with **Steve McQueen** in 1956, so they tried to
artfully pose him as a typical leading man, failing
to recognize what a unique screen presence he was.

Chapter Five
On His Way to the Top

When Steven's first movie in which he had a starring role, *Never Love a Stranger*, opened, he remembered only one critical review. The journalist claimed that Steven's "face looked like a Botticelli angel who had been crossed with a chimp."

When seeing the final cut, Allied Artists' executives knew that the film was a disaster, and they held it back from release for two entire years.

Based on a Harold Robbins novel, *Never Love a Stranger* miscast Steven as a young Jewish lawyer, Martin Cabell. His boyhood friend is Frankie Kane, played by John Drew Barrymore. Martin's sister, Julie, is played by Lita Milan, who becomes Frankie's sweetheart. When the men grow up, Frankie becomes a gangster, and Martin the district attorney wanting to bring him to justice.

Filming was in Los Angeles and New York. On weekends in California, Steven drove to Las Vegas where Neile was still appearing in a Tropicana revue.

At the gambling casinos, he proved skilled at getting rid of her paycheck. One time, when she asked him to hold her weekly check while she went to pick up a garment, he'd gambled away all of the fifteen hundred dollars in just seven minutes.

Scenes like that threatened the relationship. She loved Steven dearly, but as time went by, she became achingly aware of their different lifestyles, work habits, obsessions, and careers. The ugly word divorce did rear its head.

On location on either coast, Steven did not like the separation from Neile. "I was a thousand miles away from her, and all of my insecurities came out," he said. "Was she seeing other guys? Our phone bill went to the heavens, but she paid it. Sometimes we got into a fight, and I hung up on her."

When Steven told his biking buddies that he was starring as a district attorney, it brought a big laugh in the bar. This potboiler by Robbins, the king of all potboilers, was definitely a B-list picture budgeted at $700,000.

Steven had trouble with the bad dialogue, and especially objected to some off-screen narrator pompously intoning such platitudes as "Life is a span that links the eternities."

In John Drew Barrymore, the star of the picture, Steven met a fellow soulmate and another of the "bad boys" of Hollywood. He was born to A-list parents, his father being "The Great Profile" himself, his mother the actress Dolores Castello. In time, John Drew Barrymore became the father of actress Drew Barrymore.

Lying about his age, John joined the U.S. Navy when he was only thirteen, because he was tall and well built for his age. His film career was eventually ruined by drug busts, and he was jailed numerous times on charges of drunkenness and spousal abuse. In other words, he was, according to Steven, "my kind of guy."

During the filming of *Never Love a Stranger,* John's marriage to actress Cara Williams was eroding. Her relationship not only failed, but so did her career, as CBS executives at one time were grooming her to become the next Lucille Ball, but those plans fell through.

When the filming ended, so did Steven's friendship with John. But Steven watched with sadness as his co-star faced a bleak future in the 1960s and beyond, with more arrests for drug abuse and more jail terms. In time, John would become a derelict, retreating from the world.

Gays who first saw this movie poster misinterpreted it, thinking it was the story of a well-dressed man who picked up a psychotic hustler

"Our friendship, and it was a great one while it lasted, didn't survive because John became too weird even for me," Steven claimed. "On looking back, I think he suffered from a severe mental illness. Also, being an actor and the son of John Barrymore cast a mighty shadow from which he could never escape."

"One night in Brooklyn, John ran naked through the streets, waking up households at three in the morning. I chased after him in my car," Steven said. "I managed to subdue him, throw him into the car, and take him back to his room before the police got him."

A minor director, Robert Stevens, interviewed in Westport, Connecticut, claimed that he visited both John and Steven when they were in a room together in New York. "They were stoned and stark raving naked," he said. "This didn't mean they were having sex together, but I felt they were pretty intimate with each other." Steven even patted John on his ass. 'John may

166

be the star of this fucking picture,' he told me, 'but at night I'm King of the Road.' Read into that what you will."

The crusty Robert Bray, a former lumberjack and cowboy, was billed third in the movie. He was once hyped as the next Gary Cooper. Bray's self claim to fame was that "I fucked Marilyn Monroe when I played the bus driver in her movie, *Bus Stop*." No one knows if that were true or not.

Reached in Bishop, California before his death in 1983, Bray claimed that he felt "both Barrymore and McQueen were a couple of doped-up faggots. They weren't entirely queer, though, because each of them screwed women. If you want to know the real truth, I think they didn't bother to ask what sex they were screwing after midnight."

"In the old Hollywood, we had men like Gary Cooper, John Wayne, and Clark Gable," Bray said. "In the new Hollywood, there are a lot of girly men running around. I'd include Tab Hunter, Farley Granger, Paul Newman, and both McQueen and the Barrymore kid in that list."

Although Steven liked to hang out with John as a drinking buddy and pot smoker, he much preferred bedtime with the sultry Lita Milan. "I guess we can call it incest."

After dumping Paul Newman and Steve McQueen, **Lita Milan** set her sights on **Ramfis Trujillo** (right), son of the Dominican Republic's notorious dictator, Rafael Trujillo

The daughter of a Polish housewife and a Hungarian fur salesman from the Flatbush section of Brooklyn, Lita shot like a rocket into the film world of the mid-1950s before disappearing from the screen forever. When she co-starred with Steven, she was fresh from a recent affair with Paul Newman

| Lita Milan | Ramfis Trujillo |

167

on the set of *The Left Handed Gun* where he played a slightly gay Billy the Kid.

Lita had been a Las Vegas showgirl and model before getting cast as a spitfire *señorita* in *The Ride Back* in 1957. Ginger Rogers had advised her to "fuck your way up the Hollywood ladder."

After shacking up with Steven, Lita would soon drop both Paul and Steven when Zsa Zsa Gabor introduced her to Ramfis Trujillo. He was the dashingly handsome son of the dreaded dictator of the Dominican Republic, Rafael Leonidas Trujillo y Molina.

Her torrid romance with Ramfis led to the abandonment of her movie career. After the assassination of his father, the dictator, in 1961, Ramfis tried to seize power in the Dominican Republic. But he and Lita were forced to flee the country, going into exile in Madrid. There went Lita's dream of becoming "the Evita Perón of the Caribbean."

"Lita Milan at least had one claim to fame," Shelley Winters said. "She and I are among the very few dames who can expound on the love-making techniques of both Paul Newman and Steve McQueen. Not a lot of women can make that claim."

Even in this bad film, Steven proved that he had a certain rapport with the camera. Because of its sympathetic portrayal of Jews in New York, the film was denied a release in certain parts of the anti-Semitic Deep South. In some theaters, the Ku Klux Klan threatened to either burn or bomb a theater if *Never Love a Stranger* was shown.

Upon its lackluster release, only the novelist upon whose writing it had been based, Harold Robbins, liked it. "Unlike other adaptations of my novels, this one remains true to my original story."

At the end of the shoot, back in Hollywood, Steven agreed to meet Paul Newman in a cheap motel in Long Beach. Inside the sweaty bedroom, where a Bible rested on the night stand, Steven told Paul, "I've got every horny woman in Hollywood trying to get me to fuck 'em. I'm only one man. I need a break, a different kind of action now and then. You're the kind of change I have in mind."

During the course of the night, Steven confessed that he was involved in a torrid love affair. "She has that peasant girl kind of beauty. In bed, we sizzle like steaks on the grill." He called such encounters "fuck flings."

"What's the name of this sugartit?" Paul asked. "Sounds like I'd go for her myself."

"Lita Milan," Steven said.

Paul was stunned, but masked his surprise.

The following week, he came clean with Steven and confessed that in the case of Lita, "I've been there, done that."

"I know," Steven said. "She talked about you all the time, and I'm jealous as hell."

"Neither one of us takes our marriage vows very seriously," Paul said.

"I take one of my marriage vows very seriously," Steven said. "The part about the woman obeying the man." He told Paul that he'd confessed his affair with Lita to Neile. "Do you ever come clean with Joanne Woodward?"

"You've got to be kidding," Paul said, astonished that Steven could be that open with Neile. "Wives are creatures upon which one has to practice deceit. I don't want the truth about me ever known. It would spoil my image."

"I'm already known as a bad boy," Steven said, "so I have no prissy image to protect."

"Then the only advice I have for you is something I picked up in Louisiana," Paul said. "You'll be safe as long as you're not caught in bed with a twelve-year-old boy or a dead girl."

***

Steven followed one "quickie" with another quickie when he returned to his native Missouri to film *The Great St. Louis Bank Robbery* (1959), based on an actual attempted bank robbery that had occurred in 1953.

Not wanting to be separated from Neile, he flew every weekend from St. Louis to Las Vegas to be with her until she completed her revue at the Tropicana.

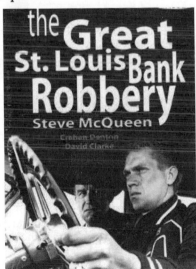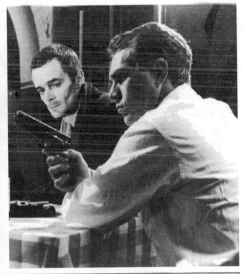

Steve McQueen, playing a blubbering bank robber, ends up a quivering, apologetic mess. He was yet to invent his super-macho image.

Somewhere along the way, he found time to teach her to drive. She wrecked the Corvette and replaced it with a Lincoln.

Steven would later say, "There wasn't anything great about *The Great St. Louis Robbery*," in which he played a former college football hero who went wrong and ended up driving a getaway car for some bank robbers.

A very unimpressive cast was assembled by directors Charles Guggenheim and John Stix. Steven was teamed with actors David Clarke and Crahan Denton. Molly McCarthy was introduced as the love interest, making one of the most uninspired movie debuts of any actress from that era. The best actors were men from the St. Louis Police Department who replicated their actual roles in solving the original crime.

The whole film ended up with a semi-documentary aura. *The Great St. Louis Bank Robbery* seemed made for the drive-in crowd that still flourished in the late 1950s. The final quarter of the film focuses on the actual foiled robbery, with Steven being the only member of the gang to come out alive. He was dragged off to the paddy wagon, his once promising life destroyed.

That was Steven's most inglorious moment in film, at least in his view. "I was sobbing, crying out, 'I'm not one of them!' Me, crying on the screen. When I saw that scene in a movie house, I practically ran from the theater. I felt my macho image had been ruined for life. Instead of marching bravely to my doom like a real man, I came off like a Nellie queen. And my friends all know how I hate Nellie queens."

One night in St. Louis, actor Crahan Denton noted that Steven was furious, raging around the set like he wanted to tear it down. He'd just spoken to Neile in Las Vegas, reversing the charges. "The bitch is carrying on like a slut," he shouted, loud enough for half the crew to hear him. "I just know it." He was so upset and angry that he couldn't shoot one final scene for the afternoon.

He was only half right. An attractive, vivacious young woman such as Neile was certain to be noticed in Las Vegas, and she caught the roving eye of film mogul and aviator Howard Hughes, who vaguely considered putting her under one of his "bondage contracts," the same he had enforced with Jack Buetel and Jane Russell since the days in the early 40s when they filmed *The Outlaw* for him.

Johnny Rosselli, the gangster, also fell for her, and actually became quite friendly and protective of her when his advances were spurned. Johnny needed to be more protective of himself, however, because his dismembered body was found stuffed into an oil drum in Biscayne Bay in Miami in the summer of 1976.

In Las Vegas, Neile also caught the eye of Elvis Presley, who told the Memphis Mafia that, "I'm gonna have that gal if it's the last thing I ever do.

And who in hell is this Steven McQueen?"

Ironically, the paths of Elvis and Steven would cross in the future, and there would be rivalry over the same woman—a different person, not Neile.

Even though Steven demanded fidelity from Neile, he didn't think the rule applied to him. During the making of the St. Louis movie, he enjoyed a brief affair with a pretty young woman he met in a drugstore when he dropped in to order a burger and a chocolate shake. Her name was Mary Wilke, and she became familiar to the cast and crew. "Steven did not try to conceal his affair from the rest of us," said co-star Crahan Denton. "I had many long talks with Mary, but I didn't tell her Steven was married. That was his business."

"I was lonely and broken hearted over my recent divorce, and Steven just moved in on me," Mary said. "We were great together. I had a little girl from my first marriage that my mother tended to while I worked. Steven played with my kid at night and brought her presents. I asked him to move in with us. As stupid as it seems now, I thought he might become my second husband. I really fell in love with him almost overnight. He was very tender. My only embarrassment came early one morning when my little girl walked in on us going at it. Steven had left the door open. He told me not to fret about it. 'Kids have to learn sometimes where a baby comes from,' he told me."

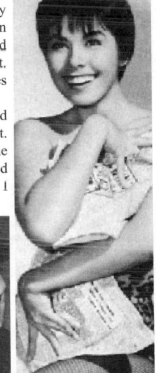

"And then one day I came home from work, and his things were gone," Mary said. "Just like that. Nothing. Not even a note. No good-bye. I guess he was a love 'em and leave 'em type guy. I watched every episode of *Wanted: Dead or Alive* on TV. I

While Steve was struggling to jump-start a career, **Neile Adams**, his wife, caught the eyes of (left to right) mogul **Howard Hughes, Elvis Presley**, and gangster **Johnny Rosselli**.

still think Steven was the cutest guy to ever become a movie star. My girl-friend preferred Paul Newman, but he looked a little too pretty for me. I heard that all pretty boys in Hollywood are gay and marry women to cover up. You can take it from me: Steven McQueen was all man."

In the spring of 1958, when Steven turned twenty-eight, Neile told him her gig at the Tropicana was coming to an end. She could at long last be what he'd wanted all along: a full-time housewife at the modest home in North Hollywood where they moved.

Hilliard ("Hilly") Elkins and the MCA agents kept mailing out his resumé and glossy eight-by-ten photographs to various studios. Only one director picked up the bait. Steven was called to his office.

The director, Edward Dmytryk, was a notorious figure in Hollywood, once blacklisted as part of the "Hollywood Ten" by the House Un-American Activities Committee. His films had included *The Young Lions* (with Marlon Brando and Montgomery Clift) and also *Raintree County* (with Clift and Elizabeth Taylor).

Steve was eager to work with Dmytryk until the negotiations became too blunt. Born in 1908, the director was from the old school of "casting couch" auditions.

"You want something I can get for you, which is a good movie role, and I want something from you," Dmytryk said.

"What do you have in mind?" Steven asked.

"I want you to take out your dick and let me suck it," the director said. "Rock Hudson got his start that way right here in this office. Look what a big star he became. Most of the country thinks casting couches are for beautiful women. But it works for beautiful men too."

"Why don't you stick a dildo up your dingleberry-coated asshole," Steven told him, getting up and storming out of the office. Behind the wheel of his car, he drove so fast he almost had an accident, even though he'd recently screamed at Neile for having an accident with the Corvette by going too fast.

Steven had reached the nadir of his early career, feeling "I was in the fast lane heading for a head-on crash. I'd bombed in New York, and, as for my starring roles in Hollywood, I was making B movies that no one went to see. So what did I do to rescue my career? I signed up for yet another B movie, which became one of the worst films ever made in the history of Hollywood."

As he uttered that gloomy forecast, he was on the verge of becoming a household name. His sudden fame would come from what he contemptuous-ly called "the little box."

***

On both the East the West Coasts, Steven encountered or set up get-togethers with his coterie of newly minted Hollywood male stars. All of them, with the exception of Monty Clift, seemed to be doing better than he was.

Steven hadn't seen Monty since May of 1956, when he was badly injured in a car accident after visiting Elizabeth Taylor and her husband, Michael Wilding, at her hilltop home for a dinner party.

He'd read that his once beautiful features had been forever altered by reconstructive surgery, which distorted his former beauty and even rendered some of his facial muscles immobile. It was painful for Steven to sit through *Raintree County*, which co-starred Monty and Elizabeth Taylor, and watch on the screen the progressive deterioration of that classic face.

He'd made several attempts to get in touch with Monty, but his calls or notes had met with no response. Steven figured that Monty did not want to face his old friends. But one day a call came in, and Monty asked him to come over.

"It was a shell of a man I saw that afternoon," Steven told his friend Sal Mineo. "Monty was drugged and drinking heavily."

At one point, Monty expressed the wish that he had been killed in that car accident. "Look at what happened to Dean. He's becoming a legend, bigger in life than he was in death. The same might have happened to me. Instead, I'm left to present on the screen what remains of my face. I feel it's all downhill from here. The roles will get more pathetic. My reputation will die. I've fucked it up. I could have become the biggest male star in Hollywood. Look at me now."

Steven tried to be as reassuring as he could, but found that none of his words caused Monty to have any hope.

After a drink, Monty got up and pulled off his bathing suit, asking Steven to take off his clothes as well. Never shy about stripping down, Steven joined him for a swim. He hoped, as he later claimed, that it wouldn't be a sexual overture. He just wasn't interested. Fortunately, Monty seemed to have lost his interest in sex.

"Did you see *Raintree County*?" Monty asked as they relaxed over drinks by the pool.

"I thought you were terrific," Steven hastened to add.

"The fucking picture was a monumental bore," Monty said. "I told Elizabeth that,

In ten seconds, a car accident robbed **Monty Clift** of his once-fabled beauty.

although I assured her she looked lovely. The God damn film editor spliced together sequences. In some frames, I had the beauty of my youth. In the next second you see what has become of my face. A ghoul. My new face on the screen is bloated, drained of emotion. I look like I have this expression of resignation. I never thought I was a sex symbol, but I knew I got parts because of my looks. Now the looks are gone. I think the roles will also dry up like my face."

"You're the finest actor on the screen today," Steven said. "Your greatest roles lie ahead of you."

"That's bullshit, and you know it," Monty said. The doorbell rang. He turned back to Steven. "I've invited our mutual friend over." Monty went to the door nude.

When Steven saw it was Marlon Brando, he didn't bother to cover up. Marlon had seen it all before.

After greeting Steven, Marlon, too, took off his clothes and jumped into the pool. After a refreshing swim, he sat between his two rival actors on a chaise longue. He wanted to talk seriously.

As Monty downed a vodka, Marlon pleaded with him to join Alcoholic Anonymous. He even volunteered to accompany him to these meetings in Los Angeles.

"Come on," Monty said. "You know I can't give up drink. Without drink, I'd probably commit suicide. It's the only thing that keeps me alive."

"I agree with Marlon," Steven said. "You can pull yourself out of this slump and reinvent yourself. It's been done before."

"You've got to give up the drugs too," Marlon urged. "You're slowly killing yourself. You've got to stop this shit."

Monty looked furious. "Why don't all of you admit the truth? With me out of serious competition, I've paved a freeway for both of you. Marlon, you can hold onto your crown. As for you, Steven, you can be the Lady-in-Waiting ready to take over the throne."

Steven flipped his dick. "This sure ain't like no lady you've ever seen before."

"I don't view you as competition," Marlon said to Monty. "A real challenge. We can be both friends and competitors like we were before. In fact, I've come over here for another reason. To talk about us doing a picture together. *The Young Lions.*"

"Yeah," Steven joined in. "Rivalry will keep both of you guys on your toes. Laurence Olivier up against Richard Burton. Me up against Paul Newman now that James Dean is out of the picture."

"None of you is making any sense to me," Monty said, staggering up from his chair. "I'm getting another drink."

Marlon and Steven, still nude, joined him at the bar.

"Listen, you little fucker," Marlon said. "I went to see *A Place in the Sun.* I wanted you to fail, but you were fantastic. You deserved your Oscar nomination. You were better than I was in *A Streetcar Named Desire.* In fact, I voted for you to win that Oscar."

Monty looked stunned. "You did? You really did?"

"Baby, at one time back in the 40s, I hated you," Marlon said. "It bordered that thin line between love and hate. You challenge me. You make me better on the screen than I would be without you."

"If I'm emerging as the greatest competition for you guys, then you've got it made in the shade," Steven said.

"You'll get there, boy," Marlon cautioned him. "Don't rush it."

Monty had been concentrating on Marlon ever since he arrived, but he looked at Steven as if seeing him for the first time. "Just what is your next picture?"

"*The Blob,*" Steven said.

Neither Marlon nor Monty had a response.

After an hour of talking, Marlon said he had to leave. Monty remained, half-drunk, on his chaise longue. Marlon turned to Steven, "Show me to the door, would you?"

After kissing Monty good-bye, Marlon walked to the door with Steven. At the door, he gave Steven a kiss on the lips. He whispered in Steven's ear "Just between you and me, Monty's a lost cause. But stand by him. Be his friend."

When Steven returned to the patio, Monty was sobbing. Steven held him in his arms.

"I want to work," Monty sobbed, "I want to fulfill my dream."

"You will," Steven said, fearing his voice carried no conviction.

***

The last time he'd be billed as Steven McQueen, the young actor led the cast of a sci-fi thriller called *The Blob*, which producer Jack H. Harris put together as a double feature with *Dinosaurus*, hoping to lure teenagers to drive-in showings.

"When Steven came into my office, he had an electric presence about him," Harris recalled. "He was different from all other movie stars, and I wasn't sure just why that was. Before he left the office that day, I decided to give him the lead."

While making *The Blob*, Steven was very difficult. "At times I thought we were dealing with Gloria Swanson. He was demanding like he was already a big star. I pitied the poor producers who would have to work with him in the future if he ever became a big star. I thought he would make it. He had the talent, the looks, and the temperament. Like most stars, he could be a pain in the ass. Throughout the film I always rushed to his side to smooth out his ruffled feathers. I must have done that at least three dozen times."

Released by Paramount in the autumn of 1958, *The Blob* was the only picture that Steven never wanted to talk about. However, it became a cult favorite, and he had never looked handsomer, beginning with his opening scene, with him kissing a girl at night in a convertible. His mid-smooch is interrupted by the nearby landing of a meteorite.

As it turns out, the meteorite contains a Jello-like creature, "The Blob," that absorbs everything in its path. Audiences were warned to "Beware of The Blob! It creeps and leaps, it glides and slides across the floor. This alien life-form consumes everything in its path, making it grow and grow into a gigantic monster." The original title for this sci-fi potboiler was *The Night of the Creeping Dead*.

Cast as a teenager, Steve Andrews, a high schooler, Steven at the time was twenty-eight years old. The camp highlight of the movie is the title song, "The Blob," by Burt Bacharach, who, like Steven, of course, would go on to greater glory.

Today *The Blob* often turns up on the list of Hollywood's Ten Worst Movies, although it has become a cult favorite, often scheduled at midnight screenings for young and usually screaming audiences.

In the biggest mistake of his career—so far—Steven was offered a percentage of the movie's future royalties in lieu of a salary. Thinking he was starring in a disaster and a box office flop, Steven took the $3,000 salary. Shot for only $150,000 in Valley Forge, Pennsylvania, *The Blob* eventually grossed more than $4 million, and is still earning money.

Steve and his girlfriend, **Aneta Corseaut,** confront a mountainous mass of homicidal Jello-O that devours everything in its path.
It was Steve's first and last monster movie

The clean-cut American boy Steven played in the film had absolutely nothing to do with the bizarre youth he'd lived. Most of Steven's co-stars, except for his love interest, Aneta Corseaut, who played the character of Jane Martin, were never heard of again after their appearance in this film.

Aneta, however, went on to work in TV movies. Three years younger than Steven, she too was from the Middle West, having been born in Kansas. Like Steven, she was making her debut in this lackluster film, and would later become famous for playing Helen Crump, the so-called love interest of Andy Griffith on *The Andy Griffith Show* (1960-1968).

Aneta was cute, not beautiful, in *The Blob*, and later in life she did admit that she could be added to the list of Steven's sexual conquest of leading ladies.

"At the time I played Jane Martin, his sweetheart, I had no idea he was a serial seducer of his leading ladies. If so, I might not have joined in the fun. He told me his marriage was a mistake, and he was in the process of getting a divorce. I believed him. He looked so sweet and innocent during his Blob period."

Aneta said Steven's wife, Neile, sometimes showed up on the set, so both she and Steven had to be discreet. "I felt sorry for her because I knew Steven planned to tell her that he was divorcing her at the end of the picture. She seemed very much in love with him, and I just knew she'd be heart-broken. I felt bad for her, and a bit guilty."

"I wasn't a very experienced woman when I met Steven," she confessed. "By the time I appeared uncredited in Mel Brooks' *Blazing Saddles*, I knew much more about men and the world. My other movie star seduction was when I worked with Robert Taylor on *The Detectives* for TV in 1962, but I think he was mostly gay, or so I heard."

"At least Steven was a much more ardent lover than Bob Taylor. If Steven had asked me, I would have waited for him until his divorce came through. As it turned out, I would have had to wait some fifteen years. The little devil lied to me, but I enjoyed my time with him immensely. He was a lot of fun. When it was over, he gave me a handshake and a kiss on the cheek. He never returned that hundred dollars he owed me, however. That guy never carried any money around with him."

Steven summed up his experiences at the end of *The Blob*. "No more will I compete on the screen with a gelatinous mass. No more will I be a teenage boy. From now on, I'm gonna be a mature man competing with Paul Newman for his roles. I'm adopting a new persona for the screen. A hero. A lover but a loner too. And from now on, I'm gonna be billed as Steve McQueen."

***

An out-of-work Steve McQueen (his new name) was driving Neile crazy. She called Cy Marsh, a William Morris television agent, who, as a favor to her, got her husband a small role in a series called *Wells Fargo*. He had only a line or two to speak, which carried a $400 actor's fee. Steve stole the scene in which he appeared with the handsome, super-macho Dale Robertson, a one-time boxer and football player from Oklahoma.

Jennings Lane at MCA saw the teleplay and thought Steve might be effective in some television shows. "I think we have a new James Dean in the making."

Ironically, on the New York stage, Steve had been told to quit imitating Dean and to find his own style. In Hollywood, imitation was no problem, since a dead Dean had become the hottest male property in Tinseltown, in the wake of the release and two Oscar nods from both *East of Eden* and *Giant*. This was the first time an Academy Award nomination for Best Actor had gone to a dead man.

With Elkins managing him, Steve was assigned Stan Kamen at William Morris to hawk him for roles. Unlike the gauche caricature of most Hollywood agents, Kamen was "buttoned down and zipped up." Along with super aggressive Sue Mengers, he became the top movie agent in motion pictures, his client roster including Barbra Streisand, Al Pacino, Robert Redford, Warren Beatty, Alan Alda, and Goldie Hawn.

More than any other player in Hollywood, Kamen may have been the key that unlocked the door for Steve in Hollywood.

Beginning in 1975, when Kamen became the head of William Morris's motion picture department, "he was one hot enchilada in this town," said Barbra Streisand in a quote attributed to her. "Everybody wanted to be represented by him."

When Steve showed up for his meeting with Kamen in a Marine butch haircut, dirty blue jeans, and a two-day growth of beard, Kamen was not put off. He later told a gay colleague at William Morris, "I like sucking off these butch types."

Later that afternoon, Kamen invited Steve to join him in a steam bath. "I like to see how my male clients are hung," he told his gay pal.

In the steam bath, Steve told him, "I want to be the hottest piece of shit walking down Hollywood Boulevard, and I want you to make me this rotten town's number one box office bonanza."

Kamen wasn't shocked by such ego blossoming. "I'd dealt with bigger shits than Steve McQueen, and I find the cocky bastard sexy."

It is not known if Steve received a few blow-jobs from Kamen, although it was widely rumored at the time that he did. Certainly, Kamen made that claim. Perhaps Steve did honor the vow he'd made to his long-ago girlfriend, Gena Gilmore, back in Greenwich Village, that he'd fuck anybody, male or female, who could advance his career.

Kamen privately told friends, "Redford eluded my net, but I got to lap up McQueen's juice on several occasions. I think he hated it, but he gave in to me. All actors who are crazed with ambition and lust for money give in at some point. The sex they have to put out is minor compared to that pot of gold waiting at the end of the rainbow."

By the 1980s Kamen's star was flickering out, as he lost clients to Mike Ovitz's CAA. Kamen's health steadily declined after he was diagnosed with AIDS, dying in February of 1986.

In the closing months of his life, Kamen revealed to a writer for the magazine *After Dark* how he launched Steve, getting him cast as Josh Randall, the bounty hunter, in the 1958 TV series, *Wanted: Dead or Alive*. From the very beginning, Kamen rejected the James Dean label and promoted Steve as "the next Bogie."

Kamen won a guest shot for Steve in a teleplay called *Trackdown*, a western TV series featuring Robert Culp as a Texas Ranger. Steve's manager, Elkins, also managed Culp, so Steve had an inside track.

Steve admired Culp's height of 6 feet, 2 inches, and his link with the Playboy mansion. He was a poker-playing buddy of publisher Hugh Hefner. "Man, there must be a lot of pussy running around that place," Steve said.

At the time, William Morris represented Four Star Productions, a company founded by actors Dick Powell, Charles Boyer and David Niven, and the actress/director Ida Lupino. *Trackdown* had evolved into a successful series, and inspired by its success, Four Star had developed a spin-off, *Wanted, Dead or Alive*.

Dick Powell, the husband of June Allyson, the MGM sweetheart of the 40s, was horrified when he met Steve. "We were looking for a Clint Walker, a Chuck Connors, or a James Arness. Big, tall, macho cowboys who would make even Roy Rogers look like a girly man. Kamen sent me this little runt who was the size of a midget with a waist that a high fashion model would be proud to own."

Director **Dick Powell**
Who needs a sphincter?

"He wasn't one of those rough-riding cowboys from the West but a Brooklyn street kid talking like a hipster. As it turned out, he even hated horses."

"Horses disgust me," Powell quoted Steve as staying. "I can't stand the way their ass puckers up when they take a dump on the streets of New York. I want to vomit watching it."

Powell not only rejected Steve, but called Kamen. "The next time you sign on with a psycho, don't send him to Four Star."

Details are murky but Kamen prevailed, eventually persuading Powell to change his mind. The rumor going around Hollywood was that the director/actor had been born with a dysfunctional sphincter—hence was unable to control his bowels. This forced him to take two different medications—one inducing constipation, another as a means of purging himself with laxatives once his intestines were ready to overflow. *Confidential* magazine had picked up on that story, which, if published, would have made Powell a laughing stock.

Joan Blondell, who at one time had been married to Powell, confirmed to the author that this rumor was true.

Kamen had a gay pal who shoveled the dirt at *Confidential*. Based on pressure from Kamen, he ensured that the embarrassing medical story about Powell would remain suppressed. Kamen was quick to point this out to Powell simultaneously with the pressure he exerted during his promotion of Steve.

"OK, fucker," Powell told Kamen, "Send the midget psycho over and we'll make a star out of him."

Two days later, Powell signed Steve to star as Josh Randall, in *Wanted: Dead or Alive* at a salary of $750 a week.

When Steve later heard how his career was launched, he told Kamen, "A rather shitty way to break into the big time," he said, referring to Powell's

Steve McQueen became a household word when he starred as Josh Randall in the popular TV series *Wanted: Dead or Alive*. Shown with his rifle, "Mare's Leg," he was hailed as "the thinking man's cowboy."

bowel movements. "But, hey, it's not important how you get to the top, only that you get there."

***

Signed for the role, Steve went to work at once. Not only did he hate horses, he had to bond with Ringo, a horse who the scriptwriters had configured as something akin to his co-star. Powell demanded that he train daily with Ringo.

"You guys will be kissing after a week or so," Powell predicted.

Steve never came to love and adore Ringo, and always ran in the other direction when the horse had to take a dump, but he did learn to ride Ringo on camera.

There was another problem. Steve had to shoot a model 92 Winchester rifle. Although he was a great car racer and cyclist, he hadn't shot a rifle since he was a kid. On an impulse, he telephoned "the fastest gun in the West," Sammy Davis Jr., whom he'd met briefly at Monty Clift's party. Surprisingly, Davis agreed to some rapid-fire rehearsals with Steve to allow him to pull off the role of Josh Randall.

During the course of their shooting together, Steve got rid of some of his prejudices against African-Americans, coming to view Sammy as a close personal friend. Davis quickly ingratiated himself with Steve, who listened to his problems.

Between shots one Sunday afternoon, Sammy confessed to Steve that "a white woman makes me feel all gooey, and I adore them. But they bring death threats." He admitted that he'd been in love with that lavender blonde, Kim Novak, but Harry Cohn, head of Columbia Pictures, had threatened to have his one good eye blinded if he continued the relationship.

"Cohn ordered me to marry a black woman, and I did," Sammy claimed. "Her name is Loray White. She was singing down at the Silver Slipper in Vegas. I hardly knew her. What I did know is that I had to get married and soon, and it had to be to a black woman."

Sammy's sincerity and his personal charm won Steve over to his side.

Sammy Davis Jr.,
"the fastest gun in the West"
(in more ways than one),
taught Steve how to shoot,
and confessed to him that white
women made him feel "all gooey."

181

In despair, Sammy later told Steve that he was going to divorce Loray after only seven weeks of marriage. "She ran up bills of $27,000 in seven weeks and charged $6,000 on my account at the Sands in just two weeks. It's bad enough that I spend my own money faster than I can get it. I don't need a woman to do that for me."

After a month of shooting with Sammy, Steve learned to shoot almost as well as the master himself.

Their bonding on the range began a long and complicated relationship that Steve never flaunted, perhaps even keeping his relationship with Sammy secret from his wives.

"I don't know if Steve was ashamed of me," Sammy once told Peter Lawford, "but he always wanted to see me on the side. In remote places. But considering what I was up to, I too needed secret hideaways. When I found out that Steve liked sloppy seconds, I told him he was in for some good times with me. You couldn't believe the white gals I was seducing."

On their final day of target practice, Steve asked Sammy why he painted one of his fingernails red.

"It's a sign we use to signal each other," Sammy said. "I'm a Satanist. The fingernail identifies me to other Satanists. I just dabble on the edges of Satanism for sexual kicks. I'm not a true believer."

***

"*Wanted: Dead or Alive* changed my life for all times," Steve said. "I would no longer be Mr. Neile Adams sponging off a broad. I would never want for a job or money ever again in my life. As for women, I always had plenty of those. After the TV series, I had to fight them off. They all wanted to get shot up with my trusty carbine."

John F. Kennedy issued marching orders to Steve: How far below did **Shirley MacLaine's** red hair extend?

The bank accounts in the McQueen household changed drastically that year, with Steve taking in a decent wage.

Still a star on the rise, Neile was touring with the Civic Light Opera production in *At the Grand*, starring (of all people) Paul Muni in his first musical. The play, headed for Broadway, was based on MGM's legendary 1932 film, *Grand Hotel*, which had starred Greta Garbo, John Barrymore, Wallace Beery, Joan Crawford, and Lionel Barrymore.

182

On the opening night of *At the Grand*, Steve brought Shirley MacLaine, whom he'd met through Sammy Davis Jr. He knew she was one of the brightest stars in musicals, and he hoped Shirley might give Neile some pointers about how she could fine tune her performance.

Three days later on the set of *Wanted: Dead or Alive*, Steve was shocked to receive a call from John F. Kennedy who remembered him. "I must say I admire you," Kennedy said. "Taking your mistress to see your wife perform," he said.

"She's not my mistress—just a friend," Steve said.

"You don't have to bullshit with me," Kennedy said. "We're talking man to man. I've got to ask you a question. Is MacLaine's pussy red? I have to know before I make plans to seduce her."

"I'm telling the truth," Steve said. "I've never gone to bed with her."

"For God's sake, man, get onto it," Kennedy urged, "and then get back to me. Is the bush red—or is it not?" He abruptly put down the phone.

The Broadway ambitions for *At the Grand* collapsed, and Steve got his wish. Neile at long last was at home barefoot and pregnant. With Steve's newfound success, they moved into the first house they ever owned, a relatively modest structure on Skyline Drive in Laurel Canyon.

As Neile neared term with her first child, she accidentally overheard Steve talking to a woman on the phone. He was trying to end the relationship with what turned out to be an extra he'd met on the set of *Wanted: Dead or Alive*. After a period of angry silence that lasted two days, she finally forgave him.

After more or less putting Neile's promising career in mothballs, Steve fathered a child with her on June 5, 1959. She was named Terry Leslie McQueen, and he didn't hide his disappointment that she'd been born a girl instead of a boy. Eventually, Neile delivered him a boy baby, as well—Chadwick Steven McQueen, but that came eighteen months later, on December 28, 1960.

While Steve was just learning to be a father himself, his years-long search for his own father, Bill McQueen, came to an end abruptly. In a suburb of Los Angeles, and through the help of a private detective, he located a woman in her late 60s who had been his father's mistress for many years.

"If you want to see your daddy, you're a little late," she said. "He died three months ago and left me with not one cent. Right before he died, he never missed an episode of *Wanted: Dead or Alive*."

It is often asked why Bill McQueen never contacted his son after he became famous. His reasons are unknown, but Hollywood history is filled with parents who abandoned children who later became famous, yet never contacted them. Guilt for abandonment? Whatever, McQueen's reasons for not contacting Steve went with him to the grave.

During the filming of the series, Steve, at least according to Dick Powell, became "the most difficult actor in the business. He was a control freak. He wanted to rewrite more of his lines than Mae West did in her heyday. He even objected to his wardrobe, calling it 'too new and shiny.' You name it—the scripts, fellow actors, even his carbine—Steve hated it. He'd already started out hating horses. In time, he hated me, and all the producers and directors. That was one hostile little brat."

"I'm gonna bring Method acting—naturalism to you—to cowboy Westerns," he threatened Powell.

"He was a perfectionist," David Niven, one of the Four Star executives said, when he came on set to watch Steve work. "I'd call his ambition titanic. Until I met Steve, I thought only actresses like Claudette Colbert had ambition like that."

In the late 1950s Steve became notorious in the industry, as "The Bad Boy of Television." He was also called a "royal pain in the ass," "a prick," "a shit-head," and "TV's temperamental child."

As author Christopher Sandford put it, "Steve's arrival on his motorbike for the day's shoot, at least early on, was the signal for muted groans, the respect accorded an admittedly gifted but temperamental child. The first cameraman on *Wanted* claimed he could tell his boss's mood by the clothes he showed up in. All-black leathers evidenced a storm—trouble ahead. A denim rig with a loud shirt was the sign of good humor—a day when he was approachable and nearly an entire episode could be shot. A neutral outfit with dark glasses signaled the unpredictable. This look was the most common."

"I was very surprised that boy would one day become the King of Cool," Niven said. "There was nothing cool about him. He was hot as a firecracker."

Ringo, his horse, seemed to sense that Steve didn't like him. He threw him every chance he got. "McQueen bit a lot of dust that first season," Powell claimed. "He also tried to bite McQueen every chance he got, and one time he stepped on his foot, breaking his big toe. Personally, I was on Ringo's side. That was one mean horse, but he was a piece of cake compared to working with McQueen."

Steve became known as "the thinking man's cowboy," his sponsor Viceroy, "the thinking man's cigarette." One Viceroy executive lamented, "Steve McQueen didn't sell Viceroy cigarettes. On our sponsored shows, he just sold himself."

Steve claimed he identified with the character of Josh Randall, and, in spite of scriptwriters, fashioned the bounty hunter to suit his own personality.

"We were both loners," he said. "We made up our own minds and controlled our own lives. He was no hero like Gary Cooper in *High Noon*. Randall was a hired hand in the game for the money. If it meant killing, he'd do the job. Unlike the tall, strapping heroes of the old movies—John Wayne, for example—I was a little guy facing big odds, and the audiences rooted for me."

Steve's Winchester 1892 Model carbine, which he called the "Mare's Leg," became part of his characterization when the show was first aired. He wore it in a holster patterned after gunslinger rigs popular in movies of the 1930s. There is something of an anachronistic touch here. The carbine was from 1892, but during some episodes, the script referred to Josh having been a Confederate soldier in the Civil War.

The series would run for three seasons from 1958 to 1961. "At long last, I'm a household name like Paul Newman," he said.

The plunge in ratings came when CBS "suits" moved the show from Saturday to Wednesday night where Steve had to compete against the wildly popular *The Price Is Right*. Ratings plummeted, and *Wanted: Dead or Alive* was cancelled after 117 episodes, airing for the final time in May of 1961. By that time, Steve no longer wanted or needed the series. He lusted to become a movie star on the big screen.

Even though his face was now recognized, and he was asked for autographs wherever he went, Steve still dreamed of the big screen. His chance came during a summer break in the TV series. Filming was scheduled to resume in the autumn.

In the meantime, he was cast as co-star in a movie opposite Frank Sinatra. Steve didn't want Dick Powell to know just how impressed he was. Perhaps as a means of downplaying its importance, he complained, "They could have given me Marilyn Monroe instead of that over-the-hill Sinatra. I bet my eyes

A lover of fast women and even faster cars, Steve would be forever identified with the original Porsche Speedster. James Dean bought one of the first models (in 1955), and Steve a '58 version equivalent to the machine shown above. It was the first car he ever purchased new. He bought it, sold it, and then bought it back.

are bluer than his, anyway."

With the bonanza of cash generated by his TV and movie roles, Steve purchased two machines—one a Porsche roadster, the other an emerald green British racing Jaguar he called "The Green Rat."

Often a beautiful woman was in the seat beside him, while Neile presumably stayed home tending those pots and pans. One starlet, Belle David, said she was picked up one night on Santa Monica Boulevard by Steve. She'd been out walking.

"When I saw it was Steve McQueen, me and my dog got in the car with him. He drove us to this motel in Malibu and checked us in. My God, he got down to action the moment we were in the room. His clothes were off. My clothes were off. As my dog barked, he did his job."

"If I had expected foreplay or dinner, I was very disappointed," she said. "After he was through, he took a whore's bath at the sink, put on his clothes, slapped my ass, and thanked me. He gave me cab fare back to where he'd picked me up. I begged him to let me stay. 'Sorry,' he told me, 'I love my wife and I'm going home to her now. See ya.'"

Although it was dangerous, especially when he was the star of a hit TV series, Steve became intrigued by the racing events sponsored by the California Sports Car Club. His super Porsche was ideal for entry in such competitions, and he learned many racing maneuvers by recklessly driving his Porsche up and down Mulholland Drive in Los Angeles at night. He was joined by other racing car drivers. To evade a patrol car, he rigged up a modification of his tail lights, allowing him to switch off the one illuminating his license plate.

This Porsche Speedster, built in 1958, became the one car (#71) with which Steve would be most closely identified. He had a racing style special windscreen installed and took off the bumpers before entering it in competition, including his first race at Santa Barbara, which occurred in May of 1959. Amazingly, competing against other more experienced sports car racers, he won.

"As I crossed the finish line, I was hooked for life," Steve said. "Sports car racing entered my bloodstream and never left it. James Dean had a Porsche, and so do I."

"Yeah, and guess what happened to Dean?" Steve's producer, Dick Powell, pointed out to him.

Call it beginner's luck, but Steve won other races he entered on the Del Mar circuit, north of San Diego, and at Willow Springs near Palmdale.

By August of 1959, the Porsche had given way to a Lotus Le Mans Mark XI. Behind the wheel of this new vehicle, he vowed to become "the top sports car racer in America."

***

For Metro-Goldwyn-Mayer, which planned a 1959 release, Steve signed to do *The Sacred and Profane*, a World War II picture with an all-star cast headed by Frank Sinatra, Peter Lawford, Charles Bronson, Richard Johnson, and Paul Henreid. The rival of Sophia Loren, Gina Lollobrigida, also starred in this epic, with location scenes shot in Burma, Ceylon, Hawaii, and Thailand. Deep into filming, the working title was abandoned, and the film was changed to *Never So Few*.

Frank Sinatra (left) and **Steve McQueen** bonded on the set of a World War II drama, *Never So Few*. "This blond kid has talent written all over his ugly kisser, but he'd better stay away from my women," Frank said.

Other actors in the dramas that ensued included **Gina Lollabigida** (top right) **Peter Lawford** (center right), and **Charles Bronson** (lower right)

John Sturges had been hired to direct this cast. Born in Illinois in 1910, Sturges would later play an important role in the Steve's future, guiding him through some of his mega hits such as *The Magnificent Seven* and *The Great Escape*.

The assistant director, Robert Relyea, would also work with Steve on some of his greatest hits in the future. At one point, Relyea introduced Steve to Brian Donlevy, an old pro whose first film was made in 1923. "I once was the biggest thing in the movies," he told Steve. "Now I take what I can get. It'll happen to you."

"Not me, man," Steve said. "I always plan to stay on top."

Steve bonded on the set of *Never So Few* with squinty-eyed Charles Bronson, over a few drinks. Bronson, still relatively unknown, was cast in a minor part. Steve later told Sturges, "Ol' Charlie and me have something in common: We both got our start hustling queers for their bread."

Sinatra was cast as a co-commander with an Englishman, Richard Johnson. Their assignment was to conduct harassing actions against the Japanese in the China-Burma-India theater of World War II. Lollobrigida, playing the kept woman of Paul Henreid of *Casablanca* fame, provided window dressing.

Even though the *Harvard Lampoon* would cite the movie as one of the ten worst films of 1959, it would help propel Steve along the road to stardom.

He got an added boost from publicity that gossip maven Hedda Hopper gave him in her columns. Many younger actors were intimidated by the notorious Hopper, who had destroyed more careers than there were stars in the heavens.

Arriving at her house, Steve took a daring approach. Instead of treating her like a queen on her throne, he came on to her like she was a cheap chorus girl. As he walked into her living room, he asked, "Wanna ball, babe? I throw a mean fuck."

Momentarily taken back, she was almost immediately seduced by his macho charm.

"You've got balls, honey," she told him when he left, as he wet kissed her. "Just like Gable, just like Coop. There are too many girly men running around Hollywood these days with names like Troy, Rory, Tab, and Rock. It's good that the movies are still attracting real he men."

Peter Lawford once said that "Steve told me he had a thing—on that rare occasion—for an antique pussy. I didn't have that fetish myself. I liked them young. He told me that one night he took Hedda Hopper to bed. I believed him. She practically gushed over him in her column. She even referred to him as 'the young gun' in print. All of inside Hollywood laughed at that. We knew what she meant."

"When Steve fucked her, I think she was seventy years old if a day," Lawford claimed. "You never knew the age of those old biddies like Hopper and Louella Parsons. They were born before birth certificates."

Upon Hopper's death in 1966, Steve anonymously took out black-bordered tributes in the trade papers, paying homage to A GREAT LADY.

***

Sinatra originally wanted to work with his Rat Pack pals, Peter Lawford and Sammy Davis Jr. But regrettably for the big spending Sammy, who desperately needed the $75,000 salary, Sinatra overheard a radio interview Sammy gave at Chez Paree in Chicago.

ANNOUNCER: *You're a big star now, Sammy. Who do you think is number one, you or Ol' Blue Eyes?*
SAMMY: *I can't lie. I think I've become number one.*
ANNOUNCER: *Bigger than Frank?*
SAMMY: *I love Frank, but I think I'm bigger than he is.*

In a rage upon hearing that broadcast, Sinatra fired Sammy and in his place cast Steve as the gum-chewing Sgt. Bill Ringa, the renegade army driver.

He had first met Steve only briefly at Monty Clift's party when he was the bartender. But he'd seen three episodes of *Wanted: Dead or Alive* and was impressed with the young actor. "The role calls for a killer with no inhibitions," Sinatra told Sturges. "Just the kind of guy Josh Randall is on the tube."

Steve took the role but was horrified to learn that it had been originally intended for Sammy. Later, when they met on the shooting range, Steve later said, "I didn't know if he was going to use his gun on me. He broke down and cried. He forgave me, though. He warned me, 'Never cross Frank.' I never did."

When Sturges hired Steve, he dropped the $75,000 to $20,000, but "Steve lapped it up," the director said. "There was a mean and hungry look in his eyes. I thought with ambition like he had, he'd go to the top."

"I feared Steve and Frank would blow each other up before filming ended," Sturges said. "They discovered a cache of cherry bombs in MGM's wardrobe of all places. They kept setting them off throughout the film."

"One day Sinatra lighted a firecracker in Steve's gunbelt when he was asleep," Sturges said. "What a wake-up call that was for him. He must have jumped ten feet in the air. Steve plotted his revenge."

"One day when Frank was in his dressing room, screwing one of the star-

189

lets, Steve threw open the door and tossed cherry bombs under his bed," Sturges said. "Frank came running out the door buck naked, still retaining his hard-on. Those rumors about what he had swinging between his legs are true. I thought Steve would be fired on the spot. Frank had that kind of power. But he broke into laughter and all was forgiven."

"Steve and Frank became kids again with each other," Sturges said. "One night both of them took turns driving up Hollywood Boulevard, mooning the nighttime pedestrians. Frank would take the wheel and Steve would moon, then Steve would take the wheel when Frank mooned. It was back to high school."

"You gas me," Frank told Steve. "I'm your new pal."

"You not only gas me, you set me on fire . . . literally," Steve said.

"Why do I like McQueen?" Sinatra asked Lawford. "Because he's as much of a bad-ass as I am, without your frilly English manners and accent. A man who knows how to stop and take a piss when he needs to, regardless of what blue noses are watching."

"What surprised me was not the friendship that developed between Steve and Frank, but between Steve and Peter," Sturges said. "Peter was English bred, urbane and sophisticated. Steve had made his living hustling and ending up in the reform school, or so he said."

"Peter was bisexual, and he was really attracted to Steve, finding him very macho," Sturges claimed. "I don't know if he were telling the truth, but Peter, who was always very upfront around me, told me that he gave Steve frequent blow-jobs during the filming. Peter claimed it calmed Steve down, made him less mean, less temperamental."

"One night when I was having a drink with Steve, I very casually asked him about Peter's accusation," Sturges said. "He was sort of enigmatic. 'Didn't you know?' he said, 'that Lawford limey is known as the best cock-sucker in Hollywood.'"

Since Steve always boasted that he'd seduced every one of his leading ladies, the question remains: Did he seduce Gina Lollobrigida? Sturges flatly asked Steve.

"I suspect Frank has beaten me to the punch," Steve said. "Sammy warned me. Don't mess with one of Frank's women."

One film critic claimed, "Ms. Lollobrigida and Mr. Sinatra did not click off screen, or on for that matter."

Actually, over the years it was rumored that Gina was seducing another star of the film, Richard Johnson, a handsome English actor who in the future would be offered the role of James Bond in *Dr. No* (1962). He foolishly turned it down because he did not want to sign a multi-picture contract.

As a point of irony, Johnson would marry Sammy's "true love" Kim

Novak in 1965, the marriage lasting only a year.

Critic Barry Norman summoned up Steve's mass appeal: "It was a clever unisex appeal. Males wanted to be him—the dames wanted to bed him, which a fair number duly did."

After attending a preview of *Never So Few* in Hollywood, Sinatra slapped Steve on the back. "The picture belongs to you, kid."

Never So Few cemented the unlikely friendship between McQueen and Sinatra. At one point Sinatra invited Steve and Neile to New York and Atlantic City where he was performing.

Steve was really awed to see how a big-time star lived, arriving in limousines, occupying presidential suites, and having bottles of champagne delivered by room service. "This is the life for me," Steve told Sinatra. Yet in spite of his fascination, Steve would never lead the life of a grand star.

***

Steve lost out on his chance to become a bona fide member of Sinatra's "Rat Pack." In New York, Sinatra asked him to appear in an upcoming film, *Ocean's 11*. CBS demanded that Steve film a dozen segments of *Wanted: Dead or Alive* back to back, upon his return from the Bob Hope Christmas Show in Alaska.

Steve drove up to the studio in his Jaguar XK-SS for which he'd paid $4,000.

He wanted to negotiate with Dick Powell to get out of his TV series. If not that, he wanted permission to take the most tempting movie offer being made. Powell turned him down on both requests.

Steve had actually committed to work for five seasons in *Wanted* if the TV show's success merited it. But he was being besieged by movie offers that were far more lucrative.

In Hartford, Connecticut, on a personal appearance tour with Neile, he devised an elaborate scheme. In a rented Cadillac, a convertible, he would stage a crash in which he would claim a neck injury, serious whiplash.

He planned to actually crash the car. In a reckless disregard of the safety of the mother of his children, he asked Neile to sit in the passenger seat with him.

June Allyson,
the nymphomaniac
who became
"America's sweetheart"
in the 1940s

Pretending to lose control of the car, he rammed it into a stone wall, narrowly missing hitting a policeman. Neile escaped unharmed, Steve with minor injuries. But he complained so badly about his neck that he sought medical attention and arrived back in Hollywood with his neck in a brace. The accident made headlines.

Elkins, Steve's manager, told Dick Powell that his star of *Wanted: Dead or Alive* was too seriously injured to do another season.

Powell suspected something and arrived at Steve's house with June Allyson to spend an evening. Both June and her husband were most sympathetic to Steve. June didn't believe Steve's act, having used an excuse of ill health with her own bosses at MGM many times over the years. Unknown to Steve, America's sweetheart during her reign at MGM was a nymphomaniac. She asked Steve to go for a walk in the garden where, it became clear, she wanted to give him a quick blow-job. He politely turned her down.

Powell knew exactly how to cure Steve's whiplash. Before the evening ended, he'd agreed to give him a substantial boost in salary, going up to $100,000 a year, and he also arranged his shooting schedule at CBS to allow Steve time to slip away to shoot a feature film.

***

Chuck Connors as "The Rifleman" also became known for a gay porno film he made early in his career. These tight jeans don't reveal that he packed another heavy gun.

Sammy Davis Jr. not only was Steve's new friend, but a long-time friend of Chuck Connors, who had become an overnight sensation on TV in the hit series for Four Star Productions called *The Rifleman*. Chuck had found more immediate success with his Western series than Steve had.

At first Steve was prepared to dislike Chuck, viewing this former baseball and basketball star as a rival. When Sammy introduced Steve to Chuck, Steve was a bit awed by this larger-than-life actor who stood 6'5" tall, weighing 215 pounds.

After about an hour, Steve put aside his resentment and fell under spell of this Brooklyn-born athlete. "At first I thought he was just another John Wayne clone, but then I learned that behind all that macho posturing was a man with a secret past," Steve said. "I think I really got to know him when Davis had to go to the clubhouse to use the toilet. When he was out of ear shot,

Chuck confided to me, 'I love Sammy dearly, but he's not my favorite singer. Frank Sinatra is. As for music, I'm still hung up on Glenn Miller and his orchestra.'"

When Steve got to know his two closest friends, Casey Perkins and Darron McDonald, he did reveal to them a small bit about his private friendship with Chuck.

"The guy was everything he appeared to be on the TV screen, but more," Steve said. "He lived in two different worlds."

As each of their Western TV series gained in fame, and as their friendship deepened, Chuck and Steve both revealed to each other that they had made porno, Steve because he was desperate for cash and Chuck "just for the hell of it," because he'd earned a lot of money from his career as an athlete.

Porno films starring Steve have never surfaced, but Chuck's brief entry in porn was used as a clip in *Hollywood Blue*, released in 1970 and shown in a Times Square theater in New York.

One time Chuck reportedly showed a clip of the film to Steve, who told his friend, "You certainly have the equipment to make it 'big' had you continued in porno."

On the day Chuck met Steve, Sammy had an appointment with a blonde—not Kim Novak—later that night. Chuck invited Steve to join him for dinner at a roadside steakhouse he patronized out in San Fernando Valley.

Since Steve never talked a lot about his secret friendship with Chuck, rich details are missing.

The director, John Sturges, knew about it, however. "Steve did not want his worlds to collide. For example, I doubt very seriously if his wife, Neile, knew about it. Steve wanted to remain a puzzle to most people. To do that, he had to keep some of the key figures in his life segregated. If all of them got together and told what they knew, maybe the final pieces of that jigsaw puzzle that was Steve could be pieced together. He was intent on seeing that that didn't happen."

Chuck became a key figure in Steve's understanding of the secret macho world of bisexual actors in Hollywood, who lived deep in the closet to protect their screen images and who only indulged in liaisons with their fellow brothers in the strictest of privacy. Until he met Chuck, and in spite of his own background, Steve still regarded homosexuals as queers to be mocked, put down, and ostracized.

Until that day of target practice with Chuck, Steve had already met the "bad boys" of Hollywood, whose proclivities toward homosexuality have been exposed over the years, notably Sal Mineo, Montgomery Clift, Marlon Brando, James Dean, and Rock Hudson.

It was through Chuck that Steve learned about the bisexuality of many of

Hollywood's leading stars of that era. On the set of *Pat and Mike*, in which Spencer Tracy had co-starred with Katharine Hepburn, the aging actor came on strong to Chuck. "I gave him what he wanted," Chuck told Steve. "I did the same for Burt Lancaster when we appeared in *South Sea Woman* in 1953."

During the filming of *The Hired Gun* in 1957, Chuck involved himself in some sexual liaisons with Rory Calhoun and Vince Edwards. When Chuck made *The Lady Takes a Flyer* in 1958, he turned down cross-dressing Jeff Chandler but went for sultry Lana Turner.

"When I did *Move Over, Darling*, with Doris Day and James Garner, I got no offers at all," Chuck said. "That was a remake of *My Favorite Wife* that in 1940 had starred Cary Grant and Randolph Scott. Had I been in that picture with those two male lovers, I'm sure both of them would have gone for me."

For the biographer, this question remains unanswered: Did Steve and Chuck have a fling? Casey and Darron claimed that Steve never said whether they did or not, but his friends just assumed they did.

Steve's director, John Sturges, thought there was a high degree of intimacy between them. "When he wasn't needed, Chuck often came onto our set for long visits with Steve in his dressing room. I think something was going on there between the little guy and the big guy."

"During the time I worked with Steve, I knew he went away for a few weekends out in the west with Chuck," Sturges said. "Steve told me they were indulging in rifle practice. Whatever they were doing, I think they enjoyed each other's company immensely. Steve pursued half the women in California but he always managed to keep up with his male bonding, and all those wives too. Frankly, I don't know how he did it."

Steve McQueen (left) and the creepy Peter Lorre, on his last legs, appeared together in a bizarre story, *Man from the South* (1960). The plot has Lorre wanting to chop off Steve's little pinky. The teleplay was part of *Alfred Hitchcock Presents.*

"As for me, I might have a piece on the side from time to time, but Steve McQueen made a career out of infidelity and was so secretive about it," Sturges said. "Had he not become an actor, he would have gone over big in espionage the way he slipped around and rarely got caught."

"If Chuck had any gay streak in him at all that was noticeable, it was his fixation on his hair," Sturges said. "If there was a looking glass somewhere, Chuck would be adjusting or rearranging his hair. Even his so-called windblown look was artfully arranged."

"From what I heard, he packed such a powerful weapon—and I don't mean his rifle—that I think he could have had any woman or gay man he encountered," Sturges said.

In the film, *Trouble Along the Way* (1953), in which Chuck had a small role in what was a John Wayne picture, the director was Michael Curtiz of *Casablanca* fame. "Stacked up against Wayne, Connors made Wayne look like a girl," Curtiz said. "Also, from what I hear, Connors has five times as much as Wayne."

***

Marlon Brando, Steve's longtime friend, lived a short distance from the McQueens on Mulholland Drive. Steve's motorcycle was seen parked outside the Brando manse on many a night. Brando was one of Steve's secret friendships. He refused to share any details of the relationship with family or friends, most of whom were unaware that he even knew Brando.

One night a member of Brando's staff heard Steve fighting with his boss. "They sounded like two shrill queens," the houseboy charged. "Brando wanted McQueen to star in an upcoming film that he was developing called *One-Eyed Jacks*. Steve adamantly refused. They reminded me of two lovers fighting, not two actors arguing over a script."

As director, Brando had promised to write in a role for Steve the equal of his, two men out in the West coping with survival. Brando's idea almost foreshadowed a future script that he'd be offered, *Butch Cassidy and the Sundance Kid*.

Long before craggy lines desecrated his looks, Steve appeared in a bizarre teleplay, *Human Interest Story* (1959) for *Alfred Hitchcock Presents*. **Arthur Hill** (right) is really an alien from Mars inhabiting the body of an Earthling.

Brando urged Steve to get out of television as soon as possible. "You need to flash on the big screen, not on some little box."

Steve did not immediately take Brando's advice.

"Just for fun," according to Steve, he agreed to appear with Neile on an *Alfred Hitchcock Presents* for television. Steve was in both episodes, Neile in one. Cast as Bill Everett, he starred in *Human Interest Story* in 1959 and played a gambler in *Man from the South* in 1960. But at this point in his life he had little interest in TV.

In the bizarre teleplay, *Human Interest Story* (1959), Steve plays a journalist who interviews a man (Arthur Hill), who claims to be an alien from Mars inhabiting the body of an Earthling. The broadcast might have been better suited for *The Twilight Zone*. Both Hill and Steve had a good script to work with, and effectively acted their roles, keeping up the suspense.

Neile joined Steve in *Man from the South* (1960), in which they co-starred with Peter Lorre. In this unlikely story written by Roald Dahl, Lorre makes a bet with Steve that he can't light his cheap cigarette lighter ten times in a row. If he does, he wins Lorre's new convertible. If not, Lorre gets to chop off Steve's little pinky.

Steve was fascinated by this Austro-Hungarian actor, who was entering the final phase of his life. He would die in 1964. Steve told Hitchcock, "I don't want to go out of life like Lorre. After all those great movies like *Casablanca*, the roles seem to be drying up for him." Steve was sad to note that in his last film, *Muscle Beach Party*, Lorre didn't even receive billing.

***

Even though Steve was still trapped in that little box, word spread quickly across Hollywood that he and Paul Newman were the hot new stars to watch. Both actors as they reached or passed the age of thirty found themselves invited to A-list parties, often attended by their screen idols.

At one party and in one night, Steve encountered some of his "fetishes" from the 1940s, a roster that included Rita Hayworth, Jane Greer, Barbara Stanwyck, and Jennifer Jones.

Throughout the evening he was most flirtatious with Rita. Every now and then their eyes would meet each other's across a crowded room. He cast his wry smile in her direction.

When he saw her standing alone for a moment, he dashed to her side and invited her out on the terrace for some privacy. Very bluntly, he told her that when he was a teenager he used to masturbate to a movie still of her as *Gilda*. "I stole it from the local movie house."

"That's the most charming thing a man has ever told me." She whispered in his ear, "Call me. I'm still hot." He could feel her slipping a piece of paper into his pocket.

The next day he shared his good luck with Peter Lawford, since he knew they'd been lovers before. "Forget it," he said. "The worst lay in the world. She was always drunk and never stopped eating."

"But my God, man, she was a real princess," Steve said. "I've gone to bed with queens such as yourself but never a princess."

Three nights later, a maid ushered Steve into Rita's living room where he found her sitting on a sofa, her feet propped under her. Except for a slash of scarlet on her lips, she wore no makeup but looked radiantly lovely with some inner glow. It wasn't Gilda. It was the real Rita Hayworth emerging from behind the glitz and glamour of her screen image.

The way she was huddled on that sofa made him think she was afraid of some impending disaster. Or else she was cold from the early winds blowing in that night. Her mind seemed to have drifted to some far-off planet—perhaps Jupiter—and she wasn't immediately aware of him. When she did become aware of his presence, she didn't seem to recognize him at first.

"Oh, you did come to see me," she said. She rose from the sofa to give him a hug and two brief kisses on each cheek. "I was hoping you'd drop in some night."

The statement startled him. His appearance here had been carefully arranged in advance. It was not a casual dropping by, but would be viewed as one of the dates of a lifetime. One by one he was getting around to those screen goddesses that had brightened many a dull night when he was taken to the movies or else slipped off and went alone. When he didn't have money back in those days, he had perfected the art of sneaking in when the ticket taker was otherwise occupied.

"My God," she said, "I'm the hostess and I haven't offered you some refreshment." She called into the kitchen and asked her maid to bring them two cups of Irish tea. When the tea arrived, Rita walked over to the bar and returned with a bottle of Irish whiskey. She poured generously into the tea. "Irish tea always tastes better with Irish whiskey, don't you agree?"

"I wouldn't have my tea any other way," he said.

For their second cup, she poured whiskey into the cup even though the tea had been drunk. He was fascinated by her as she began her dance of

Hollywood princess **Rita Hayworth** moonlighted as a painter. To Steve McQueen: "I want to paint you in the nude."

seduction. She fingered a pair of castanets on the table.

Before his eyes, she'd transformed herself not into Gilda but into Margarita Cansino, dancing with her father who'd seduced her. She was dancing without music, but this love goddess made him imagine there was music somewhere in the distance.

The dance ended in a seduction. She didn't bother asking him up to her bedroom, but let him make love to her on her large sofa. As he seduced her, he imagined all the other lovers who'd gone before, some of whom he knew, including David Niven. Others were out of his league, including Howard Hughes, Prince Aly Khan, and Orson Welles.

At three o'clock that morning, it was time for him to go. Before he left, he asked, "Is it true that a picture of you was stamped on the first bomb dropped on Hiroshima?"

"So I hear," she said. "Wasn't that a blast?" A frown crossed her face, as she realized how silly, or even how cruel, her statement was.

At the door, she abruptly asked him, "May I paint you? In the nude?"

"Sure, if you want to."

Before kissing her good night, he arranged another appointment with her.

Steve told only part of his encounter to friends, and details are missing at this point.

It seemed that he came back to Rita's home at least on six different occasions, posing nude for her, his legs spread-eagled on a bed, his arms outstretched like Christ on the cross.

Marilyn Monroe is distracted by another man as she dances in the arms of the effete **Truman Capote,** who wanted MM and Steve to star together in his *Breakfast at Tiffany's.*

In the years ahead, when Steve became a really big star and Rita was short of money, she sold the nude to a wealthy collector in San Francisco, who was rumored to have paid $100,000 for it.

Allegedly, he was "mad about the boy" and hung the painting on the wall above his bed.

It is not known if the painting exists today. When his homophobic heirs took over the townhouse after the collector's death, they found many of the walls covered with nude paintings of young men or boys. The townhouse and the antiques were sold, the paintings reportedly burned.

It is entirely possible the collector's

198

family did not know the painting above the bed was a nude of Steve McQueen and the artist was Rita Hayworth herself.

***

Still getting movie offers, despite being trapped in his TV series, *Wanted: Dead or Alive*, Steve received a phone call from Truman Capote. At long last, he had a script for a movie that, in the words of Capote, "people will be watching years from now."

To make his luncheon date with Steve even more alluring, Capote held out a surprise. "I've also invited the woman I want to play Holly Golightly opposite you."

"Just who in hell might that be?" Steve asked.

"Only the most famous woman on the planet and the sexiest female in the history of the movies."

"Been there, done that," Steve said. "You could only be talking about Marilyn Monroe."

"She never told me you two guys did it," Capote said in a somewhat petulant voice. "I thought I knew everything Marilyn did, even Joan Crawford."

"This one escaped you," Steve said. "If Marilyn told you all her bedtime stories, you wouldn't get any writing done."

"You've got a point there," Capote said.

As was typical, Marilyn was ninety minutes late. In the meantime, Capote filled Steve in on the plot of the picture. He was surprised to learn that Holly was a high-class hustler and that he'd be playing a kept man.

"This is not the kind of image I'm trying to use to launch my career into the bigtime," Steve said. "Sounds more like something Paul Newman would go for. After all, he played that hustler in *Sweet Bird of Youth*. I see my future roles as action pictures, real he-man roles, a man who does for himself and doesn't live off a woman. By the way, who do you have in mind for this rich woman who keeps me?"

"There's only one woman in Hollywood who could pull it off," Capote said, ordering another martini. "None other than Bogie's baby or former baby. Lauren Bacall."

At this point, in walked Marilyn Monroe,

The dazzlingly handsome **Jeffrey Hunter** also wanted to play the "kept man" in *Breakfast at Tiffany's*, but Truman wanted to "audition" him first to see if he was right for the part.

199

looking gorgeous and creating spectacular attention. She was wearing green. After kissing both Capote and Steve on the mouth, she sat down and asked for champagne.

"Every wardrobe designer in Hollywood tells me that green isn't a sexy color," she said. "To hell with them. I'm wearing green and making it sexy. After all, when I changed my name to Marilyn, it was considered dull, sexless. Nowadays mothers all over America are naming their daughters Marilyn after me."

She could stay only thirty minutes as she was already late for an appointment. She was more interested in drinking the champagne than in eating the peach half and a dollop of cottage cheese she was served.

"Everybody these days wants a piece of my flesh, both on and off the screen," she said. "As for my off-screen offers, I can't fuck everybody. Even Albert Einstein wants me to autograph my nude calendar for him."

After hasty good-byes, she left, trailed by Steve who had volunteered to drive her to her appointment. "No taxi is fast enough," he told her.

Capote looked disappointed that he was being left alone. He ordered another martini to compensate for his lack of company.

"Aren't you Truman Capote?" came a soft, masculine voice. Capote looked up to see a startlingly handsome face with beautifully piercing eyes, an actor who in just a year or so would be cast as Jesus Christ in the remake of *King of Kings*. "I'm Jeffrey Hunter, and I've always wanted to meet you."

"The honor is all mine, I assure you," Capote said.

Switch hitter **Brad Dexter**, former husband of singer Peggy Lee, told his best buddy, Frank Sinatra, "I never met a bordello I didn't like."

"I hear *Breakfast at Tiffany's* is being cast, and there's a role in it with my name written on it," Jeffrey said.

"We'll see about that," Capote said enigmatically. "Please sit down and have a drink with me and tell me the story of your life. Don't leave out any detail, regardless of how sordid. Is it true, for example, that both Robert Wagner and Paul Newman are madly in love with you? And did you know that Marilyn Monroe and Steve McQueen just departed my table? Steve is gay, you know?"

"I didn't know," Jeffrey said. "But I'll certainly spread the word across Hollywood. Before the rooster crows in the morning, all of Tinseltown will know."

Jeffrey Hunter, Jesus Christ reincarnate, was a man of his word.

After mulling it over for three days, Steve called Capote and bowed out. "The part is not for me. What about George Peppard? I think he'd be perfect."

A few weeks later, Capote called Steve again. "George has agreed to do it. He's a living doll. Very handsome, very sexy, just the kind of Marine hunk a woman would keep. Patricia Neal, not Bacall, is going to be his female patron. But the studio doesn't want to go with Marilyn. I'm so sad."

"Why not?" Steve asked. "Don't tell me she couldn't pull off a hooker role. She could rely on her own background."

"Marilyn would have been absolutely marvelous," Capote said. "She wanted to play it too. Paramount double-crossed me and cast Audrey Hepburn. Audrey is an old friend and one of my favorite people, but she's wrong for Holly."

Before he rang off, Capote, ever the voyeur, had to ask the question. "Did you and Marilyn get it on again?"

"In a way," Steve said. "She was late, as usual, for her appointment. I drove her there breaking all speed laws but I wasn't arrested. On the way, she took it out and gave me her usual skilled job. I nearly wrecked my Jaguar."

***

Robert Vaughn, one of its co-stars, was convinced that *The Magnificent Seven* would fail at the box office. Today it's the second most frequently played film on television, trailing Bogie's *Casablanca*. It also was a "star maker" not only for Steve but for James Coburn and Charles Bronson.

Producer Walter Mirisch had arranged for United Artists to put up two million dollars for the 1960 release of this film. He hired John Sturges, who had directed Steve in *Never So Few*, to cast the other six cowboys after Yul Brynner had signed to play the lead role of "Chris," a shoot-to-kill cowboy who dresses in black and almost never removes his hat to show his bald head.

The Western, which became a classic, was based on Akira Kurosawa's celebrated *Seven Samurai*. Brynner arrived on the set gloating over his Oscar win for *The King and I*.

The plot swirls around seven cowboys of widely mixed backgrounds and personalities, each a gunslinger, hired by a Mexican border town to halt periodic forays on the pueblo by *banditos*.

Robert Vaughn learned the hard way that whenever Steve McQueen accompanied him to a Mexican bordello, it's prudent to carry extra *dinero*.

This was Brad Dexter's last major film role. After that, he would spend most of his life as Frank Sinatra's professional buddy. Sinatra put him on the payroll after he saved his life from drowning off the coast of Malibu.

It was Vaughn himself who got Coburn cast, tracking him down to Greenwich Village where "he was shacked up with a colored chick smoking dope."

Three years younger than Steve, Horst Buchholz was once called "the most beautiful man in Berlin." In time he became known as "The James Dean of German Cinema." He was introduced to American audiences in *The Magnificent Seven*.

The "services" of German actor **Horst Buchholz** became a bone of bitter contention between Steve and Yul Brynner, the feuding co-stars of *The Magnificent Seven*.

In the battle for Horst, Steve's charms won out over those of the bald-headed wonder.

In the film he played Chico, an inexperienced Mexican youth who dreams of becoming a gunslinger. Although he was married when Steve met him, Horst was a notorious international homosexual and had countless affairs with men. In 2000 he openly admitted to "bisexuality" for the first time in the German tabloid *die Bunte*.

Eli Wallach, the second lead, after Brynner and before Steve, was signed to play the Mexican *bandito* who terrorizes a village with his gang.

Sturges wanted—and finally got—Steve for the third lead, offering him $65,000 for his appearance in the film. He was given the role of Vin, a fun-loving, muscle-bound Mexican/Irishman. In the Japanese movie, this role was made famous by Toshiro Mifune.

With his rising status in Hollywood, Steve bought a larger house for his growing family, moving to 2419 Solar Drive in Nicholas Canyon. It cost $65,000. One reporter said Steve's house "cranes over Hollywood like a hippie Berghof."

At long last, after years of delay, shooting began near Cuernavaca, lying some fifty miles outside Mexico City.

Even before filming had begun, lawsuits kept popping up, threatening to shut down production. The most serious one was filed by Anthony Quinn, who claimed that Kurosawa had sold him the rights to the screenplay. A judge later dismissed Quinn's claim.

Steve enjoyed working again with Bronson and the associate director, Robert Relyea. He'd also become close friends with Coburn.

In Cuernavaca, Steve checked into the Pousada Jacaranda along with most of the cast. Brynner and Horst preferred to rent private houses. On his first night, Coburn spotted Steve slipping off to his room with a young Mexican *señorita.*

"Mexico is great," he told Coburn the next day. "You can get all the pussy or pot you want with a mere flick of the finger. But I've got to watch my step. My old lady is planning to come down on weekends."

According to Vaughn, from the very beginning "Steve was determined to steal the picture out from under Brynner. Damned if he didn't do it."

"You gotta make my part better," Steve told Sturges. "I'm not going to be Brynner's ass-wipe."

During the shoot, Steve also asked Sturges to cut some of his dialogue. "Movie acting is reacting. Silence is golden on the screen."

"You would have loved making silent films," Sturges shot back.

After observing him closely, the co-star, Eli Wallach, claimed that "McQueen was the best reactor of his generation."

Its gay wardrobe master claimed that *The Magnificent Seven* was actually the average measurement of penis sizes for this splendid array of talent.

Left to right: **Yul Brynner, Steve McQueen, Horst Buchholz, Charles Bronson, Robert Vaughn, Brad Dexter,** and **James Coburn**

Steve was a scene stealer. In one shot, while Brynner was magnificently leading his posse, riding tall in the saddle, Steve behind him lowered his cowboy hat into a mountain stream, filling it with water and, without missing a beat, putting it back on his head, as water cascaded down, soaking him.

At first Brynner and Steve were on speaking terms, as he regaled Steve with stories of his life. "I was once addicted to smoking opium," Brynner said. "I became friends with Jean Cocteau. We smoked opium together."

"I bet she was one hot *puta*," Steve said.

"Cocteau is a famous French writer, a man."

"Were you also his lover?" Steve asked.

"No, I'm not a homosexual," he said. "Those are malicious lies spread about me. If you want my qualifications as a straight lover, just ask Tallulah Bankhead, Anne Baxter, Ingrid Bergman, Joan Crawford, Marlene Dietrich, Judy Garland, Gina Lollobrigida, Maria Schell, and Nancy Reagan."

"I've fucked a lot of those same ladies myself," Steve said, exaggerating, of course. "I don't have any inspiration to get around to Nancy Reagan. But Judy Garland's A-Okay."

The next day Brad Dexter told Steve that Horst's rented car had been seen every night parked in front of Brynner's rented hacienda. "Horst is gay, you know, and Brynner is taking full advantage of getting a hot piece of Kraut ass. First, Marlene, now Horst. In spite of all those A-list pussies he's fucked, he also likes boy ass. I heard he fucked your pal, Sal Mineo, when he was only thirteen and appearing on Broadway with the kid in *The King and I*."

The legendary Mexican beauty **Dolores Del Rio**--fabled as "The Timeless Wonder"--told Steve, "I was Elvis Presley's mother in *Flaming Star,* but I can be more than that to you."

"I'll file that away for future use," Steve told Dexter.

It was not characteristic of Steve, but he tipped off the press about a feud with Brynner. "I think, in this film, I represent a threat to Mr. Brynner," he said. "He doesn't ride very well and he doesn't know anything about quick draws and that kind of thing. Well, I know horses and guns. I'm in my element and he isn't. I guess I make him nervous."

Brynner's response? "Arrogant little shithead. I heard he used to sell his dick on the open market to any buyer with a ten-dollar bill."

The day after a story about the Brynner/McQueen feud appeared in the press, Brynner confronted Steve on the set. Brynner grabbed Steve by the shoulders and spun him around. "I'm an established star, and I don't feud with actors in bit parts. I'm too big for that. Call the paper and admit you lied."

"Take your fucking hands off me, or I'll rip you bald," Steve said, injecting both a threat of violence and humor into the confrontation. "Don't you ever touch me again, you fucking faggot!"

From that day and until the end of the shoot, there was a real—not an imaginary—feud between the two stars. Steve could never settle for a mere confrontation. He wanted "major payback time," he told Dexter.

"To get even with Brynner, Steve started using all his charm and male flash to win over Horst," Dexter claimed. "He came on strong. He turned the kid's head around. After about a week, Steve's rented car was parked in front of Horst's rented hacienda. Brynner was left out in the cold, but he recovered quickly. In a week or so he was seen keeping company with this beautiful green-eyed *mexicano* boy."

"I don't know what was going on between Steve and Horst," Coburn later recalled. "Frankly, I think in the beginning Steve didn't give a rat's piss about Horst emotionally. He only wanted to take something away from Brynner and humiliate him. Maybe Steve thought he would be the better man by stealing Horst. Unfortunately, Horst's emotions got tangled with. I heard he fell big time for Steve. But after the movie wrapped, Steve dropped Horst like a gringo dump after he's had too many hot Mexican chili peppers."

Whenever he was free, Steve liked to share many a tequila with Bronson. He learned that he'd been a coal miner. Born to a couple from Poland and Lithuania, one of fifteen children, he told Steve he was so poor that at one time he had to wear his sister's dress to school "because I had nothing else. When the boys made fun out of me, I beat the shit out of them."

He also claimed that he learned "to hustle queers" while serving in the United States Air Force as an aircraft gunner. "I found out soon enough that many civilian guys are only too willing to part with a ten spot to get the chance to suck an airman's dick."

During the shoot in Mexico City, Brad Dexter, who knew the city intimately, took Steve on a tour and taught him such delights as the pleasure of "sensual" pedicures or massages from a fourteen-year-old Mexican beauty with Jane Russell sized breasts.

He also took Steve along with him to attend a party at the elegant home of Dolores Del Rio, who had been born in 1905 but still retained her regal beauty.

She told them that she had just finished an American film. "It's called *Flaming Star*, and I played Elvis Presley's Indian mother."

That night she screened *Bird of Paradise*, her most famous film in which she played a Polynesian girl opposite Joel McCrea. It had been shot in 1932 as an early talkie.

Brad told Steve, "I think she dips her face in porcelain. She never ages. Of course, she never appears in daylight either. She's strictly a lady of the evening. She's also rich. You should become her kept boy and retire from Westerns."

That night, Brad later claimed, Steve stayed in Del Rio's luxurious bedroom, which had a special refrigerator to chill vintage champagne.

"We bathed in rose water—stinking stuff—and a maid came in and sprinkled fresh rose petals in our bath," Steve said. "Those petals didn't cover up my big hard-on. Later, we retired to her satin-sheeted bed, which also was covered in rose petals. That bitch sure liked her roses. We fucked until dawn. Some of these antique pussies I like at times can go at it longer than a young *puta*."

In another wild Mexican adventure, Robert Vaughn, in his memoirs, *A Fortunate Life*, related how Brad took Steve and him "to one of the finest brothels in North America." In his account, Brad, Steve, and Vaughn were welcomed by the blonde-haired madam "like visiting dignitaries." He also noted that the parade of young women, beautifully dressed, groomed, and sent out for inspection "could have passed for finalists in a Miss Universe pageant."

Instead of **Glenn Ford** in a top hat, this movie poster could have depicted Steve McQueen opposite **Bette Davis**.

Brad disappeared with two raven-haired beauties, leaving Steve and Vaughn alone with seven hot *putas*. Instead of making a selection, Steve wanted all of them. Vaughn admitted that because of their massive consumption of tequila, they did "more laughing than humping."

When it came time to pay the bill, Vaughn learned about Steve's notorious habit of not carrying any money with him. The bill came to $700, and Vaughn had only $400 on him, and couldn't lend Steve the *dinero* he wanted.

Steve was surrounded by beefy *mexicanos* who looked like they wanted to slit his throat. "Steve was virtually kidnapped and was being held for ransom," Sturges said. "He tried to run away but was caught in the garden. Vaughn made his escape. Steve was brought back into the house and buggered by one of the tough security guards, or so he told me. When Steve was allowed to place a phone call to me, I sent over ten one-hundred bills to buy his freedom."

"When I found him in his hotel room, the

sheet on his bed was covered with blood," Sturges said. "The buggery had set off those hemorrhoids that he was always bitching about. I took him to a hospital. I told him that in the future when he visited whorehouses, take along some money. But when he got out of the hospital with his sore ass, he never followed my advice. That guy simply refused to carry money on him."

The Magnificent Seven opened in a massive blitz of saturation screenings across the nation. By the time the final bill for promotion came in, it came to almost a million dollars, which was extremely rare for a film release in the autumn of 1960. In spite of the reviews, many of them hostile, the film was a box office bonanza.

After the release of *The Magnificent Seven*, Bronson called Steve to read him what a reviewer had said about him. "Charles Bronson's rugged looks look like a Clark Gable who has been left out in the sun for too long."

In spite of their differences filming together, Brynner recognized the box office clout of Steve and urged him to sign on for *The Return of the Seven*, shot in 1966. "After all, you were my *protégé* on the first version, and now your star is the equal of my own."

Steve politely bowed out, blaming other commitments. Later, he called Sturges. "That pig called me his *protégé*. What an asshole! Down in Mexico, behind his back, I always called him a pig because he resembles one. On second thought, I thought he looks like a circumcised prick. The plot of this new script is also a horse's ass, and you know how disgusted I am by horse assholes, especially when they're taking a dump."

***

At the cancellation of his series, *Wanted: Dead or Alive*, and the completion of *The Magnificent Seven*, Steve danced a jig of joy.

"Free at last," Steve. "I'll owe Josh Randall a kiss for making me a star, if only on TV. But now I can become a big-time movie star. Watch out Paul Newman. I'll be fucking your ass all the way to the box office. I've got a real chance to grab that brass ring, and I'm gonna go for it. I'm the best grabber in Hollywood. A hundred years from now the movie world will be talking up Steve McQueen."

In spite of his optimism, there would be a few rough bumps on the road to his horizon.

Say that it isn't so!
What really happened during Steve's interview with gossip maven
Hedda Hopper?

207

***

When he returned to Hollywood, one of the first calls Steve got was from Miss Bette Davis. She was all business with a script she wanted to film with him. No mention was made of their rendezvous in Maine when he was appearing in a play there with her husband, Gary Merrill.

Meeting her at a Santa Monica restaurant, he was eager to see what was on the table. He was now a movie star searching for his next role. She gave him only a mild kiss on the cheek before sitting down opposite him at a table with a view of the Pacific.

Somewhat reluctantly, she had agreed to film a *Pocketful of Miracles* for Frank Capra. It was a remake of the 1933 *Lady for a Day*, in which May Robson had given a brilliant performance. Bette would be "uglied up," as she put it, to play Apple Annie, a Damon Runyon character. She wanted him to play "Dave the Dude," a racketeer who turns her into a lady. "You'll not only get star billing after me, of course, but you'll get to fuck Ann-Margret, who'll be making her first film."

Steve was intrigued, and the idea of working opposite a first-rate star, even though a fading one, appealed to him. He'd never seen the original but on Bette's advice alone, he agreed to star in it with her. She said that Frank Capra had already approved the casting of him and would meet with him at his earliest convenience to discuss the role.

After telling Bette how much he wanted to work with her, he kissed her good-bye. But two days later, he received another call from her. The producers, Franton Productions, had not seen *The Magnificent Seven* yet and didn't think Steve had "enough star power" to carry this Technicolor production, which would eventually be released by United Artists in 1961. Both Frank Capra and Bette were overruled.

The "suits" requested Frank Sinatra but he turned it down, not really wanting to play a Broadway gangster.

"Steve got a knock in the mouth the moment he got back to town," John Sturges said. "He wasn't quite the big star he thought he was. He was on the way, but not there yet."

Steve read in the trade papers that Glenn Ford had been signed to star in the part, and he'd cast his girlfriend, Hope Lange, opposite him.

When Bette encountered Steve at a party after *Pocketful* was wrapped, she said, "I had the dressing room next to Glenn's. That son of a bitch moved me out and gave my dressing room to that Lange bitch. That's Hollywood for you. You're on the way up and I'm on the way down."

"I'm even looking over a script that would star Joan Crawford and me,"

208

Bette said. "I need the money but I don't know if we can find a director with enough balls to tangle with the two of us. I'm calling Crawford and telling her that if anyone asks, I'm the pretty one."

"Is there a part in it for me?" Steve asked.

"No, the leading role for the man is a closeted homosexual," Bette said. "I've told people who ask that the only bona fide male heterosexual in Hollywood still left is one Steve McQueen, so I think you'd better find a more macho role."

"And do I have such a role for you," came the familiar voice of Hedda Hopper behind him. She'd glided silently into a position within earshot, as she often did at parties, and caught some of their dialogue.

Bette had always had a troubled relationship with Hopper, especially when the columnist practically called for Bette's resignation from the acting profession after the disastrous release of *Beyond the Forest*. After air brushing Hopper's cheek with a faux kiss, Bette hastily retreated to the other side of the room.

Steve, who claimed he adored Hopper, gave her a sloppy wet one.

"I'm here with one of my best friends tonight," Hopper told him. "It's Ronald Reagan, and he's a dear. He was talking about this script for *General Electric Theater*, and I told him you'd be ideal for it."

"But, Hedda, I'm sorta getting out of television these days."

At that point he turned around to stare into the smiling face of a former movie star. "Hi," he said, "I'm Ronald Reagan. Nancy and I saw you in *The Blob* and thought you were terrific."

***

When he wanted to, Reagan could turn on the charm, which he did upon meeting Steve. "He was old Hollywood, and I was the new breed, and we weren't comfortable with each other," Steve later told John Sturges. "But we agreed to meet for lunch the next day at the Brown Derby."

Over lunch Reagan showed up in a suit and tie, Steve preferring jeans and a T-shirt. The former movie star was not making films but was the host of *General Electric*

Ronald Reagan in his heyday as a pitchman for General Electric

Steve to Ronnie: "No TV viewer would believe that you and Nancy could have given birth to me."

209

Theater on TV.

Even before he pitched a new script to Steve, Reagan spoke of the many big stars who'd appeared for *General Electric*, including Joan Crawford, Joseph Cotten, Jack Benny, and Alan Ladd.

"Nancy and I will play your parents in this new teleplay," Reagan told him. "It's about redemption. How a young man with the proper guidance can turn himself around."

"Instead of just entertaining, I think more and more our teleplays should be moralistic," Reagan told him. "We can entertain and enlighten at the same time."

"I don't like preachy movies," Steve said.

"I don't mean preachy like getting up on a soap box," Reagan said. "Scripts can be handled with greater delicacy."

Steve didn't want to go there, so he quickly changed the subject, trying to find some common bond with Reagan. He asked him if he felt that a TV series, such as both of them had done or were doing, destroyed one's chance on the screen.

"I'm getting no big screen offers," Reagan said. "It's true. Most movie producers don't want television performers on the silver screen. After *Hellcats of the Navy*, which I made with Nancy back in '57, the offerings have been few and far between."

Steve decided to be blunt. "I think you and me are in different boats, sailing down different rivers. You were a movie star who turned to TV to get work. I was in a TV series wanting to break out and become a big-time movie star. I mean, splashed up there in glorious Technicolor, my face as big as a horse's ass."

"I know I'm not a good pitchman for returning you to the TV screen, but the young kid you played in *The Blob* seemed just right for our drama," Reagan said. "Why don't you take the script home and consider it?"

"It's a deal. But without reading the script, I suspect it's not for me. Besides, nobody would believe that you and Nancy could give birth to a son like me."

Reagan chuckled but seemed uncomfortable and embarrassed.

"Actually, my real mother was a whore," Steve said.

Reagan looked shocked. "You're joking, of course."

"Not at all," Steve said. "I meant every word I said." Once Steve saw that he could shock Reagan, he couldn't let go. "I was also a male whore. In fact, I worked in three bordellos in my day, all the way from Havana to Texas."

"Now you're putting me on," Reagan said. "There's no such thing as a male whore. It would be physically impossible."

Now it was Steve's turn to chuckle. "That reminds me of something I heard at a party in New York. Marlon Brando told us that Queen Victoria signed a law outlawing homosexuality between men but didn't think a similar law was needed for lesbians. According to Brando, the Queen said 'sex between women is impossible.'"

"If you want to shift this conversation into homosexuality, you're talking to the wrong actor," Reagan said. "I mean, I've lived in Hollywood for years, and I know of such things. I don't understand the perversion, and I don't plan to wrap my mind around it. If you've ever been involved in it, I hope you'll put it behind you and enjoy a happy family life with your wife and kids."

"I just might do that," Steve said, rising from the table. "It's been great meeting you. Movie star of yesterday meeting star of tomorrow."

"The script?" Reagan asked. "What about the script?"

"Hollywood is full of actors," Steve said. "You don't need me." He looked down at Reagan, who seemed confused by Steve's hostility. "I hope you've saved up your money, because after you go off the air, sooner than later I suspect, I think you're finished. Maybe you could go into the insurance business. Maybe real estate. I suspect you won't get any more film roles unless you're cast as a villain."

Far from being insulted, Reagan in 1964 wrote Steve a note when he'd become a big star. "I'm appearing in this picture with Lee Marvin called *The Killers*. It's based on a story by Ernest Hemingway. I play a villain, a first for me. Actually the film was made for NBC-TV, but is considered too violent for the home screen. I slap the hell out of Angie Dickinson. I've been watching old movies of James Cagney and Edward G. Robinson. You gave me good advice—I mean, about becoming a screen villain. I think a whole new career is opening up for me. No more Mr. Nice Guy."

In response, Steve sent a postcard. On it, he wrote:

RONNIE, BABY, YOU'RE A PISSER.
YOU'RE NOT WASHED UP YET.
LOVE AND KISSES,
STEVE MCQUEEN.
P.S. LET'S YOU AND ME GET IT ON SOMETIME.

"Coffee and me for breakfast?"
Some Steve McQueen fan clubs claimed that, in spite of the scar on his right cheek from a
motorcycle accident, that this was the sexiest picture for
which their idol ever posed.

Chapter Six
"An Actor Who Races, or a Racer Who Acts?"

Steven must have been high on marijuana the day he told director Richard Thorpe that he would star in the so-called comedy, *The Honeymoon Machine*, for Metro-Goldwyn-Mayer. "When I saw the final cut," Steve said, "I never thought it possible, but I hate this film more than *The Blob*."

When he'd signed on the dotted line, the shooting title of the film had been *The Golden Fleecing*. The movie, ostensibly set in Venice, was shot on an elaborately reconstructed Hollywood sound stage. It looked like a cheap production. To establish the actual scenery of Venice, MGM used old grainy CinemaScope travelogue footage as a backdrop for this farce.

Several gay reviewers noted that the only good thing about the film was that Steve appeared "topless," establishing a pattern he'd repeat in almost all of his future movies. The word "topless" showed a shifting in vocabulary usage of the 60s. Before that, men without their shirts appearing on screen were referred to as bare-chested.

The plot, such as it was, was about a Navy man, who uses his ship's computer to break the bank at a chic casino in Venice. Cary Grant was offered the script but asked the director, "Was the writer of this screenplay on something when he came up with this piece of shit?" George Wells wrote the screenplay, but it was based on a play, *The Golden Fleecing*, by Lorenzo Semple.

Since it was set during the paranoid peak of the Cold War, the Soviets got written into the plot, their brass thinking that the computer signals Steve transmitted indicated plans for an impending nuclear attack by the United States.

Steve agreed to play the role of Lt. Fergie Howard for a fee of $100,000. For his supporting players, Thorpe signed on a talented

213

cast, including Brigid Bazlen as the female lead.

Brigid had just signed a contract with MGM wherein she would appear in three movies. Although she had high hopes for stardom, her star burned out quickly. The pretty little starlet had become known for lip-syncing "I'm a Little Blue Fairy" in a Chicago children's show. Her mother, *Chicago Sun-Times* writer Maggie Daly, warned the director "not to let McQueen fuck my daughter and get her pregnant."

From all reports, Thorpe was unable to keep Steve from mating with Brigid. "She was cute stuff and I was hot and horny," Steve later said. "Besides, I've always wanted to fuck a Blue Fairy."

Worried that her daughter would fall for a married man, Maggie herself flew from Chicago to Los Angeles. She showed up unexpectedly on the set dressed in a Dior suit, mink coat, and black gloves.

After meeting Steve and having a reunion with her daughter, she asked Thorpe for lunch and an interview. Over her chicken salad, she told the director, "I don't blame Brigid for losing her heart to this guy. I could go for Steve myself."

Thorpe later told Steve what the columnist had said. "I think she's well preserved and just as good looking as her daughter," Thorpe said.

Shortly before closing time, Frank Sinatra dropped by to wish Steve well. He and Maggie shared a warm, affectionate embrace. Later, with Steve, he said, "You should not always go for the daughter and neglect the mother, especially when she looks like Maggie. Chicago is Marshall Fields, the Wrigley

Steve's leading lady on *The Honeymoon Machine* was **Brigid Bazlen**, seen on the left as "The Little Blue Fairy," in a kiddie show.
Teamed with Steve, and under the glare of cameras in the right-hand photo, above, she fizzled during their carefully scripted "honeymoon in Venice."

Building, and Maggie Daly. Why don't you and Maggie join Eva and me for dinner?" Sinatra was referring to Eva Gabor.

The next day Steve called Sinatra. "You're right. The mother was much more experienced and a lot more fun than the daughter."

"See what I told you," Sinatra said.

Paula Prentiss and Jim Hutton, who'd just made the successful *Where the Boys Are* (1960), also joined Steve in the cast. Hutton at 6'5" towered over Steve. He was tall and gangly, and was being groomed as a successor to James Stewart. That dream never came true. Paula stood 5'10" so she was almost a match for Jim. Steve didn't plan to pursue her—"she's too tall for me"—even though she'd later be voted one of the 100 sexiest female stars in film history.

In the film, Steve was no Jerry Lewis, although at times he seemed inspired by this comedian, as he mugged and smirked his way through the film, overplaying scene after scene when a little subtlety might be called for.

Jim Hutton (upper left), "the new Jimmy Stewart," screams when he reads the reviews of *The Honeymoon Machine*. Jack Weston (upper right photo), playing a hapless sailor in the movie, is carried out by (left to right), **Paula Prentiss, Brigid Bazlen, Steve, and Jim Hutton.**

Steve (lower left) works out to keep in shape as a comedian, but he didn't shape up enough. Lower right: **Steve, Hutton,** and an unidentified actor clown around in this lackluster farce.

At that point in his career, Steve hadn't built up a loyal fan base, and the movie-going public stayed away in droves, perhaps influenced by blasts from critics. The cruelest slap in the face came from *The Saturday Review* that suggested that Steve "go back to TV westerns and selling cigarettes."

Almost passing unnoticed by the rest of the crew, Steve dropped Brigid the day he met a beautiful extra on the film. Her name was Sharon Tate. They would begin an on-again, off-again torrid affair that would last up until the year she was murdered.

Her enormous brown eyes and large, dazzling smile captured Steve's heart. Although she had given birth to two sons in the 50s, these pregnancies had not harmed her shapely figure's measurements of 36-22-35.

"She bathed me in a body soap called Milk & Pearls," Steve told Thorpe the next day. "I can really go for this *puta*. She's a great piece of ass. She's a little too philosophical for me, but other than that I love her madly. She says things like 'beauty is something you see, love something you feel.' Shit like that. I'm taking her riding up in the hills tonight."

"You have a wife and children," Thorpe said, challenging him. "Or does that matter?"

"Of course, it does," Steve said. "I love them dearly. But I don't want any woman to start thinking she owns my dick."

***

With Sharon Tate, Steve would often drive into the desert and just disappear, telling family and friends that he just wanted to be by himself. During the making of his next picture, *Hell Is for Heroes* for Paramount (a 1962

release), he totaled three rental cars the studio had arranged for him.

"He took them on dirt tracks, bad trails where even his motorcycle wouldn't go," said James Coburn, one of his co-stars on the picture. "Sharon told me at one point that she was never going to ride with him again."

Steve maintained distant relationships with other members of the cast who included singer Bobby Darin playing a serious role, Fess Parker, Bob Newhart, and Harry Guardino. But Steve quickly found another riding buddy among his co-stars, and his name was Nick Adams. Coburn saw a potentially dangerous liaison developing with Nick.

"He latched onto Steve the way he'd attached himself to James Dean and Elvis Presley," Coburn claimed. "The guy was a star-fucker. The sex didn't matter. Nick seduced anything in his pathway. In Steve he saw the next Dean and a possible bread ticket for the future. Nick became Steve's doormat. Steve always wanted a doormat, if not at home, then outside the home."

At the debut of his career, when Nick arrived in Hollywood completely broke, he hustled older gay men who picked him up in cars along Santa Monica Boulevard. He told Sal Mineo, who became his lover, "I was the highest-paid stud on the block, getting fifty dollars a lay when my competition was selling it for five or ten dollars at the most."

Nick told the author, "Steve and I both came from the school of hard knocks. He was raised on a hog farm, and I came from a gritty coal mining town in Pennsylvania."

In one of his first interviews, Nick said, "Movies were my life. You had to have an escape when you were living in a basement. I saw all the Cagney, Bogart, Garfield pictures, the ones where a guy finally got a break. Odds against the world—that was my meat."

One way he won Steve over as a friend involved convincing him that he was the heir apparent to all those tough guys Nick had seen in the movies.

Biographer Albert Goldman once wrote that Nick was "forever selling himself: a property which, to hear him tell it, was nothing less than sensational—the greatest little actor to hit town in years. In fact, he had very little going for him in terms of looks or talent or professional experience. He was just another poor kid from the sticks who had grown up dreaming of the silver screen."

"I no longer have to hustle my pecker," Steve told Nick. "Today I put my pecker where I want it—or else it's no dice. Of course, Hollywood still fucks me in the ass, but now I make them pay for it."

"Steve took me to car races, and we bonded, though we often picked up girls," Nick said. "I long ago learned that Steve liked sloppy seconds. I'd always go first. Sometimes we didn't

Nick Adams made a name for himself by taking **Natalie Wood**'s virginity before moving on to **James Dean, Elvis Presley,** and **Steve McQueen.**

need these whores—just each other."

In the winter of 1960, Steve had formed Scuderia Condor Enterprises, his own production company, taking the name from the Scuderia automobile in Italy, a division of Ferrari. It was on a loan-out, a combined deal between Paramount and Condor, that he accepted the role of Private Reese in *Hell Is for Heroes.*

Arriving on the set, Steve had "gone Hollywood," as his enemies claimed, at least in some small way. He'd just purchased a weekend home in Palm Springs, though it had cost him only $26,000. He called his new lifestyle "Candyland."

Following *The Magnificent Seven*, where he'd established himself on the big screen as a Western hero, Steve was now anxious to become a screen hero of World War II, a reputation he would establish in a trio of back-to-back pictures.

He got his wish. In his next movies, he came to personify the fighting man of World War II, a lone wolf who says little and lives by his own code.

Set in Germany in 1944, the plot was by Robert Pirosh, who wrote *Battleground* (1950) starring Van Johnson.

Hell Is for Heroes tells of the plight of seven men who are forced to hold their position for two days against invading Nazis who far outnumber them.

The first week of the shoot, Steve clashed with Pirosh, demanding script changes. As a master sergeant during World War II, Pirosh knew a lot more about war than Steve, as the screenwriter and sometimes director had seen action in both the Ardennes and Rhineland campaigns.

When the writer, with some justification, refused to make the changes,

Steve (left photo) throws the fatal hand grenade that concludes *Hell Is for Heroes* for him.

During filming, actor **Nick Adams** (above photo, left) moved into Steve's innermost circle like a tyrannosaur seeking lunch.

Steve had Paramount fire him. Of course, Nick stood by Steve in all his battles, and, along the way, urged Steve to have extra scenes written in for him.

Throughout the shoot, Steve would also tangle with Henry Blanke, his Berlin-born producer with such notable credits as Bogie's *The Maltese Falcon*, plus several films such as *Juarez* and *Old Acquaintance* that starred Bette Davis.

Before he was fired, Pirosh was also set to direct the film. After a short delay, Paramount sent in Don Siegel, who in short order would also clash with Steve. The difference was that Siegel stayed "through the bloody end" (his words) whereas Pirosh did not.

Before tangling with Steve, Siegel had just completed what is considered Elvis Presley's best picture, *Flaming Star*, released in 1960. Today the director is known mainly for the cult classic, *Invasion of the Body Snatchers* (1956).

Siegel and Steve got off to a bad start. "I was too honest with him at first. I told him, 'most of my pictures, I'm sorry to say, are about nothing. Because I'm a whore, I work for money. It's the American way.'"

"I made a mistake in telling Steve that," Siegel said. "I sent the wrong signal to him. After that, he walked around the set with the attitude that the burden of preserving the integrity of the picture was on his shoulders. All the rest of us, in Steve's view, were company men ready to sell out, grind out an inferior picture for a few bucks. Eventually, however, after many a fight on the set, Steve and I grew to like each other."

Siegel noted the growing intimacy between Nick and Steve. At one point he saw Steve stuff two pieces of Juicy Fruit gum into Nick's mouth. "I like to chew the stuff but I don't want all the sugar in my mouth," Steve told Siegel.

"Nick actually chewed the gum, getting rid of most of the sugar flavor, then gently placed it between Steve's lips where he chewed it for most of the afternoon," Siegel said. "I'd never seen anything quite like that before. The memory has always stuck in my mind. In addition to appearing in our movie, Nick was also Steve's caterer. If Steve wanted a cold drink or whatever, Nick brought it to him. He practically moved into Steve's dressing room. At one point, I warned Steve to be a bit leery of Nick. He had a reputation of attaching himself to stars like Dean or Presley and using them."

"Don't you worry your Cambridge-

Steve (left) teamed with **Fess Parker**, of Davy Crockett fame, to create this World War II drama that helped establish Steve as an action hero.

educated little head," Steve told Siegel. "I've got Nick Adams under perfect control. If I commanded him to eat my shit, he'd do it for me. The boy knows what none of you other fuckers know, and that is that Steve McQueen is the greatest actor ever to hit this town. Even Spencer Tracy agrees with that."

"*That* Steve McQueen," Siegel said upon recalling their time together. "No wonder the producers in the future wanted him for *Dirty Harry*, which eventually went to my dear buddy, Clint Eastwood. As for Steve, I can only hope and pray that his dick is as big as that ego of his."

Steve at first didn't like such an impressive line-up of talent. He remained friends with Coburn, but seemed to resent most of the other actors. He approached Siegel and asked, "Why can't they just film the whole fucking picture around me? They don't need all these other bantam roosters. One big rooster is enough to take care of the henhouse."

He told Siegel that he thought Fess Parker was a "fuckhead." Steve seemed to resent this former college football player from Texas, probably because he loathed his link with Walt Disney and his incredible success with the Davy Crockett series, a craze that had swept the nation in the 1950s.

He found Bob Newhart, making his film debut, "a pussy." Newhart managed to work a telephone act into *Hell Is for Heroes*, and this later became his trademark on TV.

Steve and Bobby Darin, both actors with tremendous egos, clashed during the first week of shooting. Darin told Siegel, "Steve McQueen is nothing but a second-rate jerk."

On hearing that, Steve approached Darin one hot afternoon when the temperature reached 117°F in the woods of Redding, California. "Paul Newman told me that your *puta*, Sandra Dee, likes to get fucked with his dick more than she does with yours."

In *Hell Is for Heroes*, **Bob Newhart** perfected his famous telephone routines, and **Bobby Darin** (right) became Steve's Enemy no. 1

Darin punched Steve in the nose, bloodying it. Steve struck back with a powerful blow to Darin's stomach. Seeing the fight, Coburn intervened and broke up the two men. Darin lay on the ground, looking as if he were suffering a heart attack. An ambulance was summoned. Steve was unaware that Darin suffered from a heart condition aggravated by a bout with rheumatic fever during childhood. He was to die in 1973 following open heart surgery.

When he heard the news, producer Henry Blanke called from Paramount.

"Great work, McQueen. You've been on the set for only four days, and you nearly killed your co-star."

The picture was originally called *Separation Hill*, but Steve didn't like the title. Nick agreed with him, telling Steve "it sucks." Paramount changed it to the rather bland *The War Story*, which Steve also didn't like. Nick backed up Steve in this opinion too.

Steve heard that Paramount was shooting a picture called *Hell Is for Heroes*, starring Edmond O'Brien. "Clanking his balls," as Nick put it, Steve demanded that title for his own picture and the studio caved in, re-titling the O'Brien movie *Man Trap*. Nick, of course, applauded his action.

Goaded on by Nick, Steve continued his clashes with Siegel. In response to his every move, Nick assured Steve, "You're the greatest."

Steve's onscreen dialogue was mostly confined to a "Yep" or a "Nope," which brought comparisons to screen legend Gary Cooper.

His wife, Neile, often showed up on the set to join the actors in the buffet line for lunch. A rare picture exists of Neile, Steve, and Nick together on the food line.

Because of all the production delays, most of which were caused by Steve, and the film's slim budget of two and a half million dollars, Blanke threatened to shut down the picture. He had the backing of the suits at Paramount.

Blanke appeared on location in Redding and ordered grips to seize the cameras. Confronting them, Steve pulled a branch from a tree. He drew a line in the dirt. "Any shithead who steps over this line is gonna end up in the hospital where I put Darin."

Blanke and his men backed off and drove back to Los Angeles. Steve had won. The picture was completed.

***

When John F. Kennedy flew into Los Angeles, Steve sent a request, via Frank Sinatra, to the president, hoping that JFK would remember who he was. *Hell Is for Heroes* was based on a true incident in World War II, showing the heroism of American soldiers fighting against overwhelming odds. Since it was a true story, Steve thought the president might film a brief prologue to introduce the film. Without seeing it, and based on Steve's recommendation, he agreed to do it.

"Steve got a ten-minute invitation to have a drink in Kennedy's presidential suite," Nick told the author. "JFK talked about his favorite subject, Hollywood pussy."

According to biographer Christopher Sandford, JFK also asked Steve, "Don't you find you get a headache if you don't have at least a poke a day?"

Allegedly the President and Steve tallied up their scoreboards for the previous year, each of them estimating between 200 and 300 conquests, an astonishing figure. Obviously, each of the men was exaggerating.

Actually Steve's real goal involved not having more seductions than Kennedy but "to have more pussy than Frank Sinatra."

"In the pussy department, Sinatra was definitely his role model, not the President," Nick claimed.

According to Nick, during Steve's brief meeting with Kennedy, he thanked him for agreeing to film the prologue for *Hell Is for Heroes*, but went one more. A movie was going to be made of Kennedy's role as a naval hero in *PT-109*.

"Steve practically begged JFK to let him play the Navy hero," Nick said. "Kennedy told him he'd have one of his staff get back to him on that. What he didn't tell Steve was that Paul Newman also wanted the role for himself. Jackie wanted Warren Beatty. She sort of had a crush on him. Kennedy, however, without informing any of these actors, had already settled on Cliff Robertson."

"Steve's feelings were badly hurt," Nick said. "He felt JFK had really let him down, and he didn't have any trouble switching his loyalty to Lyndon Johnson when Kennedy was assassinated. Steve asked me to go see *PT-109* with him. We thought Cliff Robertson was awful, and both of us agreed that the movie sucked, not that there is anything wrong with sucking."

Steve prevailed on **John F. Kennedy** to introduce *Hell Is for Heroes* to movie audiences. But the president was less receptive to having Steve portray him in *PT-109*.

It has been reported, but never completely confirmed, that President Kennedy screened *Hell Is for Heroes* at least a dozen times at the White House. Jackie Kennedy gave her own review, "That boring old thing."

Biographer Sandford got to speak to one of Steve's dozens of conquests, a woman named Natalie Hawn. She discovered that Steve, known as the quickest draw in Hollywood, was "something similar in bed." He admitted to Hawn that he'd hustled both men and women in New York when he was down on his luck.

Even with the President of the United States recommending *Hell Is for Heroes*, the "suits" at Paramount weren't that impressed with their own movie. While in the White House, Kennedy filmed a brief introduction to the movie, praising the bravery and courage of the American G.I.s who fought on the battlefields of World War II.

Paramount released it as half of a double feature, pairing it with *Escape from Zahrain*, a film about prisoners escaping from a Middle Eastern jail that starred Steve's nemesis, Yul Brynner, and his friend, Sal Mineo.

Both movies died a quick death and were eventually assigned to the graveyard of endless TV re-runs.

In time, *Hell Is for Heroes* gained a long-awaited audience, including director Stanley Kubrick, who said that Steve's was "the best portrayal of a solitary soldier I have ever seen."

***

In the same year, 1962, Steve filmed another World War II movie, *The War Lover,* this one shot at airfields in Eastern England and released by Columbia. It was made with the cooperation of both the USAF and the Royal Air Force.

In addition to discovering England, Steve found out—to his joy—that filming would be next to the challenging Brand Hatch racetrack. "The way a gambler is attracted to Las Vegas, Steve is attracted to race tracks," said director Philip Leacock.

The producer of the film, Arthur Hornblow Jr., was not thrilled about Steve's car racing. He'd taken out an insurance policy for Columbia. In Steve's contract, he could be sued for two and a half million dollars, the cost of the picture, if he were injured or incapacitated during the shoot.

When Steve learned that Hornblow was the producer, he had high hopes for the movie. Hornblow, once married to "the Queen of Hollywood," Myrna Loy, had been nominated for the Best Picture Oscar four times, including for the thriller *Gaslight* (1944), starring Ingrid Bergman.

During his first meeting with Hornblow, Steve was his prickly self. "We have something in common," he said to his producer. "We've both fucked Veronica Lake." It was Hornblow who'd renamed Constance Ockelman Veronica Lake.

Steve wasn't impressed with Philip Leacock, the Londoner assigned to direct *The War Lover*. Raised in the Canary Islands, Leacock was known for making films about children. "This is not a film about kids," Steve reminded him.

Leacock later told Hornblow, "I think

McQueen is a prick, but since the lead in the picture is a prick, he can just play himself and we'll come out just fine. As you know, I wanted Warren Beatty but he pulled out."

The weak script was by Howard Koch and based on a novel by John Hersey, the novel reading far better than the screenplay.

A heartbroken Robert Wagner, suffering from the breakup of his marriage to Natalie Wood, arrived in England. He and Paul Newman were close friends, but he didn't bond with Steve that well, finding him "very self-conscious and very competitive, even about small things. Steve was such a complicated man, always looking for conflict and never really at peace. That kind of personality can be very wearing, to say the least."

In time, Steve and Robert became friends. Robert claimed that Steve was sympathetic about his failed marriage. "I think he trusted me as much as he trusted anybody, which wasn't all that much."

What Steve didn't tell Robert was that he planned to seduce Natalie himself as soon as the first opportunity came up.

When Robert remarried, this time to Marion Marshall, Steve and he became much better friends, even biking buddies riding "our motorcycles in the desert together," which was followed by drinks and dinner. Rumors swirled around Hollywood that they were having a big gay romance, but this gossip was never confirmed. Steve was so touchy about the subject that when Sal Mineo inquired about the status of the McQueen/Wagner friendship, and slyly suggested something might be going on, Steve punched him out.

"Love Triangle" (left to right),
Steve, Shirley Ann Field, and **Robert Wagner)**
was a concept that existed only in the script.

In real life, and offscreen, Steve
willingly relinquished the beautiful British actress to Robert.

Except for Robert, the rest of the cast was virtually unknown. The female lead and love interest for both Robert and Steve was a rather wooden English actress, Shirley Ann Field. The former "Miss London" had been raised in an orphanage, along with her brother, who was later murdered in the United States.

Field had made a name for herself when she was chosen by

Laurence Olivier and director Tony Richardson to star in *The Entertainer* (1960).

When Steve met Field, he said he could no longer keep his vow of seducing all his leading ladies. He did not like her or her stage-trained English style of acting.

He complained to Leacock, "She's cutting off my balls. Our styles don't match. She thinks she's still playing opposite Olivier and doesn't take to my more laid-back King of Cool style."

She didn't give him a good review either. "All I got out of my love scenes with McQueen—or was it rape?—was a cut lip. He's no kisser like Robert Wagner."

Steve was cast as Captain Buzz Rickson, "a pilot who can make a B-17 stand up on its tail and dance." His character, a real hot shot, takes "orgasmic delight" in flight and air battles. He loves planes and war, not human beings, except perhaps for himself.

"A real son of a bitch," claimed one critic. An underground paper in Hollywood said, "Steve McQueen is a Grade A asshole both on and off the screen."

All the sympathy in the film went to Robert, playing Lt. Ed Bolland. He gets the girl, meaning Field, both in the movie and off stage.

Steve noted that Robert made a quick recovery from his heartbreak from Natalie. Robert claimed, "I liked Shirley a lot." He was also rumored to have fallen for Joan Collins during his stay in England.

"He's one busy man," Steve told Leacock. "Makes me long for the bachelor life. A guy can't have all that much fun lugging around his ol' lady and two kids."

The McQueens lived in England from September of 1961 to March of 1962, first stop the elegant Savoy Hotel on the Strand.

One night around midnight Steve brought some racing buddies back to his suite at the Savoy. The men were hungry, and Steve agreed to cook them some scrambled eggs on an illegal hotplate he'd smuggled into his suite. He could have called down for room service, but he was always tight with a pound. The draperies caught fire.

In his underwear, Steve ran out in the hallway looking for a fire extinguisher. Regrettably two elderly English ladies spotted him and were horrified, reporting to the manager that "some naked savage was running through the hallway, intent on rape." How they suspected rape is not known.

The next day the manager kicked Steve out of his suite, suggesting that some other address in London might be more suitable. Steve had attended a masquerade ball, unusual for him, on Chester Square. Complete with trench coat, he'd come as Bogie in *Casablanca*. Later, he reportedly said, "I got to feel up Queen Victoria."

He noticed a four-story townhouse for rent. When he inquired, it belonged to Lord John Russell, who was willing to lease it for $1,200 a month. Steve accepted the deal and moved his family in.

Back on the set of *The War Lover*, Steve McQueen became known as "the Ugly American." When Leacock told Steve that's what the crew was calling him, he quipped. "Good. That means I'm in character."

***

While in England, Steve rejected the limousine with chauffeur that the studio provided. For transportation, he purchased two vehicles, a twelve-speed, four-wheel-drive Land Rover and an 1,100-cc formula Jr. Cooper, a fast British racing vehicle, both of which he eventually shipped back to California.

Against all advice, Steve indulged in some British car racing on week-ends. In one close race, he came in second to Pat Cooper, the top woman driv-er in Britain. "He was furious," Leacock recalled.

"I was beaten by a fucking bitch," Steve said. "A dyke, no doubt."

In these races in Britain, Steve began to wear fire retardation, asbestos-lined driving suits. These suits, along with early exposures to asbestos in the military, may have ultimately shortened his life. Of course, his habitual smok-ing of three packages of cigarettes a day was a major cause as well.

Steve made an astonishing statement to Robert, telling him, "The only time I can relax is when I'm going 130 mph."

Steve spent many an evening with the celebrated Stirling Moss, the most famous race car driver in the world. "We talked about cars and women—in that order," Moss recalled.

Moss took "quite a fancy to Neile," but, amazingly, he never aroused jeal-ousy in Steve. He told Robert, "I find it a harmless, amusing flirtation. I don't think he ever took off Neile's panties."

A potential disaster loomed one afternoon when the brakes on Steve's Mini Cooper locked on him.

A London sports writer witnessed what happened next. "As he hurtled downhill, off the road, McQueen did a superb job of propelling the Cooper between poles and metal signs that could have demolished it. He controlled the slide until the final instant, looped and slammed the car at an angle into a dirt embankment. The Cooper snapped around like a top, whirling, and bounc-ing, but miraculously did not turn over."

Steve injured his lower lip and was worried what the director would think, since he was scheduled for close-ups when he reported to work Monday.

Leacock saved the day by shooting scenes of Steve wearing an oxygen mask in the cockpit.

It was in that cockpit where Steve filmed the dramatic conclusion, as he ordered the men of his crew, including Robert, to bail out of his doomed Flying Fortress. He rode the B-17 to his death, crashing into the White Cliffs of Dover.

Before heading back to London, Steve fired his long-time manager, Hilliard Elkins. He resented his manager running up too many expenses for him to pay.

In the future, he'd rely on Stan Kamen at William Morris. The agent sent potential scripts first to Neile for her approval. If she liked a script, she'd pitch it to her husband, who relied on her professional opinion.

After getting rid of Elkins, Steve called Kamen. "Get me more money, and then more money, and right before you've bled the bastards dry, top it off with another $50,000. Make the cocksuckers pay if they want to see my puss on the big screen." Remembering Kamen's sexual proclivities, Steve added, "Not that I have anything against cocksuckers."

Both Steve and Robert were horribly disappointed at the box office failure of *The War Lover*. "Steve and I thought it was a fine novel but a terrible adaptation," Robert told writer Warren G. Harris. "We were willing to sit it out until a better script could be developed. But at the time, the head of the studio said, 'Trust me, a picture with two great guys like you can't miss.' It did."

The War Lover was more popular with Brits than Americans. Steve's most cherished review was printed in *Life* magazine. He's "an oddball who combines the cockiness of Cagney, the glower of Bogart, and the rough diamond glow of Garfield."

Life devoted a cover story to him, even running a picture of him lying in a tub with Neile.

It was a time of career crisis. Whenever he could, which was often, he escaped to the desert with his buddies. "But I can't do that forever. I need a hit."

Even though his friends assured him that *The War Lover* would make him a bona-fide A-list movie star, he was painfully aware that of all the films he'd made, only *The Magnificent Seven* had been a success. Yul Brynner claimed that he was the reason for the good box office on that film.

"How long will producers keep offering me scripts?" Steve asked Kamen. "If I let you suck my dick again, will you get me a bigger part?"

That offer might have been motive enough for Kamen. He called Steve the next day. "John Sturges will be phoning you this afternoon. Don't run off on your bike. And, Steve, don't forget, you'll owe me one."

"I'm a man of my word," Steve told him.

At lunch, Steve had told Neile, "I've got to find the one role that can put me over the top, the big one."

As if destiny heard his call, his friend and former director John Sturges called exactly at three o'clock that day. He immediately pitched a script to Steve called *The Great Escape*.

"Not another World War II picture," Steve said. "People used to say that Errol Flynn single-handedly won World War II. Soon they'll be saying that about Steve McQueen."

"We've got a great supporting cast lined up," Sturges said. "James Garner, Charles Bronson, Richard Attenborough, James Coburn, David McCallum."

"Hell, man, that sounds like another boys' dormitory movie to me," Steve said. "I need a vehicle that focuses on *me*, not every other male face in Hollywood."

Sturges was persistent and finally got Steve to sign on the dotted line. It was good that he did. *The Great Escape* finally freed Steve from the little box and propelled him into international stardom.

Before flying to Germany to begin filming *The Great Escape*, Steve had some serious racing to accomplish. In March of 1962, in a cross-country motorcycle race, the Four Aces Moose Run, he came in third. "I'd have won but the assholes gave me a bad starting position," Steve claimed. "They resented me because I'm an actor." He also claimed that one of his close friends, stunt rider Bud Ekins, had taught him the finer points of dirt-cycle racing.

Through an arrangement with his new friend and racing champ, Stirling Moss, he was off to Sebring, Florida, to compete in the twelve-hour automobile endurance race as a member of the British Motor Corporation (BMC)

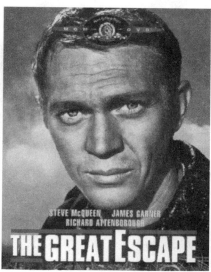

team. The main event took place on a Sunday a few weeks later, when Steve was teamed with John Colgate, of toothpaste fame, riding side by side in the same Austin-Healey. Steve and his partner were heading to the finish line when a defect in the casing caused a massive oil loss. He was bitterly disappointed at the loss, caused by a mechanical failure.

In late spring of 1962, after his Cooper arrived from England, Steve entered it in a car-racing competition at Del Mar, 20 miles north of San Diego. During the big event on Sunday, a water leak brought him down, that and the fact

228

he caught a rock in his goggles, which blinded him, sending him into the bushes. Fortunately, he was not injured.

In spite of his losses, he was flushed with success as he drove back to Los Angeles. "I was burning with car-racing fever."

As a racing car driver, Steve found a new identity. He told writer William F. Nolan, "I was no longer just an actor; I was a man who raced, and that was important to me—to have this separate identity."

Waiting for him at his manse was an attorney for United Artists with a restraining order. The studio could not risk the star of *The Great Escape* having a motor vehicle accident. "It's either sports racing or motion picture acting—the decision is yours." the attorney demanded.

Steve had the weekend to make up his mind. "It was the most painful decision of my life," Steve later said. "I came very close that weekend to giving up acting forever. If I had done that, I'm sure I would be a mere footnote in motion picture history. I thought about security for Neile and the kids. I finally pledged to give up racing."

He called Stirling Moss that night. "Take note, my retirement from racing is not forever. One day I might even combine car racing in a movie. That would be like having my cake and eating it too."

***

Sturges wasn't the only one who wanted Steve to appear in a movie. Tennessee Williams admitted that "I got a hard-on watching McQueen in *The War Lover*." He wanted him to appear in "my strictly heterosexual movie," *Period of Adjustment*.

He would be teamed with Jane Fonda. Steve had seen her play a whore in *Walk on the Wild Side*, and he'd come home and chastised Neile for not having "a fuckable ass like Jane Fonda." He was "hot" to do a film with Fonda, but the studio rejected him as the male lead, awarding it to his friend and rival, Tony Franciosa, instead.

A very tempting offer came his way to film *The Victors*, co-starring Sophia Loren, Ingrid Bergman, and Simone Signoret.

"If I make this movie, my pecker will fall off," he jokingly told Stan Kamen. It was a tough decision but he decided to stick with Sturges and *The Great Escape*. Steve regrettably turned down *The Victors*, his role going to his long-time companion George Peppard. Peppard didn't end up with the original cast, as the leading female roles were later assigned to Melina Mercouri, Romy Schneider, and Jeanne Moreau.

"What the hell!" Steve said, on learning of the new cast. "I would have fucked all three of those women too. Lucky George."

The suits at United Artists found the title, *The Great Escape*, misleading, since fifty of the prisoners were executed in a mass killing by the Gestapo. Only three ever made it to safety; the other twenty-six men were returned to the high-security camp to wait out the war.

In spite of reservations, UA agreed to put up four million dollars for the production, which was a slim budget since it involved shooting in Europe.

Steve flew to Munich with Neile and his children. Once there he drove to the village of Deining where he'd rented a manor house. The villagers had been alerted to his arrival and greeted him with an oompah band. He was grandly escorted to his temporary headquarters where he tossed red roses to his well-wishers from a balcony.

The actual shooting was at nearby Geiselgasteig.

In spite of a serious racing injury of champ Stirling Moss, Steve drove recklessly every morning between Deining and the studios at Geiselgasteig. One morning he crashed into a herd of cattle crossing a narrow road. Sturges arranged a settlement with the farmer. Steve invited all the crew for steak dinners, since the dead cows, after payment had been made, belonged to him.

Often he was chased by the Bavarian police. In all, he accumulated forty speeding tickets during the shoot. On location, he suffered two major car crashes, totaling his vehicles. "And people said what a good driver he was," Sturges said in despair. "He was King of the Road, ready to crash into any obstacle that blocked him."

On the set, Steve had a reunion with James Garner, Charles Bronson, and James Coburn. "I hope Munich has enough beer in stock for all of us," Steve said. "So far, I haven't run into any drug dealers in Deining to supply me with my stash of marijuana. Guess I'll have to grow it myself."

It was **Steve's** idea to insert what became the most dramatic sequence in *The Great Escape*, his attempt to escape in a purloined Nazi motorcycle. In the film, he has a choice--face the Nazis or attempt to jump over two high barbed wire barriers. He hurdles over the first barrier, but the second is too high. He falls to a crashing halt and is entrapped in the barbed wire.

Steve also enjoyed working again with his friend, Robert Relyea, who was assigned as the assistant to Sturges. At one point during the filming, when no one else was available, Relyea had to stunt crash an airplane.

When the British actors arrived in Bavaria, Steve called them "fucking candyass limeys," but he later bonded with the talented actor, Richard Attenborough. Even so, he warned Sturges, "We've got to de-ball these Brits and make the Yanks the heroes."

In spite of its flaws—mainly a lack of character development in its key players—*The Great Escape* was a first-rate adventure film. With such a talented cast, Steve, as Captain Virgil Hilts—also known as "The Cooler King"—had a rough time trying to keep the focus on himself.

The plot had been based on a true-life adventure during 1944 when some Allied POWs, both American and British, tried to escape from a specially constructed compound some ninety miles southeast of Berlin. Sturges opted to build his camp, Stalag Luft III, in Bavaria, because he could film more dramatic scenery, ranging from "castles in the sky" to towering alpine peaks.

To adapt the novel to the screen, Sturges hired James Clavell, who would later achieve fame as a novelist with such titles as *Shogun* and *Tai-Pan*. W.R. Burnett was also employed in the adaptation, and it was this writer who would clash so often with Steve.

On the first day of shooting, Steve noted to Bronson, "I guess Neile can sleep peacefully at night since there are no women in this film. Perhaps I can pick up some Bavarian peasant girl in the village."

Steve's character, a wise-cracking loner, had become an archetype—super brave, cocky, macho—in movies with themes based on World War II.

In his first major picture, Steve lacked the power at that time of a really big star. Despite that, however, he was difficult and overbearing. W.R. Burnett, who worked on the original screenplay, called him "an impossible bastard." Every morning Steve demanded rewrites before filming began, causing endless delays.

Steve complained constantly that his character had not been fleshed in properly. He objected to the way he marched helplessly to the "cooler" or brig without

In this scene from *The Great Escape*, **Steve** is not playing baseball, but surrendering to his Nazi captors. When he's confined to the brig, he endlessly tosses a baseball against the wall to preserve his sanity.

protest. "I should at least put up a fight," Steve told Sturges. The director reminded him that if he did, the Nazis guards would shoot him. "You've got a point there," Steve said, backing down.

The cooler evoked memories of his own incarceration in the brig when he'd served in the U.S. Marines. As a "bit of business," Sturges devised a gimmick where Steve would endlessly toss a baseball against the wall and catch it in his mitt. He didn't like performing this "senseless" stunt, but Sturges prevailed. A scene with the catcher's mitt, in fact, brings the movie to its conclusion. To Sturges, Steve's tossing that baseball, an American symbol, showed the stamina of the Allied soldier, refusing to give in to Nazi domination until the very end.

"Listen," Steve said, "pay me my $100,000, and I'll catch all the balls you throw at me."

Although it might not have been appropriate to 1944, Steve insisted that his wardrobe consist of a sweatshirt, leather jacket, and beige chinos. He also cut down his dialogue to short sentences. "I prefer to convey the mood with my face, not dialogue," he told Sturges.

Even though Garner was Steve's friend, Steve complained to Sturges that Garner as "The Scrounger" had a more defined role than his. He even objected to Garner wearing a white turtleneck sweater, because it was "too eye-catching" in Steve's competitive view.

He also resented that Garner too had become interested in car racing. "I think Steve viewed that as an invasion of his turf," Sturges said.

His hair dyed blond to match Steve's, stunt man **Bud Ekins,** Steve's close friend, performed the most dangerous stunt of the film--an attempt to jump over the highest part of the barbed wire. Movie audiences believed that it was Steve who performed this feat.

Steve became furious when he learned that after his opening sequence, he would not appear again until thirty minutes later. He demanded that new scenes be written in for him. When they were not immediately forthcoming, Steve, in a "temperamental diva rage," as Sturges put it, bolted from the picture.

His William Morris agent, Stan Kamen, had to board the next plane from Los Angeles to Munich "to smooth out Steve's ruffled feathers."

When Kamen arrived in Munich, Steve met him at the airport. En route to the set, Steve raged, "Garner's stealing the picture out from under me. The billing should read, JAMES GARNER WITH HIS PUSSY BOY STEVE

232

McQUEEN.

Steve's walk-out paid off. Sturges ordered new scenes inserted for him.

"Perhaps because Steve had been abused all his life, he suffered from acute paranoia," Coburn said. "If everything was going right, he felt something was wrong. If there was no trouble, he had to stir up some. Why he didn't get banished from motion pictures early in his career before he became a big star is a mystery to me."

Even before Kamen's plane had landed back in Los Angeles, Steve had walked off the set again. He'd seen the latest script changes and claimed they were "shit—pure shit."

"I quit," he said.

Sturges called to his departing back, "You're not quitting. You're fired."

Informed of the latest mishap, Kamen in Los Angeles caught the next plane back to Munich to negotiate with Sturges over Steve's unprofessional and irresponsible behavior. The beleaguered agent managed to calm Steve down and to get Sturges to rehire his star.

Kamen's most convincing argument to Steve was, "Make this picture. It'll be great. You'll be the first star to emerge from television to become a bona fide movie star." Steve liked the sound of that.

"Originally the film did not entirely revolve around Steve," Sturges said. "At the end of the shoot, most of it did. He saw to that. But we went through hell and back with him. It turned out to be a great film, but he took three years off my life."

"People call me selfish, a screen hog," Steve told Coburn. "I'm not being selfish, I'm protecting myself. I learned as a kid that if I don't protect Steve McQueen, no one else in hell is going to do that. I was once gang raped. I know what happens to a guy when he lets his defenses down. I want to get them before they get me." He never said who "them" was.

Based partly on his eagerness to complete the film before Steve could sabotage it further, Sturges was "all ears" when Steve wanted to rewrite part of the script. He wanted his escape at the end of the film to be a spectacular motorcycle race across the beautiful summery countryside of Bavaria, with Nazis in hot pursuit. Most of the motorcycle riding was performed by Steve himself, although Sturges was afraid his star might injure himself.

Even though handsome actor **James Garner** was a friend, Steve threw a fit when he perceived that Garner was stealing *The Great Escape* from him. Steve thought that the white turtleneck made Garner look too dashing.

At the end of the chase, Steve finds himself trapped between the Nazis and two large barbed wire barriers. Revving up his cycle, he passes over the first barrier. But the second barrier is impossible. Steve bravely makes the attempt but falls into the barbed wire, where he is trapped in the coils, coming to a crashing halt.

Even daredevil Steve knew he couldn't pull off this stunt, not that Sturges would let him. He flew his cycle-riding buddy, Bud Ekins, to Munich to perform the jump of sixty feet over the high barbed wire fence.

What became the most famous scene in the movie was actually performed by a double, although the public gave Steve credit for it. However, on Johnny Carson's *Tonight Show*, Steve admitted that Bud was the real daredevil.

At one point Steve put on a Nazi uniform and became his own pursuer after himself on the motorcycle. He could do that because his face was carefully hidden from the cameras.

"It was an amazing stunt he pulled off, "Sturges said. "Steve McQueen chasing Steve McQueen. Maybe that was the story of his life."

After the success of *The Great Escape*, Steve proclaimed, "I'm bigger than Paul Newman. In fact, I'm the biggest fucking movie star in this big fucking world, and any man who says I'm not can eat my shit."

***

Judy Garland waited in a limousine for a lover man, any lover man. Steve volunteered.

In spite of the failure of many of his films, Steve in the wake of *The Great Escape* flew into Los Angeles thinking he'd "arrived" as an A-list star in Tinseltown. He still felt insecure, as he would all his life, but secure enough to invest $300,000 into a mansion for Neile, his two children, and himself in 1963.

He called his ivy-clad, eighteen-room manse "The Castle," and it came complete with its own cloisters and an Olympic-sized swimming pool where Steve often swam nude, once to the delight of a photographer. The location was on three acres opening onto Oakmont Drive in fashionable Brentwood, a leafy suburb of Los Angeles. James Garner, who'd just filmed *The Great Escape* with Steve, was his nearest neighbor.

There was a parking lot big enough for a dozen cars and Steve needed these spaces for his ever-growing collection of machines that ranged from a Lincoln to a dune buggy, and which overflowed his garages.

In his newly acquired mansion, he had visions of becoming not only the top box office attraction in America, but a movie producer as well. He changed his production company's name from Condor to Solar, Inc.

"At this point in his life, Steve's ambition knew no bounds," said James Coburn. "He wanted the moon today, perhaps Jupiter tomorrow."

As the 1960s deepened and became more political, many of Steve's friends urged him to take political positions. Among these advocates were James Garner, Marlon Brando, and Tony Franciosa.

Steve did not appear at the famous march of celebrities on Washington on August 28, 1963, although his name appeared on the list of expected guests. He was a no-show. But since his name was on the list, the FBI created a file on him, viewing him as a potential threat, "someone to watch."

Steve never liked to be drawn into political controversies. He was always embarrassed at being asked political questions, or even questions in general. He knew he was not educated, so he didn't like to speak out on issues.

He still hung out with grease monkeys, but A-list Hollywood began to show up at his door to party. Jane Fonda (of "the great ass"—Steve's words) turned up, representing the far Left, but John Wayne also drove up to his door, representing the conservative Right. Zsa Zsa Gabor put in an appearance. Steve and the Hungarian talked about Porfirio Rubirosa. Joan Collins arrived, looking gorgeous, and taught Steve how to do the Watusi.

Milton Berle showed up, and, as a joke, danced with Steve. "I've unzipped my pants," he whispered in Steve's ear. "You can reach it and grope me if you want. That way you'll know if the legend's true." Even Pat Boone appeared. "What's that candyass doing here?" Wayne asked.

Steve not only invited A-list stars, but in a few short months he'd be receiving invitations himself from A-list personalities ranging from a president of the United States to the princess of Monaco.

"Not bad for a kid from the reform school," Steve boasted to his wife, who went around in the briefest of miniskirts. Frank Sinatra showed up one night and introduced Steve to his pal, Dean Martin. "Dino," instead of saying hello, asked Steve, "Got anything decent to drink in this joint? I don't go for that rotgut shit Frankie drinks."

Sammy Davis Jr. arrived late one night and whispered in Steve's ear, "Judy Garland is waiting outside in a limousine," he told Steve. "She wants me to fuck her. I'm a bit used up today. Would you go out and do the job for me? I promised her I'd ask you."

"Dorothy in the *Wizard of Oz*?" Steve said. "My favorite picture when I was a kid. I will gladly oblige."

Without telling Neile, Steve secretly attended the notorious parties thrown by Rock Hudson. These two hot box office attractions still talked about making a picture together. One night at Rock's house, the star of *Pillow Talk* bluntly asked him, "Who in Hollywood would you like to meet that you haven't already met?"

"Mae West," Steve blurted out.

"An odd choice but I can arrange that," Rock said. "Mae and I became great friends when we sang 'Baby, It's Cold Outside' at the Oscar show in '59. By the way, why oh why would a guy like you want to meet Mae West?"

"I've always wanted to see her in person," Steve said. "I have this secret to share with you. Every time there's a full moon, I have this lust for antique pussy."

***

Two weeks later, Mae West in her apartment in Ravenswood settled back on her white sofa and told Steve and Rock Hudson, "I didn't have to take off all my clothes like the gals do in movies today. Men imagined what was underneath."

Rock's memory of that night with Mae differed from Steve's. "Although heavily made up and with her age disguised, Steve and I sat there for hours as an old lady told us amusing stories of her life—and what stories. She had us laughing hysterically. Mae was a lot of fun. I never knew what Steve saw in her. To me, it'd be the same as going to bed with your grandmother."

Rock Hudson and **Mae West** sing "Baby, It's Cold Outside" to Oscar night audiences around the world. "He's one hunk I didn't seduce," Mae later said. "I heard he was strictly for the boys."

"Censorship, dearies, was invented both on Broadway and in Hollywood to suppress me," she told Steve and Rock. "I always believed in keeping the censors raging and the fans coming." She said the word "coming" in her most suggestive style. "Greer Garson and I could say the same line. No one took notice if Garson said it. Let me say it, and they call the police."

Steve very gently helped ease her up when she obviously had to excuse herself to go to the toilet. When she came back, both Steve and Rock rose to their feet until she was seated comfortably.

"What sign are you?" she asked Steve.

"Aries," he said.

"That's one of the great sex signs in the

Zodiac," she said. "No wonder an Aries is born under the sign of the Ram. How appropriate. Guys born under your sign know what they've got and know how to use it. When an Aries man decides he wants a woman, he almost always gets her. An Aries man never leaves the bed of a woman until he has completely satisfied her."

"I'm a Scorpio," Rock said. "What kind of man am I?"

"When a Scorpio guy gives you everything he's got, you're bound to get plenty," she said.

Before the night was over, Mae advised Steve, "Never change your image. Find an image and stick to it. In other words, don't try to be a Katharine Hepburn and impersonate a Chinese coolie. Hepburn's a dyke, you know. I wouldn't let her get near me. Marlene came on to me too. I don't go that route."

"I'll tell you right now the image I'm going for," Steve said. "A man of few words on the screen, but one whose face registers what he's feeling. I want to be directly honest with the camera and a bit world weary. How do you think I come off?"

"Squinty eyed and a touch simian," she said, "and I mean that in the most complimentary sense. Would you go nude on camera?"

"If the director says so, I'll flash my wares," he said.

"Good to know that," she said. "I'll be your director later tonight. As for me, I'm a woman of taste. I believe you can be risqué without being vulgar. I would never do a role that's against my image. My fans wouldn't allow it. When Billy Wilder offered me the role of Norma Desmond in *Sunset Blvd.*, I turned it down. Do you think my fans would accept Mae West as a has-been?"

"You are eternal, Miss West," Steve said.

"Call me Mae," she said. "We might get better acquainted later tonight so we should be on a first-name basis."

As the evening wore on, Mae became more provocative. "Now Rock here, or so I hear, likes the boys. I see nothing wrong with that. Remember I was in the theater for years. The gays remain my best and my most loyal fans. When the cops on Broadway used to beat them up, I told 'em that the fellahs were really women in men's bodies. So when they were beating up a homo, they were in fact beating up on a woman."

"Mae, I don't think it quite works that way," Rock said, "but thank you for stopping the beating of those boys back then."

She turned her attention to Steve and appraised him for the first time that evening, the way she looked over men when she auditioned them to be a muscleman in her act.

"I felt she was undressing me," Steve later told Rock.

"I'm not a good appraiser of horse flesh," she said. "Leave that to John

Wayne. But I know man flesh when I see it. Mr. McQueen, unless my radar fails me, I think you're all man."

"Thanks," he said. "I am."

"You may be a little on the runty side," she said, "but some of you shorter guys deliver where it counts. While some of the big guys like Rock here fall short."

"Let's not call my legendary ten inches short," Rock said defensively.

"Ten inches," she said reflectively. "I've known bigger but ten inches are just fine. My lowest rating is seven and a half. If a man has less than that, I'm not interested."

"Neither am I," Rock said.

"Hey, guys," Steve said, "let's stop all this gay talk. I didn't come here for that."

"And just why did you come here, dearie?" she asked.

"To pay tribute to you, and tell you how much I loved your image on the screen," Steve said.

"There's just one way I like a man to pay tribute to me," she said. "Why don't you and I have a little sleepover tonight?"

"I'd be honored," he said.

"I'm out of here," Rock said. "Three on a match is bad luck."

Rock called Steve the next day for a full report, but didn't get it.

"I've heard a lot of stories that Mae is really a man in drag," Steve said. "I can vouch for her. She's all woman, and that's all I have to say on the matter. Except she has a script she wants me to read. She thinks now that I'm big box office, me and her might star in a picture together. We're still talking about the billing. She wants it to be Miss Mae West with Steve McQueen."

"I'm sure you guys will work it out," Rock said. "What's the name of this upcoming epic?"

"*There's Sex in Your Stars!*" he said.

"Sounds like it will be your next big hit," Rock said before ringing off.

***

Steve, in his own words, was "sitting pretty on top of the world." Among the many offers he was weighing was a starring film role from John Sturges to do *Vivacious Lady*, despite Steve's unprofessional conduct on *The Great Escape*.

238

In charge of his own production company, Solar, Steve was receiving screenplays coming in over the transom. With his new-found loot, at $300,000 a picture, his business manager was investing in restaurants, an office building, a bowling alley, and even a Christmas stocking factory.

The time had come for him to return to the screen, and once again he made a disastrous choice, signing up for another comedy, a Blake Edwards production called *Soldier in the Rain*. Instead of having top billing, he had to stand in the very large shadow of Jackie Gleason.

Based on William Goldman's novel, the movie wavered from sentimental drama to high comedy. Comedy was never Steve's *forte*, and it took the making of *Soldier in the Rain* to convince him to bow out of this medium forever.

Gleason played a swinging sergeant, Steve his loyal admirer. "We'll become another Gable/Tracy," Gleason assured him on the first day of shoot under the direction of Ralph Nelson. Nelson, an award-winning director from TV's Golden Age, was guiding Sidney Poitier to Oscar glory in the 1963 *Lilies of the Field*.

The first meeting between Steve and Gleason hadn't gone well. Steve astounded Gleason with his opening greeting, which he might have meant to be funny. "They told me Goldman's novel is tinged with homoeroticism, whatever in the fuck that means," Steve said. "If you think that entitles you to suck my dick on this picture, dream on big boy."

"The little fucker," Gleason told Nelson. "I should have sat on him and squashed him right on the spot, but decided I want my paycheck more than the satisfaction of flattening him out."

"Gleason also liked a gag, and finally Steve won him over by mooning all the time," Nelson said. "I saw more of Steve's ass than I did of my wife's during our brief marriage." He'd wed Celeste Holm in 1938, the marriage lasting less than a year.

When the suits from Allied arrived on location, and Nelson threw a big party for them, Steve appeared, dropped his pants and mooned all of them, letting "the biggest fart of my career," and then disappeared into his dressing room.

Steve told Nelson, "I turned down both John Sturges and Frank Capra to work on this piece of shit. You know why I decided to go for it. Allied offered

Jackie Gleason cuddles up to **Tuesday Weld** in *Soldier in the Rain,* although Steve was more her type.

me 20.5 percent of the net."

While making *Soldier in the Rain*, Gleason encountered Bobby Darin, who had completed *Hell Is for Heroes* with Steve. Gleason told the singer, "I think Steve is his own worst enemy."

"Not while I'm alive," Darin shot back.

Steve had many a sleepless night making *Soldier*. When he was frustrated, he'd call his agent, Stan Kamen. He frequently taunted him about his homosexuality. "Guess what I'm doing right now, baby," he'd say to Kamen. "I'm playing with my big hard-on, thinking of your lusty lips wrapped around it. If you were here tonight, I'd shoot my biggest load down your gullet."

"What do you want, Steve?" Kamen asked. "It's the middle of the night."

"If you don't come up with a better movie for me next time, you'll be reduced to handling only Margaret O'Brien." Steve slammed down the phone.

Deep into the shoot, Steve began to resent his character of Supply Sergeant Eustic Clay, a hapless hick half-wit.

Writer W.J. Weatherby claimed that the movie didn't do "much for Gleason's Hollywood reputation, but McQueen didn't dare to play any tricks with Jackie. He recognized the tough kid from Brooklyn in Gleason."

"My two stars didn't become bosom buddies," Nelson said, "but they didn't exactly kill each other, either, although Gleason almost ran over Steve in a souped up golf cart."

A young Adam West, the future Batman, appeared briefly as Captain Blekely in *Soldier in the Rain*. Steve didn't care about that. He was entranced by the female lead of the picture, Tuesday Weld.

When Steve first heard of the name Tuesday Weld, he joked to Nelson, "Why didn't she call herself Wednesday Weld? That way, her initials could be W.W."

When he actually met the doe-eyed, beautiful blonde, he'd been given a lot of reports on her from his friends, including Sal Mineo and John Drew Barrymore, even Frank Sinatra.

Fresh from a torrid affair with Elvis Presley, her co-star in *Wild in the Country* (1961), Tuesday, though still young, was already a survivor. She'd had a nervous breakdown at age nine, began drinking heavily at ten, made her first suicide attempt at twelve, and debuted on-screen at thirteen.

As Tuesday herself admitted, she lost her virginity at age twelve to a guy who turned out to be gay. "As a teenager, I was a wreck," she admitted. "I drank so much I can't remember anything."

Nelson claimed that Steve had an affair with Tuesday. Gleason agreed. "He got to her so fast that it was like he was shot out of a cannon," Gleason said. He said he'd heard that the McQueen/Weld affair continued through the making of *The Cincinnati Kid*.

Steve was jealous of Elvis, a rivalry that would soon intensify. Tuesday had already praised Elvis in the press. "He walked into a room and everything stopped. Elvis was just so physically beautiful that even if he didn't have any talent, just his face, his presence, was enough to get him by. And he was funny, charming, and complicated, but he didn't wear it on his sleeve. You didn't see that he was complicated. You saw great needs."

When Steve read Tuesday's comment about Elvis in the press, he tossed his paper on the floor and pissed on it.

Except for the claims of Nelson and Gleason, two key players in the film, actual details of Steve's alleged affair with Tuesday will have to remain as rumor.

Soldier in the Rain was released on November 27, 1963 in the immediate wake of the assassination of John F. Kennedy. The critics, taking time out from watching Kennedy's death on the news, savaged the picture, and *Soldier in the Rain* remains one of Steve's biggest mistakes on the screen. Arthur Winsten of the *New York Post* claimed that the failed movie "would set back the star's blossoming career one giant step."

Critic Casey St. Charnez found that Steve played his role so broadly "he comes off like Gomer Pyle with a permanent adolescent erection."

In spite of the box office failure of the picture, Steve was hailed as "a man's man and a woman's dream." He turned them down, but reporters wanted to interview this new "Bad Boy of Hollywood." He was getting copy which in the past would have been reserved for Dean or Brando. *Newsweek* claimed he looked like "a young Eisenhower after sophomore year at San Quentin."

Although he remained furiously jealous if any man paid the slightest attention to his wife, he kept up his philandering, which Steve said had actually begun on his honeymoon when "I slipped away to fuck a Mexican waitress."

Neile allegedly called him "a male nymphomaniac—a fuck 'em and leave 'em sort of guy." Reportedly, he shared the details of many of his sexual conquests with her, although he never suggested that he might be intimate with one of the homosexuals or bisexuals for which he continued to express extreme disgust.

He and his bisexual friend, Peter Lawford, often laughed at the secrets they shared. "The wives are always the last to know," Lawford said.

Still happily married to Neile, still a devoted father to his children, Steve was about to experience a new love entering his life to complicate an already complicated existence.

It would be *Love With the Proper Stranger*.

***

Steve didn't want to do another war movie—"I've already won World War II for America," he said—and he was no good at comedy, as proved by *The Honeymoon Machine* and *Soldier in the Rain*. He ordered his agent, Stan Kamen, to get him something else, "perhaps something in a more romantic vein."

Coincidentally, just such an offer came in from the team of Alan J. Pakula and Robert Mulligan, the guiding lights behind the Oscar-winning adaptation of Harper Lee's *To Kill a Mockingbird*. Even though it dealt with abortion, "it was a romance of sorts," according to the Broadway playwright, Arnold Schulman, who wrote the screenplay.

Playwright James Leo Herlihy's *Blue Denim* had already made it to Broadway, depicting the story of a teenage abortion. But *Love With the Proper Stranger* was the first major film to bring this taboo subject to the silver screen. To make abortion appear as unattractive as possible, Mulligan ordered an angular and shadowy set for the abortionist that evoked *The Cabinet of Dr. Caligari* (1919).

Mulligan was drawn to the script because it was the story of "falling in love in reverse—of having an affair, and then, through the stress and results of the affair, falling in love." Writer Schulman nicknamed the script, *A Funny Thing Happened on the Way to the Abortionist*.

From the beginning, the female co-star was Natalie Wood, the former child actress who'd been married to Robert Wagner, with whom Steve had filmed *The War Lover*. At the time, Natalie was

Natalie Wood   Steve McQueen

Love With The Proper Stranger

viewed as a "hot" property, having garnered two Academy Award nominations for *Rebel Without a Cause*, with James Dean, her lover, and *Splendor in the Grass* with her lover Warren Beatty.

As she arrived in New York to film *Love With the Proper Stranger*, Natalie was in the throes of recovering from her ill-fated romance with Beatty.

Mulligan's first choice for the male lead was Beatty. The director wanted to take box office advantage of the affair of the two stars, which was played out in movie magazines across the country. Beatty bowed out because of his commitment to film *Lilith*.

Mulligan's second choice was Paul Newman, who might have played the part of Rocky Papasano more effectively than Steve. "One Rocky was enough for me," Paul told Mulligan, turning it down.

"But your first Rocky was a boxer," Mulligan protested.

"Your Rocky is still Italian," Paul said, refusing for the second time.

After that turn-down, Mulligan contacted Steve who read the script. With Neile's stamp of approval, he signed on the dotted line for $300,000 in cash.

Even before Natalie met Steve, New York columnist Dorothy Kilgallen, Natalie's most rigid critic, predicted a "romantic *contretemps*."

After flying to New York, Steve said, "It's good to be back on the streets of this old city. After all, that's where I got my start. It's home to me."

"I'm here to make a film about love and abortion," he said. Then he added something that shocked readers at the time. "Love and abortion," he repeated. "A great combination."

Was he actually inserting a plug for abortion? When there was fallout over this remark, Steve was forced to add, "The film is about love winning out over abortion."

Privately he told Mulligan, "I don't know how many gals have aborted my babies, but there have been quite a few."

The film was pioneering on other fronts as well, suggesting that women are the sexual equals of men and should have the same rights to sleep with men if they chose. That right, of course, was for sexual pleasure alone, not love.

Steve had had many long talks about Natalie with her then-husband, Robert Wagner, during the filming of *The War Lover* in England.

In Natalie, Steve met his female equal. He took pride in bedding all of his leading ladies, and she attempted to bed all her leading men.

Mulligan introduced Steve to Natalie, and her opening line to him was deliberately designed to shock. "Did you fuck R.J. when you guys shot *The War Lover*?" she asked.

"I didn't," Steve said, without losing his cool. "But I did see him in his underwear, and he looked like he had a very fuckable ass."

"Everybody says that," she said enigmatically.

All memoirs recording events of that time report how Natalie flirted outrageously with Steve on the set. But he allegedly turned down her availability because of his friendship with Wagner.

"Yeah, right," Mulligan said

On screen, **Natalie Wood** was seduced and impregnated by the character played by **Steve**. Off screen, she was merely seduced, but didn't end up pregnant.

years later at his Connecticut home when asked about that story. "They were fucking so much in her dressing room during the shoot that I privately advised Steve, 'Save some of your juice for the camera.'"

Neile herself claimed that Natalie developed a crush on Steve. "She tried every which way to ensnare Steve short of using a butterfly net, including resorting to adolescent tricks like sticking her leg out of her trailer steps, pretending she was talking to someone inside just as Steve would pass by." Neile claimed that Steve resisted Natalie's advances, although he did, eventually, "succumb to Natalie's charms, but that was years later."

"It wasn't years later," Mulligan said. "Steve McQueen could never resist succumbing to any beautiful woman's charms. He had absolutely zero resistance. I can't tell you how many times I caught him walking up Natalie's trailer steps to get to that much overused honeypot. I must say Natalie sure had a taste for beautiful men. James Dean, Robert Wagner, Warren Beatty, Steve McQueen. God knows who was next on her list."

Natalie's sister, Lana Wood, weighed in with her opinion. "I saw Natalie and Steve working together and sensed an intimacy that went beyond the camera."

Steve and Natalie had to be discreet because Steve's "ol' lady," Neile, was frequently on the set.

After the humiliation of being dumped by Beatty, Natalie wanted to maintain her credentials as a sex symbol. Even though Steve had a wife, snaring him gave her "an opportunity to prove that she could get any man she wanted, even if it meant breaking up a marriage," said author Warren G. Harris.

During the course of their affair, Natalie confessed to Steve that "two of my lovers were offered the script before you." She named them as Newman and Beatty. "I never mind sloppy seconds," he told her.

Natalie had turned down *Charade*, which went to Audrey Hepburn, who teamed with Cary Grant. Instead she took the role of a Macy's salesgirl in *Love With the Proper Stranger*, who has a one-night stand with Rocky (Steve) and becomes pregnant by him. Most of the storyline concerns a possible abortion.

Steve and Natalie were teamed with co-stars, Edie Adams, playing Steve's stripper girlfriend, and stage actor Tom Bosley, who went on to greater fame as the father on the TV sitcom, *Happy Days*.

Edie found Natalie "emotionally unstable and willing to plunge into any affair to forget Beatty. Steve was the first sexy man who crossed her path."

"For a lot of her characterization, Natalie drew upon her ill-fated romance with Beatty," said costar Bosley.

A close friend of Marilyn Monroe's, Edie often had long talks with Steve about the fallen screen goddess. Even though he didn't know Marilyn very well, he was greatly saddened by her death in August of 1962. He felt, based on very little evidence, that she had been murdered. Between takes, Steve and Edie developed conspiracy theories about who murdered Marilyn.

Costume designer Edith Head was brought in to handle wardrobe, although Natalie complained to Steve that "the old dyke handled me improperly during my fitting." There is no evidence that this was true. From all reports, Head was the ultimate professional.

One of the most memorable scenes in the film was when Steve as Rocky shows up at Natalie's workplace with a picket sign reading BETTER WED THAN DEAD.

The "cum shot," as Steve called it, was his kiss with Natalie. Both were on their knees. Critic Casey St. Charnez called it "that popcorn-selling, theater-filling, studio rent-paying kiss." The image of these two beautiful stars kissing became one of Steve's most popular movie posters.

By the film's end, even Mulligan conceded that, "It's Natalie's picture. She beats Steve to the finish line in all ways." Her role won her her third Oscar nomination, though she lost the prize to Patricia Neal for *Hud*, in which she co-starred with Paul Newman.

Although the film was nominated for five Oscars—none of which it received—Steve was left off the list that year. He was furious, telling Mulligan that Academy members "are nothing but fucking assholes, each one covered with more dingleberries than the next."

He didn't get the kind of reviews he dreamed of, with Bosley Crowther of *The New York Times*, calling him a "face-squinching simpleton."

His favorite critique was in *Saturday Review*, which suggested that as an actor he might give Marlon Brando a few lessons.

Paul Newman and Steve got together for a beer, or whatever, to commemorate how the Academy had completely ignored them. "Maybe you and I should stop playing Italians," Paul advised Steve. "I thought you looked about as Italian as Jerry Lewis."

"See me at payback time for that sassy remark," Steve said.

"I'm going to give up anything with Stranger in the title," he told Paul weeks after filming ended. He was, of course, referring to *Never Love a Stranger*, in

Edie Adams, playing Steve's stripper girl friend in *Love With the Proper Stranger,* mulled over murder conspiracy theories associated with the death of their mutual friend, Marilyn Monroe.

which he was cast as a Jewish district attorney, and also to *Love With the Proper Stranger*, in which he played an Italian jazz musician.

Despite its flaws, *Love With the Proper Stranger* became a minor hit and established Steve for the first time as a romantic hero in films.

Steve not only seduced Natalie, but would do so in the future. The question remains, why? He later said, "I never saw what was so great about Natalie. She was short, and lousy in bed."

***

For months some strange man had been following Steve but at such a discreet distance that there was never a confrontation. One night Steve dined with Neile in a restaurant. The man entered and sat at a far and distant table. Hot-tempered Steve was tempted for a face-to-face encounter, but realized he might have a gun.

When driving, Steve was vaguely aware that someone was following him. Since he was King of the Road, he could usually outsmart another driver, or at least outrace him.

One night Steve went for a nude swim in his pool, and sensed that he was being observed. He heard no movement, saw no sign of human life, but still he feared for his safety. Someone had slipped by the gate and entered his heavily secured compound. He just knew it. Perhaps it was that strange man who had been following him for months.

Steve's rear bedroom had a large window that opened to the sounds in the canyon below, where wild dogs barked at night. Far from disturbing him, he found some solace in these lost dogs, wandering at night to scavenge whatever food they could for survival.

He was a rich man today, but once he'd been like one of those dogs embarked on a relentless search for food and, ultimately, survival.

It was on one blistering hot night that he heard a sound. Rising nude from the bed—he always slept in the nude—he tiptoed through the dimly lit hallway.

The sound seemed to be coming from his front door. A prowler had evaded his security and even his guard dogs and was jimmying the lock on his front door.

Acting impulsively, he rushed to his hallway cabinet and removed his 9mm Mauser. Slipping through a side door, he sneaked up behind the stranger and put the gun to his head.

"Don't move! You fucker!" he shouted at the intruder. "I'll blow your brains out." His shouts had awakened the house. When someone inside, perhaps Neile, realized what was going on, the Brentwood police were called.

Steve later claimed, "If the asshole had resisted, I swear I would have killed him."

When the police arrived and were let in, they apprehended Alfred Thomas Pucci, an unemployed Italian immigrant.

When he was grilled at police headquarters, he told the department that he'd followed Steve for months. "I've seen all his films," Pucci said, "and his face is beautiful. It's the face of the most understanding man I've ever seen. I knew that if I could get inside his house and meet him man to man that he would understand me. I have deep problems. Steve can help solve them for me. I just know that. My brain just seems to bubble at times."

Pucci was sentenced to three months in prison, and Steve's lawyers obtained a restraining order against him. After his release, Pucci just seemed to disappear and was never seen again.

However, demented fans would continue to pursue Steve throughout the rest of his too-short life.

He was fiercely protective of Neile and the kids. "No one harms my family," he said. He had installed elaborate security measures, including cameras and guard dogs, on his property. "No President of the United States is better protected," he boasted.

He was long used to demented fans raiding his garbage cans when they were put out on the street for collection. These fans were hoping for some souvenir to save.

One crazed young girl, about eighteen, threw the garbage all around the street. When a neighbor spotted her, the police were called.

At police headquarters, the girl claimed that she was hoping to find some nude Polaroid shots of her film idol that had been carelessly tossed out in the garbage instead of shredded.

Indeed Steve had been known to take such candid Polaroid shots, so the girl's dream was not beyond the realm of possibility.

***

Steve was itching to begin another picture and to launch another affair. He was sitting around the house too much or else racing too dangerously. Director Robert Mulligan and producer Alan J. Pakula called to offer him another role, that of Henry Thomas in *Baby, the Rain Must Fall*, adapted from the Broadway play, *The Traveling Lady* by Horton Foote.

His co-star was the lovely and talented Lee Remick. The bleak location would be Bay City, Texas, a state from which he'd fled so long ago.

He may have been disappointed by the public's reception of his role in *Love With a Proper Stranger*, but he was ill-prepared for the hostile reviews he'd receive for *Baby, the Rain Must Fall*. In fact, that reception would be so venomous he temporarily retired from motion pictures.

His portrayal of the long-suffering Henry Thomas was described as "sad sack, ill fated, and emotionally immature." Hollywood insiders, at least those who saw this failure of a picture, claimed that Steve was miscast.

On the other hand, Remick was perfectly cast as the loving wife of ex-con Steve. In her slow, enticing way, a bundle of loveliness and charm, she stole the picture right from under him.

"Oh, my God," Remick said upon meeting Steve. "I think I have Southern Gothic written on my forehead. This script is even complete with a mad woman in the attic. How Southern can you get?"

Steve played a country singer, and, amazingly, did his own singing in the picture. "I decided not to pursue it as a career," he later said. He also learned to play the guitar, working with Billy Strange as his technical adviser.

Actually it was Glen Campbell who coached Steve in his country singing, although he never got any screen credit for his work.

Steve liked the sound of his own voice, but Mulligan called Steve's first attempt to sing "like a hog at slaughter time on his uncle's farm in Slater, Missouri."

It was only two weeks into filming that Steve learned that Mulligan had originally offered the role to Elvis Presley.

In *Baby, the Rain Must Fall*, Steve plays an ex-con, a role that should have suited him easily. Released from prison, he is tracked down by his wife, "The Traveling Lady," who brings along their little daughter to a remote town on the Texas plains.

There she encounters a sympathetic Don Murray, playing "Deputy Slim," who befriends her. Remick's character wants to start life over again with Steve, although the audience already knows right from the beginning that his fate is doomed.

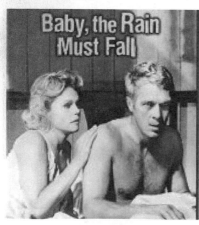

A child actress, Kimberly Block, played Steve's daughter in the film. "Margaret O'Brien she was not," Steve said. He should know. After all, he'd worked with the child actress of all child actresses, discounting Shirley Temple, of course.

Lonely and alone in this bleak Texas location, Steve quickly graduated to the nurturing breasts of Remick. "She is one of the warmest, sweetest creatures I've ever made love to," Steve told Mulligan. "I can see why you chose her for this part. When you bed her, she makes every man feel like his pecker is three inches longer than it is."

Both Steve and Remick knew that their affair was "just one of two lonely hearts coming together under the bright stars at night over the state of Texas," Mulligan claimed. "Both of them let me know that it would be over by the end of the shoot when Steve would go back to Neile and the kids."

Remick was married to Bill Colleran, an American TV producer with whom she had both a son and a daughter.

Mulligan also revealed Remick's hidden agenda. "Right in the middle of shooting, I had to grant her a week's leave of absence. Unknown to Steve, she had to fly to Los Angeles to shack up with Robert F. Kennedy. They were having an illicit affair."

"Lee was usually a sane gal, but she lost her marbles over Kennedy," Mulligan said. "Believe it or not, she had convinced herself that Kennedy was so in love with her he was going to divorce Ethel and marry her.

"'Oh, Lee,' I cautioned her," Mulligan said. "'You wouldn't want to be the stepmother of that brood of kids.'"

"She was absolutely convinced I didn't know how sincere Kennedy was in his commitment to her," Mulligan said. "I thought he was just making idle promises to get in her pants. I knew that Lee was headed for heartbreak, and I tried to warn her, but she wouldn't listen. As for Steve, I don't think he knew about Lee's affair with the attorney general, and I also don't think he would have given a hot damn either way."

Mulligan called a "wrap" of *Baby, the Rain Must Fall* in May, 1963. Steve would not work again until early in 1965. During the previous year he'd made three feature films, or thirteen feature films in his entire career, plus a hit TV series.

Back in Brentwood, and feeling guilt over his adulterous affair, Steve confessed to Neile. She later said, "There was no reason for me to find out except for his compulsion to tell me. Not to hurt me—just to make it all right for him. But I knew then that as long as I was around, Lee Remick would never do another movie with Steve McQueen."

Allegedly, Neile sabotaged Remick's

Lee Remick played Steve's long-suffering wife in *Baby, the Rain Must Fall*. She's seen here with child star Kimberly Block, cast as Steve's on-screen daughter. Lee made herself available to Steve off screen as well, except whenever RFK called.

chance to appear again opposite Steve in his film, *Tom Horn*, even though by that time (1978) he and Neile were divorced.

Columbia held *Baby, the Rain Must Fall* until 1965 before releasing it to virtually no box office. It would be Steve's last black-and-white film, and his last movie for some time.

Marlon Brando called with his review. "Now I've seen the Stanley Kowalski of the Texas plains, ugly dirt roads and all that shit. After looking at that countryside, I can only be grateful that Tennessee Williams set us in New Orleans. Actually the whole thing reminded me of my home state of Nebraska. Nebraska is a place you don't want to visit. It's a place you want to leave."

A surprise call for Steve came in from Elvis Presley. "I could have acted the role better than you, but I have to admit you've got me beat in the singing department. See you around, kid." He hung up.

Steve went into what is now known as his paranoid retirement.

Chapter Seven
King of the Box Office

Before he experienced what had been a near-fatal motorcycle accident in East Germany, Steve had had one of the greatest summers of his life. He was at the peak of his power as a major movie star.

It had begun in August, 1964, when the president of the United States, Lyndon B. Johnson, had telephoned him. This was the third president that Steve had directly conversed with, Harry S Truman and John F. Kennedy being the other two.

Johnson wanted Steve and Natalie Wood to host a cocktail party in Beverly Hills as part of his campaign that year for the presidency. As vice president, he had filled out the term of the assassinated JFK, but had never been officially elected president by the people.

His seventeen-year-old daughter, Luci Baines Johnson, would be the guest of honor. LBJ knew the political implications of what he was doing. As cameras clicked, Steve danced the night away with her, doing the Watusi, making front pages across the country.

The night of the bash, Steve quickly learned that the Secret Service name for Luci was "Venus." He also learned that Luci had this "thing" for Sara Lee angel food cake. The kitchen didn't have it, so Steve sent out for it.

The President's daughter was trying to be glamorous, and dancing with Steve created a chic new image for her. She was yet to meet Hollywood stylists who would get rid of her Dallas bouffant hairdo and pluck her eyebrows, or subdue her "oil baroness makeup."

"I can't have an affair with you," Luci whispered in his ear. "Daddy hates actors and anything Hollywood. But I love it. I'm having a great, grand time."

One of the evening's highlights came when the Secret Service arrived with a package of venison sausage that LBJ had ordered flown in from his Texas ranch. "It was lip-smacking good," Steve later claimed. "We got greasy lips and did a lot of kissing before the rooster crowed."

Later, Steve told his friends, Casey and Darron, "I plugged her before the sun that had risen in Washington finally made it to the Pacific Ocean."

This claim definitely cannot be confirmed and is probably Steve's fantasy. If he did indeed seduce her, it is not known where this brief affair would have occurred, and if it had, it would definitely be categorized as one of Steve's *liaisons dangereuses*.

***

Shortly after the party he co-hosted for the President's daughter, Steve was about to meet a blonde bombshell at the Whiskey à Go-Go, a nightclub owned by one of his best friends, Elmer Valentine, an ex-cop. It was the summer of 1964.

A clone of Marilyn Monroe and the chief rival of Jayne Mansfield, Mamie Van Doren was a bosomy platinum blonde who appeared in some of the cheesier Hollywood fare of the late 1950s.

Nicky Hilton, Elizabeth Taylor's first husband, said "Mamie was a hot number. She knew how to make a man feel like a man."

Her other conquests included Burt Reynolds, Joe Namath, Elvis Presley, Robert Evans, Tony Curtis, Warren Beatty, Johnny Carson, Steve Cochran, and even boxer Jack Dempsey. She almost seduced Rock Hudson but he prematurely ejaculated as she tried to guide him inside her. Mamie revealed that tantalizing tidbit about Hudson within her very candid memoirs, *Playing the Field,* published in 1988.

Luci Baines Johnson--known as "Venus" to the Secret Service--dances the Watusi with Steve, complete with her bouffant hairdo and "oil baroness" makeup.

Both Steve and Mamie that summer roamed the dance floors of Whiskey à Go-Go, looking for adventure. In response to a tap on her shoulder, Mamie turned around to stare into the icy blue eyes of Steve, who invited her to dance.

After many dances, Steve made his pitch and Mamie invited him to get into his Ferrari and follow her in her creamy white Jaguar into the Hollywood Hills.

"As we kissed," Mamie wrote in *Playing the Field*, "I felt him growing hard against me." Somehow she managed to stave off his passion on their get-acquainted night with the promise

252

of more to come scheduled for another day.

Two nights later found Mamie and Steve gyrating once again across the floors of Whiskey à Go-Go. After working up a sweat, he invited her to a party at the home of Jay Sebring, one of his newest and best friends.

Sebring was the most celebrated hairdresser in Hollywood, and he not only cut Steve's hair but even picked out his underwear for him.

Within the hour, Mamie found herself in the Tudor mansion once occupied by Paul Bern and Jean Harlow, the reigning goddess of the 1930s silver screen. The ill-fated Bern/Harlow marriage lasted only two months, ending in September of 1932 with Bern's death from a gunshot wound in the head—either a murder or a suicide, depending on which theory you believe. Ironically, Mamie's choice of platinum blonde hair had always been inspired by Harlow's.

That evening's party evolved into an orgy, and Steve lured Mamie into dropping a tab or two of Sandoz sunshine. She hesitated because of what she'd heard about bad LSD trips. But Steve was very persuasive.

Finally, he lured her into the bedroom where the corpse of Paul Bern had been found thirty-two years previously. "Once again, I could feel the sizable hardness of his cock against my leg," Mamie wrote in her memoirs.

That night Mamie did not meet an impotent Steve McQueen the way Harlow had in Bern on their wedding night.

In Mamie's words, with both of them hallucinating on acid, they kept making love "through the psychedelic night."

In the early hours of the morning, she woke up, imagining that the dead body of Paul Bern lay crumpled on the floor. In a panic, she awakened Steve, who bounded out of bed to confront Bern's nude corpse, only to discover that it was actually a pile of dirty laundry.

After that bizarre night, Mamie asserted that she and Steve continued an affair that lasted for six months, although he made it clear to her that he did not plan to divorce Neile.

She later admitted that the attraction was purely sexual. "He was a man of great energy and imagination who was unabashedly wonderful in bed." She turned down future drug use, but he continued to take LSD, and, for his added sexual pleasure, he used a lot of amyl nitrite.

Blonde bombshell **Mamie Van Doren** believed that if you had 'em, don't keep it a secret. Steve turned out to be all man in the same bedroom where the impotent Paul Bern had committed suicide (or was it murder?) after a honeymoon with Jean Harlow

"As we were about to reach a climax, Steve would crack open one of the glass vials of amyl nitrite and inhale the vapors deeply."

After the affair ended, Mamie claimed that, "I have never been one to remain in a love affair with a married man who is unwilling to leave his wife. But I missed him when it was over."

***

Sharon Tate (top photo, left) and **Jay Sebring** during those happy, halcyon weeks before their brutal murders. Sebring (pictured in both of the pictures above) not only trimmed Steve's golden locks, but staged S&M orgies for him.

Steve was still slipping around Los Angeles and dating Sharon Tate whenever he could. On one particularly hot night in August, 1964, he invited Sharon to Whiskey to meet Jay Sebring.

"Even though he was a hairdresser, Jay was rather masculine and quite attractive," Sammy Davis Jr. said. "He'd served in the Navy for four years where he'd developed his hairdresser skills. Kirk Douglas liked him so much he got him the job of being the hair stylist for *Spartacus*. The only thing I ever had against him was that Jay was born in Alabama."

One night Sebring and Steve arrived "stag" at Whiskey à Go-Go. Since Sebring was a known bisexual, many of their friends just assumed they were having an affair, especially since they seemed so intimate with each other.

"Jay was really sucking up to Steve," said Sammy Davis Jr., who was often at the disco. "I think every time Steve had to take a leak, Jay went with him to the men's room to take his dick out for him. Now that's what I call a good friend."

Sharon walked into the disco alone and headed to the table where Steve and Sebring awaited her. "Meet Miss Richland of 1959," Steve said in lieu of a more formal introduction. "She's an actress now but wants to be a psychiatrist. She once worked for Pat Boone but don't hold that against her."

Nick Adams had always hated Sebring, thinking that Steve had more or less dropped their friendship to hang out with him. "Sebring

254

is nothing but a cheap star-fucker," Nick said. Of course, the same claim had been made about Nick. "He was a leech. He sucked up to Steve all the time. Or any movie star for that matter."

"Sharon Tate was really impressed with Jay, and they started seeing each other, but not as man and woman but as two men and one woman," Nick claimed. "All three of them were having sex together. It was the talk of Hollywood. Steve's wife must have heard about it. How could she not?"

"I knew Sebring only briefly," Nick said. "The fucker came on to me one night. I told him to go home and stick a dildo up his ass. He didn't hide the fact that he'd go to bed with a man or woman. He had only one requirement. That they be a movie star. His friendship with Steve was the best thing that ever happened to him. He told hopefuls that he was Steve McQueen's haircutter. He used Steve as an advertisement. When Steve called him, Sebring dropped his hair-cutting scissors and came running. You know what the big attraction was? It sure wasn't haircutting. Sebring always had plenty of white powder to bring Steve. He became hooked on cocaine."

"People said I was jealous of Sebring, but that was a lie," Nick claimed. "I'm a star. He's not. Just a skinny little hair-cutter. Someone told me he wasn't very good at cutting hair, but great at ass sucking."

***

In September of 1964, Steve was selected to become a member of the U.S. Cycle team for the International Six Day Competition Trial in what was known at the time as The German Democratic Republic—East Germany. He was filled with joy to have been chosen for this team, which included his closest friend, Bud Ekins.

Representing America, Steve would compete against the Soviet Union, the United Kingdom, Sweden, Poland, and other nations.

For a motorcyclist, running this race was the highest honor. Launched in England in 1913, the competition was a grueling 1,200-mile jaunt through rough mountainous landscapes. Each member, including Steve, had to race against the time clock with the intention of traversing a minimum of 200 miles per day.

The Six-Day Trial, centered near the ancient city of Erfurt in East Germany, was conducted during the height of the Cold War, which involved Steve in a complicated hassle at the border with armed guards. His team was delayed for nearly five hours before they were allowed into East Germany.

As they made their way along heavily patrolled roads behind the Iron Curtain, they were followed by a police guards on motorcycles, who wanted to ensure that members of the U.S. team didn't veer off the Federal highway.

"I was scared shitless," Steve said, "that I was going to be arrested and thrown in the brig. Of course, I was used to that both on and off the screen. Breakfast began every morning with a cup of black, muddy coffee and a cold slice of eel."

After the first day, it became clear that the British team presented the most formidable challenge. By the end of the second day, the British and U.S teams were in a dead heat tie.

At the beginning of the third day, Steve had high hopes that the Americans would break free and outrun Britain. But a few hours later, the American team's best motorcyclist, Bud Ekins, broke his leg and had to drop out of the race. By the fourth day, all hopes hinged on Steve, who by default was now viewed as the best cyclist on his team.

The fourth day dawned gray under threatening clouds. A bad omen, Steve told his team, fearing that by mid-afternoon the ground would be slush mud.

"I was riding well, heading for the finish line," Steve later recalled. "I could see victory ahead. Then all of a sudden tragedy struck."

In Steve's own words, as related to William F. Nolan, he was pumping his Triumph to go at maximum speed, or "riding the edge," as he put it, heading for the finish line, making up for time lost when he'd broken a chain and had to take time out to repair it.

This Triumph motorcycle looks relatively harmless in this photo, but in East Germany it almost took Steve on "the last mile" as he flirted with death.

"Then, on the brow of a slope lined with spectators, along the narrow lip of a pine-thick ravine, this guy on another bike cut right across the course," Steve said. "He didn't hear me or see me. When he saw me bearing down on him, he hit the panic button. He cut left at the last split second and side-swiped me. My Triumph sailed over the side of the ravine, buzzed off into space, and I unloaded in midair."

When he regained consciousness in a hospital, he heard the grim report. His cheek was open to the bone. His lips were split into four parts, and his two front teeth were missing. That was not all. Neither of his kneecaps had any skin on them.

"Oh, God, I'll become another Monty," Steve cried out. His East

256

German nurse didn't know what he meant. But Steve's greatest fear was that his face had been damaged so severely that plastic surgeons could never completely restore it, and that he would look as drawn and lacking in emotion as Monty's face did in *Raintree County* after the plastic surgeons finished with him.

"I didn't think the scar would heal properly, or could be erased," Steve remembered. "I thought the only role I could play in the future was that of *Scarface*."

From his hospital bed, he demanded the best plastic surgeons in East Germany, "the best money can buy."

***

As he lay in an East German hospital, waiting for his bandages to be removed, Steve called Neile. "I've done it to myself. Wrecked my face. That's the same as wrecking my career."

When fellow cyclists visited him in the hospital, he told them that "Frankenstein is waiting to take off his bandages."

To an East German doctor, who spoke English, he had long talks, confiding in him why he constantly risked his life either racing motorcycles or sports cars. "An actor is a puppet, manipulated by a dozen other people," he said. "Auto racing or even cycle racing has dignity. But you need the same absolute concentration that an actor has to have. In racing, as in acting, you have to reach inside yourself and bring forth a lot of broken glass."

On another day, he attempted once again to explain his love of racing. "Racers I know aren't in it for the money. They race because of something inside of them. They're not courting death. They're courting being alive."

Later, he'd remember those days recovering in a hospital bed as the "worst of my life, with the exception of the days after I was gang raped."

"I climbed so far," he later told Neile, "and now I fear it'll all be taken away from me. Steve McQueen, big time movie star. Male sex symbol of America. Now, women will run at the sight of me. What if I end up as a monster?"

With his East German doctor, he seriously talked about suicide. He even begged the doctor to give him something so he could die a painless death if his face would be riddled with scars that even a plastic surgeon couldn't remove.

His moment of truth came when the bandages were removed. Except for some red spots, his face had been restored. "It's a miracle," Steve shouted, rising from the bed. His doctors had never seen a face so mutilated that had healed so quickly.

Unlike Monty Clift, who never really recovered his facial beauty, Steve emerged "from those beauty butchers" with his looks intact. Doctors, themselves amazed at the outcome, assured him that except for some tiny lines, he would look more or less as he did before the accident.

Totally nude, and in front of two nurses, Steve looked at himself in the mirror. "I'm beautiful again. I'm beautiful! I'm still the sexiest man on the planet, with the most beautiful face. Paul Newman, eat your heart out. You have a girly boy's face. I'm a real man with a man's face. A man's beauty. They've restored me and given me back my face."

Neile joined Steve for a trip to Paris for the French premiere of *Love With the Proper Stranger*. The paparazzi didn't even know he'd had plastic surgery.

His TV series, *Wanted: Dead or Alive*, had been wildly popular in France. As he walked the Champs-Elysées, he was mobbed by adoring fans. He had dethroned Marlon Brando to become France's favorite foreign movie star. Rejected for so many years of his life, Steve loved the adoration, although he complained at first that he hated being recognized and hounded.

He was the toast of Paris, and was seen at the celebrated Maxim's Restaurant. Hordes of fans gathered in front of the swanky Hotel Crillon which at that time was favored by visiting movie stars. Steve waved to his faithful devotees as he came and went from the place de la Concorde in the heart of Paris.

"My God," Steve said before retiring in his suite at the Crillon for his final night in Paris. "I've become more famous than Marie Antoinette. Speaking of that bitch, just who was she exactly?"

***

With his wounds healed, Steve finally agreed to return to work to star in a gambling picture, *The Cincinnati Kid*, set in the French Quarter of New Orleans. He liked the $350,000 salary, but feared that he would be compared unfavorably to Paul Newman's *The Hustler*.

A Filmways-Solar picture, the movie, set for a release in October of 1965, would be distributed by Metro-Goldwyn-Mayer. He still had a grudge against MGM, claiming the studio "fucked up my career when I was cast in *The Honeymoon Machine*."

Steve would be working with an all-star cast, one of the most talented troupes assembled for any movie in the mid-60s, but there was conflict from the beginning.

His biggest disappointment came when Spencer Tracy, relying heavily on the advice of Katharine Hepburn, turned down the co-starring role of Lancey

258

Howard, called "The Man." The aging Tracy did not feel that his role was a real star part and certainly nothing equal of "The Kid." Steve seemed desperate to want to co-star with Tracy, and made a surprisingly generous offer to him. He would even allow Tracy to have star billing. In response, the grand old star sent him a "maybe next time" letter.

The co-starring role went instead to veteran actor Edward G. Robinson. After initial jitters about working with "this young upstart," Robinson came to like and admire Steve. "He comes out of the tradition of Bogie, Gable, Cagney, and even myself. He's a stunner."

Charlton Heston called Steve before filming began to warn him about the director, Sam Peckinpah. Heston claimed that during the making of *Major Dundee* (1965), he had become so furious with Peckinpah that he'd threatened to take his cavalry sword and plunge it through his heart.

On the first day of shooting, Steve fought with Peckinpah over the script. Steve wanted many changes, even though some of the most talented writers in Hollywood—Ring Lardner Jr., Terry Southern, and Paddy Chayefsky—had sweated and labored over the scenario.

In particular, Steve wanted his lines cut down. "I want to act the picture, not talk it." He also demanded that a fight scene with a switchblade knife and

Scenes from *The Cincinnati Kid* (top row, left to right): **Steve McQueen, Edward G. Robinson,** and **Karl Malden** interacting with **Steve.** Robinson thought Steve was following in Bogie's footsteps.
Bottom row, left to right: **Tuesday Weld** during bathtime with **Steve, Ann-Margret** (center photo), and (lower right), **Tuesday Weld with Ann-Margret,** a duo hailed by one critic as "the two sexiest broads in America."

a rusty razor blade be inserted at the beginning of the movie. "My fans expect it of me," Steve told Peckinpah.

There was yet another major disagreement. Steve wanted the film to be shot in color, so that the playing cards would stand out. Peckinpah wanted to capture the gritty Depression Era of New Orleans and demanded that it be filmed in black and white.

At this point, the film's producer, Martin Ransohoff, based on "conceptual differences" of how the film should be structured, was losing patience with his director. The end was near.

At the time, Ransohoff was promoting the career of Sharon Tate, wanting to turn her into "the next Marilyn Monroe." He told Peckinpah that Sharon would be ideal cast as Steve's girlfriend, Christian Rudd.

Since he was sleeping with Sharon and admired her talent, Steve wanted to cast Sharon too. But Peckinpah insisted that she was far too inexperienced to carry off such a role, so he cast Tuesday Weld instead. Steve was sorry to see Sharon go but had "fond memories" of Tuesday Weld when they'd filmed *Soldier in the Rain* together.

Unexpectedly, at great expense and without getting permission, Peckinpah filmed two separate nude scenes, which was a very provocative thing to do in an A-release film of 1965. One involved a rich Southern gambler, William Jefferson Slade, as played by Rip Torn, in bed with a black prostitute. Even without the nudity, that would be shocking enough for the times.

Even though Peckinpah didn't want Sharon for one of the leads, he also filmed a nude scene with her. The up-and-coming actress had no objection to taking off her clothes in front of the camera, as readers of *Playboy* discovered when they picked up that magazine in March of 1967.

Director **Sam Peckinpah** had a well-deserved nickname, "Bloody Sam." He liked to see beautiful women take off their clothes in front of a movie camera.

Ransohoff ordained that he would not allow either nude scene to be inserted into the picture. Even in the best of times, Peckinpah had an obstinate and abrasive edge to his personality. Fueled by booze and marijuana, he stood his ground. His argument with Ransohoff soon escalated into a physical altercation that included Peckinpah's punching Ransohoff in the nose, bloodying it. Taking poetic license, Peckinpah later claimed, "I stripped Ransohoff as naked as one of his bald lies."

Based partly on that episode, he became known in the business as "Bloody

Sam," a reputation enhanced by the 1969 release of his dark, gritty, and nihilistic western, *The Wild Bunch.*

After their fistfight, there was a production delay when Ransohoff shut down the picture. A young and at the time inexperienced Norman Jewison, a former taxi driver, was hired. Steve was skeptical of Jewison right from the beginning. "Isn't he the fart who directs all that Doris Day shit?"

Jewison got the cameras rolling again, although the final cost of the picture went over budget, reaching $3.3 million.

At long last Steve greeted his fellow cast members, "I'm having a hot reunion with Tuesday Weld," he claimed to Karl Malden, whom he'd known since he was a struggling actor.

"But since I didn't see anything, I'm not sure which member of the cast he was seducing," Malden said. "Ann-Margret never looked sexier than she did in this film, and I thought Steve, who told me that she was 'everybody's wet dream' would surely fall for her. I'm not certain, but I got the impression that she didn't fancy Steve at all. I think she was still hung up on Elvis Presley," Malden said. Malden thought Tuesday Weld, though one sexy woman, looked rather wholesome in the film. "But Ann-Margret gave every card player on the set a hard-on." Malden played her sugar daddy in *The Cincinnati Kid.*

Film critic Pauline Kael summed up Ann-Margret's appeal. "She comes through dirty no matter what she plays. She does most of her acting inside her mouth. She gleams with built-in innuendo. Men seem to have direct-action responses to her. They want to give her what she seems to be asking for."

Joan Blondell, who'd lost her husband, Michael Todd, to Elizabeth Taylor, had a reunion on the set with Edward G. Robinson. They had last worked together in the 1936 *Bullets or Ballots.*

Steve was fascinated by her stories about James Cagney, with whom she'd worked. She said, "Jimmy Cagney and Eddie Robinson had voices that were

Joan Blondell (left) was cast as "Lady Fingers" in *The Cincinnati Kid* alongside **Cab Calloway** playing "Yeller." The American jazz singer and bandleader, Calloway discussed African-American penile size with Steve. Joan also went "penile," raising the subject of male circumcision.

as important as the characters they played. You know what you were getting, even before you paid for the ticket." With her blonde hair, big blue eyes, and big smile, Joan impressed Steve with her humor. She told him that she called the four ex-husbands of Bette Davis "The Four Skins" since they were all Gentiles.

"Even though we were friendly," Joan said, "I don't think Steve really liked to hang out with women. He much preferred to hang out with men. He liked women only for one thing, or so I gathered. I told him that whatever he did with women, don't do what Mike Todd did to me. He gambled away all my life savings and once held me out a hotel window by my ankles until I forked over the last thousand dollar bill I had."

The son of a shoemaker, Jack Weston had worked with Steve on the ill-fated *The Honeymoon Machine*. After *The Cincinnati Kid*, Steve would request that he be cast again with him in *The Thomas Crown Affair*.

"I liked McQueen," Weston told playwright James Leo Herlihy and Tallulah Bankhead, as well as Joan Blondell, when he toured with them in *Crazy October*, a play that never made it to Broadway. "But when I heard he fucked guys, I just couldn't believe it."

"Believe it, *dah-ling*," Tallulah said. "For example, one way you can always tell a homo in Britain is that he has a wife and two kids—just like McQueen himself."

The American jazz singer and bandleader, Cab Calloway, was somewhat taken back by Steve's direct approach. The first time he met him on set, he came up to him and asked, "Is it true all you black dudes have bigger dicks than us white boys? Shall we whip it out and take measurements?"

"I didn't show him my dick," Calloway said, "but I did sing to him one of my classics, 'Reefer Man,' about a man who likes his marijuana. Even though he handled himself rather well, Steve was stoned during the entire making of *The Cincinnati Kid*. But what the hell? It was the 60s. Everybody was stoned back then."

Steve liked to shock people when he first met them. He walked up to Rip Torn and said, "I've never fucked your wife but I'd like to." He was referring to actress Geraldine Page.

"Sleeping with Geraldine is a man's job," Torn shot back.

"We have a best friend in common," Steve said, trying another approach. "George Peppard. I bet I'm a closer friend of his than you are."

Once again, Torn won the round. "Perhaps so," he said. "At least I don't fuck George."

It was after movie audiences saw the self-controlled character he played in *The Cincinnati Kid*, that Steve became known as "The King of Cool."

In 1965, at the age of thirty-five, Steve could at last tell his old-time friend, Marlon Brando, "to eat my dust." Of course, when Steve said it, he didn't use the word "dust."

From Europe to Japan, he was hailed as the favorite American movie star. Even in 1963, during the most intense period of the Cold War, the Soviet Union had awarded him a Best Actor prize at the Moscow International Film Festival, the first U.S. citizen so honored.

In May of that year, he flew to Nice, where he drove to Monaco to attend that principality's Grand Prix. Princess Grace invited him to a dinner party at the palace where she presided with Prince Rainier.

Steve and Neile met the royal couple and an array of European royalty, some of them from kingdoms which had disappeared after World War II.

The evening was marred when Freddy Heineken, of the famous beer brewing family, took too keen an interest in Neile. In anger, Steve challenged him to a duel. Yes, that's right, a duel.

Some men intervened to cool the King of Cool's temper. Steve was gradually eased out the door, escorted by security guards. A disaster was averted.

Steve would later brag to his Grand Prix pals that he seduced Princess Grace. How he managed such a high profile seduction, with his wife in tow, was never fully explained. There is no evidence to suggest that he did seduce Her Serene Highness.

However, his claim cannot be easily dismissed. Both the Princess and Steve were among the skilled seducers of their era, and they operated in secret and were famous for covering their trails.

Ever since her days in Hollywood, Grace had been rather sneaky in arranging a discreet rendezvous here and there to seduce a married man. Perhaps she did pull it off.

Peter Lawford once quoted her as saying that she considered Steve as "an exceedingly attractive man in a devil-may-care sort of

When Steve was invited to visit the royals, **Prince Rainier** of Monaco and his beautiful princess, **Grace Kelly,** he made a spectacle of himself. He challenged a beer baron to a duel and possibly seduced her Serene Highness as well.

way. I knew the old Gary Cooper, so I was eager to meet the man hailed as his replacement."

In the future, when Steve would meet his friends, Casey and Darron, he told them that "Grace was all prim and proper—white gloves and all that—but once you got her alone in a bedroom, and took her panties off, she was a raging wildcat."

Although that evaluation might have been true, it was more properly and accurately attributed to Gary Cooper, not Steve. His story of his seduction of Grace Kelly might well have been one of his sexual fantasies. There is also the possibility that he might have been telling the truth.

***

Steve wasted little time in returning to work after his European jaunt. For half a million dollars and a motorhome, he signed to star in *Nevada Smith*. The script by John Michael Hayes was a spin-off from Harold Robbins' best-seller *The Carpetbaggers*, based loosely on the character of the eccentric billionaire Howard Hughes. The star of that blockbuster, and the actor portraying Howard Hughes, had been Steve's bosom buddy, George Peppard, who kept popping in and out of his life.

Steve's title role of Nevada Smith was based on a minor character from *The Carpetbaggers,* a role which had in the 1964 original been played by fad-

Steve, pictured in the Louisiana swamps with **Arthur Kennedy,** felt right at home filming *Nevada Smith.*
The film brought back memories of his own incarceration as a switchblade-wielding teenager when he was part of a street gang.

264

ing matinee idol Alan Ladd. This would be the second Robbins-inspired character that Steve had brought to the screen, having appeared in *Never Love a Stranger* early in his career.

In essence, *Nevada Smith,* which was eventually released in 1966, was a "prequel" to *The Carpetbaggers*, although that term would not be invented until 1979. Steve's tight-lipped, craggy Western hero, if he could be called that, bore no resemblance to the original Nevada Smith as played by Alan Ladd.

As a revenge-seeking half-breed pursuing the killers of his parents, Steve in his title role of Nevada Smith evokes Josh Randall, the bounty hunter he'd portrayed in his TV series *Wanted: Dead or Alive*.

Locations included a swamp near Independence, Louisiana as well as various places in California, including the Inyo National Forest. These were just some of the four dozen sites used in the film.

Steve knew many members of a cast that encompassed nearly seventy speaking parts. They included his long-standing colleague Karl Malden, Arthur Kennedy, Martin Landau, Howard Da Silva, Raf Vallone, and Pat Hingle.

Steve's big challenge didn't involve any of these character actors, but the fiery director, Henry Hathaway, who was under contract to Paramount, which planned a summer release in 1966.

Like the rest of Hollywood, Hathaway had heard about how difficult Steve was to work with. Hathaway had begun his career as a child actor in Westerns before World War I, and he was one crusty, tough, old Californian (born in 1898).

He was fond of saying, "There's lots of nice guys walking around Hollywood, but they're not eating." He also said, "To be a good director you've got to be a bastard. I'm a bastard and I know it."

On the first day of shooting, he invited Steve in for what he called a "Come to Jesus talk."

He began by telling the star, "I clank the *cojones* on this picture. If you have a problem with that, I'll punch you in the kisser right now and you'll be a bloody mess before I finish working you over. I've directed everybody from Marilyn Monroe to John Wayne, from Gary Cooper to Marlene Dietrich, so I want you to know I'm not impressed with some sawed-off runt like you. Even Mae

In *Nevada Smith,* **Steve** had to participate in love scenes with **Suzanne Pleshette,** but felt embarrassed because he'd been her longtime "Big Brother" and didn't like coming on to her romantically.

West thought she could tell me what to do, but the cunt learned different."

At long last Steve had met a director who could control him. He buckled under and listened to Hathaway's direction. By the end of the picture he was calling his director Dad, and Hathaway was referring to Steve as "my son."

Steve had met his leading lady, Suzanne Pleshette, at a Greenwich Village party when she was only fourteen years old. He rescued her from the "clutches" of an older man and took her back to her home on a motorcycle.

"Beginning that afternoon, Steve always told me I was his baby sister, and he was going to look after me," Suzanne said. "As the years went by, I became family to Steve, Neile, and their children. I was there, for example, when Terry was born."

"When I told Steve that I'd been cast as his love interest in *Nevada Smith*, he said, 'Oh, shit! We've got kissing scenes together.'"

When the actual kissing scene was filmed, it was the worst of all Steve McQueen kissing scenes. "He was an awful kisser," said Suzanne.

"It was like kissing my baby sister," Steve told director Hathaway. "That's incest, man!"

"Steve always claimed he seduced all his leading ladies," said Suzanne. "Take my name off that roster. It didn't happen. We never thought of each other as sexual objects, and I think our love scenes together sort of showed that."

In 1964 Suzanne had married Troy Donahue, whose onscreen dynamic with Sandra Dee was becoming a fading memory with audiences. Still defining himself as her big brother, Steve had called her when he'd heard that she had started to date Troy. "He's a girly man," he told her.

Heartthrob **Troy Donahue**, once married to **Suzanne Pleshette**, depicted above, won high praise from Rock Hudson for his skill in the oral arts.

"You're confusing him with another blond, Tab Hunter," Suzanne said. "Troy is straight."

"Like hell he is," Steve said. "Rock Hudson told me he's one of the best cocksuckers in Hollywood and has a really tiny dick."

Suzanne didn't listen to Steve and married Troy anyway. She later called Steve and said, "Everything you said about him turned out to be true. Our marriage ended acrimoniously after just eight months." Steve had predicted that it would last only three weeks.

Since Steve didn't have a leading lady to seduce on this film location in the steamy swamps of Louisiana, he called on Neile to fly down. At first she resisted, claiming she had to remain in Brentwood with their two children. Finally, Steve demanded her presence on location, and prevailed.

He told Hathaway, "I just can't function when my old lady's not around. She digs me, understands my moods, keeps me in balance. She even brings me Mexican beer. And she's sexier than any movie starlet! Man, we *need* each other!"

Neile's sojourn in the muggy, oppressive swamplands of Louisiana was brief, but Steve took full advantage of her visit to assert his conjugal rights.

Before and after her visit, he drove to New Orleans on the weekends looking for sex. He always found what he was looking for. "Even in the whorehouses, I got it for free," he told his "Daddy," the director Hathaway. "What *puta* wouldn't want to sleep with Steve McQueen, famous movie star?"

"During those long hot nights on location, I had many talks with Steve about cars and women, his two favorite subjects," Hathaway recalled. "Except for his wife, Neile, I got the impression that he hated women. He used them for sexual relief and discarded them quickly. I gathered that sex was just mechanical with him. He wanted to shoot his load, pull out, and say thank you, then be on his way. I know he didn't respect women, except, for some curious reason, Suzanne. He was her big brother, always protective of her."

"When he flew down to Louisiana, Steve said he had sex with a stewardess on the plane," Hathaway said. "He told me he'd seduced dozens of women on airplanes, screwing them in those cramped, little bathrooms. He defined himself as president of the Mile High Club."

"It's just a game to play," Steve told Hathaway. "I always return home to my old lady and my kids. That's where my heart is. Everything else is called getting a piece of pussy. My fuck flings are meaningless. I'm a man who screws, not a man who loves, except for Neile, of course. She gives me a long leash. Otherwise, our marriage could not work."

Deep into the shoot, Steve realized that he was in a long-winded horse opera, and he struggled to make his character as vivid as possible, hoping it would save the picture.

In June of 1966, a press preview of *Nevada Smith* was staged on the Paramount lot. In the middle of the show, a fire of unknown origin broke out on the adjoining sound stage. A hero on the screen and off, Steve pulled off his jacket and tried to save both property and lives. Fortunately, all 1,500 guests escaped without bodily harm.

Director **Henry Hathaway** was the only helmer who could tame Steve. On the first day of shooting, he informed his star that he was the only man on the set who was allowed to clank *cojones*.

To those viewing *Nevada Smith* today, the

scenery is far less dramatic than it was at the time of its original release, because the footage was shot with EastmanColor stock, which began to fade within a year.

Nevada Smith was a huge hit with international audiences, especially in Europe and Japan, but received a gloomier reception in America. Wanda Hale, of the *New York Daily News*, called it a "tedious Western with too little suspense and too much talk." There were those who also objected to the violence.

By this point Steve had established a loyal fan base which flocked to see the movie despite its negative reviews.

He was besieged by film offers, one of the most tempting originating with Audrey Hepburn, who wanted him to co-star with her in *Two for the Road*. She conveniently didn't tell him that she had previously offered the role to Paul Newman, who had rejected it after he'd had a brief affair with the enchanting star.

Steve's most tempting offer came from producer-director Robert Wise, who had first cast him in *Somebody Up There Likes Me*.

"I'm sending a script over to you," Wise told him over the phone. "It's got 'Best Actor, Steve McQueen, Oscar winner' written all over it."

***

The final personalities from his childhood in Slater began to fade away. Before any more films could be made, Steve had to deal with death, many deaths.

Steve's great uncle, Claude Thomson, had died in 1957, leaving his estate, which included his 360-acre farm, to his wife, Eva Thomson. Eva had sent Steve a card informing him of his uncle's death, but he had not made a pilgrimage home for the funeral.

For years his grandmother, Lillian Crawford, had lived in an insane asylum in Fulton, Missouri. Neither her grandson, Steve, nor her daughter, Jullian Crawford, had ever visited her there. One building at the Fulton compound was filled with inmates judged by the courts as "criminally insane."

Steve did not support Lillian in this institution, although her closest friend, Helen Kettler, said, "Miss Crawford loved that little boy." The county paid six dollars a month for her room and board. In lieu of family visitors, Helen visited Lillian every other week. During their times together, Lillian maintained that her father had left a will and that she owned half of her brother's estate, but Eva had taken everything from her.

In the wake of Claude's death, Eva had married a much younger man, John Simmermon. As she drove throughout the county, she always bragged about the "virility" of her new husband.

Believing Lillian was completely sane, Helen investigated Lillian's claims. She finally dug up in a courthouse the will of John W. Thomson, father of both Lillian and Claude. Indeed, as a probate judge later discovered, Lillian had been deprived of her inheritance.

Eva was "in raging fury," but Judge Thomas J. Boland of the Probate Court of St. Louis restored Lillian's inheritance. Helen was instrumental in getting her transferred to the St. Joseph Home in Jefferson City, which was run by a Catholic order of very gentle nuns. With these kindly sisters, Lillian was able to live out the final months of her life in a place of tranquility and beauty. The compound was set on a riverbank and heavily planted with flowers.

As it turned out, however, Lillian was not completely sane. Despite the fact that her father had died and been buried in 1916, she wrote Helen that she'd seen him alive around the end of World War II.

When the estate was finally settled, Lillian got the proceeds from the sale of nearly one hundred acres of rich agricultural land.

She'd pledged to give the inheritance to the Catholic sisters when she died. In her will, she also remembered her daughter, Jullian, leaving her exactly one dollar.

Lillian died on July 26, 1964, with Helen her only mourner.

Calling Helen from San Francisco, Jullian protested the will and threatened to sue. She didn't want "any God damn Catholics taking money that rightfully belongs to me."

Judge Boland agreed that Jullian, if she sued, would have a strong case, so it was decided that Jullian be cut in on the estate. In late September of 1965, a check was mailed to Jullian at her address in San Francisco.

***

Relations between Jullian and Steve had never been good. Throughout the 60s, he had his business manager send her money on occasion, but there was never a personal note. "The memories are too painful," Steve told not only Neile but close friends of his.

For her final years, Jullian had moved into a small apartment close to Fisherman's Wharf in the North Beach section of San Francisco. Her rent was ninety dollars a month, which Steve paid. He'd even advanced her the money to open a small clothing boutique at one point, but it had gone bankrupt.

The dozens of men who had passed through Jullian's life when she was a prostitute were bad memories she tried to block from her mind. She had grown obese and tried various crash diets, but always remained plump. She spent her days sewing clothing.

The checks from Steve, for some reason, stopped coming in July of 1965.

Until her inheritance arrived, Jullian managed to eke out a meager living on Social Security and from making dresses for her friends.

She bragged to these friends about what a "bigtime movie star little Steven has become." She sat through each of his pictures many times, telling patrons that "Steve McQueen is my son." No one seemed to believe this fat old bag lady, especially not when she claimed that the secondhand Volkswagen "bug" she drove up and down the hills of San Francisco was a gift from Steve.

On October 14, 1965, Jullian took a taxi to the Harbor Emergency Hospital. Collapsing in the hallway, she was rushed to the emergency room. When she regained consciousness, she complained to the doctor that she was "suffering a headache that I can't stand—it's so painful." He accurately diagnosed that she was experiencing a cerebral hemorrhage.

Her doctor called an ambulance, and, with red dome light flashing, she was transferred to Mount Zion Hospital.

A nurse searched through her purse and found a letter from Steve's business manager to Jullian. A quick call was made to Los Angeles. The manager conveyed the emergency to Neile at Brentwood, who promptly called Steve.

"Your mother's dying," she told Steve. "She has only hours to live."

Both Neile and Steve flew to San Francisco, arriving there shortly before midnight. When doctors assured him they were doing all they could for her, Steve rented a room in the hospital where he stayed for her final hours. He was allowed to go into Jullian's room, but she'd already sunken into a coma from which she never recovered.

The following afternoon, Jullian's doctor came into Steve's hospital room. "We did what we could," he said. "Your mother has passed on."

Steve didn't cry, but he told Neile, "She never came to. I was never able to tell her that I forgave her. And she didn't have a chance to tell me that she forgave me."

In all of her fifty-five years of life, Jullian had never known the peace which came during the final hours of her life. She died in her sleep.

Flying back to Los Angeles, Steve told Stan Kamen that he would give no interviews. As much as possible, he didn't want details of Jullian's life to be investigated by the press. He made arrangements for her to be buried at Forest Lawn.

Steve personally selected an expensive coffin and requested that it not be covered with roses, but with simple daisies. "Back in Missouri, a daisy, not a rose, was always her favorite flower."

He also asked that no clergyman or priest be allowed to preside. Standing with Neile and his two children, he watched Jullian's coffin lowered into the earth. For the first time, he began to cry, although those in attendance didn't know if he were crying for Jullian or the pain of his early years.

When she was six feet into the ground, Steve asked that he be allowed to stand at her graveside alone. When he later joined his family in a waiting limousine, he said, "Maybe she loved me a lot more than I loved her." His soft voice sounded as if he were choking. "I wish we'd known each other better."

Storm clouds had formed on the horizon. As the limousine drove away under threatening clouds, Steve said, "I don't want to speak of Jullian ever again."

There was a footnote. Steve never heard from Eva again, but a friend of hers wrote Steve that "she's growing worse by the month and is in a wheelchair. She'd love you to come for a visit." He did not respond.

Another letter came in, the friend begging Steve to send Eva money. She was being forced to sell all the jewelry Claude had given her, even the antiques he'd brought back from New Orleans.

In 1975, Steve was notified that Eva had died. He did not send flowers, not even a note. "The last of the Thomsons have departed Slater," said the mayor at her funeral. "They were part of the legacy of this town, especially Claude. Steve McQueen is a bigtime movie star now. I guess he doesn't have time for little folks like us."

Steve never heard that speech given at Eva's funeral. "They're all dead," he told his second wife, Ali MacGraw. "I'm all that's left."

As he said that, he could hardly have known that he had only five years to live.

✳✳✳

Director **Robert Wise** (left figure in top photo, above) coaches sailor boy **Steve** in *The Sand Pebbles,* the only film for which Steve would ever be nominated for an Oscar. An on-location overview shot (immediately above) evokes mainland China, even though it was actually shot on Taiwan.

For *The Sand Pebbles*, Steve made his best deal yet, getting $250,000 in cash up front and participation in the gross. In all, he may have netted $750,000 on the film. "I'm about to become a million dollar baby," he claimed to friends.

Wise told Steve that "I dashed off" *The Sound of Music* just to get the chance to produce *The Sand Pebbles*." What he didn't tell Steve was that he'd offered the starring role first to Paul Newman, who turned it down.

The movie was from a screenplay by Richard Anderson, who based it on a novel by Richard McKenna. It was set to open right before Christmas in 1966.

McKenna had risen from the ranks of a simple sailor to hit it big—bestselling novel, serialization, $300,000 for the screen rights. But he didn't get to enjoy this new-found lotto. He died before filming began.

When Wise got Anderson's screenplay, he told Steve, "It's as thick as a God damn phone booth." The final cut ran 193 minutes, or as Judith Crist of *The World Journal Tribune* put it, "over three hours of tedium."

Just as he was studying the script for *The Sand Pebbles,* yet another offer came in. Joseph E. Levine wanted him to star in a very different type of movie---*The Ski Bum*, based on a Romain Gary novel. Levine claimed, "I want McQueen because he has a ton of sex appeal and a ton of box office clout." After mulling it over, Steve

Despite the coziness of this boating scene, no off-screen romance ever developed between **Steve** and his co-star, **Candice Bergen.**
He thought she was "one horny broad" and suggested that she get it on with his cronies.
Playing a loner (top photo, above), Steve was interpreted as "restrained, honest, and heartfelt" by critics, who also asserted that the film itself was a "blood-spattered, schmaltz-spangled compendium of screenplay clichés."

opted to go with Wise.

Neile also got one of her few film offers après marriage, turning down the female lead in *Southwest to Sonora*, which would have cast her opposite Marlon Brando. Steve was adamant that she not accept the role. Neile herself told Wise that, "I don't think a married man should ever be left alone for more than two weeks."

Privately Wise said, "Two weeks? I think Steve McQueen can meet a gal, fuck her, and wash his dick in the sink—all in one hour or less."

The role of a sailor, Jake Holman, was Steve's toughest to date. The setting was 1926 China on the Yangtze River. The 150-foot steel-hulled U.S. gunboat, the *San Pablo*, was a vital prop. Costing $250,000 to build, and an authentic replic of one type of U.S. navy gunboat used in China in the 1920s, it was the most expensive prop ever constructed for a movie.

After its mission with the film was finished, the *San Pablo* later operated behind Vietnam battle lines as a floating bordello. A loner at heart—a role perfect for Steve—Jake was a machinist. He befriends "Frenchy," a sailor in love with a Chinese girl, Maily, who has been sold into prostitution. The English actor, Richard Attenborough, was cast as Frenchy, and he and Steve had a reunion and talked about their making of *The Great Escape*.

Steve (left) and English actor **Richard Attenborough** reunited on location for *The Sand Pebbles,* having starred together earlier in *The Great Escape.* Attenborough plays "Frenchy," a sailor who falls for a Chinese girl, Maily, who has been sold into prostitution.

Richard Crenna was cast as Captain Collins. Even though Crenna found his first talks with Steve comparable "to conversing with a Zulu warrior," the two actors eventually became friends. "But," Crenna added, "you had to maintain a friendship only on *his* terms, not yours."

Candice Bergen, the daughter of the famous ventriloquist, Edgar Bergen, was cast as a missionary teacher called Shirley Eckert.

Candice may have been one of the few leading ladies to escape Steve's butterfly net of seduction,

Steve peers through the lens of a camera. On every picture he made, he tried to take over the director's job.

although he urged her to "get it on with my buddies."

He was referring to six stunt men, each an ex-Marine he'd flown to Taiwan to "hang with me" during the shoot. "Elvis has his Memphis Mafia, and I have my personal honor guard," he told Candice.

After turning down the Brando film, Neile had come along with the cast for the filming in Taiwan.

Steve arrives with a duffel bag to board the gunboat *San Pablo*. He got the role because Paul Newman turned it down.

Clowning around, Steve sits under a giant sculpted elephant, a moment of levity within an otherwise grueling day of shooting on *The Sand Pebbles*. "I fought off Asian queers and deadly bamboo vipers," he later reported.

She may have suspected that Candice had plans to seduce Steve. His first impression of Candice, as revealed to his wife, was that "she's one horny broad." Candice wasn't all that broad at the time, as she was only nineteen years old.

A bright, intelligent actress, Candice painted a more brilliant word portrait of Steve than any of his other female co-stars. "Coiled, combustible, he was like a caged animal. Daring, reckless, charming, compelling; it was difficult to relax around him—and probably unwise—for, like a big wildcat, he was handsome and hypnotic, powerful and unpredictable, and could turn on you in a flash. He seemed to live by the laws of the jungle and to have contempt for those laid down by man. He reminded one of the great outlaws, a romantic renegade; an outcast uneasy in his skin who finds himself with sudden fame and fortune. One had the sense that it came too late and mattered little in the end. And that he tried to find truth and comfort in a world where he knew he didn't belong."

That's what Candice thought of Steve. As to what he thought of her, we have only a cryptic comment from the director, Robert

Wise. "Steve told me that Candice was 'one cool, classy lady, but too much of an outspoken feminist. I think women should be kept in their place.'"

Candice said that Steve and his boys spent their nights in Taipei "on the prowl, roaming the city, drinking, heckling, picking fights, and pummeling."

The little city at the time was famous for its bordellos, and Robert Wise, claimed that "the gals in those brothels worked overtime when Steve and his ex-Marines hit town."

Steve had stashed Neile and his two children in a rented one-room villa in the middle of a rice paddy infested with deadly bamboo vipers.

After moving in, he called Wise. "Less than a week ago I was at a black-tie dinner at the Bistro in Beverly Hills, chatting the night away with Princess Margaret, making Lord Snowdon jealous. Just between us roosters, I think the royal bitch has the hots for me. I'm kissing Elizabeth Taylor—finally, she knows who I am—embracing Frank Sinatra, getting propositioned by both Rock Hudson and Laurence Harvey, and being asked by Judy Garland to throw her another fuck. Now here I am stuck in this hell hole."

Steve told Wise, "I fucked a lot of Chinese pussy. Back in the Marine Corps, the guys who'd served in Asia told me that their pussies are slanted. But they're built just like a regular *puta*."

For such a privileged child, born to Beverly Hills royalty, Candice could be earthy at times. Commenting on her less-than-voluptuous figure, she said, "I'd like to have tits." Years later, meeting Steve at a Hollywood party, she told him that, "I may not be the greatest actress on the screen, but I'm the greatest at faking on-camera orgasms. Ten seconds of heavy breathing. A roll of your head from side to side, then a simulation of a slight asthma attack. And then you perform the ultimate, what the French call, 'the little death.'"

Built for $250,000, the gunboat, *San Pablo,* was at the time the most expensive movie prop ever constructed. It later saw duty as a floating bordello during the Vietnam war.

The film itself faced endless delays and production hurdles, including temperatures that ranged from sultry hot to freezing rain.

Wise had to supervise 1,500 natives in different outfits, very few of whom spoke English. "It was a nightmare," he later said.

Wise and Steve battled over how certain scenes would be filmed. The director knew how to deal with Steve, filming his cut and the star's cut. In every single case, Wise proved to be the better director and none of Steve's versions were used in the final print.

At the end of *The Sand Pebbles*, which depicted China on the brink of a Civil War, Jake, as played by Steve, dies heroically, providing cover for Candice, playing the schoolteacher whom he has come to love.

Back in the United States, Steve still had some final shots to be filmed in the studio. Rare for him, he gave a brief interview to the press. "*The Sand Pebbles* was my toughest assignment yet," he said. "I had my skull twisted a couple of times, got sick, inhaled tear gas, worked myself dingy, fought off some tiny-dicked Asian queers trying to check out my American pecker in latrines, and ended up exhausted back in the States. In fact, when I landed in Los Angeles, I kissed the ground when I got off the plane."

Reporters ran the interview, removing the reference to the penile measurements of Asians and the attack on homosexuals.

***

At long last, Steve meets **Elvis,** learning that he had wanted many of the roles into which Steve had been cast. After a drug-enhanced night, Steve found himself waking up the next day in the nude with "The King."

The next day Steve was driving around in a maroon-colored, mid-60s Corvette Sting Ray coupe when he stopped on Beverly Glen for a red light.

Checking out the black limousine alongside him, Steve squinted his eyes and peered into the rear of the vehicle. "Elvis, is that you?" Steve asked.

According to Elvis' bodyguard, Sonny West, as related in *Elvis: Still Taking Care of Business*, Elvis rolled down the window and said, "Hey, Steve, whatcha doin'?"

Steve said he was in town for the final in-house shooting of *The Sand Pebbles*. Elvis said he was on his way to MGM Studios. As the cars behind them blew horns after the light changed to green, Sonny wrote down Elvis' address. "The King" wanted to meet on Saturday for a drink.

Sonny later claimed that Elvis had been fascinated with the screen persona of Steve ever since he'd watched each episode of *Wanted: Dead or Alive* on TV. He'd also ordered *The Great Escape* screened for him at least six times at the Memphian Theatre in Memphis.

"I always thought Elvis was a little professionally jealous of McQueen," Sonny said. "Steve got a lot of plum dramatic roles in the 1960s that appealed to Elvis, including *Baby, the Rain Must Fall*, which Elvis very badly wanted to do."

If this were so, and apparently it was, it explained Elvis' bitchy phone call to Steve about his singing in *Baby, the Rain Must Fall*, where Steve had played a country singer.

Promptly at eight o'clock, Steve arrived at Elvis' rented home. Sonny was nowhere in sight, but another member of the "Memphis Mafia" ushered Steve into a back bedroom where Elvis lay nude on a bed getting a work over by a Japanese masseur.

"Come on in, kid," Elvis said, not bothering to rise. "I even found out the name of your favorite poison." Another guard seemed to appear miraculously with a cold Mexican beer, the kind Steve liked.

"It's great seeing you, big guy," Steve said. "When it comes to singing, you're my favorite."

"Of course, I am," Elvis said, giving him a wink. "That just shows you have good taste."

The two rivals sat and talked for about fifteen minutes until Elvis finished his massage. He rose from the bed and wrapped a towel around his nude body. "You wanna go next? The guy's really good."

"Sure, I'd love it." Steve stood up and removed his blue jeans and T-shirt, peeling off his jockey shorts. Elvis waited for the unveiling. Steve couldn't help but notice that he got a thorough checking from Elvis before "The King" headed for the bathroom for a hot shower.

At the door, Elvis called back to Steve. "Watch out where Tokyo Rose puts his hands. He's queer as a three-dollar bill."

"I know that," Steve called back. "That's why they become masseurs in the first place. To get their faggoty hands on our red-blooded, heterosexual bodies."

"You got that right," Elvis said, before disappearing into the bathroom where Steve soon heard the sound of the shower. As Steve had anticipated, Elvis sang in the shower. The sounds of "All Shook Up" came from the master himself.

Emerging from his shower and still toweling himself dry—with a pink towel, no less—Elvis patted Steve's ass and told him to meet him in the living room when he was through.

After he had showered himself, Steve left the room, neither tipping nor thanking the young Japanese male who sat rather forlornly in the corner. Throughout the entire session, he hadn't said one word.

Steve put back on his jockey shorts and jeans, but came out shirtless to join Elvis, who sat in a big chair in his jockey shorts. He was listening to a recording by Little Richard.

"Do you hate fags as much as I do?" he asked Steve.

"I think they're the most repulsive shits on earth," Steve said. "They'd be okay in my book if they stayed with their own kind and didn't try to mess around with us straights."

"My sentiments exactly," Elvis said. He called to one of the guards. "Get this Missouri mule here another beer, fucker."

The beer arrived with two capsules. "What in hell are these?" Steve asked.

"Your ticket to paradise," Elvis said. "All you have to do is swallow them. Don't tell me you're a sissy. Swallow the fucking things."

On a dare, Steve swallowed the capsules, downing them with a hefty swig of Mexican beer.

Before he and Elvis became completely wasted, Elvis expressed his admiration of Steve on the screen. "That Colonel Parker has caught me by the *cojones*, and he likes to squeeze and twist them every day of my life. I want to be a serious actor, but this clodhopper sticks me in one silly little piece of fluff every time. I watch guys like you and Newman get all the juicy parts, and I'm left with the shit end of the stick."

"Don't you have the power to tell the good colonel to shove a dildo up his ass?" Steve asked. "A fourteen-inch black dildo."

"He's got shit on me," Elvis said. "Pictures. Blackmail. Stuff like that. I can't break from the asshole. He decides what scripts I can do. One scenario has me abandoned as a foundling in a gypsy camp. They raise me to become a gypsy singer and dancer. Shit like that."

As Steve began to feel the effect of the drugs, he said something he'd later regret. "Why don't you kill Col. Parker?"

"And go to jail?" Elvis asked in astonishment.

"C'mon now," Steve said. "I didn't mean for you to kill him. Have someone else do it. Remove yourself from the scene as far as possible. Frank Sinatra told me it happens all the time in Las Vegas. It could be a car accident. That's right. A car accident. Things like that are easy to arrange."

"You've got me thinking, boy," Elvis said. "You're good. Have some more of these dolls."

"What do you mean, dolls?" Steve asked. "You got chicks stashed here?" One of the Mafia guards emerged with two more capsules. Steve swallowed them, washing them down with the beer.

Elvis was rather wasted at this point. "Dolls, they're called. Pills, baby. Feel good pills."

Somewhere in the night, Steve blanked out. He didn't remember when or how. When he came to, he found himself in a darkened room. The clock on the stand said it was two o'clock. Since he'd been with Elvis at two o'clock in the morning, it must mean it was two o'clock in the afternoon.

He turned over to see Elvis snoring in the bed beside him. Steve realized he was nude. Someone had pulled off his clothes.

Gently he slipped from the bed. He didn't see his clothes anywhere. He tiptoed into the hallway where the Japanese boy was waiting with fresh coffee and orange juice. On a table next to the boy Steve recognized his clothing.

Without speaking to the boy, he walked over and slipped into his jeans, putting on his shoes. "Did you strip Elvis and me down last night and put us to bed?" Steve asked.

"Yes, sir, that's my job here," the boy said in an accented voice.

Steve looked at him very skeptically. "And what else did you do? Did you give me and Elvis blow jobs, you little faggot?"

"I do my job," the boy said defensively. "I do whatever Elvis tells me to do."

"That's not answering my question," Steve said. "On second thought, I don't want to know. I'm out of here. Thank Elvis for his hospitality."

The bright light of a Los Angeles afternoon blinded him when he went outside. Getting into his car, he wanted to drive along the coast and feel the air from the Pacific blowing over him. He hoped that bracing air would brush away the cobwebs of the night.

It was another of those nights that happen so often in Hollywood that you don't want to remember and hopefully will forget.

***

In 1967, for the first time in his life, Steve was honored with an Academy Award nomination as Best Actor. In all, *The Sand Pebbles* would receive eight nominations, including Best Picture, losing out to *A Man for All Seasons*.

Steve faced stiff competition from Richard Burton in *Who's Afraid of Virginia Woolf?*, Alan Arkin for *The Russians Are Coming*, and Michael Caine for *Alfie*, losing to Paul Scofield for *A Man for All Seasons*.

Steve was bitterly disappointed at the loss, feeling he deserved that year's Oscar after all the grueling months he'd spent on Taiwan trying to bring life to his character of Jake.

As a consolation prize, Steve, along with Julie Andrews, won World Film Favorites at the Golden Globes.

Wise later said that "Steve was so pissed after his failure to win an Oscar that he announced his retirement from the motion picture industry."

***

During his hiatus from "fairy directors and producers"—his words—Steve tested cars and motorcycles during the summer of 1966. He even toured "God's country" in Montana and parts of Southern Canada.

Neile made a brief comeback in summer stock when a troupe revived *Pajama Game*. Appearing in the role she'd performed so successfully on Broadway, she was in her element again until storm clouds gathered in the McQueen home. "I'm a selfish, chauvinist pig," Steve told his friends. "I demanded she come home and take care of me and the kids."

Declaring to the press that "I'm a loser no more," Steve pressed his footprints into the wet cement in the forecourt of Grauman's Chinese Theater, a symbol declaring that he'd made it in Hollywood.

Wearing a (fake) Phi Beta Kappa key, in a scene from *The Thomas Crown Affair*, Steve, a high school dropout, cuts a dapper figure in his tailor-made suit. Partly because he dropped his motorcylist's mumble, it was his most dashing and polished role.

During the summer of his "exile" from Hollywood, Steve told Paul Newman he'd read more than one hundred scripts, "each of them more shitty than the one before."

"Count yourself lucky, kid," Paul told him. "Guess how many actors are hanging out in the Hollywood Hills waiting for a call from some casting office."

The only script that caught his attention was eventually released in 1968 as *The Thomas Crown Affair*. The director and producer, Norman Jewison, although having worked with Steve before, had been eager to cast Paul Newman in the role. He turned it down. Even Jack Lemmon was considered for the role, at least for a day. Jewison then offered it to Sean Connery. "He fiddled, faddled, and diddled with us and finally rejected it," Jewison said. Rock Hudson was considered, even Jean Paul Belmondo.

At one point, in a startling bit of casting, talk show host Johnny Carson was offered the title role.

Waiting for the ski season to begin, and clearly bored, a Boston lawyer, Alan R. Trustman, decided to write his first screenplay, originally calling it *The Crown Caper*.

About the last person Jewison and especially the writer Trustman wanted was Steve McQueen. "We didn't think it was his kind of role," Jewison said. "When you think of a dapper, suave, elegant, impeccably dressed man, you don't think of Steve. But for reasons not clear, he wanted the role. He was very persistent. He persuaded us he could do it. And, my God, he did."

Steve was cast as a self-made millionaire who was clearly bored with the good life and plots "the perfect crime," a $2.5 million bank hold-up where the robbers have never met before.

Debonair and sophisticated, he has an elegant Beau Brummel wardrobe of $3,000 suits that would have put Cary Grant to shame.

A gentleman of taste and culture, Thomas Crown was a connoisseur of beautiful women and vintage wine. "Wardrobe even supplied me with silk drawers so I could 'feel' the part," Steve said. "The suits were tailored to my body, and my shoes were handcrafted in Rome. I had to learn to play polo like my late friend, Porfirio Rubirosa. If Rubi had been alive, I would have hired him to teach me how to play. I even had to learn sky diving and I hate heights."

"I was high society, man," Steve said. "Contoured silk shirts, Boston ties. I looked fucking dapper. If only Princess Margaret had seen me dressed as Thomas Crown, she would have dumped that Lord Snowdon in a second. I was even fit to meet her sister, the Queen of England, no less. And, guess what? This ninth grade school drop-out wore a Phi Beta Kappa key across my vest. Of course, I had no problem driving the Rolls Royce."

The film was shot in Cape Cod and Boston, the polo sequences near Hamilton, Massachusetts, "where my red blood met all the bluebloods at the Myopia Hunt Club," Steve said. "In my specially designed wardrobe, I was hot shit."

Jewison, surprisingly, considered the French sex kitten of the day, Brigitte Bardot, for the role of Vicky Anderson, an insurance investigator who tracks down her man, falls in love with him, and solves the crime. This emancipated woman makes FBI agents look like bumbling idiots. The character of Vicky Anderson was a female version of James Bond.

Bardot was not available. Eva Marie Saint was another hot possibility to play the female lead, but Jewison changed his mind after Faye Dunaway became such a big star in *Bonnie and Clyde*.

Few women in the films of the 60s were as well dressed as Faye in *The Thomas Crown Affair*. She became known as "the clotheshorse of the 60s." Women in the audience gasped at her entrances, wondering, "What will the bitch wear next?"

Steve felt that in spite of his character's "outer fur, Thomas Crown is my kind of cat, a rebel against the establishment. Okay, so I didn't go to Dartmouth."

As compensation for his involvement, he was offered a $750,000 base salary by United Artists, plus a gift of the dune buggy used in the film and all those tailored suits he wore. However, since he used his own watch, he billed production $250.00. Add to that his $500,000 annual salary from Solar Productions, and he became one of the most highly paid movie stars in Hollywood. The studio invested $4 million in the film, but early returns produced a payback of $14 million.

Steve did not have a smooth transition adjusting to Faye's professionalism—her perfect memory of her lines, her rigid adherence to the script. He was more spontaneous.

Jewison felt that Faye wasn't taken in by Steve's facile seductive charm. "Maybe that's why they were so good together on film. It's the love story between two shits."

Dunaway on McQueen: "He stimulates that cuddly feeling. He's the misunderstood bad guy you're sure you can cure with a little warmth and home cooking."

Faye not only had a beau at the time, and Steve a wife in residence, but she claimed that he didn't know how to deal with an intelligent woman, one "not inclined to the old male-female games that he knew how to win. I don't think Steve ever truly relaxed around me, nor I him."

Steve and **Faye Dunaway** look like they're falling in love on the screen in these scenes from *The Thomas Crown Affair,* but apparently, they didn't. According to Faye, "I've had work, possessions, love, sex, and men. I worked during the day, and I had a man to share my bed at night becasue I need love and sex--but never one without the other."

In the bottom photo, **Steve** and **Faye** focus on the sexiest chess game in film history.

In one dramatic scene, Steve piloted a dune buggy across the sands of Cape Cod. Her nerves shattered, Faye sat in the seat beside him. He later claimed she deserved the Purple Heart for riding as his passenger.

"I dug my heels into the floorboard and hung on for dear life," she said. "It was terrifying, yet at the same time it was terrific fun. All the thrills and chills of a ride on a roller coaster."

At one point, with the dune buggy hurtling toward the ocean at 60mph, the steering wheel jammed. Both stars ended up in twenty feet of water.

The film's "chess-and-sex" scene became one of the most immortal in film history.

Faye told Jewison that she always "thought that what is hinted at is infinitely more provocative than what is revealed." In the chess scene, she carried through on her thought to the ultimate extreme.

She appeared in a backless diaphanous chiffon gown, colored a pinkish beige. An antique cameo brooch was pinned to the front of the gown. Not a word is exchanged for the next five minutes, as Thomas and Vicky enact one of the greatest scenes of sexual tension between stars.

The individual moves within the chess game that Dunaway and McQueen played in the movie were directly copied, play by play, from one of history's most discussed and most analyzed chess competitions. It occurred in Vienna in 1899 between chess masters G. Zeissl and Walther von Walthoffen, although it's certain that the McQueen/Dunaway re-enactment of the match was more sexually suggestive. In the immediate aftermath of their onscreen chess replay was "The Kiss," the longest in screen history.

Faye in her memoirs described her reaction to "The Kiss": "It begins with the briefest of touches, his lips barely pressing mine. Then we both move in on each other in what was meant to be the longest, most passionate, most sensual, most erotic kiss in the world. I'm told it was. Then the camera

"The Kiss" as it came to be called, was the longest in film history. It firmly established Steve as a romantic matinee idol. The never-ending smooch originated with the chess game, a five-minute sequence that evoked comparisons to the famous eating scene in the movie, *Tom Jones*. For the first time in an A-list movie, tonguey kisses are clearly highlighted.

starts spinning around us, as if we are wildly spinning. Then we become a thousand prisms of light, a starburst of color, as the kiss goes on and on."

It took eight hours to film and three days to set up. "I never got a hard-on," Steve confessed, "only chapped lips."

After viewers saw the two stars "eating each other's face," rumors spread that they were involved in a torrid affair. However, no smoking gun has emerged. "Steve is married and everything," Faye said. "I didn't date him. To me, any married man is trouble. I don't want any part of such clandestine relationships."

Upon its release, comparisons were inevitable between *The Thomas Crown Affair* and Alfred Hitchcock's *To Catch a Thief* (1954) with Cary Grant and Grace Kelly.

Critic Pauline Kael, the lady of the barbs, weighed in with her verdict. "Pretty good trash." Arthur Winsten of the *New York Post*, delivered an even more pointed barb. "McQueen, dashing around with verve, unlimited energy and bright, inquiring eyes, makes you wonder if he knows he's hatching something almost akin to a turkey."

Regardless of what the critics said, the public, especially women, flocked to movie houses across the country. A group of Southern society women, calling themselves the "Belles of Memphis," named Steve "The Sexiest Male Alive."

In Plains, Georgia, a future U.S. President, Jimmy Carter, for reasons known only to himself, saw the picture sixteen times.

The film won the Academy Award for Best Song with its "Windmills of Your Mind," sung by Noel Harrison, son of Rex Harrison. The music was by Michel Legrand, lyrics by Alan Bergman and Marilyn Bergman.

A lackluster remake was released in 1999 starring Pierce Brosnan and Rene Russo. In a surprise appearance, Faye Dunaway appeared as the therapist for Thomas Crown.

No biographer of former president **Jimmy Carter** has ever asked the big question: Why did he go to see *The Thomas Crown Affair* sixteen times?

Did he fall in love with Faye Dunaway, or *--surely not!--* with Steve?

When he saw the final cut, Steve pronounced *The Thomas Crown Affair* "the favorite of all my movies. In my spiffy clothes, I think I looked far sexier than Faye, especially in that scene where I stripped down with her for the sauna. I got an erection just watching myself on the screen. The sauna was God damn hot but so was this country boy."

***

As the summer deepened, so did Steve's drug habit, enough to alarm Neile. "More and more, he depended on his 'weed' to get him through a day," she said. "He took cocaine the way a person might casually drink a Coca-Cola." When challenged, Steve would launch one of his imitations, perhaps John Wayne, telling her, "A cowpoke has to do what a cowpoke has to do."

Jay Sebring was a frequent visitor, arriving with comb and scissors to do Steve's hair, perhaps to brighten it, making it even blonder than it was. Sebring always carried small "packages of the white stuff."

Sometimes Sebring and Steve would disappear from the house. Perhaps unknown to Neile, the two men were often having a three-way with Sharon Tate.

Even though he had friends, Steve remained somewhat of a loner, disappearing on his motorcycle and riding by himself "into nowhere," as he called it. One night in 1967 changed his life. He acquired two friends in the desert, and "The Three Musketeers," as they called themselves, were born.

Darron McDonald and the much younger Casey Perkins entered Steve's life one night when they were driving home to their trailer about twenty-five miles east of Palm Springs. Casey made his living "pumping gas," and Darron worked as an auto mechanic. Both of them owned motorcycles, and each of them shared the joint ownership of a pickup truck.

Darron had picked up Casey as a hitchhiker when he was only fourteen years old, and the two young men had been living together ever since. Casey had run away from "home," but he never exactly said where home was.

Like Steve, Darron, born in West Los Angeles, never knew his father. And, like Jullian, Darron's mother supported herself as a prostitute working Pershing Square.

"As we headed home one night, it was already dark," said Darron. "Suddenly in our headlights, a guy emerged standing beside his motorcycle. He looked stranded. I stopped the car and asked if he wanted a lift. I told him he could get in, and we'd hoist his motorcycle onto the back of our pickup."

"Thanks, guys," Steve said, introducing himself.

"My God, he looked a little beat up, and we didn't recognize him at first," Casey said. "Both Darron and I almost shouted at the same time. *Steve McQueen!* Darron asked him, 'What in hell is a big-time movie star like you doing out here all alone in the desert?"

"We lifted his motorcycle into the back of our truck," Casey said, "and he joined us up front. I'll always remember that night. Just as Steve crawled into the seat with us, Hank Williams on our radio was singing 'two-dollar bills to

285

boot.'"

"We'd seen three of Steve's movies," Darron said. "We told him he was our favorite star. He seemed to love hearing that."

"Pretty soon we were talking about Hollywood pussy," Casey said. "We asked him about all the hot tamales he knew. He told us that he regularly banged Liz Taylor, and that Marilyn Monroe had been in love with him. At that time, we didn't know he was married with two kids."

"We told him that about ten miles up the road was a filling station next door to an all-night diner," Darron said. "He could get gas there and also have some supper with us if he wanted to. I was floored when he accepted our invite. A big movie star like that willing to hang out with two country boys."

"It was amazing," Casey said. "Before I finished off my last chicken leg, Steve bonded with us. Even though he was a movie star, we had a lot in common. All of us were high school dropouts. We didn't have much money, and since he was making millions, I thought he'd pay for dinner. We were really surprised that he didn't even have Hank Williams' two dollar bills in his pocket. Here he was in the middle of the desert completely broke. We paid for dinner and also picked up his gas bill for his cycle."

"I thought he'd roar off and we'd never see him again," Darron said. "But he seemed to want to hang out with us. We told him we had some good, cold beer waiting for us in our trailer. I'll be God damn, he agreed to go home to our dump. I felt ashamed to show him where we lived. The trailer had seen better days, and there was only a cactus at the door, that and our barbecue pit in the front yard."

"We had quite a lot of beer that night, and talked until about three o'clock in the morning," Casey said. "We invited him to sleep over and apologized for the lack of bedding. 'Don't worry,' he told us. 'I'll join you guys.' Mother fuck. He stripped off his clothes with me and Darron. We always slept buck-ass naked. Our small bed in the back would sleep one comfortably, two in a pinch. But Steve was a great sport. He crawled in between us and, drunk as a skunk, he slept the rest of the night away. After that close contact, Steve the next morning said that made us 'asshole buddies.'"

"Christ, he went into the kitchen and even made our coffee and cooked some eggs for us," Darron said. "For such a big-time movie star—maybe the biggest box office star in the world—he was so God damn down to earth I couldn't believe it. Before the morning ended, we'd forgotten about him being such a big star and were talking to him like he was a regular guy. We talked mainly about pussy, cars, and cycles."

Darron and Casey drove back in the pickup heading for work in Palm Springs. Steve on his motorcycle rode along with them. When they got to the outskirts of Palm Springs, he told them he had a small house there and gave them his address. He also learned the address of the place where they worked, and said he'd drop in Saturday at five o'clock when they got off from work.

"I couldn't believe it," Darron said. "I mean he could be spending Saturday night in the arms of Elizabeth Taylor, and he wanted to spend it with us. We were thrilled and couldn't think of anything else. Casey warned me not to get my hopes up too high. He feared that once he got back to Hollywood and all those movie stars, he'd forget about us."

"Lo and behold, when five o'clock came that Saturday, Steve showed up in a Porsche," Casey said. "We thought he might have Elizabeth Taylor in the car with him, but he was alone. He invited us for a steak dinner at this little joint he knew down the way. It was a great steak. Thank God that me and Darron had just got paid that Saturday because once again Steve didn't have any money on him. We paid for his dinner, but was glad for the company."

"Instead of hitting the bars," Darron said, "he wanted to drive back to our dingy little trailer and hang out there. We were potheads and always had plenty of weed there. That night Steve introduced us to cocaine. He'd brought some little white packets of the stuff. He pulled off his clothes, and we got down and dirty that night. We talked a lot about pussy, and all of us got hot."

"Steve suggested a circle jerk," Casey said, "and we were all for that. When all of us got hard, Steve wanted to measure himself against us. Darron won that round by an inch, and I came up a bit short. But it was all in good fun."

In looking back on their long relationship, when Darron and Casey tried to pitch a memoir to Manor Books in the 1980s, Darron said, "We were buddies for life. But not in the way we thought. When we first met Steve, we thought he'd be taking us to parties where we'd meet all these big movie stars. But we remained his secret friends."

"Except for Jay Sebring, we never met any of his friends and were never introduced to any of his three wives or his kids," Casey said. "Maybe he was ashamed of us. I don't know. During all the time we knew him, he never had any money. He was always hitting us up for money, which was a bit strange. But he had moments of real generosity. He gave us something big each Christmas. One year he bought us new motorcycles. Another year he bought us a new car. It was secondhand but like new. His greatest gift to us two years before he died was a new mobile home."

"With Steve, it was never about the money," Casey said. "We loved the guy and had the greatest times of our lives with him. He was one wild boy, let me tell you that. We did things together and went to places that I hope no one ever finds out about. It was a wild time—orgies, lots of dope, plenty of sex. No movie stars, but Steve knew where the action was. He had some sort of radar to guide us there."

In summing up his offbeat relationships, Steve told his friend, William F. Nolan, that "maybe they run a garage or race bikes. Guys like that, when it gets down to the short stroke, they'll give blood. They'll put their *life* on the line for you. Same as you will for them. You don't find many like that but when you do, you hang tight with 'em because you know you've got the real thing."

***

Steve might be riding the heap of Hollywood stars, but one morning at breakfast with Neile he began to learn the price of fame. It was a different era. Studios no longer had most stars under contract, and there was no department to cover up embarrassing incidents such as a male star running over and killing someone while drunk, or another male star getting caught in bed having sex with an eight-year-old boy.

With fame came an increasing attention focused on Steve's background, which to some observers was notorious.

In January of 1968 an underground book, *Hollywood Homos,* was published and distributed under the counter at newsstands along Hollywood Boulevard and other places. It was an exposé of gay Hollywood, and its editors ran pictures and identified "The Top Homos of Hollywood." As of this writing, the author of that book is still alive, and, for reasons associated with an FBI investigation at the time, still denies authorship or any involvement with it at all, for that matter.

An anonymous call came in to Steve the morning the book hit the stands. He was having breakfast with Neile. In her memoirs, she quoted the caller as telling Steve: "I thought you'd like to know that your name is on the list." The caller abruptly hung up.

Sometimes the wife is the last to know. Neile wrote, "No one in his right mind would ever think of Steve as gay. I mean, *Steve*!!" Yet, some of the great womanizers of Hollywood had secret gay liaisons, including the likes of Errol Flynn and others.

But instead of letting the book die on the grapevine, "Steve became possessed" in Neile's words. "His ego couldn't handle the innuendo. It seemed to violate everything he stood for—most notably his macho image."

During earlier, more naïve eras, it was presumed that gay men were effeminate—never macho. That myth, of course, was exploded decades ago, but not where Steve was concerned. He ordered his attorneys to track down the source of the publication. It was traced to a mailbox in West Hollywood.

The list, in no particular order, included the following celebrities:

ROCK HUDSON
TAB HUNTER
MONTGOMERY CLIFT (deceased)
RODDY McDOWALL
PAUL NEWMAN
STEVE McQUEEN
SAL MINEO
YUL BRYNNER
MARLON BRANDO
JAMES DEAN (deceased)
FARLEY GRANGER
RORY CALHOUN
GUY MADISON
TROY DONAHUE
PETER LAWFORD
ROBERT WALKER (deceased)
TOM DRAKE
CARY GRANT
RANDOLPH SCOTT
GENE KELLY
FRED ASTAIRE
GEORGE CUKOR
DAN DAILEY
TYRONE POWER
ERROL FLYNN
ROBERT TAYLOR
WALT DISNEY
NICK ADAMS
VAN JOHNSON
JEFFREY HUNTER
JOHN DEREK
ANTHONY PERKINS
CESAR ROMERO
SPENCER TRACY
CLIFTON WEBB
GEORGE NADER

Each of the names ran with a picture, often a nude, and a small profile, outlining the gay relationships and activities, however provocative or illegal in some cases, of each of the stars named. In Steve's case, it cited his intimate relationship with certain male stars, including Sal Mineo, Montgomery Clift,

Underground Book
Outs Hollywood Homos

| Rock Hudson | Tab Hunter | Montgomery Clift | Roddy McDowall |

| Paul Newman | Steve McQueen | Sal Mineo | Yul Brynner |

| Marlon Brando | James Dean | Farley Granger | Rory Calhoun |

| Guy Madison | Troy Donahue | Peter Lawford | Robert Walker |

Tom Drake

Cary Grant

Randolph Scott

Gene Kelly

Fred Astaire

George Cukor

Dan Dailey

Tyrone Power

Errol Flynn

Robert Taylor

Walt Disney

Nick Adams

Van Johnson

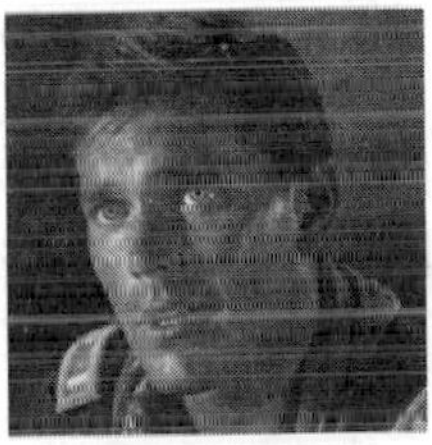
Jeffrey Hunter

John Derek

Anthony Perkins

Cesar Romero

Spencer Tracy

Clifton Webb

George Nader

Paul Newman, and Marlon Brando.

The book also wrote of Steve's involvement in Cuban porno, his work in three different bordellos (suggesting that he might have been for hire himself), and his former role as a male hustler to both men and women.

The writer ended the book with a postscript: "This is only the tip of the iceberg," the back page read. "Many more stars—both on the A-list and B-list—will be exposed in a subsequent edition. YOU KNOW WHO YOU ARE!"

The date of that publication marked the beginning of speculation on the alleged closeted homosexuality of both Paul Newman and Steve McQueen. From that date forth they would be labeled as "Friends of Dorothy" in the underground press throughout the 70s and 80s. FOD, of course, was a reference to the character that Judy Garland played in *The Wizard of Oz* and was a code word for gay. So prevalent was the gossip that all McQueen biographers, if only to deny it, had to deal with the subject of his potential homosexuality.

The publication of that underground exposé was perhaps the beginning of the end of Steve's marriage to Neile. She noticed the subtle changes that began to occur in their relationship, beginning when he went to San Francisco for location shooting of *Bullitt*, his next film.

He began by asking her to fly to San Francisco only on weekends, claiming that he would be too busy during the week. Later she'd learn that Steve was not sitting home alone during week nights in San Francisco.

He embarked upon what became the most promiscuous era of his life. Since it was the wild and woolly late 1960s, and he was a big-time movie star, he found the sexual conquests almost too easy for him.

"When he walked into a room," Rock Hudson said, "it wasn't whether Steve would make out, it was which woman he would choose for the night. Or should I say women. He was never happy with just one after that stupid book came out. It's like he had to prove something. Screw four women in one night to show the world he was super macho. I almost felt sorry for him. He seemed desperate, and I don't think he enjoyed the sex all that much. How can you when you're doing it not to have fun but to prove something to yourself?"

In contrast to Steve's reaction to the book, Roddy McDowall told the author of this biography, "It made no difference to me that my name was on the list. Let's not kid ourselves. Hundreds of insiders in Hollywood could have compiled that list. The people on that list were commonly gossiped about."

"From various sources, I'd heard dozens of stories about Steve, including the fact that he hustled men," Roddy claimed. "Later they called Steve the King of Cool, for reasons I don't understand. He wasn't cool at all if someone accused him of being gay. Cool would be to brush it off, ignore it. If you went ballistic at the charge, that aroused suspicions. Didn't Steve understand that?

He should have."

Sal Mineo, whose name was on the list, recalled getting a desperate call from Steve. "I was delighted to hear from him," Sal said. "But when he arrived one night at my house, I was almost frightened. He looked like a madman. He told me to get in his car. I knew something was wrong. Out on the open highway, he floored the accelerator, passing everything in sight. It's a wonder both of us weren't killed. Amazingly, the highway patrol didn't chase us. He came to such an abrupt stop along the beach that he nearly threw me through the windshield."

Steve turned to Sal. "Why did you do it, you fucker?"

"Do what?" I asked.

"Get my name on that list, and don't tell me you don't know what list I'm talking about," Steve said. "All of Hollywood is talking about nothing else."

"Like hell I talked to any writer," Sal protested. "My name's on that list, and exposure damages me as much as it does you."

"It took about two hours, but finally I was able to convince him that I had nothing to do with it," Sal told the author. "I told him to let it blow over, but he wouldn't listen."

"I found his behavior a bit pathological," Sal later said. "Not that I'm a shrink, I never knew what there was in Steve's past that made him so uptight about homosexuality. There were rumors that he was gang raped as a kid. But I think it was deeper than that. Of all the people on that list, Steve had the biggest struggle coming to terms with his own desire. There were parts of himself that he just couldn't face."

"After that exposure, he began to drop former friends and even denied knowing some of us," Sal said. "Of course, he couldn't deny knowing me, because we'd made a picture together."

"He stopped seeing us one by one, like he didn't want to be associated with the lavender brush," Sal confided. "Marlon Brando, Rock Hudson, Peter Lawford, all of us fell by the wayside. He still saw Paul Newman and George Peppard. Of course, poor Monty had died in 1966, and James Dean was long gone. So he didn't have anything to fear from them."

Several mysterious visitors came calling on **Nick Adams** just prior to his death. Nick had shot to fame playing Johnny Yuma in the hit TV series, *The Rebel*. Appearing at Nick's home, Steve brought a warning from Elvis, who demanded that Nick abandon his plan to publish a tell-all *exposé*.

293

"I thought Steve was pathetic," Sal said. "You didn't have to be a shrink to know that his raging homophobia was a kind of self-loathing. God, he must have hated those dark desires he had. No one else paid any attention to that stupid book, although whoever the shit who compiled that list of homos knew what he was talking about."

"Beginning that night, the last time I saw him, Steve was no longer in to certain friends who might call," Sal said. "All of us got the message. He didn't want to have a thing to do with us. It was sad, really, how some of us were dropped. He still hung with Jay Sebring, but Sharon Tate was the beard for that relationship. Everybody knew that the haircutter had the hots for Steve. I heard that Steve ended up hanging out with grease monkeys. God knows what he and his grease monkeys were doing with the axle grease."

Biographer Christopher Sandford summed up Steve's position in life in the late 1960s. "McQueen's omnisexual days, when he'd soul-kissed James Dean and hustled around New York, were long since over. Even at that sorry pass, he'd never been out and out gay, just voraciously greedy. Whereas back when he'd attended bisexual orgies, at least one of them, in the Gramercy Park Hotel, was surreptitiously taped by the FBI."

***

Late one night Steve received a call from Elvis. He sounded drugged. "I hear your boy, Nick, is writing a book." He was obviously referring to Nick Adams. "He won't be the first asshole who's tried to write an exposé book about me."

A close bond was formed between **Elvis** and **Nick Adams** on the first night they met. Nick told Natalie Wood, "Elvis is going to replace Jimmy in my life." He was referring to James Dean.
The relationship eventually soured, and Nick's life ended in tragedy when he was found dead in his cottage in Beverly Hills.

"I'm sure he'll treat you kindly," Steve said. "Nick's a nice guy. He won't tell *everything*."

"Like hell he won't," Elvis said. "I've seen the fucker. He threatened me, demanded $100,000."

"Nick must be desperate to do something like this," Steve said.

"He is," Elvis said. "He needs money and he's blackmailing me. Would you get over there tonight and talk some sense into his fool head? You've gotta warn him; if he goes ahead with this stupid book, it might be the last one he'll ever write." Angered, foggy, and confused, he slammed down the phone.

294

Hurriedly getting dressed, Steve rode his motorcycle to 2126 El Roble Lane where Nick lived in a rented house.

Nick seemed startled to confront Steve at this time of the night, but he let him in. Wandering around in his jockey shorts, Nick seemed alone in the house.

Steve wasn't much for small talk at a time like this. He got right down to business, asking what kind of memoir Nick was writing.

"I take the advice of Mae West," Nick said. "Keep a diary while you're young, because it will keep you when you get old."

Steve warned Nick that he was racing down a dangerous road. "You know, of course, that that old geezer, Col. Parker, will never let a book like yours get published."

"I'm not afraid," Nick said defiantly. "They'll either pay up or suffer the consequences."

"I've warned you," Steve said. "Now it's up to you. If you go forward with this thing, you'll be cutting off your head. That brings up a point. Am I written up in this fucking homo book?"

There was a smirk on Nick's face. "Not if you don't want to be," he said.

"Well, I don't want to be," Steve said. "I'm a private man. I'm already in that fucking book about Hollywood homos. So are you. Neile and everybody else in Hollywood knows about that book. Do you want another scandal?"

"I will see to it that you're not in the book," Nick said. "If I write about us, it'll greatly increase my sales. Without you, the book won't sell as well. Will you agree to make up the difference in my lost sales?"

"Exactly what kind of loss are we talking about?"

"About $100,000 worth," Nick said.

Steve rose from the sofa. "You're getting nothing from me. Not one God damn red cent."

"Then you can read about yourself," Nick said. "It's pretty juicy stuff."

"You must be really hard up to want to pull this shit," Steve said.

"I didn't become a star like you guys," Nick said. "Too many people blocked my way. They didn't want me to get ahead. It's payback time. I need money and I'm gonna get it one way or another."

"You've been warned," Steve said, moving toward the door.

"Do you want me to send you a free copy," Nick asked. "Or do you want to pay for your order for an autographed copy right now."

"There will be no book," Steve said in a low voice.

"How can you be sure?" Nick said. "I've already started it."

"Col. Parker, one way or another, will stop you. Watch your step, kid. You're gonna get your *cojones* caught in a wringer. You're just a coal-mining kid from Pennsylvania. You're playing with the big boys now."

Nick stood up, as if to confront and defy Steve. "I'm not running scared."

"You should be." Those were Steve's final words to Nick. He would never see him again.

On February 6, 1968, Steve received another call from Elvis. "Your boy's committed suicide. I've just heard the news. There was no suicide note."

After a search of the house, the police found no pills, bottles, syringes, or needles. Missing were his journals and unfinished manuscript.

Steve confided the whole story and his theories about Nick's death to Casey and Darron. Until he died, Steve believed that Col. Parker had Nick knocked off.

Steve's ultimate take on the mysterious death of Nick—homicide or suicide—was what he told his friends. "If you fly too close to the sun, you'll likely to catch fire."

***

Even though he resisted playing a cop—"my young fans will turn against me"—*Bullitt* would become Steve's fifth box office bonanza in a row. He knew it would be "my picture," since his Solar Productions controlled it, even though it was financed by Warner Brothers.

Originally Warners had signed a six-picture deal with Steve, but after *Bullitt*, the contract was cancelled. Steve fought against Warners during the making of *Bullitt*, the way he'd fictionally battled the Nazis in *Hell Is for Heroes*.

He cast himself as Frank Bullitt, a rebel cop who was "tough as nails." The plot concerned his investigation of the death of a Mafia mobster.

The movie was based on a novel, *Mute Witness*, by Robert L. Pike. The Boston attorney, Alan R. Trustman, who had written the screenplay for *The Thomas Crown Affair,* was hired to adapt *Bullitt* for the screen. His

Steve (top photo) in his classic role as Frank Bullitt in the picture *Bullitt.* As the humorless rebel cop, Steve practically directed himself in this hit movie.

In the scene in the bottom photo, **Steve** reunites with his friend, **Robert Vaughn**, who plays a cold and oily politico opposing Bullitt's every move.

convoluted plot turned out to be somewhat incomprehensible but, nonetheless, it played well on the screen.

Steve's longtime friend, Robert Relyea, was executive producer, and the job of director went to an Englishman, Peter Yates. His super hits such as *The Deep* (1977) and *The Dresser* (1983) lay in his future.

As anyone who has seen *Bullitt* knows, the spectacular car chase through the hilly streets of San Francisco was the highlight of the movie. In fact, Yates was hired as the director because Steve had been impressed with the car chase in the English film, *Robbery*, shot in 1967. Flying to San Francisco, Yates was assigned to helm his first American movie.

Steve and Yates agreed to hire the stunningly beautiful Jacqueline Bisset as Steve's love interest. Her part was mostly decorative, however. Yates told him, "People are inclined to be skeptical about Jacqui because she's so beautiful. But she has that quality of intelligence that goes with the face and makes it something more."

For his co-star, Steve teamed once again with Robert Vaughn, who had worked with him on *The Magnificent Seven*.

Vaughn played Walter Chalmers, an ambitious politician with no morals. Although it's a libel of the true character of Robert F. Kennedy, some of the young Kennedy's persona is reflected in Vaughn's interpretation "smart, charismatic, and ruthless," as the actor himself described it.

The legendary car chase (the two photos on the left, above) helped make *Bullitt* an international hit, and brought riches to its star.
In the photos on the right, Steve is seen in bed with the beautiful **Jacqueline Bisset**, and getting dangerously close to a Pan American jet as it takes off.
Steve performed this stunt himself, and it nearly killed him.

The hills of San Francisco were used as the dramatic backdrop for the car chase. Of course, local policemen had to clear the area of pedestrians. Both Steve's car and the vehicle he's pursuing literally became airborne from the top of the city's hills.

Bud Ekins, who had jumped that tall barbed wire in *The Great Escape*, was called in again to drive Steve's car in the most dangerous sequences. A hairdresser dyed his hair blond to match Steve's.

The car chase took three weeks to shoot, and, in the words of Yates, "it devoured automobiles." A hand-held camera was used in a vehicle going more than one hundred miles per hour. Taking up at least twelve minutes of film time, it inspired many other car chase motion pictures of the future, notably *The French Connection*.

Steve used a souped-up 390 GT Mustang for his chase against the bad guys in a 440 Magnum Dodge Charger.

In addition to the car chase, Steve demanded that he, not a stunt man, film a dangerous sequence on a runway where he narrowly misses getting run over by a 707 taking off. He's chasing a Mafia gangster across the airport runway who tries to kill him. Falling belly down, Steve just managed to escape the 250-degree surge of heat from the 707's jet pods.

With the risks he took, refusing at times to use a stunt man, Steve could easily have met a violent death. He later said, "It's the hardest million I ever earned."

Often Steve invited Neile to join him on location. But on *Bullitt*, he suggested she fly to San Francisco only for the weekends, as he needed time alone to plot the tough location shots.

The question remains, did Steve want to keep Neile at bay while he seduced Bisset and other women?

He was quoted as saying, "Of all the females I've made films with, she had the greatest body." That tells a lot but doesn't fully suggest seduction, although it certainly hints at it.

In turn, Bisset called him "a beautiful, beautiful man."

Biographers have claimed that Bisset and Steve had an affair during the making of *Bullitt*. Marshall

Throughout his career, legendary beauties of the screen pursued Steve aggressively. He told friends, "I had to fight them off." With **Ava Gardner**, his resistance was low.

298

Terrill has suggested that it was because of that affair that Steve didn't want Neile in San Francisco on a week night. Christopher Sandford claimed that the twenty-three year-old "substar" forgot her antagonism with Steve "just long enough to fall in bed with him."

The author, living in San Francisco at the time, talked to many members of the cast and crew. Nearly eighty percent of them claimed that Bisset and Steve were locked into an affair, the other twenty percent having "no comment." There was a universal fear of their boss, Steve himself.

Casey and Darron, Steve's new friends, claimed he boasted of an affair with Bisset, going into rather graphic details.

The beautiful star told gossip columnist Rona Barrett, "It was confusing to me because he spoke in American slang, and I could hardly understand him." Perhaps she understood the universal language of the bed, if indeed an affair did take place. Steve always claimed, "My best way of communicating with a woman is from a position on top of her."

Once, upon her arrival in San Francisco for one of her visits, during a stay in Steve's rented apartment, Neile emerged from the shower. On a night table in the bedroom, she found a hair brush with long blonde hairs, admittedly not Bisset's, but some other woman's. Furious, she waited for him to return from the day's filming

When he walked through the door, she threw the hair brush at him and caught the next shuttle flight back to Los Angeles.

He was not a lonely bachelor for long. Just as he was planning his evening as a free man, a call came in for him. He'd already instructed the switchboard not to put anyone through to him unless it was the president of the United States or his trusted friend, actor Don Gordon, who'd been cast as Detective Delgetti in *Bullitt*.

"Yeah, what's happening?" Steve in a gruff voice demanded to know of the party calling. "Who is this?"

"I'm the Tarheel Bitch, Ava Gardner, and I've just seen you kissing Faye Dunaway in *The Thomas Crown Affair*. I'm staying at this suite at the Mark Hopkins. Why don't you come up and see me sometime? Or has that line already been used by another actress?"

Steve, in *Bullitt*

Chapter Eight
The Tragedy of Stardom

Even though she was dangerously on the road to turning fifty years old, Ava Gardner was one of the world's most glamorous women. Sultry, tempestuous, and a vision of ravishing beauty, she was still a screen goddess, although her allure was fading.

Instead of meeting her in her suite at the Mark Hopkins Hotel, as she had suggested, he'd invited her for a visit to his rented apartment, where they'd attract less attention.

Barging into Steve's apartment, she said, "Who do you have to fuck to get a drink around here?"

That opening line was his cue to recognize her as a hard-living, hard-loving woman who enjoyed life to the hilt. From that point on, she would be blunt with him to the point of outrage.

Normally, he did not like liberated women, certainly not one as flamboyant, though compelling, as Ava. He was impressed, however, that she'd chosen him, a woman who lived life by her own rules and had been pursued obsessively by every man from Howard Hughes to Frank Sinatra.

With drink in hand, she kissed him on the lips. "I'm just a li'l hillbilly gal, but that's what attracts 'em, honey chile."

"Thanks for dropping by," Steve said. "I can't believe I'm sitting across from Ava Gardner. *The* Ava Gardner. You're sitting here but I'm not really seeing you. Images are flashing before me. That department store mannequin come to life in *One Touch of Venus*, that mysterious beauty who came out of the night in *Pandora and the Flying Dutchman*."

"Honey, I didn't give a damn for any of those pictures," she said. "To me, movies are just a way to earn a quick buck. If it hadn't been for movies, I would have become a prostitute. I'm not your typical movie star like my bosom buddy, Lana Turner. I don't slash my wrists or overdose on sleeping pills."

"Maybe you and I should make a film together," he said. "I think we'd look great up there on the screen."

"The only film I know we could do together is *Sweet Bird of Youth*, me playing the over-the-hill actress and you the handsome young gigolo. But that's already been done with your buddy, Paul Newman. Newman's OK but he needs to let himself go more in bed. Loosen up and get lowdown and dirty."

"Now you're talking like you're my kind of woman," he said, getting up and moving to sit beside her on the sofa.

"I just had to meet you," she said. "Watching you with that bitch, Faye Dunaway, and that *kiss*," she said. "I turned to my date when I saw that kiss, and said, 'Sugar, buy me some of that.' No woman in the world should have to live out her life without at least once getting to know Steve McQueen. Don't you agree?"

"I can't get around to all of them," he said. "But I try. C'mon, let's go to dinner and then see what happens. My ol' lady is back in Los Angeles. She'll never know unless I confess."

"And don't do that, sugartit," she said, "especially when you run into your old buddy, Mr. Frank Sinatra. Frankie likes to cut off the peckers of guys I sleep with."

"I need mine," he said, "so I'll be careful."

Two biographers have discovered the affair of Ava Gardner with Steve. Lee Server who wrote the definitive book on Ava, *Love Is Nothing*, stumbled onto it. But the liaison merited only a line. "There were one-night stands here and there: In Los Angeles with a young Steve McQueen—he complained to friends that she had all but assaulted him."

After seeing Steve McQueen emote with Faye Dunaway in that long, smouldering kiss in *The Thomas Crown Affair*, sultry beauty **Ava Gardner** wanted in on the action. Author Lee Server called his biography of Ava *Love Is Nothing*, but that is not what Steve experienced when she came to call on him. It was the beginning of a long but relatively secret affair between this famous couple.

Christopher Sandford also discovered the involvement, defining the forty-six year old Ava as one of Steve's sexual "predators." He quotes Steve as saying, "You got to sit and tell some dope [about] how she's a great actress, and at the same time you got to keep from being raped."

Actually, Steve's involvement with Ava endured on and off for a number of years, and evolved into one of his major relationships of the 1970s. However, for murky reasons of his own, he kept the ongoing trysts a secret, feeling that there was something "dirty" about it.

***

At the peak of his career, when he was the reigning as king of the box office, Steve made a major mistake. He turned down *Sundance Kid and Butch Cassidy* (its original title). But not at first.

Both Steve and Paul Newman had originally been the leading choices to play the cold-blooded killers in the film version of Truman Capote's *In Cold Blood*. Capote himself wanted Steve and Paul, although the producers feared they were too well known. Eventually, the roles went instead to Robert Blake and Scott Wilson.

When both Steve and Paul saw the finished result in 1967 after the film was released, they regretted turning down the roles. They vowed that if a good script came along featuring two equal male parts, they'd go for it.

Over the years Paul had maintained a friendly rivalry with Steve. When Paul was filming *Winning* (1968), Steve, now number one at the box office, called Paul. "Hey, it's lonely at the top, old pal, old buddy," Steve said. "Come for a motorcycle ride with me in the desert. I'll fuck you in the sand until you get cactus up your ass."

"Dream on, faggot" Paul said.

Although they talked "dirty" to each other, each man, although a rival, still maintained a deep and abiding love and respect for each other. Paul

In the advertisement above for *Butch Cassidy and the Sundance Kid* starring **Paul Newman** (right), the depiction of **Robert Redford**'s face (left) might easily have been replaced with that of Steve McQueen. But after some stupid arguments over who'd get first billing, Steve pulled out of the picture, a decision that cost him one of the most memorable roles of the 1960s.

303

liked Steve so much that in the months ahead, he would invite him to join him as an investor in a new film production company.

When Steve went to see Paul's film, *Winning*, his take on a race car driver, Steve was clearly jealous that his rival had beat him to the screen with a picture about his own favorite sport.

As a drunken, stoned Steve was seen leaving the movie theater, a reporter asked him if his interest, and that of Paul's, in sports car racing expressed a death wish.

"Either of us can fuck anybody in the world we want," Steve said. "All we have to do is call 'em on the phone, and they come running. There have been rumors about Paul and me, about most actors. There have even been suggestions that we're not masculine. Out on those race tracks, we show those faggot reporters who's the man, baby."

Marlon Brando was asked to star in *Butch Cassidy and the Sundance Kid*, but bowed out, claiming, "I'm just too tired to make another God damn movie." He called Paul and told him of his decision to withdraw his name from the roster of candidates. "Why don't you get Steve McQueen to play Sundance?" Brando asked.

Richard Zanuck of 20th Century Fox called George Roy Hill, who had signed on as director of the Butch and Sundance film. "Newman and McQueen are two of the world's biggest stars," Zanuck said. "With those guys on the marquee, millions around the world will flock to see them. Of course, there will be the problem of top billing. They're both number one."

Meeting with the "suits" at Fox, Zanuck claimed that "McQueen is a born screen cowboy," citing his role in *The Magnificent Seven*. He contacted Steve directly and sent over a script, bypassing his agent.

Three days later, Steve called Zanuck. "I'm your Sundance. Draw up the contract. I don't work cheap. Remember that."

For years Paul and Steve had discussed appearing in a film together, and the roles of Butch and Sundance now seemed to provide that chance. In dialogues night after night, they became so fired up over the movie's possibilities that Paul proposed that they acquire the rights to the script themselves, each of them investing $200,000 from their own pockets. Steve rejected that idea.

The question of billing kept coming up, Steve demanding top billing but Paul refusing to relinquish his star status. Fox intervened when they heard of this argument and proposed a staggered but equal billing.

After endless debates with himself, and after negotiating an agreement with Paul to appear opposite him, Steve suddenly and impulsively rejected the movie offer. "There's no way in hell that I'm gonna play Newman's bitch," Steve told the stunned executives at Fox. He had finally figured out that *Butch Cassidy and the Sundance Kid* was the story of a love affair between two homosexual outlaws.

Many months later, after it had become obvious that *Butch Cassidy and the Sundance Kid* had been a staggering success, Paul called Steve to chide him. "How does it feel to be dethroned, old buddy, old pal?" Paul asked. "And to think you could have been riding in the saddle with me if you'd signed on as Sundance."

"Wasn't my role Butch?" Steve asked, "With you playing that faggot, Sundance? You might be number one at the box office—at least for 1969—but my dick is bigger than yours, and there's not a God damn thing you can do about that, fucker. Say, kid, since you're now the Queen of the Box Office, let's get together for some beer. I'll let you feel it under the table so you'll know what a real man is like." Having uttered that, he put down the phone.

***

It was 1969. Steve began to believe the publicity defining him as the "King of Cool." To keep abreast of the times, he increased his drug consumption, and he also changed his look. Encouraged by Jay Sebring, he let his hair grow longer. Jay also selected a different wardrobe for Steve.

As he moved into middle age, Steve began to dress more like a rock singer in the Haight-Ashbury district of San Francisco. Even though he had as his best friend the most celebrated men's hairdresser in California, Steve let his own curly hair grow frizzy over his ears.

He appeared with bracelets and love beads, and Jay fitted him with skin-tight jeans designed to reveal the outline of his genitals. In the "head" shops of San Francisco, where he spent more and more time, he became intimately acquainted with joss-sticks and incense, experimenting with various aromas to determine which of the array put him in the most seductive mood.

One night, fans spotted Steve walking the streets of San Francisco in a caftan. On other occasions, he dressed as a Navajo Indian. He told his friends, or anyone who'd listen, that the Navajos were "God's chosen people," and the only ones in America who still had their freedom.

Joan Crawford had her own opinion about "hippie" Steve as well as other stars of the New Hollywood. "He is nothing but a thirty-nine-year-old juvenile delinquent who can utter only ten words in every film he does. Directors, or so I am told, even have a hard time getting that out of him."

Many of Steve's friends did not approve of his relationship with Sebring. "He was a starfucker," said Nikita Knatz. "Steve was just one in the stable. Sebring was a nothing, a skinny little haircutter with nothing to offer. I would not buy a used car from him. I did not dislike him, but he just didn't impress me. He was a bloodsucker, a leech. He knew how to party, how to leech. He was a drunk and was made out to be a hero."

Sebring was extremely beholden to Steve, who was one of the keys to the hairdresser's success, having persuaded Frank Sinatra, Peter Lawford, Paul Newman, and other clients to have their hair styled by Sebring. Steve's friend, George Peppard, had once flown Sebring to London and back just so he could style his hair. The cost was $25,000.

Sebring and Sharon Tate once joined Steve and Neile in a rented villa at Diamond Head, right on the beach, a scene straight from *Blue Hawaii*.

Living next door was Judy Garland. She was with the fourth of her five husbands, Mark Herron. They were sharing a rented villa with Judy's children. On his second night in Hawaii, Steve managed to slip away for an hour-long seduction of Judy. "She begged me for it," Steve told Sebring. "For old time's sake. I've plugged her before."

Judy's marriage to Mark wasn't going well, and she poured out her troubles to Steve, who threatened to come over to her villa "and beat the shit out of Mark."

"Why do you always marry faggots?" Steve asked Judy.

"I wouldn't exactly call Sid Luft a faggot," she told Steve.

One night Sebring and Steve were sitting on the porch of Steve's rented villa when they heard Mark and Judy engaged in a bitter fight next door. Lorna Luft, Judy's daughter, recalled that night in her memoirs when she ran out into the living room to discover both Judy and Mark covered in blood.

The following afternoon, Lorna returned from the beach to find smoke billowing from the house. Her mother rested comfortably under a large hat with sunglasses on a chaise longue. She announced that she was burning Mark's clothing.

Next door, Steve saw the smoke billowing over his stone wall. He rushed to the rescue, hosing down Judy's rented villa.

Even as he struggled to put out the flames, Judy warned him, "Don't be a hero. This isn't the movies. Just sit down and wait for the fire department to come—after all, it's their job, not yours."

Steve finally gave in, no doubt thinking Judy was insane. He sat down with her and Lorna, waiting for the fire department.

Ultimately the fire department arrived, but Judy's plan backfired. The smoke was sucked through a shaft leading into her closet, and ruined all of her own clothing, as well as Mark's. After extinguishing the blaze, the firemen lined up to ask for Judy's autograph. By that time, Steve had retreated next door. "I don't give autographs," he said.

Lorna later claimed that this experience was Steve's early rehearsal for a future movie, *The Towering Inferno*.

Steve grew morbidly obsessed with the idea of turning forty, and spent more and more time in front of the mirror, looking for signs of age.

"He met fear with bravado," said his friend, Von Dutch. "More women, more drugs, more power. He could have anything he wanted. So he wanted more: more money, more cars, more girls. One alone isn't enough. Now he needs three, four, a thousand sports cars, twenty broads, a different one for every hour of the day and night." His behavior was compared to a spoiled Emir out of *The Arabian Nights*.

"When Steve switched from cocaine to heroin, he was no longer the King of Cool," Casey said. "His mood was black. His two favorite words to everything from the outside was 'Fuck you!' He was obsessed that the underground press was claiming that he was a homosexual. 'After all the pussy I've had, how can they call me a faggot?' He kept repeating that as if he could hardly believe it."

Deeper and deeper into mid-life crisis, he faced the restrictions of marriage as a family man with two children. "I'm missing out on the parade," he told Casey and Darron. "Life is a merry-go-round, and I've fallen off the hobby horse while every other fucking bastard is out there having a great old time."

When Sammy Davis Jr. came to see him, Steve definitely lost his cool. "Oh, Sammy, Sammy," he said, "my mother drank herself to death, and I think that's what's happening to me. I want bigger and bigger thrills. I can't race a car fast enough these days. My fuck flings are getting more and more boring. People piss me off except for a few good buddies here and there. I want to tell the whole world to go fuck itself."

"I'm getting more and more violent with some of the birds I let fly into my coop," Steve continued. "One time I picked up this bitch in Haight-Ashbury. When I got her alone and in bed, I found her cooze was the size of the Lincoln Tunnel in New York. I know it wasn't her fault,

Unaware of Steve's affair with his former wife, Ava Gardner, **Frank Sinatra** a longtime friend, accidentally encountered Steve at the Los Angeles airport, wandering in a drug-induced daze. Steve didn't know where he wanted to go, but Sinatra purchased him a ticket to San Francisco. Finally, Steve told Sinatra that he was going to hell.

but I beat the shit out of her and kicked her out of my room. I told her to go get off on the nearest telephone pole."

Frank Sinatra, who had not learned about Steve's affair with Ava, ran into him at the Los Angeles airport. He later told Peter Lawford and Sammy Davis Jr. that, "Steve didn't even know where he was going. He didn't have a ticket, and I could see he was freaked out on cocaine or something. I told him I'd buy a ticket for him if he'd tell me where he wanted to go. He looked at me with vacant eyes, 'Where does anyone want to go?' he said to me. 'To hell—that's where all of us are going sooner than later.'"

"I decided to get him a ticket to San Francisco and to see that he got on the plane," Sinatra said. "I slipped a stewardess a hundred dollar bill to see that he was taken care of. I'd heard about the film he'd shot up in San Francisco. When I asked him about it, Steve couldn't even remember the name of the fucking movie."

Steve's old friend, Peter Lawford, encountered him at a West Hollywood bistro. "At first I didn't recognize him," Peter said, "when he came to join me at table. His look was completely different. He was stoned. As we chatted, I came to believe that Steve had gone stark raving bonkers. But the pot can't call the kettle black. So was I at the time. Nobody was getting through an entire day without being stoned. Steve told me that one-on-one sex was passé. Orgies were the way to go."

Stan Kamen, who had done so much to promote Steve's career, said, "With success, Steve's ego became so inflated that I feared for his downfall. After fabulous success in Hollywood, a fall from grace is always inevitable. Steve's mistake was in thinking his good luck would go on forever."

"More and more when he called me in the middle of the night, I was talking to Mr. Ego," Kamen said. "His psychosis was showing. Knowing I would forgive him for any of his shit, he always ended our phone chats, some of which lasted two hours, with a 'fuck you, cocksucker.' Lovely boy. I didn't want to deflate his ego, but I've sucked bigger dicks than his, notably Rock Hudson's."

Sometimes, instead of attending an orgy, Steve openly dated just one woman at a time at rather public places like the Whiskey à Go-Go.

Steve stunned patrons of the Polo Lounge when he showed up in Beverly Hills with top model Lauren Hutton, known for her ads for Revlon cosmetics.

Long before readers of *Playboy* were treated to her charms, Steve got a sneak preview.

One night he made a head-turning scandal when he appeared with Lauren Hutton in the Polo Lounge.

Thirteen years younger than Steve, Lauren was a top fashion model for the Ford Agency and Revlon cosmetics. As such, she was the first model to negotiate a major cosmetics deal, and thanks partly to her measurements of 33-23-34, she also became a *Playboy* bunny. In time she would be ranked number thirteen on Chanel 5s "World's Greatest Supermodels" list.

At the time Steve dated her, she had just finished playing the only major female role in *Paper Lion* (1968), starring Alan Alda.

Steve told friends that Lauren reminded him of his Myrtle Beach flame of yesteryear, Suellen. Both women were natives of South Carolina.

Allegedly, Steve sparked Lauren's interest in motorcycle riding, which would cause her to make headlines at the age of 55 when she was involved in a serious motorcycle accident while on a 100-mile ride near Las Vegas with Dennis Hopper and Jeremy Irons.

It is not known if Steve implanted his homophobic views onto Lauren, but she did raise the ire of the gay community when in 2000 she attacked gay writers for stereotyping single women as sluts on *Sex & the City*. "It's written by guys who happen to be gay, who are sluts," Lauren charged. "That's what I think. Let's face it, most men are sluts. That's what testosterone is supposed to do. You have a bunch of guys who are sluts, writing for women and telling them they are supposed to act like this." After the uproar, Lauren denied she was a homophobe.

Of course, all of Steve's drug abuse and public philandering had impacted his marriage. "My life was being thrown into disorder," Neile said. "I was feeling disconnected from the man I had married. At times it felt as though I were living with a stranger."

When the McQueens purchased a larger and more secure vacation home in Palm Springs, Steve asked that it be "my pad," and that it be decorated in a masculine style.

The end of the relationship was near.

***

Without forewarning, Steve's long-term relationship with Sharon Tate and Jay Sebring ended abruptly and tragically. In a communal desert compound in Death Valley, a "dirtbag psycho" named Charles Manson was plotting a mass murder.

After Sharon married the director, Roman Polanski, the budding star's friendship continued with Sebring and Steve. Both men were frequent visitors at the sprawling French provincial-style house at 10050 Cielo Drive, in Benedict Canyon, Los Angeles, that Polanski and Sharon had rented.

Before Sharon moved in with her husband, the house had been inhabited by such luminaries as Cary Grant and Henry Fonda. Its most recent inhabitants had been Candice Bergen and her lover, Terry Melcher, son of Doris Day, and an influential force in the music industry.

After submitting the music he'd composed and recorded to Melcher, in the hopes that he would make him a star, Manson, who envisioned himself as the next Bob Dylan, had sat by his phone for days waiting for a call. No such call was ever made. When Manson tried to reach Doris Day's son by phone, Melcher was "not available." Manson plotted his revenge.

It was later revealed that Steve's name was also at the top of the list of Charles Manson's death targets. Three months prior to his disappointment by Melcher, Manson, who also fancied himself as a screen writer, had sent a script to Solar Productions. After weeks went by, and he hadn't heard from Steve, he confronted him one morning in front of the Solar offices as Steve was getting out of his car.

When Steve refused to speak to him, Manson shoved him against his vehicle. Reacting to that, Steve plowed his fist into Manson's face, bloodying his nose.

Back at his dusty commune, surrounded by his disciples, Manson informed his followers that he wanted to kill both Steve and Terry Melcher.

On the night of the Manson-orchestrated murders, Steve was scheduled to visit Sharon Tate at her new (rented) home on Cielo Drive with the understanding that Jay Sebring would also be there. But before heading there, en

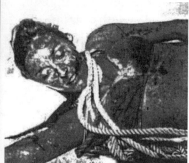

The beautiful actress **Sharon Tate** (left and right photos) was near term with her child, fathered by Roman Polanski, when goons directed from afar by **Charles Manson** (center photo) broke into her house, murdering not only Sharon but friends of hers who included Jay Sebring.

Steve was on his way to that doomed party until he was lured away by a spontaneous pickup. His adultery saved his life, or else he, too, would have been one of the murder victims.

route to a bachelor pad he'd rented close to the CBS Studios in West Hollywood, he was mugged. He turned over his money to the muggers. When the muggers took off, he followed them in his car. Catching up to them, he threatened them with a gun, demanding "my bread back—and *now*." The muggers returned his money and fled.

To cool off, he stopped in for a beer at Sif's Tavern on Third Street, where he met an actress, reportedly Maria Douce. After two or three Old Milwaukees, he invited her to his bachelor pad. That invitation saved his life. He never showed up at the party at Sharon's house and didn't call either. Likewise, Roman Polanski was out of town on the night of the fateful party.

Around eight o'clock on the morning of August 9, 1969, the Polanski maid, Winifred Chapman, arrived at the Polanski house on Cielo Drive.

She discovered the lifeless and grotesquely mutilated bodies of Jay Sebring and Sharon Tate, as well as Abigail Folger, the coffee heiress, and her boyfriend, Wojiciech (Voytek) Frykowski.

The body of another victim, Steven Parent, was discovered outside the house. Shortly after his car had pulled into the driveway the previous night, the Manson killers had fatally shot him.

After learning about the murders, Steve called Darron and Casey, asking them to come to his house. When they got there, he gave them the keys to Sebring's home and told them to go there at once and "clean house"—that is, remove any illegal drugs. He feared many packets of cocaine or other paraphernalia had his fingerprints on them. Two hours later, when the police arrived to search Sebring's house for clues, all the drugs had been removed and delivered to Steve.

Because he was so closely linked to Sharon and Sebring, Steve feared being affected by the public fallout from the Manson murders. But in the ensuing aftermath, his nocturnal activities and drug abuse escaped any direct police scrutiny.

The official report on Sebring, however, declared that, "he was considered a ladies' man and took numerous women to his residence in the Hollywood Hills. He would tie the women up with a small sash cord and, if they agreed, would whip them, after which they would have sexual relations." The official reports did not mention that Steve had been a visitor at many of these kinky S&M orgies.

Steve told Casey and Darron something he never told the police, fearing an entanglement he didn't want. "He was very worried that news of his involvement in the life of Sebring and that Tate woman would become public, because reporters were crawling all over the place," Casey said. "The three of them had been seen many places together. Dozens of people had observed Steve disappearing into various bedrooms with Tate and Sebring."

At the time of her brutal murder, Sharon was pregnant. Steve believed that the child might be his, or possibly Sebring's. "Publicity like that I don't need," he told his trusted friends.

On August 9, 1969, less than 24 hours after the murders at the Tate/Polanski household, Manson's goons broke into the Los Angeles home of Leno LaBianca, a rich supermarket owner, and murdered him and his wife, Rosemary.

Darron said that Steve told them that two nights later, he received a sinister telephone call from an unknown male who predicted, "You're next," before hanging up. "From that day forth, Steve never went out without a gun, and he had security measures at his home beefed up."

Writer Dominick Dunne later recalled the tension that swept over Hollywood in the wake of the Manson clan's murders. "The shock waves that went through the town were beyond anything I had ever seen before. People were convinced that the rich and famous of the community were in peril. Children were sent out of town. Guards were hired. Steve McQueen packed a gun when he went to Jay Sebring's funeral."

Steve was not the only celebrity who reacted fearfully. Frank Sinatra went into hiding, and Mia Farrow, Sharon Tate's friend, was too afraid to attend her funeral. Jerry Lewis installed an elaborate alarm system around his property with closed circuit TV. Connie Stevens converted her Beverly Hills home "into a veritable fortress."

"Friendships ended, romances broke up, people were abruptly dropped from guest lists, parties canceled—for with the fear came suspicion. The killer or killers could be almost anyone," or so claimed Vincent Bugliosi, prosecutor at the Tate-LaBianca trials.

Heavily armed, Steve attended Sebring's funeral. Neile sat next to Warren Beatty. At one point an unknown, uninvited mourner rose to his feet and threw himself on Sebring's coffin, crying out and sobbing hysterically. Steve immediately jumped to his feet, his pistol pointed directly at the head of the mourner. Security guards rushed to have the intruder removed from the funeral.

Also present at the Wee Kirk O' the Heather Chapel at Forest Lawn were Paul Newman, Henry Fonda, and George Hamilton, each of them former Sebring clients.

Steve, along with 150 other mourners, also attended Sharon's last rites at the Holy Cross Cemetery. Celebrities included Roman Polanski, who broke down several times during the ceremony, Yul Brynner, James Coburn, Lee Marvin, Peter Sellers, and Warren Beatty.

Later it was discovered that it had been Susan Atkins, a member of Charles Manson's "family," who had murdered Sharon and her unborn baby. She named as her accomplices Charles (Tex) Watson, Patricia Krenwinkel, and Linda Kasabian. Atkins also implicated Charles Manson, the ghoulish but charismatic patriarch of the gang, as the orchestrator of the plot.

By the time it was discovered that Atkins had played a significant role in the Tate murders, Atkins had already been arrested and sent to prison for her involvement in an earlier murder, the torture and killing of Gary Hinman on July 25, 1969. Manson claimed that Hinman owed him money and had dispatched Atkins and other followers to torture and kill Hinman two weeks before the Tate-LaBianca slaughter.

While in prison, Atkins confessed to her cellmate, Virginia Graham, that she had personally killed Sharon Tate, and that she was one of Charles Manson's groupies. Not only did she confess that, but Atkins told Graham about how—in addition to Sebring, Tate, and the LaBiancas—the Manson gang planned to dispose of other high-profile victims.

One of these plots involved a conspiracy to mutilate and murder Elizabeth Taylor and Richard Burton. After tying them up, according to the carefully choreographed plan, Atkins was going to heat a knife red hot and ruin Taylor's beautiful face. She was then going to carve the words "helter-skelter" on her forehead before gouging out her eyes. Manson, according to Atkins, had taught her how to do that.

Then she was going to castrate Burton, placing his penis and Taylor's eyes in a bottle. "And then I was gonna mail the bottle to Eddie Fisher."

Another of her intended victims was Tom Jones. At knife point, she was going to force him to have sex with her. "Just as he is climaxing, I'll slit his throat." What she didn't describe was how she was going to get the singer, under those circumstances, to produce an erection.

For Frank Sinatra, she had planned an even more horrible death. After kidnapping him, they would strip him and hang him nude from a rafter where the Manson gang would play an album of his as they skinned him alive. With Sinatra's skin, they planned to make purses and sell them at high prices at hippie shops "so everyone would have a little piece of Frank."

For Steve, Atkins claimed the Manson gang was planning an excruciatingly horrible death "because the son of a bitch had rejected Charlie's screen play."

It is mind boggling to contemplate a more horrible death than that of Sinatra. However, a police warden interrupted Atkins and Graham before she could relate the contemplated details of Steve's ghastly death.

It wasn't Atkins, but another member of the Manson gang who leaked the details of how they planned to kill Steve. Gang members would strip him, secure him, and then literally eat flesh from his body until he died, while making an attempt to keep him alive as long as possible while "we enjoyed our meal of his flesh."

When she was free to do so, Graham reported Atkins' confession to prison authorities, who then arrested Manson and his gang.

According to Casey, when Steve was informed of the fate that might have been in store for him, "he went into a state of shock. He was stoned for days and wouldn't eat."

"You guys are always playing that song from *Hair*, about the dawning of the Age of Aquarius," Steve told Casey and Darron. "Well, my friends, the age has dawned and died with the murders of Sharon and Jay."

***

In the wake of the Manson-ordered murders, Steve "went sort of wild," Casey claimed. "I'd never known him so self-destructive. He was certain that something would happen to him in the near future that would cut short his own life. That made him more and more determined to crowd more adventure into his life. He became reckless. 'You've got to live for today,' he told us. 'What if you don't have a tomorrow?'"

"One night Steve drove us out into the desert where we camped for the night," Darron said. "He made us strip down and told us we were going to sit here and smoke dope until the sun 'rolled its lazy ass from the New York islands to the Pacific coast,' his words. He brought Navajo blankets for us to ward off the desert cold."

"That night in our tent he fucked both of us and made it hurt real bad," Darron claimed. "He said it was an old Navajo custom. The young braves had to submit to the chief to show their loyalty. He bit both of our lips and told us we had to endure the pain and the blood to show our complete submission to him. 'Remember this, guys,' he told us, 'in the future you don't even go take a piss without asking my permission. I'm the boss. I'm in complete control. If you ever forget that, I'll kill you.' I thought he meant it, and I was scared. But then we decided that Steve had taken too much acid."

"Increasingly Steve talked about bubble asses," Casey claimed. "He told us that he was getting off fucking asses these days more than entering through the front door. He said that Jane Fonda's ass was his dream ass."

"One wild night, he plotted we'd kidnap the Fonda bitch, take her to the desert, strip her down, and fuck her ass for hours until she was bleeding profusely," Casey said. "That was one wild fantasy. One night all three of us sat around the campfire jerking off just thinking of all the things we would do to Fonda when we kidnapped the slut and turned her into our sex toy."

"All women are whores," Steve told Casey and Darron. "They were put on this world just to be used by man. Abusing them is part of the fun. The bitches love it. Jay Sebring has taught me one thing, and that is a woman likes

314

to get the shit beat out of her before she's fucked. Remember that."

"Steve was always testing our loyalties," Casey said. "One night he told us that to prove our love, he was going to shit in each of our mouths and make us eat it. It took a lot of drugs before each of us agreed to do it. I thought it was the most disgusting thing I'd ever heard."

"He brought two bottles of Tequila which he claimed we could use to clean out our mouths," Casey said. "At one point I vomited, just thinking what I was going to have to do. Darron was crying like a baby. Still, we were prepared to do this disgusting act. Fortunately, we didn't have to. He told us he was just joking. He wanted to test our loyalties, and we passed the test. 'We're blood brothers to the end,' he told us. He then took a pocket knife and cut our wrists. We blended our blood with his."

The casualness with which Steve approached sexual encounters became legendary. As related by writer Christoher Sandford, one acquaintance Steve met at a disco said, "I'd sit in a chair sometimes and talk to Steve while he was giving it to some snatch. I'd watch TV and sit in that chair, because he wanted somebody to talk to. Two, three women at a time. He'd be fucking one, rubbing up another, and we'd be calmly laughing and chatting to each other."

Even his own daughter, Terry, admitted that her father "hated" all women except herself. As always he remained a loving father to both his son, Chad, and his "little girl," who wasn't so little any more. His children were growing up before his eyes, which at times caused Steve to go into panic.

Although Steve and **Jane Fonda** (left photo) knew a lot about each other, they apparently never "connected." He told his friends that Fonda had "one of the great asses of Hollywood--and I'm an ass man myself." Plans Steve made with his friends to kidnap Fonda for immoral purposes never evolved into anything more serious than a drug-induced fantasy.
Steve wasn't alone in fantasizing about Fonda. The right-hand photo shows how a cartoon version of Fonda's famous *derriere* was emphasized in the marketing of the Italian release of one of her films.

"The idea that his children would grow up one day and make him a grandfather was more than he could take," Casey said. "'Come that day, I'll be old,' he said. 'With gray hair. I think I'll kill myself before I grow old,' he told us."

Many biographers have noted Steve's fondness for group sex and how he liked to share a woman, or several women, with his male buddies. Writer Penina Spiegel quoted one of Steve's intimates, saying, "He liked showing off his body and his peepee. The first guy to take his shirt off was Steve, the first to drop his pants was Steve."

Spiegel reports one particularly graphic description from one of Steve's biker buddies: "I've been in a room with McQueen, three or four guys, one chick. One guy had it up her cunt, she was jacking two guys off, sucking another guy off. One guy was jacking off on her. She loved it. Steve and I had some good times together . . . two, three girls at a time. He was screwing some broad from behind, she was sucking my cock, and we were looking and talking to each other. She was just a piece of ass, that's all."

More and more of Steve's friends reported his growing interest in "poop shooting," as one of his intimates called it—that is, sodomizing women who often weren't partners in love, but victims.

As the months went by, Steve grew increasingly obsessive about all the rumors circulating through Hollywood that he was a homosexual. "The more he heard shit talk like that, the more he wanted to prove the gossips had got it all wrong," Darron said. "He was a man for the ladies, and he proved that almost every night by serial seductions of whores he picked up."

"On some nights, though, he'd be tired," Casey said. "He often picked up girls, tossed them in the back seat of his car, but kicked them out before we brought them to a motel. On a few nights, he just wanted to spend the evening talking to us, because Steve knew he didn't have to prove anything with his good buddies."

"Steve was very virile," Casey said. "He didn't go into all that girly boy shit. Hollywood, in case you didn't know, is filled with fags. When we weren't with Steve, a lot of queers tried to pick us up. We pretended to go along with it. But we'd get a queer somewhere alone and beat the shit out of him. Steve told us he did the same thing when he was in the Marine Corps."

According to Sammy Davis Jr., one night at Whiskey à Go-Go, Frank Sinatra impishly asked Steve if he'd ever had a gay experience.

"Stevie went ballistic," Sammy said. "He and Frankie never spoke to each other for two years after that night. Peter Lawford and I had to restrain Steve. He was actually going to pick a fight with Sinatra. That Steve McQueen had his hang-ups. You know what I think? I think the lady doth protest too much. Even Frankie's had his cock sucked a few times by guys. We all do that."

"If he was a queer, he'd be begging for us to plug him," Darron said. "He

316

never did that. So, he got off watching us plug a chick. A lot of guys get off doing that. Haven't you heard that porno is a big business? He never let us use a rubber. Just as we were about to explode inside a woman, he'd yank us off the bitch and let us shoot in his mouth. That way, we didn't make the gal pregnant and we got to shoot our wad in a warm mouth. It was great! We did the same for him when he'd plow a woman. He told us that's what asshole buddies do for each other, and he was right. I loved having sex that way with him helping us. It was much more fun when all of us had sex together."

Casey also claimed more or less the same experiences with Steve. "He'd like to bring a chick to our mobile home to share her with us. He'd jerk us until we were hard, then insert our dicks into the bitch of the night. While we screwed the whore, he would fondle our balls. Not to get off on doing that. That's a stupid idea. He was just trying to make us blast off faster so he could mount the chick himself. He wouldn't let us use rubbers. He'd have us pull out and squirt into his mouth just at the moment of blast-off. Do you think he did that because he liked it? Hell, no! He was being a good buddy. That's not what I call queer. After all, we had a chick in the bed with us."

When some of his biker friends made jokes about homosexuals, Steve never joined in the mocking laughter. "Cut the shit, guys," Steve told three of his biker friends one night. "Can't you guys talk about pussy. Why do you have to talk about faggots all the time? The way I see it, you guys must have an obsession with them."

These attacks on his friends were hardly a defense of homosexuals. "He loathed gays so much he couldn't even stand for them to be mentioned," Darron said.

"Steve hated queers more than he hated anything else on Earth," Darron claimed. "He despised the bastards, and thought they were the scum of the earth. He told us one night in the desert that his greatest thrill would be to take a bomb and toss it into a disco where dozens of guys were dancing together. Could you just imagine the sound that three hundred screaming queens would make as they were blasted off the face of the Earth?"

None of his closest pals seemed to equate his interest in watching his buddies have sex and getting turned on by seeing their erect cocks in action as being homosexually inclined.

His close friend, Elmer Valentine, claimed, "When people say Steve was homosexual—he absolutely was not. Absolutely. I personally know there were times Steve and I fucked in the same room." Valentine's quote appeared in Spiegel's book. "Steve and I fucked in the same room with different girls. He liked to switch girls, but there was never a sign of homosexuality. I'm an ex-cop. I know when someone's homo."

"Even if Steve *were* gay, he wouldn't have let himself be," Valentine told

317

Spiegel. "He was such a macho bastard that if he *had* that tendency, he wouldn't have done it."

"After Steve's death, a lot of people, especially those publishers we talked to in New York, said Steve's relationship with us was homosexual," Casey said. "That's pure bullshit. Steve always made a difference between asshole buddies who helped each other get off, and queers who sought out other men to fuck them. As any fool can see, private stuff going on between straight buddies and what queers do are two God damn different things."

***

In 1969, nearing the end of his marriage, and before he went off to shoot his next film, Steve asked Neile to join him on a vacation in Europe. He had accepted an invitation to visit the beautiful actress, Claudia Cardinale, and her producer husband, Franco Cristaldi, in Rome. Steve and Neile had met the married couple at the 1964 presentation of the Oscars.

In Rome, he discovered that Cardinale lived in one villa, Cristaldi in another about a mile and a half away. Steve suggested that this living arrangement might be the clue to a happy marriage.

Even though living apart from his wife, Cristaldi was highly protective of his "possession." Steve and Neile were forbidden to even take her to lunch alone.

Steve learned that she'd been born to Sicilian parents in Tunisia, and that she didn't learn to speak formal "mainstream" Italian until she began pursuing a film career in Italy when she was sixteen.

Invited to dinner at her farmhouse-style retreat, she served Steve and Neile her favorite meal. She personally made the dry martinis before dinner, and her maid served caviar for hors d'oeuvres. Steve never liked "these fish eggs." That was followed with a small lobster and a steak alla Florentine, which she served with a rich, Tuscan red wine.

Long hailed as one of the world's great beauties, Cardinale sexually aroused Steve. There were rumors of a "Love in the Afternoon" tryst, and Steve himself claimed he had a brief fling with the star. However, this might have been his fantasy. There is no evidence that he was sexually involved with her at all.

Cardinale and Steve agreed on one aspect of movie making—"no nudity" for them in any of their films. "I'll never reveal my body in a film," she told Steve. "Mystery is important."

"I'll never show my pecker either," Steve said.

"What is a pecker?" Cardinale asked.

"I'll show you sometime," Steve shot back.

***

After a visit with the movie queen and her jealous husband, Steve and Neile flew to London, where they were entertained by Steve's former co-star, Richard Attenborough.

While Neile was out shopping, Steve slipped around London to call on his aging flame, Ava Gardner.

Steve found Ava living in a luxury flat on Park Lane with her pet Corgi, Cara, who immediately pissed on the leg of Steve's blue jeans. The once sultry movie star welcomed him with a long, lingering kiss.

Virtually retired from motion pictures, her days as the reigning beauty of the screen were now a memory. She still looked gorgeous and well preserved, but years of late nights and drinking had put their mark on her once-lustrous skin.

"I have given up the bullfights in Spain for tennis tournaments," she told Steve. "Sinatra and I are no longer tabloid fodder. That hellish relation I had with George Scott visits me only in a nightmare."

"You mean there are no more men in your life?" he asked her, "except me, of course."

"There is an occasional man," she said. "I don't think I can go cold turkey on men." Cuddling her bare feet under her legs, she looked impish. "And an occasional woman."

He seemed surprised. "I thought that was just Hollywood gossip."

"Afraid not, sugartit," she said "Most of the men escorting me to the ballet or theater are homosexuals," she said.

"I have no use for those kind of guys," he said. "They turn me off."

"You're too young yet," she said. "As you get older and it gets more difficult for you to get erect, you'll find there's nothing like a pretty boy cocksucker to make you rise to the occasion. Peter Lawford swears that's true."

"Let's change the subject," he said. "I don't have all afternoon. I'm here with my ol' lady. Why don't we retreat to the bedroom?"

"I thought you'd never ask," she said, rising from the sofa.

Born of Sicilian parents in Tunisia, sultry beauty **Claudia Cardinale** briefly lit up the screen. Meeting Claudia and her husband at the 1964 Oscar ceremonies, Steve accepted an invitation to visit the famous pair in Rome. At her farmhouse retreat on the outskirts of the city, she served him caviar, but he didn't care for "fish eggs." That afternoon, he had to explain to the actress what a "pecker" was.

319

After making love to her, he was attracted to his own image in the full-length mirror that stood near the door to the bathroom. He surveyed his body, as he so often did. "I'm getting on in years," he said, turning to look back at her, her body covered with a sheet. "I ran into Tennessee Williams the other night. He's in London with some young, cute guy. He said time is our enemy, an enemy we can never escape."

"Oh, darling," she said. "I've already faced the enemy of time. Every morning I stare into that mirror, I confront time. It's a little different for me. You weren't called the most beautiful woman in the world. You don't have to see the ravages of beauty reflected in the most minute detail as your face is blown up looking like a horse's ass up there on that unforgiving screen, all in glorious color showing every imperfection."

Later, when both of them had showered and Steve had dressed, she joined him the living room for more champagne. She was wearing only a robe.

"After all those bullfighters you had in Spain, I was afraid they'd be a tough act to follow," he told her.

"Don't let that bother you," she said. "Ernest Hemingway told me most of them pad their suits of light."

"Glad to hear that," he said.

After finishing off the bottle of champagne with him, she opened her robe. "Mickey Rooney always praised my big brown nipples. He said when aroused they stood out like some double-long, golden California raisins."

"They still do, baby cakes," he said, moving toward her.

***

While he was in London, a personal note was delivered to Steve. He tore it open to read: REMEMBER ME? CALL ME.

It was signed Gia Scala.

At the bottom she listed her phone number. He rang her up late that night. Of course, he remembered her. Between 1952 and 1954, during his early years in New York, he'd had an on-again, off-again affair with her.

Tall, dazzling, green-eyed, and a beautiful brunette, Gia Scala had been born in

Fresh out of the Marine Corps, Steve had fallen in love with the tragic actress **Gia Scala**. He even asked her to marry him. She turned him down, but years later, in London, she told him that she'd decided to accept his proposal. It was too late: he'd moved on. But before he dumped her forever, he bluntly asked Gia, "Am I better in bed than Brando?"

320

Liverpool to an aristocratic Sicilian father and an Irish mother. She grew up in Messina, on the eastern coast of Sicily. At the age of fourteen, she migrated to New York, where she attended Bayside High School in Queens, graduating in 1952.

While studying acting with Stella Adler, she'd met the ex-Marine, Steve himself, and he'd fallen in love with her. At one point, he even asked her to marry him, but she turned him down. That made him bitter and crushed his ego, but the affair continued, although in the years ahead he'd go for months without seeing her.

She was first discovered as a professional "quiz kid" on *The Arlene Francis Show*, which led to a contract with Universal International. Newspapers hailed her as "the next Ava Gardner."

During the making of *The Big Boodle* (1957), she claimed that Errol Flynn raped her, though she didn't press charges. She was seen around town dating the handsome actor, George Nader, but later learned that he was a homosexual involved in an affair with, among others, Rock Hudson.

Gia had dropped from Steve's radar screen until he heard that Marlon Brando was dating her, even though at the time he was married to Anna Kashfi. That piece of news aroused Steve's interest in Gia once again.

In Hollywood, Steve called Gia and, in secret, began to date her, even though she had married actor Don Burnett in 1959. As a newlywed, she didn't feel compromised by her simultaneous relationships with Steve and Brando. As a means of massaging his ego, she told Steve that despite earlier affairs with Glenn Ford, Robert Mitchum, and Richard Widmark, "you're the best."

Always threatened by a woman of his being involved with another man, Steve pressed her for details about her previous relationships. And because he viewed Ford, Mitchum, and Widmark as "granddaddies of yesterday," his main interest focused on Brando. One night he bluntly demanded of Gia, "Am I better in bed than Brando?"

She assured him that he was, and he felt proud of that, repeating her assessment and boasting about it to his friends.

Somehow Brando discovered that Steve was once again dating Gia. He called Steve one night to talk about Gia. By that time, Steve had already grown disenchanted with Gia because of her excessive drinking. Expecting to encounter a jealous former friend, Steve was astonished at Brando's frankness. "You can have her. I wish you'd take her off my hands." Referring to his wife at the time, Anna Kashfi, Brando went on to say, "She's bonding too closely with Anna."

"Now that the two of you have hooked up again, it's time for me to leave," Brando told Steve. "Her husband should be doing his duty so the poor girl doesn't have to run outside the house to get fucked. Tonight I'm going to tell Gia it's all off between us."

"Oh, pal, old buddy," Steve said. "Frankly, I want you to take her off my hands. She drinks like a fish. I don't like my broads to drink, not even a glass of wine. I'm dropping her, but I'm afraid that if I do, she'll threaten to kill herself once again."

In 1958, in the wake of the death of her mother, Eileen Sullivan, Gia had attempted suicide.

"Every person on this earth should have the right to kill himself," Brando said. "If Gia wants to go, let her. Don't stand in her way. I don't want her, and I'm telling her so."

Sometime between the late 1950s and the early 60s, both Brando and Steve had cut off their relationships with Gia. That, along with a medley of other disillusionments and disappointments that included the deterioration of her marriage, proved too much for her delicate nerves. She made another attempt at suicide by slashing her wrists, but was rescued in time.

In 1969, encountering her in London, Steve was shocked at her appearance. Years of massive alcoholic consumption had taken a toll on her fresh-faced beauty. Her career was also on the skids, as was her marriage to Don Burnett.

"Don is leaving me and wants a divorce," she said. "I know now that I was wrong to turn down your offer of marriage. I've thought it over night after night, and I want to marry you after all. I'm divorcing Don, and you can divorce Neile."

"No way," he said. "I love my wife and kids. Besides, my offer of marriage was made back in 1954. My world is very different now."

She was bitterly disappointed at the rejection. Her deep-rooted insecurities were more obvious than ever, and she seemed to be suffering from severe emotional problems. No temple of mental health himself, he suggested that she "go to a shrink," but she adamantly refused.

She cried and threatened suicide, but he refused to give in to her wishes. He did promise to send her a check for $10,000, a promise he kept through his business manager.

She begged Steve to take her back. He would later tell friends, "In London, I had the real Ava Gardner. I didn't need what the press called 'the second Ava.'"

It was raining in London when he told her good-bye. She clung to him and begged him to divorce Neile and marry her.

"My wife and family mean too much to me," he said.

"All my life I regretted not marrying you," she told him, kissing him on the lips. "I dream of you every night. Every girl has a man who got away. For me, you're that man." She was crying when she left him to walk alone in the rain, having refused his offer to get her a taxi.

It was a scene straight from a tear jerker movie.

When film roles dried up in England, she returned to California, hoping to jump-start her career. Steve was surprised that in the spring of 1971, Anna Kashfi took custody of Gia, her husband's former mistress. One can only speculate about why Kashfi put aside her jealousy and befriended Gia. At least the two women had lots of material for dialogue—Brando himself.

But Kashfi's love and support couldn't piece Gia together again. On the night of April 30, 1972, a friend found her dead in her home in the Hollywood Hills. An overdose of liquor and drugs was blamed for her death at the age of thirty-eight.

Scenes from *The Reivers* (1969), based on the writings of William Faulkner. Upper left: **Steve** is shown with the African-American actor **Rupert Crosse,** who plays Steve's sidekick in the movie. The real "star" of the film was a lemon-colored replica of a 1905 **Winton Flyer,** one of the world's first automobiles. Shown in the photo on the upper right, it was specially built for the movie, and ended up in Steve's private collection.

In the lower photo, **Steve,** with child actor **Mitch Vogel,** is on his way to his favorite whore house, where the kid begins to learn some of the facts of life.

Steve seemed rather callous in his reaction to her death. He called Brando, saying, "Getting a woman for guys like us is about the easiest thing in the world," Steve said. "Getting rid of them is something else again."

Before leaving London, Steve held a press conference. He startled reporters by claiming, "I've got a feeling I'm leaving stardom behind and becoming more of a filmmaker than an actor. After all, I'm no matinee idol, and I'm getting older." He was nearing birthday number forty.

When asked about his sex appeal, Steve demurred. "People say I have this sexy thing for the girls. I'm not aware of it."

As always he avoided political questions. "Politicians are drowning in their own spit," was his only comment.

***

As King of the Box Office, Steve had his choice of film scripts, and he turned down offers to appear in such ultimately successful pictures as *The Wild Bunch* and *Ryan's Daughter*. He would later regret not campaigning for *Easy Rider* (1969), the tale of two cyclists chucking it all to discover the real America. The movie brought glory to Peter Fonda and Dennis Hopper.

Steve was offered, and accepted, a lead role in *The Reivers,* a poignant turn-of-the-20th-century coming of age story based on William Faulkner's last novel—one for which he'd won a Pulitzer Prize. Foolishly, Steve agreed to be directed by Mark Rydell, a former actor from whom he'd stolen Neile way back in 1955. The project's credentials were pristine, and even the pay was good, including a $700,000 payment for Steve up front. *The Reivers* would represent Steve's final attempt to do comedy. At this late point in his screen career, he had at last learned what not to do onscreen in attempts to be funny.

Making *The Reivers* was not a happy venture for either Steve or Rydell. "He was hard and he could be mean, and he did have my back to the wall sometimes," Rydell said. "He wanted to feel that nothing could happen without him. He was an entirely instinctive actor. He never learned his lines and after one, or at the most, two takes, he wasn't any good."

At first, both Rydell and Steve had high hopes for the film. The script had been written by topnotch screenwriters, the husband-and-wife team of Irving Ravetch and Harriet Frank Jr., both Faulkner specialists. Previously, they had adapted Faulkner's *The Long, Hot Summer* for Paul Newman and Joanne Woodward, and had also won an Oscar for best screenplay for *Hud*, also starring Newman, Steve's eternal rival. But to virtually everyone on the set, it soon became obvious that the movie's plot was being too greatly altered from Faulkner's original.

The Reivers was released on Christmas Day of 1969. Fortunately for the original author of the novel, Faulkner, who died in 1962, never lived to see his Pulitzer Prize-winning novel bastardized on the screen. Faulkner had set his story in the venerable old town of Jefferson in Yoknapatawpha County, Mississippi. The actual shooting occurred in Carrolltown, Mississippi, and also at the Walt Disney Ranch in California.

Faulkner had crafted the focus of his novel on its protagonist, 11-year-old Lucius, as played in the film by child actor Mitch Vogel. But during its tweaking and multiple rewrites, the script was configured so that the character of Boon Hogganbeck, as interpreted by Steve, became the star. Hogganbeck had originally been described by Faulkner as "tough, faithful, brave, completely unreliable, six feet four inches tall, two hundred and forty pounds with the mentality of a child." Steve didn't measure up to that description.

One of the film's most skilled performances was delivered by an actor who never appeared on screen. The veteran dramatic actor Burgess Meredith was hired for the off-camera narration.

The film also starred Will Greer, who would gain far greater fame years later when he played Grandpa Walton on the hit CBS-TV series *The Waltons*. Sharon Farrell was cast as Corrie, Boon's love interest who just happens to be a whore. In a role originally intended for Richard Pryor, Rupert Crosse played Ned McCaslin, Boon's sidekick.

Many critics thought the real star of the movie was a 1905 lemon colored Winton Flyer, one of the first automobiles. It was so highly prized by Steve that he acquired it and kept it for a while within his personal automobile collection.

The film's highlights included the yellow Winton Flyer getting caught in a mud trap, and eleven-year-old Lucius winning a horse race.

Emerging from a decaying old Mississippi house, Steve is first seen hastily buttoning up a feedsack shirt. He yanks a yellow rose off a bush as he rushes along. "He is pure country boy, with Mississippi mud between his toes," Rydell said. As filming progressed, however, Rydell became less and less impressed.

After the first week of shooting, Rydell realized that Steve "was Ham City. He played Boon too broadly, overacting throughout the film. His entrance, though, had a quality of lovable rambunctiousness."

Steve was holed up in the tiny town of Greenwood, Mississippi, in a run-down two-story motel where he was besieged day and night by Peeping Toms wanting to get a look at a genuine Hollywood movie star. To keep him company, Neile arrived two weeks later, accompanied by the actor and martial arts expert Bruce Lee.

It was Jay Sebring who had introduced Steve to Bruce Lee months before he became famous. Both Sebring and Steve had seen Lee's performance at the

Long Beach International Karate Championships, and Steve was particularly impressed. He too wanted to learn karate.

Between takes, Steve wanted to train with this Chinese American martial arts expert, a practitioner of Wing Chun and founder of the Jeet Kune Do concept. In time, he would be considered the most influential martial artist of the 20th century and a cultural icon.

Steve particularly admired Lee's body, which one doctor described as being, "as muscled as a squirrel and as spirited as a horse."

"I'll always remember my first lesson with Steve," Lee recalled. "He came before me and said, 'Baby, here I am.' The man was a fighter and very determined. If there was one thing he hated, it was to lose. The son-of-a-gun had more toughness in him than any of my other students."

During his training of Steve, Lee shared his philosophy with him. "Use only that which works and take it from any place you can find it."

During the early 1970s, Bruce Lee's hard-hitting action movies would elevate him to the status of an international star and a martial arts legend.

Defined by *Time Magazine* as one of the most influential people of the 20th century, he's revered as one of the major cultural icons of Asia.

When Lee became a movie star in Hong Kong, he was hailed as "The Steve McQueen of Asia." "I'm now bigger star than you are," Lee wrote Steve when his movies began to take off.

"It was payback time," Lee later said. "I had tried to get Steve's Solar Productions to produce my first movie. Steve turned me down. He said, 'I'm in the business of being a movie star, not making one.'"

In spite of their rivalry, Steve maintained his bond with Lee. When his friend died in the summer of 1973 at the age of 32, Steve was a pallbearer at his funeral. Steve was convinced that Lee's untimely death was the work of the "Oni" (Japanese for demons or evil spirits). It is not known who taught Steve about the Oni.

***

As filming progressed on *The Reivers*, Steve and Rydell clashed frequently.

Neile was kept awake at night by Steve's ongoing denunciations of "your old boy friend." At one point, when Steve saw the rough footage of the film, he demanded that Rydell be fired. But the director appealed to the backers of the movie, Cinema Center Films, and kept his job.

Rydell later claimed Steve was "going through his looney-bin period." Since he was "king," Steve took advantage of his position to dress down Rydell and his directorial judgment in front of cast and crew.

On one occasion, Steve shouted, "You're not directing a pack of lesbians here." He was no doubt referring to Rydell's last film, *The Fox*, a well-crafted tale of lesbian love.

Rydell and Steve had another clash over a beautiful girl (name unknown) who had been cast in the picture. When Rydell came on to the young actress, she flirted back. It was only later that the director learned that she'd been sleeping with Steve. "From that point on, I knew Steve would make my life hell. It was back to the mid-1950s and we were locking horns over a woman again."

Born in Sioux City, Iowa, and ten years younger than Steve, Sharon Farrell was married to John Boyer when she made *The Reivers*, and apparently she had no off-screen romance with Steve. "Another leading lady who got away," Rydell allegedly said. Obviously he knew of Steve's reputation for seducing his leading ladies.

Farrell had made her acting debut in the 1959 film, *Kiss Her Goodbye*. Today, she is known mainly by fans of the long-running TV soap opera, *The Young and the Restless*, on which she labored from 1991 until the millennium.

The Reivers was not a success, but did "respectable" business in some cities, most of it because of Steve's enormous box office clout.

Loyal Steve McQueen fans went to see the film, hoping to witness their hero in action again. By the thousands, fans were disappointed. The film never caught on with the general public, ending Steve's great run of luck at the box office.

Rupert Crosse received a nod as Best Supporting Actor by the Academy. Thousands in the African-American community were rooting for him to carry off the Oscar, but he lost to Gig Young for *They Shoot Horses, Don't They?* Steve was not nominated. "I'm not surprised," he said. "The Academy is run by a pack of fags."

Back on the West Coast, Steve couldn't sleep one night and stood on his private balcony overlooking the ravine from "The Castle" in Brentwood. He told friends the next day, "Two visions came to me last night, and I'm in deep shit."

Casey and Darron knew he'd taken acid the night before, so they attributed little importance to what he was saying.

"First, I think my short reign as the King of Hollywood is about to end," Steve said. "Second, this beautiful angel came to me. She told me I have only ten more years to live."

***

327

By February of 1970, Steve, mainly because of the success of *Bullitt*, released sixteen months previously, was at the pinnacle of success. He emerged as the Golden Globe World Film Favorite in a poll taken in more than forty countries. Despite the fact that he now demanded a fee of one million dollars per picture, he was flooded with scripts. "I'm turning them all down," he said, "and heading to France to make the greatest car-racing picture of all time." The film would ultimately be entitled *Le Mans*.

Before leaving the States, he wanted to indulge in some serious racing of his own, both on his motorcycle and in a sports car.

Neile had always feared that her husband would be killed "racing some contraption." Steve himself admitted that, "When you race bikes, you break bones." The same could have been said of the dangerous sport of car racing.

In a cycle race at Lake Elsinore, some 70 miles southeast of Los Angeles, his prediction came true. The course itself was not just rugged, but a disaster, with desert trails spread over a choppy terrain that included drainage ditches. At one point there was a steep 500-foot plunge into the town of Elsinore. Some 500 riders, both experienced and neophyte, competed in this one hundred mile race, facing obstacles which at one point included a 180-degree hairpin turn.

Having officially entered middle age, Steve took control of his Motocross Husky with its 405-cc engine. In his own words, he described his accident in the fourth lap. "I was coming out of a wash under a bridge with this road dip ahead, and I took one of those big jumps where you're sure you're going to make it but you don't. I didn't. My cycle nosed into the dip which was really deep. I went ass over the bars of my cycle into the spectators. They weren't hurt but I was. My left foot was busted in six different places."

In the hospital, he made a rash decision. The Sebring International 12-hour Endurance Race in Florida was coming up in only two weeks. He was going to enter, broken foot and all.

Steve showed up at Sebring with what he called "my Frankenstein boot" on his left foot.

With his broken foot, Steve competed in the twelve-hour race at Sebring, driving a Porsche 908 with professional driver Peter Revson. His fellow driver was a millionaire sportsman/racer.

It was the most painful race he'd ever run, and at one point his plaster cast melted. "The pain was messing up my concentration," Steve said. Even so, he didn't want to turn the wheels over to Revson until he'd endured as much racing as he possibly could.

Steve finished a close second behind Mario Andretti, who had vowed, "I will not be beaten by a God damn movie star."

The heir to the Revlon fortune, Revson later died in the flames of a fatal crash while participating in yet another race.

Back in California, as Steve prepared to fly to France, his obsession with reckless racing continued, along with his obsessive pursuit of women, which at this point was virtually dooming his marriage to Neile.

He told his friend, the writer William F. Nolan, that it was "kinda spooky the way women chase me. They bribe their way into your hotel room, hide naked under the bed. And they're not too subtle about letting you know what they want. Females can be very aggressive."

Once in Le Mans, while filming, he continued to address this point to a journalist from a London tabloid. "It's very hard to say no to women sometimes. Some are very beautiful, and I'm no saint. Marriage is really difficult when you're in the public eye."

"Just when McQueen thought he was King of the World, I had some bad news, crippling news, really," said William Haher, who was his new business manager. He'd just completed a review of Steve's finances. Driving to "The Castle" in Brentwood, he informed both Steve and Neile, "You guys are technically broke."

"Where in the fuck did all the money go?" Steve shouted, his paranoia bursting out in full force. "I want to get to the bottom of this. There will be jail time for the fuckers who screwed me over."

If anybody had been mismanaging Steve's money, it was the star himself. He'd been recklessly spending it and wasting it, not even setting aside enough to pay the Internal Revenue Service.

"I think McQueen thought it was a gravy train of perpetual motion," Haher said. "Spend like hell all the money you want today, because tomorrow that gravy train would arrive with a fresh supply of bucks."

Steve had been maintaining nearly forty-five employees, either as domestic servants or as professional associates. The grandeur of his lifestyle didn't match that of Louis XIV at

Steve (right) showed up at the races in Sebring, Florida, in a "Frankenstein boot" that protected his shattered left foot. Along with **Peter Revson** (left), he drove in his Porsche 908 in an endurance race that lasted twelve hours. The heir to the Revlon fortune, Revson would go up in fatal flames in a subsequent race.

Versailles, but it was a formidable payroll nonetheless.

"Steve thought the release of *Le Mans* would supply him with a lot of money," Darron said. "*Bullitt* was still a big hit, and he also thought he'd get rich off that movie, too, because the bucks were still rolling in from around the world."

While Solar Productions still gave the impression of being a hot property, it went public early in 1970. When 300,000 shares of the company's common stock went on the market, selling for nine dollars a share, *Variety* hailed Steve's decision as "gutsy."

The move netted Steve a million and a half dollars, with the company itself taking in about a million. The remainder of the money was earmarked for developing future film projects and other expenses. But despite the windfall, Steve and Solar still weren't flush with cash, as there were enormous bills to be paid. As soon as money appeared in Steve's personal account or the company's business account, it seemed to get spent.

Finally, in 1970, Steve's long-cherished dream came true. Cinema Center Films finally green-lighted the film *Le Mans*, promising Steve a budget of seven and a half million dollars, with warnings not to go over that.

Steve would be flying to Paris, with a promise to send Neile and his two kids by ship.

"When we told him good-by before he headed for France," Darron said, "he had high hopes for that racing picture. We knew he was frightened at the idea of running out of money, losing his home and all his cars. But the thing that got him was turning forty. He didn't want to grow old."

"Can you guys picture a gray-haired Steve McQueen?" he asked Casey and Darron. "Hell, ten years from now I'll be playing Paul Newman's father. Fuckwit has discovered the Fountain of Youth." Fuckwit was his nickname for Newman—his friend and constant rival.

Steve's parting words to his friends were, "I can't grow old . . . I just can't. I should follow the advice of James Dean. Live fast, die young, and leave a beautiful corpse."

***

When Steve landed in France, he was all set to begin filming *Le Mans*, but there was a problem. He didn't have a finished script. He'd hired his mentor, John Sturges, as his director. To this old pro, he said, "The script is in my head."

The director had handled such stars as Burt Lancaster, Kirk Douglas, Frank Sinatra, and Spencer Tracy. "We had scripts in those days," he told Steve. Almost from the beginning, Sturges feared that working with Steve this time around was going to produce a disaster for both of them. But at least in the beginning he kept his cool with the "King of Cool," who was anything but.

For his vehicle of choice, Steve selected a durable 917 Porsche. Priced at $75,000, it was the world's fastest sports car, able to sustain speeds of an astonishing 240 mph.

He'd wanted to enter the actual race at Le Mans, not a simulated one, but Cinema Center Films nixed the idea, fearing he might lose his life or be seriously injured. "What a blow that was to me," Steve later said. He was depressed for days and very hostile to the crew as they began their preparations for the filming of *Le Mans*.

His Porsche was allowed to take part, finishing a respectable ninth, despite the spoiled aerodynamics and frequent stops to change film rolls. The drivers assigned were Jonathan Williams and Herbert Linge, but, according to a persistent rumor, Steve slipped into the car and secretly became one of the drivers after all.

The Porsche 917 that Steve drove in the film would later pass through a series of owners before ending up in the possession of Jerry Seinfeld.

The film had the feel of a documentary, depicting an auto race in the '70s on the world's hardest endurance course: Le Mans in France. The competition goes on for some 24 hours on 14.5 kilometers of cordoned country road. Every few hours the two drivers per car alternate. The 1971 action film featured footage that had been shot during the actual 1970 race.

Steve's friend and rival, James Garner, actually beat him to the screen with the 1966 release of *Grand Prix*, directed by John Frankenheim and co-starring Eva Marie Saint. Unlike *Le Mans*, Garner's film focused on the per-

Jerry Seinfeld is the owner of this 917 Porsche, which Steve drove during the ill-fated film *Le Mans* (1971). The relentlessly boring film was an artistic and financial disaster, and was shot primarily as a means of indulging Steve's passion for auto racing. Throughout the film, Steve merely poses for the camera, never really acting his part, not that there was ever much plot to work with.

sonal lives of auto racers and their loves, and later won Oscars for editing and sound effects.

Steve was extremely jealous of Garner for "beating me to the punch." In a veiled reference to Garner's film, the French press dubbed Steve's *Le Mans* "*Petit Prix.*"

The plot, such as it is, focuses on Steve's main character, Michael Delaney, who has a strong rivalry with the Ferrari team driver, Erich Stahler, as played by Siegfried Rauch.

A German film and television actor, Rauch famously appeared in Hollywood war films in the 1970s, usually as a die-hard Nazi. Although rivals on film, Rauch and Steve became friends off-screen, and Rauch later named Steve as the godfather of his son Jakob.

For the female lead, if it could be called that, Steve wanted Diana Rigg, who had other commitments. A beautiful model, Maud Adams, later a Bond girl, was tested. She was far too tall for Steve, even if he wore lifts. He finally found a short, relatively unknown actress, Elga Anderson, and offered her the role, which she accepted.

Born in Germany, the slender blonde had appeared in several French films during the 1950s and 60s. She was also a singer, having recorded the title song for *The Guns of Navarone* in 1961.

"The first day I met McQueen, he invited me into his rather luxurious trailer," she said. "I thought he wanted to talk over the script, but he practically raped me. I wanted the part and I finally gave in to him. But I much prefer the love-making of Peter Gimbel." She was referring to an actor she later married.

While promoting *Le Mans* for Cinema Center Films, she'd met Gimbel while he was hawking another movie, *White Death*. They didn't marry until 1978, a union that would last until his death in 1987.

During an argument, as reported by Elga, the subject of Steve's sparse dialogue came up. "My God, man, it's a talking picture," Sturges said. "Sound has come to film. You're not Rudolph Valentino. You have to say something. Utter one, two, or even three words of dialogue. Say something, anything, even if it's not more than 'excuse me, I've got to take a shit.'"

"I don't need dialogue to convey my character," Steve told an exasperated Sturges before walking away.

When *Le Mans* was finally completed, it contained fewer than one hundred and fifty lines of dialogue.

Viewing the film on DVD today, patrons can expect almost no love story. They get racing, lots of it, and lots of the noise associated with it. In fact, the first thirty minutes of the film contain no dialogue at all, only the roaring sounds of cars.

Steve uttered the only memorable quote in the film: "A lot of people go through life doing things badly. Racing's important to men who do it well. When you're racing, it . . . it's life. Anything that happens before or after . . . is just waiting."

Sturges found Steve impossible, "a complete diva, a complete asshole." One afternoon Sturges announced to his staff that he was going home. His secretary thought he meant back to his temporary quarters. Instead the director journeyed to Paris where he flew back to Los Angeles. His final words were, "I'm too old and too rich to put up with McQueen's shit."

After Sturges' departure, the film floundered, expensively, for two full weeks. At the beginning of the third week, Cinema Center Films replaced Sturges with Lee H. Katzin.

When he arrived on the set to re-establish order, Katzin stuck out his hand, calling the star "Steve." Grabbing him by his necktie and choking him, Steve informed him, "It's Mr. McQueen to you, and don't you ever forget that!"

"Katzin was a complete candy-ass," a production assistant claimed. He did not want to be named. "He was basically a hack, more a quickie TV director than a movie helmer. He finished the picture with McQueen, but most of the time he went around licking the dingleberries off McQueen's crack."

As John Sturges had warned before departing, "There will be casualties. Steve is obsessive in pursuing realism, but realism can kill."

British driver Derek Bell suffered severe burns on his face and hands, and Porsche driver David Piper had to have his right leg amputated after a pile-up on the track.

"That could have been my fate," Steve said.

***

Before Neile arrived on the set with their children, Steve had a brief affair with the Swedish actress, Louise Edlind, who'd been cast as Mrs. Anna Ritter in *Le Mans*. A woman of elegance, education, and refinement, she became a member of the Swedish Parliament in 2003, losing her seat following the 2006 elections.

One night, Steve invited Edlind and his young assistant, Mario Iscovich, to "go for a spin" in the nearby countryside. Steve often

Elga Anderson was cast as the thankless female lead in *Le Mans* when Steve's first choice, Diana Rigg, bowed out. A beautiful blonde from Germany, Elga claimed "I was practically raped" by Steve when he met her. She much preferred the lovemaking of actor Peter Gimbel, whom she later married.

333

required young Mario to go out on a date with him, serving as his "beard," hoping to avoid suspicion. Traveling at top speed into a curve in the road, Steve lost control of the car and rammed the vehicle head-on into a tree.

Even though Edlind and Steve crashed right through the windshield, landing on the hood, they escaped with only minor cuts and bruises. Mario, however, had a broken arm. After their injuries were repaired at a local hospital, Steve and Edlind were released, but Mario had to remain behind for five days.

During Mario's stay in the hospital, Steve never went to see him, but told Edlind that he was worried that the boy might sue him.

When Mario returned to work, Steve accused him of coming on to one of the young women who frequented the set as one of Steve's groupies. The charge was completely false. Steve's attack on Mario grew so severe that he told him he was quitting and flying back to America. After having served Steve long and faithfully for many months, he could no longer tolerate the abuse, much less Steve's "I'll die tonight" kind of driving. Mario was a friend of Neile and was also tired of lying to her about Steve's many conquests.

From the race tracks of Le Mans to the innermost circles of the Swedish Parliament, actress **Louise Edlind** was rumored to have had an affair with Steve during the shooting of their ill-fated film. In intelligence, elegance, and refinement, she dated "down," during the time she spent dating Steve. Although he pictured himself as a great driver, he often crashed whatever vehicle he was piloting, as he did during one road rampage with Edlind.

Steve became "the king of his castle" when he rented the 14th-century Château Lornay, which stood in beautiful meadows around Vire-en-Champagne. He'd told John Sturges, "The kids will love it, a chance to live in a real castle." When the McQueens moved in, they heard strange noises at night, convincing them the castle might be haunted. There were other problems. Neile woke up one night in bed with Steve to find their room filled with bats.

On the few nights Steve came home, a family dinner was served in a room dating from the Middle Ages. But as filming progressed on *Le Mans*, the château became the setting for some of the most violent disagreements of their fifteen-year marriage. Steve later said, "It was a castle, not a home. A lot of bad memories there, not only for myself, but for its previous occupants. The damn building was cursed."

Shortly after Neile arrived from the States, Steve had abruptly informed her that a lot of women would be visiting him in his customized trailer. For the duration of the shoot, she was to stay at the château and wait for him on the nights he might decide to come home.

Those were heart-breaking words for her. She remembered fleeing to a strange car, perhaps one owned by a member of the film crew, and sobbing for hours. In her words, "I cried my heart out."

Once, on an occasion when he returned to the château to spend the night with Neile and the kids, the evening had gone fine until the kids turned in for bed. He apologized for having hurt her, and, as she put it, "he cradled me in his arms."

Since he was away so much, he asked her if, during his many absences, she'd ever gone to bed with another man. Eventually, through cocaine, he wore down her resistance, forcing her to admit to an affair.

After her confession, Steve left the room and returned shortly thereafter with a pistol which he pointed at her head. "Who is the fucking bastard?" He yanked and pulled on her hair and slapped her repeatedly until she blurted out the name of Maximilian Schell.

After calling her every filthy name in the dictionary used to describe a bad woman, from whore to cunt, he stormed out of the château and disappeared into the night in his Porsche. She had no idea when he was coming back to the château, or even if he were going to return at all.

Instead of hiring assassins to kill Schell, Steve called him and asked him to perform some high-speed driving for his film. Schell discreetly turned down the offer of a movie role under Steve's supervison.

On reflection, Neile remembered all too vividly how the affair with Schell had begun. While she was vacationing with Steve in their Palm Springs house, she'd discovered a strange dress in the closet of their bedroom.

Fueled by anger, she returned to Los Angeles where she booked a flight to New York for some relaxation and shopping. She was furious at Steve for betraying her once again. Not only that, he didn't even bother to clean up evidence of his adultery.

On the flight back to Los Angeles, she encountered Maximilian Schell, who had recently won an Oscar for his performance in *Judgment at Nuremberg*.

She found the Austrian actor dark, handsome, intelligent, and most romantic, referring to him in her memoirs as a "charming Casanova." On the westbound flight to the coast, she also said Schell made her feel "wanted, pretty, and feminine." She couldn't say that of Steve these days.

By the time the plane landed in California, she had agreed to a tryst at the Beverly Hills Hotel.

After mulling it over, she had decided, "At least I have gotten Steve where he lives, the son-of-a-bitch!" Regrettably, in the wake of her brief affair with

Schell, she found herself "guilt stricken and feeling even emptier than before."

The day after their confrontation, Steve and Neile announced their separation to the press. Actually they didn't separate, but flew instead to Morocco for a shared two-week vacation, hoping to patch things up. While there, Steve visited the local bordellos, insisting on very young girls, and, so it was rumored, young boys who agreed to "perform vile acts a female whore won't do."

After their return to France, the McQueens heard that a confrontation was looming with the backers of the *Le Mans* film.

At one point, Cinema Center tried to open negotiations with Robert Redford to fly to France and star in the picture. For two weeks, the suits planned to fire Steve and replace him, if not with Redford, then with another racing car driver, Paul Newman. He was seriously considered, although no offer was ever made to him. Corporate executives booked tickets to France, where they planned to drive to the set for a showdown.

On the set, with stern faces, the executives met Steve in his luxurious trailer, which they were paying for. Members of the production staff in France had reported to the brass back in Hollywood that Steve was not only being unreasonable, but irrational to the point where his sanity was in question.

The meeting with the executives went badly for Steve, with the film backers holding the ultimate ace—that of shutting down the whole picture unless Steve gave in to their demands.

Steve lost the round. If the picture were to continue, he would have to make enormous concessions, including the loss of his $750,000 salary and his profit participation. He also had to surrender creative control.

During his marriage to Neile Adams, Steve conducted numerous adulterous affairs. But Neile had only one relationship outside home, and that was with the handsome Austrian actor **Maximilian Schell.** In her memoirs, she doesn't name him, but refers to him as "a charming Casanova." After Steve learned about her brief fling, he never really forgave her. Steve may, in fact, have been plotting Schell's death when he offered him a dangerous role in the film, *Le Mans.*

No longer was he a producer, script writer, and director. He was reduced to the status of a mere actor, who was told to do what he was ordered to. He fumed, spat, and cursed, but to no avail. In the end, he caved in.

Faced with continuing losses, and

stripped of his salary, Steve was in a firing mood. He not only fired members of the crew on the film set of *Le Mans*, but he sent word back to his business manager, William Haher, in Hollywood to "pink slip" dozens of employees from Solar Productions.

After all his years of service, after virtually making Steve a movie star, Stan Kamen in Hollywood opened a cable to read:

DEAR STAN,
YOU'RE FIRED.
STEVE

When Steve finally returned to the château for a night with Neile, he discovered that she'd flown to London. It was only later that he learned that she'd gone there to abort his third child.

Steve was asked if *Le Mans* destroyed his marriage to Neile. "It sure put the cap on it," he said. "I don't think Neile ever got the image of me hot-ass-in' that 917 down Mulsanne at 200-plus out of her mind. I laid the whole package on the line for that one—my career, my money, my marriage, even my life. I went balls out on *Le Mans*."

He had reached a low point in his career and marriage, and he didn't know how he was going to crawl out of the hole he'd dug for himself.

On three separate occasions, he nearly had fatal car accidents. Back in California, he confessed to Casey and Darron that "the third one was no fuck ing accident. For at least five brief seconds, I considered killing myself in a fiery crash."

***

Reportedly, John Sturges, when seeing its final cut, called *Le Mans*, "McQueen's eight-million-dollar home movie. It was a God damn ego trip for the conceited bastard. I told the asshole we needed some storyline, some fucking plot. The picture is a disaster. So is Steve McQueen. If I sound bitter, I am."

Before flying back to Sweden, her film work finished, her affair with Steve over, Louise Edlind warned him, "Beware of what you want for you shall surely get it."

Le Mans had been his dream. At the end of filming, he was a bitter man. Aside from his conflicts with Sturges and his many budget excesses, there had been a strike by the entire crew. Once it was released, almost no one except car-racing fanatics, went to see *Le Mans*.

Surely *Le Mans* was a sad film for Steve. During its production, he ended his long-standing friendship with John Sturges, engineered the demise of Solar Productions, and, most costly of all, destroyed his marriage to Neile.

With a length of 106 tedious minutes, *Le Mans* opened on June 23, 1971. Howard Thompson of *The New York Times* dismissed it as "a bore," and Kathleen Carroll of the *New York Daily News* accurately claimed that it "appears to be an excuse for Steve McQueen to indulge his passion for auto racing."

Jay Cocks of *Time Magazine* thought Steve's style of glacial cool had gone too far, reaching "the point of impenetrable mannerism. He only stands in front of the camera and allows himself to be photographed."

Marlon Brando went to see Steve in *Le Mans*. He later told his friends, "This is about it for Stevie as a bankable star. But who in hell wants to be bankable? Ugly word."

Le Mans opened with what had become a Steve McQueen trademark, a close-up of the back of his head. It reminded some long-time fans of the opening scene in *The Blob*.

One critic said, "McQueen's mistake in *Le Mans* was turning around and showing us his face. It was dead. The film died with it."

***

On hand to greet Steve when he flew into Los Angeles from France was his new agent, Freddie Fields, known as "The Barracuda."

Fields was not only a film producer but a theatrical agent as well, and he had been instrumental in the careers of Henry Fonda, Judy Garland, Marilyn Monroe, Robert Redford, Fred Astaire, and Barbra Streisand. He was called one of Hollywood's greatest wheeler-dealers. At one time, he had been married to the actress Polly Bergen.

He showed Steve two newly optioned books, *The Getaway* and *Papillon,* that he wanted him to read.

Also waiting for Steve was a greeting from the Internal Revenue Service, informing him that Solar Productions owed two million dollars in back taxes.

Le Mans had crippled Cinema Center Films, and knocked Solar Productions down with a death blow. It was a box office disaster.

After the making of *Le Mans*, Steve abandoned the sport of car racing altogether.

Back home at "The Castle," Neile tried to hold onto a disintegrating marriage and signed up Steve and herself for consultations with a marriage counselor. When Steve met with his friends, Casey and Darron, he told them that Neile was "a whore" and a "dirty cunt." His friends did not point out all his many indiscretions.

Steve told one counselor, "I will never forgive the bitch for betraying me with this Austrian Nazi."

Steve grew more and more violent, his moods shifting. Neile began to fear for her life and the safety of Terry and Chad. She later confessed in her memoirs, "It was likely I would wind up dead." She even considered asking a judge to grant a restraining order against Steve.

On occasion, he slapped her and pulled her hair. Separation appeared inevitable.

Deserting "The Castle," Steve moved into a tiny, dark, and damp guest cottage he'd rented in Pacific Palisades. Darron and Casey were his most frequent guests along with a string of anonymous women, who would go back to wherever they came from and claim, "I fucked Steve McQueen." Casey and Darron kept Steve supplied with drugs.

At Steve's hideaway cottage, Casey and Darron noticed that the women he brought home to entertain them kept getting younger and younger. "Through Sebring, Steve had learned a lot of dirty games and he forced us to go along with them," Darron claimed. "Sebring had taught him that all women were whores, and many of them who were came to his cottage. I mean, they didn't charge but they were still whores."

"Steve had developed this kinky habit of wanting to piss in a girl's mouth," Darron said. "I couldn't believe how many went along with this crap. He also didn't want to wear rubbers. A lot of aspiring young actresses in Hollywood had to get an abortion that year."

"A few of them decided to have Steve's child," Casey said. "There are probably several kids running around the country today that could call Steve Dad."

A psychiatrist agreed that it was all right for Steve and Neile to "date," but on those occasions the name of Maximilian Schell always popped up. He had never forgiven her, and friends of Neile suspected that he never would.

There was some hope that the marriage might be saved when Steve on March 24, 1971, celebrated his 41st birthday. A producer and former agent at William Morrow (name unknown) called Steve and asked if he could drive by briefly en route to dinner with a friend.

"Bring him along, it's okay," Steve said. It turned out that the friend coming with him was none other than Maximilian Schell.

After hanging up, Steve went ballistic and physically attacked Neile. Hauling her to a bedroom, using caveman techniques of pulling her by her hair, he began beating her, calling her a whore. "Are you now letting him come to my house to fuck you?" he shouted at her.

If Schell had arrived on Steve's doorstep, Neile feared that Steve would have shot him with one of his many assault weapons.

Fortunately, Neile fled from the house and Schell never showed up. Just as Steve had managed to avoid being murdered by the Charles Manson sickos, so Schell had inadvertently escaped with his life.

Steve went back to living in the dank cottage, and his visits to "The Castle" continued to be volatile. Steve slapped Neile the way his "stepfathers" had beaten up his mother, Jullian Crawford. The pattern he'd observed as a boy was repeating itself in his adult life.

One evening turned especially violent. It was Memorial Day, 1971. Once again, after dinner, Steve began attacking Neile for her intimacies with Schell. In the courtyard of "The Castle" he kicked her and knocked her down, bruising her legs. He screamed "whore" so loud the neighbors heard him.

That was the night when she finally faced the truth, telling him that she had to leave him for good. "If I don't leave, someday you'll kill me," she quoted herself in her memoirs.

He calmed down and seemed to understand. Her last words to him were, "Good-bye, my husband, I love you. Take care of yourself."

After telling her, "I will always love you," he left without saying another word

When he drove back to his cottage, the phone was ringing. He picked up the receiver, thinking it was Neile.

"If I come over tonight, it won't be *Love With the Proper Stranger*," came a soothing, seductive voice. "We know each other too well for that."

"Surely this is not Natalie Wood," he said. "Like Elvis tells you, I'm lonesome tonight."

"Even as we speak, I'm on my way out the door," she said before hanging up.

Chapter Nine
A "Love Story" with Ali MacGraw

Steve's Solar Productions, and even one of its small commercial spinoffs, Solar Plastics, had closed their doors. Steve also seemed to be shutting down his life. He became obsessed about back taxes. In the future he would pay his taxes as money was first earned. He'd read about too many movie stars, such as Judy Garland, who'd gotten into serious trouble with the Internal Revenue Service.

Cash poor, he was leading the solitary life of a bachelor. The obsession with orgies had faded somewhat in the wake of the grisly murders of Sharon Tate and Jay Sebring.

After the abject failure of *Le Mans*, he needed a good movie role to propel him back into the running.

All that was released was a minor film, *On Any Sunday* (1971), about motorcycle racing. Running only eighty-nine minutes, it was produced, directed, and narrated by Bruce Brown.

Brown was an American documentary film director, the pioneer of such surf films as *Slippery When Wet* (1958) and *The Endless Summer* (1964). Steve didn't expect much from *On Any Sunday*, although in time it came to be regarded as the best motorcycle documentary of all time.

Initially, Brown had found it hard to get financial backing for *On Any Sunday*. Finally, knowing that Steve was a rider, he arranged a meeting with him.

"He liked my concept for the film," Brown said. "Then he asked me what I wanted him to do in the movie. I told

him I wanted him to finance me. He laughed at me. 'I star in movies, I don't finance them,' he told me. As a joke, I said, 'Okay, then you can't be in the movie.'"

"The next day he called me back and green-lighted the project," Brown said. "He also said he'd appear as a cyclist in the film."

During the shoot, Steve opened many doors to Brown that might otherwise have remained shut. Through a contact, Steve arranged for Brown's crew to film a sunset riding shot on the beach at the Camp Pendleton Marine Corps base in California.

In the actual movie, Steve appeared in several sequences, including the moto-cross footage that begins the film. "That million dollar body was on the line that day," Brown said.

Steve expected low box office, but ten million dollars in domestic rentals more than made up for his original $300,000 investment.

The film as a documentary was for the most part favorably reviewed except for Jay Cocks of *Time*, who attacked Brown for including "every conceivable cliché of documentary filmmaking." He even criticized the musical score, claiming it sounded like "The Glory of Tupperware."

Although the film made a reasonable profit, Steve got none of the money. All his profits went to pay back taxes.

***

Playing "sex kitten" with a French poodle, **Natalie Wood** had a "fuck fling" with Steve McQueen after her divorce from Robert Wagner and before her remarriage to the same actor.

On a scale of one to ten, Steve gave her a "three."

Robert Wagner was in England working on *Madame Sin,* in which Bette Davis starred as the leader of an Asian espionage ring. At the time, he was involved in an affair with Tina Sinatra, daughter of Frank Sinatra, but he was still eager to learn who Natalie Wood, his former wife, was dating. Rumors were swirling about Steve and Natalie, so he called her, hoping for the truth.

Perhaps Robert was thinking about getting back together with her, perhaps even remarrying her. "Are you seeing anyone at the moment?" he asked bluntly.

She frankly admitted that she was dating Steve McQueen. Robert sounded shocked, considering Steve a friend and viewing the seduction of his former wife as a betrayal of that bond between them.

Before ringing off with Natalie, Robert held out the possibility of a reconciliation between them in the future.

Natalie admitted to her friends that "I'm only having a fling with Steve," a harmless diversion that they'd begun many years previously on the set of *Love With the Proper Stranger*.

She also confided to friends that when she played on-screen love scenes with Steve, she had used her relationship with her estranged lover, Warren Beatty, for inspiration.

In *Natasha, The Biography of Natalie Wood*, Suzanne Finstad, claimed that Natalie "thought the world of Steve" and viewed him as "one smart cookie."

After a few high profile dates between Natalie and Steve, including their well-publicized entrance into Chasen's, Hollywood gossip columnists were crowing over a big romance.

Some reporters viewed Steve's buying Natalie a pair of $1,000 solid gold sunglasses as tantamount to an engagement ring.

Casey and Darron, who were privy to the relationship, claimed that Steve felt Natalie was falling in love with him. "But Steve wasn't serious about Natalie and didn't think their relationship had a future," Darron said.

"I'm between acts," Steve told his friends. "Natalie will be just one of many women checking in and out of my life. I've had better sex with most gals than I've had with Natalie. She doesn't know how to make love. I think she and Robert Wagner would rush into the bathroom, brush their teeth and gargle, then go to bed, have sanitized sex, and then rush back to the bathroom to shower. Natalie even thinks rimming is dirty."

After about two weeks, Steve drifted away to the arms of Mary Wilson, a member of The Supremes, and Natalie retreated to the bed of Jerry Brown, the governor of California.

Allegedly, when Steve next encountered Robert, he is reportedly to have said, "I was just keeping it warm for you, old pal, old buddy. No hard feelings, ok?"

***

Once Mary Wilson met singer Tom Jones in his skin-tight pants, she claimed in her memoirs, *Dream Girl: My Life as a Supreme*, that it was love at first sight. His reputation as a lover, not to mention his legendary endowment, had preceded him.

But like the candle that burned at both ends, the relationship flickered out. Jones put it bluntly to her that he wasn't going to leave his wife.

On the rebound from her aborted love affair with Jones, Mary admitted that she fell in and out of love with three men in a row: Steve McQueen, Flip Wilson, and Jack Lucarelli, the latter an actor who performed stunts in film and on TV. He was also a producer and director.

Casey and Darron were in a state of shock when Steve told them he was dating an African American woman. "I didn't know he went for black chicks at all," Darron said. "They certainly weren't our thing. We lived in an all-white world. Every club we went to, even the restaurants, had only white patrons. We often used the word 'nigger' around Steve, and he never seemed to object to it."

Two of Steve's closest biker pals were shocked when he started dating "a black chick," **Mary Wilson** (top photo), a member of The Supremes, starring Diana Ross.

Steve described Mary as "a white person living in the body of a black female."

"Frankly, during the brief time Steve was going with that Supreme gal, we didn't see much of him for a few weeks. He seemed to sense that we didn't approve of the relationship, and he didn't rub it under our noses."

"I thought if he wanted to date one of the Supremes, it should be Diana Ross," Casey said. "She seemed far more glamorous to me than Mary Wilson."

Because Casey and Darron weren't privy to the details of Steve's affair with Wilson, and she wasn't helpful in her memoirs, details are sketchy about the romantic twosome. "Steve never talked about it, except one night when we were stoned," Darron said.

"Mary is different from most black women," Steve said. "She is actually a white person living in the body of a black female. She is glamorous and beautiful just like Marilyn Monroe but in a very different way. She and The Supremes, especially Diana Ross, are trying to teach the world that black is beautiful."

"Everyone, especially black activists, wants Mary to go political and take a stand for civil rights," Steve said. "But I think she just wants to do her job, which is to sing. Can you believe that some motherfuckers are attacking her for not being black enough?"

"When Steve hooked up with Wilson, and news got into the columns, he told us he was getting hate mail," Darron said. "He met with Sammy Davis Jr. to talk over how he handled hate mail when he was involved with that lavender blonde, Kim Novak. Amazingly, Steve told us that Sammy advised him to drop Wilson if he wanted to remain a big star in the movies."

"A piece of pussy, especially a black pussy, just isn't worth risking your career," Sammy told Steve, or at least that's what Steve claimed.

"Frankly, we were glad when Steve and Wilson broke up," Cascy said. "We didn't know her and didn't have anything to do with her. But we wanted Steve back for ourselves. We missed him. We wanted him to pick up white girls again, broads all three of us could enjoy."

It was weeks later before the name of Mary Wilson surfaced again. "It was just a fuck fling," Steve said. "Dating black is not my thing: I want my future women to look like Jacqueline Bisset."

***

When Steve learned that the hip and highly irreverent TV cult variety show, *Rowan & Martin's Laugh In* (1968), had been their favorite show, he admitted to having had an affair with the tiny-framed, pixie-like Judy Carne. She became famous for her phrase, 'Sock it to me!" at which point she was doused with water, or in some other way assaulted.

Carne quickly rose to flower power stardom, but her career faltered when she left the show after two wildly successful seasons. She'd never regain that early acclaim.

Steve caught Carne between marriages, the first to actor Burt Reynolds (1963-1965) and the second to producer Robert Bergman. The marriage to super macho Reynolds ended in tempestuous headlines in the tabloids, each member of the marriage charging the other with various indiscretions. She accused Reynolds of throwing her against a fireplace

The "Sock It To Me!" girl, **Judy Carne**, in a peaceful moment with her husband, actor **Burt Reynolds.** This picture was taken before the marriage turned poisonous.

After the bitter divorce, Steve moved in to sock it to Judy personally.

and cracking her skull. He countercharged that he could no longer tolerate her drug-taking.

When Steve first met Carne in the late 60s, her short kinky haircut came courtesy of Vidal Sassoon, the famous English hairdresser, with whom she'd been involved romantically. Her big smile and ninety-pound frame enticed Steve, reminding him of his wife, Neile.

Steve had hung out with Carne on several occasions when she was dating one of his best friends, the famous racing car driver, Stirling Moss. After Burt Reynolds, she'd had several affairs, and there had always been a sexual tension between Steve and Carne. He felt flattered that she had been attracted to him, because she'd turned down a number of other suitors, including Desi Arnaz, Sr.

One night in Los Angeles, the sexual tension that had long been simmering between Steve and Carne bubbled to a boil when he followed her home to her Laurel Canyon nest. She found his rugged charm similar to that of Reynolds.

As she related in her memoir, *Laughing on the Outside, Crying on the Inside*, "We stood there staring into each other's eyes for a few moments, and then it felt as if a valve had been released. We embraced and dropped to the floor, landing softly on the cushions and fusing ourselves together. It happened magically and spontaneously, and since we knew it might never happen again, our lovemaking at that moment was vital to us. We fulfilled a mutual longing that had built up over the years, an attraction that evolved from a tender friendship and didn't demand more than we were prepared to give."

"Steve never wanted to talk too much about Carne," Darron said. "He did

In photo above, **Barbra Streisand** places her hand on Steve's chest. Rumors swirled around Hollywood that she did far more than that. Pictured here are the four chief honchos of the newly formed First Artists, Inc.: (left to right), **Steve, Paul Newman, Barbra** herself, and **Sidney Poitier.**

Barbra (above) made it known to prospective lovers that she preferred circumcised men.

say one day that she represented the flip side of glamorous Tinseltown."

Within the context of their friendship, her drug taking had never bothered him, because he was perpetually stoned himself. However, he did become alarmed for her sake when he heard that she'd moved from a frequent ingestion of marijuana and hallucinogens to a full-fledged heroin addiction.

"I pray I never end up begging for a handout and walking up and down Hollywood Boulevard, reminding people that I used to be Steve McQueen," he said.

Burt Reynolds and Steve never became friends, although Carne once revealed that both of them had "nice asses."

Burt became famous for posing nude for *Cosmopolitan* magazine. He became so celebrated for this layout that he once said, "When I die, what they're going to write on my tombstone is HERE LIES BURT REYNOLDS: THE FIRST GUY TO POSE NUDE IN A MAGAZINE."

What isn't known is that the editors had first asked Steve to pose for the centerfold, but he turned them down.

He sent the editors his brief rejection with a note, "The only women who are going to feast on my dick are those I'm fucking."

***

Jointly with Paul Newman and Sidney Poitier, Barbra Streisand formed First Artists Productions in the early 70s. By having their own production company, each of these stars would retain creative control of their movies.

Within two years, both Steve and Dustin Hoffman would join the company. Each of these actors agreed to make three films for the company, in which they agreed to forego their salary in return for 25% to 33% percent of each movie's gross.

At its inception, First Artists was inspired by United Artists, the company established in 1919 by Mary Pickford, Charles Chaplin, D.W. Griffith, and Douglas Fairbanks Sr. In contrast, First Artists was actually set up as an elaborate tax dodge.

From all reports, Barbra had not been that impressed with Steve until she and her husband, Elliott Gould, screened *Bullitt* in October of

Freddie Fields, nicknamed "The Barracuda," was the agent for both Barbra and Steve. He once secretly compiled a list of Barbra's lovers, stating that they ranged from Elvis Presley to Bill Clinton.

1968. She found him sexy, which made Gould angry and jealous.

Steve caught up with Barbra on the rebound from her affair with Ryan O'Neal, whom she'd met when they starred together in *What's Up, Doc?*, a movie she later referred to as "a piece of shit."

Steve had actually met Barbra in 1967 when she'd arrived in Hollywood to film *Funny Girl*, a musical melodrama based on the legend of Fannie Brice.

Its producer was Ray Stark, a powerbroker known for his Machiavellian ways, and one of the last great Hollywood moguls. He was an ogre of male chauvinistic casting couch entitlement, and had already molested Barbra when she auditioned for him. To welcome his star to Hollywood, Stark had pitched a tent on the grounds of his elegant Holmby Hills estate and hired an all-girl orchestra to perform for guests who included Marlon Brando, Rosalind Russell, Ginger Rogers, Robert Mitchum, James Stewart, John Wayne, Gregory Peck, and a surprise guest, Steve McQueen, an actor who didn't really like to go to Hollywood parties.

At first he had found Barbra a bit snobbish and contemptuous of Hollywood, but since he also held Hollywood in contempt, that wasn't necessarily a strike against her. She told him that she was living in Beverly Hills in a manse that had once been occupied by Greta Garbo. "The woman had taste," she told Steve. "Something I haven't seen too much of around here."

"At long last I'm taking Marlon Brando's advice and dating Jewish girls," Steve told Casey and Darron. "Most Jewish gals want a man to be circumcised."

"I wouldn't know about that," Darron told him. "I only fuck Gentile bitches."

Freddie Fields ("The Barracuda"), who at the time represented both Steve and Barbra, recalled later in his life (he died in 2007) that Steve was added to Barbra's alleged list of seducers, others of whom included Robert Redford, Warren Beatty, Richard Burton, Sidney Chaplin (son of Charlie), Clint Eastwood, Richard Gere, Don Johnson, Kris Kristofferson, Liam Neeson, Anthony Newley, Ryan O'Neal, hairdresser Jon Peters, Elvis Presley, Omar Sharif, comedian Tommy Smothers, and Pierre Trudeau, the prime minister of Canada. One night, when Hillary was away from Washington, Barbra was alleged to have visited the presidential bedchambers of Bill Clinton.

The McQueen/Streisand romance was short-lived, but Barbra did call Steve in 1973 when she learned through the testimony of White House counsel John Dean that both of them were on Nixon's enemies list. They shared the honor with, among others, Jane Fonda, Carol Channing, Paul Newman, Gregory Peck, Tony Randall, Dick Gregory, and Bill Cosby.

"I'm scared shitless," Barbra told Steve. "Are we safe? Nixon will stop at nothing."

"I don't know about you, but I view it as a badge of honor to be on his fucking list," Steve said. "Trouble is, I'm the most apolitical figure in the world. How did I get on that list? It's not true that I fucked Pat Nixon."

***

Despite their bitter separation, and despite the many beatings and denunciations, Steve was shocked when Neile filed for divorce in October of 1971. At first he couldn't believe it. For more than fifteen years she'd patiently endured his endless transgressions, seemingly always forgiving him for whatever he'd done.

She had loved him as she'd loved no other man, and over the years his serial adultery had caused her endless pain. Perhaps he couldn't understand that she wanted a more orderly life. She'd even given up a promising career for him. There was talk during her heyday on Broadway that she'd become the next Debbie Reynolds.

Of course, as the years passed and she tested the possibility of a show-biz comeback, she obviously discovered that there wasn't as intense a demand for her services as there had been when she was a much younger performer.

"As far as I'm concerned, Neile was a saint in the relationship," said Freddie Fields. "So, she fell off the wagon one time and had a brief fling. Compare that to Steve's track record. He fell off the wagon at the rate of two or three times a day. How much could one woman take? She was also a good and faithful mother, keeping the home fires burning while Steve was off doing God knows what."

Some Hollywood wives who had divorced stars warned Neile of what a lonely road she'd be traveling when she could no longer call up a restaurant and reserve a table for Mrs. Steve McQueen. She was also warned that many so-called friends would drop her from their social lists.

"That, of course, is a painful reality of

Neile Adams was headed for Broadway stardom the night she met Steve in a New York City restaurant. He proceeded to systematically derail her career as they entered into a tumultuous marriage. She had to accept that month after month, year after year, he was the eternal unfaithful husband.

Hollywood," Fields said. "When you're no longer the wife of a box office champ, no one wants you. It's always been that way in Hollywood. Even so, being married to a star isn't all that great if you're suffering emotional pain almost daily, especially if you're being physically abused. Steve was clearly the villain the marriage, not Neile, who was both a good wife and mother."

Neile and Steve continued to make love after their divorce, but she diverted her attentions to a surgeon, David Ross, and soon, to the surprise of Terry and Chad, Ross became a live-in daddy. Neile had given Steve a gold Saint Christopher's medal, inscribed with the words TO PART IS TO DIE A LITTLE.

"And that's what I did after leaving Neile," Steve told Darron and Casey. "I died a little until Ali MacGraw brought me back to life."

The divorce was extremely painful for Steve as well. He was also financially strapped. Although he'd refused in the past to appear in commercials, he accepted a one million dollar offer from Honda in Japan, with the iron-bound clause that the ensuing advertisement would only be shown in that country.

Dozens of picture offers were flooding into the "The Barracuda's" office, so the major issue revolved around when, and not whether, Steve would return to work.

"I had every intention of getting him a million per picture," his agent said. "All he had to do was sign on the dotted line."

In 1971, Steve turned down films which included *Play Misty for Me*, a suspense drama which became a big hit for Clint Eastwood. Steve feared that the part of the woman was stronger than his. He wanted to make *Yucatan*, a film about an Indian well in Mexico filled with ancient jewelry, but the project proved too costly to film. One of the first films he wanted to do for First Artists was *American Flag*, written by Elmore Leonard, the story of a western mining town. But Steve rejected the script.

According to California law, their property was equally divided between Neile and Steve. Steve told Fields, "Neile deserves every cent. Without her, I probably wouldn't have climbed the Hollywood ladder at all."

The terms of their final divorce settlement was announced on March 14, 1972, with Neile getting one million dollars.

Alimony payments would start at $7,000 per month for the first months, scaling down eventually to $2,000 a month by 1982, at which time Steve would have been dead for two years. The McQueen's Brentwood mansion was sold to Zubin Mehta, at the time the music director of the Los Angeles Philharmonic, and his wife, Nancy.

Even though Neile was a strong woman, friends of hers reported that she appeared emotionally fragile after the breakup. On some occasions the mere

350

mention of Steve's name could cause her to burst into tears.

Divorces, of course, often involve bitter custody battles over children. Not so in the case of Steve and Neile. He was allowed to see Chad and Terry whenever he wanted, and his children could stay with him for as long as they wanted. It was a very loose arrangement based on the good will of both parties.

Steve's dating of famous women such as Barbra Streisand and Natalie Wood had not worked out or at least never developed into anything serious. But a new and beautiful woman had entered his life. Complications arose when it was discovered that Elvis Presley shared Steve's interest in an actress named Barbara Leigh.

***

It was time for Steve to go back to work. He was offered the role of a cop in *The French Connection*. He turned down the role of Popeye Doyle, which, as interpreted by Gene Hackman, became an international hit. "No more cop roles for me," Steve told his agent Freddie Fields.

After signing with First Artists, Steve was almost immediately disappointed with the new company's first releases. One of these was Paul Newman's *Pocket Money* (1972). Co-starring Lee Marvin, it emerged as one of the most boring of Newman's many movies. Steve was also not impressed with Barbra Streisand's *Up the Sandbox*, or with Sidney Poitier's *Buck and the Preacher*, both of them released the same year.

Steve had really wanted to star in *McCabe and Mrs. Miller*, but his ally, David Foster, wanted Warren Beatty for the part.

Foster, of course, was the Canada-born musician, record producer, composer, singer, songwriter, and arranger who was known as the "master of bombastic pop kitsch" and a key player in the careers of Janet Jackson, Barbra Streisand, Peter Allen, and John Travolta.

Known as "Bloody Sam," **Sam Peckinpah** was an American director and screenwriter who frequently worked with Steve. He was known for films loaded with violence in his revisionistic approach to the Western genre, and for his behind-the-scenes battles with Steve over scripts and direction.

He eventually succumbed to alcoholism, drug addiction, mental illness, manic depression, and paranoia.

Steve decided to appear as the star of a movie called *Junior Bonner*, playing an aging rodeo star.

Originally producer Joe Wizan had wanted Robert Redford to star as the rodeo cowboy, but he turned it down. "Not my thing," he said.

The role of Junior Bonner, that of a laconic, living embodiment of the code of the once-golden Old West who now must confront the fact that he's a living relic, had already been brought to the screen before. Just name the names: Joel McCrea, William Holden, Robert Ryan, and Randolph Scott.

In the film, Junior Bonner's goal is to ride a bucking Brahma bull named Sunshine for eight seconds. No cowboy had ever been able to stay on this beast for that amount of time.

Steve had agreed to star in the film for a half million dollars. As a result, he was the only one associated with the film who made any money. *Junior Bonner* grossed only two million dollars worldwide, and in terms of box office receipts, was one of the most disastrous movies he'd ever made.

One factor that hurt *Junior Bonner*'s box office was the sudden release of several other rodeo pictures. They included James Coburn in *The Honkers*, Richard Widmark in *When the Legends Die*, and Cliff Robertson in *J.W. Coop*.

Sam Peckinpah, the fiery helmer who almost got to direct Steve in *The Cincinnati Kid*, signed on as director. He cast two very talented veteran actors, Ida Lupino and Robert Preston, as Steve's co-stars. There was a minor part for a beautiful girl, and he and Steve set out to cast the role.

Once a fabled beauty, **Ida Lupino** dared to look her age in *Junior Bonner,* where she clashed repeatedly with Peckinpah, but got along with Steve.

She told him that early in her career, her agent had promised that she'd evolve into "the Janet Gaynor of England." "Everyone wanted sweetness and light," Ida said, "but since the age of thirteen, I opted for hooker roles instead."

By the time he met Ida Lupino, Steve had abandoned his interest in "antique pussy." Otherwise, Lupino might have been a candidate for seduction.

She was fifty-four when she played Steve's mother, and there was only a fifteen year difference in their ages. Actually she did look like his mother, because she wore no makeup and a red wig, and didn't try to conceal the bags under her eyes.

Meeting her for the first time, Steve said, "Hi, Mom, gimme a kiss." Although that approach was a bit fresh, he kept a respectful distance from her throughout the remainder of the shoot.

Lupino, a director in her own right and once a fabled beauty, did clash with Peckinpah, who kept embarrassing her in front of the crew. On the first day he made a sarcastic comment about the way she'd applied her lipstick. When Steve felt the director was harassing Lupino, he intervened, telling Peckinpah to lay off.

At one point, Lupino walked off the picture, until roses, champagne, and an apology brought her back. "Ignore Bloody Sam," Steve told her. "He's a fucking macho pig."

Peckinpah had seen Barbara Leigh playing the role of Rock Hudson's wife in *Pretty Maids All in a Row,* which had been released by MGM in 1971. Roger Vadim, the French director who'd discovered (and later married) Brigitte Bardot, the sex kitten, had originally spotted Barbara walking along the beach at Malibu, and cast her in the role.

Barbara's memoirs, and what a story, were chronicled in rich detail in 2002 as *The King, McQueen, and The Love Machine, My Secret Hollywood Life with Elvis Presley, Steve McQueen, and James Aubrey.*

Aubrey, nicknamed "the Smiling Cobra," was the president of MGM and the inspiration for Jacqueline Susann's novel, *The Love Machine.*

In this candid memoir, she writes of how she tried to balance three lovers at the same time: Steve McQueen, Elvis Presley, and James Aubrey.

Born in Ringgold, Georgia, in 1946, one of six children, she was sent to an orphanage in Miami when it was ascertained that her mother could not support all those kids by herself.

At the age of fourteen, Leigh married her sister's ex-boyfriend. At the age of seventeen, she became a mother.

Shortly after moving to Los Angeles, she got a divorce. After a stint working in a doctor's office, she became a model, which led to a glam-

Actress and model **Barbara Leigh** was cast as the romantic lead opposite Steve in *Junior Bonner.* Before filming had begun, she was already his number one bedmate.

Steve, however, wasn't her only love. During her torrid romance with Steve, she was screwing around with Elvis Presley and James Aubrey (head of MGM) on the side. But which of the three made her pregnant?

orous career, with her appearing in TV commercials across the country. She also got some minor roles in films.

Before Steve, there was Elvis. According to Joe Esposito, one of Elvis's closest pals, The King met Barbara in 1970 when he was performing at the Las Vegas International Hotel. She came to his show and later joined the celebrities, fans, and groupies who gathered in Elvis' dressing room where he held court after the show.

According to Esposito, she was definitely Elvis's type, being a brunette with sensational good looks and a beautiful figure. After their initial meeting, an affair soon followed. Their torrid romance lasted on and off for two years, as Elvis got all shook up over Barbara, but also shared his manly charms with other beautiful women along the way.

Barbara received a call from Peckinpah's office to come for a reading for the role of Charmagne, who plays Steve's girlfriend in the movie. Appearing at producer Joe Wizan's office in Studio City, she was shocked to encounter not only Peckinpah but Steve.

Steve read lines with her during the twenty-minute audition. When Peckinpah rose abruptly and dismissed her, she knew she'd lost the part.

In the parking lot, Steve ran up to her. He more or less admitted that she'd been turned down by the director, but he asked her out for dinner anyway. In the office she'd regarded him as "charming and sexy." And although she knew

A southern belle from Georgia, **Barbara Leigh** wrote an autobiographical tell-all book entitled *The King, McQueen, and the Love Machine* about Elvis, Steve, and James Aubrey (aka the Love Machine). She provided intimate details about what it was like for an upcoming starlet to crawl between the sheets with this trio of icons. She recommended Elvis for kissing, Aubrey for technique, and Steve for nonstop sex.

he was married at the time, she accepted his invitation, figuring she'd some-how manage to work Steve in between her dates with Elvis and Aubrey.

Their rendezvous that evening was at a restaurant in the resort of Malibu. He'd picked the place because of its intimacy and privacy, hoping he would-n't be hounded by fans seeking autographs. Over dinner the two bonded, learning that they'd each come from white trash backgrounds.

She'd deliberately turned down his obvious invitation for sex that night, not wanting to spoil the possibility of an affair with a one-night stand. After kissing her "again and again," he made a promise to call her tomorrow.

Driving home in a car Elvis had bought for her, she thought only of Steve, calling him "a rebel, boy-man, a bad boy. He had a wild aura about him. I just knew he would be good in bed."

The next morning a ringing phone woke her up. It was Steve calling for a date that night. At that time Steve was leading a pre-divorce bachelor life in his dank cottage in Pacific Palisades.

Over dinner at an Italian restaurant he admitted what she already knew. Peckinpah wanted the actress, Tiffany Bolling, for the role of Charmagne. "I held out for you," Steve said, "but he's the director."

Bolling was a strikingly beautiful, blonde-haired actress, who shot to fame as a cult favorite of 70s B-movie buffs in a handful of trashy drive-in flicks.

Sexually, Barbara managed to hold Steve off until yet another date sched-uled for the following Saturday night. After dinner, he carried her, without preliminaries, over the threshold of his house and right into bed.

As a lover, on a scale of one to ten, she gave him a ten. "He was wild, provocative, and passionate. He took pride in his body; he was stocky and strong. There was longing in his ice-blue gaze, a slight sadness. We fit perfect-ly as lovers."

In remembering his love-making, she definitely considered Steve "great in bed, a little on the rough side, like the Heathcliff character from *Wuthering Heights*."

From the film set of *Junior Bonner* in Arizona, Steve called Barbara unex-pectedly. He informed her that Tiffany Bolling had become ill, and that she'd been assigned the role of Charmagne. Barbara was overjoyed.

She became Steve's leading lady both on and off the screen.

***

Upon her arrival on location in Prescott, Arizona, Barbara was greeted with a big wet kiss by Steve in front of the crew, a clear symbol of their mutu-al involvement. Now that Neile had faded into the background, he could be more open in his relationships with women.

Barbara quickly learned that Steve, Robert Preston, Ida Lupino, and Sam Peckinpah were all heavy drinkers. It was 100-proof Smirnoff vodka that would eventually destroy Peckinpah's career.

Barbara spent her nights with Steve in his rented villa, discovering that he didn't like foreplay as much as Elvis, preferring instead to get down into the "bad boy action" fast.

Whenever he made love to her, she noticed a loaded sawed-off shotgun in bed beside them. He was still traumatized by the murder of Jay Sebring and Sharon Tate.

During the course of the shoot and Barbara's affair with Steve, she confessed to maintaining other ongoing affairs with both Elvis and James Aubrey. If he seemed threatened or jealous, he didn't show it. Unlike his response to Neile's confession of an affair with Maximilian Schell, Steve did not go ballistic upon hearing of Barbara's other romantic links. Both Elvis and Aubrey constantly called Barbara while on location, leaving messages.

Steve called Elvis "a guitar hick," and Elvis referred to Steve "a motorcycle hick."

A problem arose when Elvis wanted to fly to Prescott to shack up with Barbara, who was already shacked up with Steve. To prevent his arrival, she had to confess her affair with Steve. Elvis said good-bye coldly and hung up the phone.

When Barbara Leigh met **Elvis,** the attraction was immediate. "He was a passionate lover when he wanted to be," she claimed. "He was also gorgeous, the most beautiful man I'd ever seen."

James Aubrey (aka "The Cobra") was head of CBS and later of MGM Studios. He's remembered today as the honcho who oversaw the dismantling of that failing studio as a means of saving it from financial ruin. With Barbara Leigh, he became a key player in the decade's steamiest love triangle.

She thought Steve was falling for her, and there was talk of their living together. Unlike James Aubrey, Steve wasn't refined in his manners. She claimed that he could be "crude, boorish, and coarse," citing examples of eating his food with his feet on the table. She also claimed he "spit whenever he wanted to and cussed like a sailor."

After Barbara's part on *Junior Bonner* was finished, she stayed on with Steve for another week, spending her final night making love to him. As she described in her memoirs, "After smoking a joint and drinking tequila, we sweated the night away with nonstop sex."

Back in Hollywood, Barbara could no longer keep her affairs secret from her other lovers after columnist Rona Barrett published the details of her on-location tryst with Steve. It was the talk of Hollywood. Naturally, well-meaning "friends" called Neile with the news.

In Los Angeles, Steve moved to a much more upmarket house in Coldwater Canyon, fleeing from the dark and moldy cottage along the Pacific Palisades. Before that, and for a brief time, he lodged at the Chateau Marmont, where everybody from Paul Newman to Marilyn Monroe had at one point in their lives sought lodging.

When Steve returned to Los Angeles, he called Barbara and told her how much he missed her. He suggested a reunion at his vacation home in Palm Springs.

Complicating matters, after a long delay, Elvis seemed to have forgiven Barbara and called her, suggesting they meet for an off-the-record weekend in Palm Springs. The song's refrain of "torn between two lovers" fitted her life perfectly, except in her case, there were three lovers.

She pleaded other commitments in New York to Elvis and postponed their rendezvous. After completing her commercial in New York, she did meet with Steve in Palm Springs, settling into his home where both Frank Sinatra and Bob Hope were neighbors.

When Steve suggested they should live together, Barbara rejected the idea, not wanting to eliminate Elvis or even Aubrey from her life. He finally rebelled. As a super macho, Steve didn't like the idea that he was being "worked into" Barbara's schedule between her other two lovers.

It was the hardest decision of her life, but Barbara decided that if forced to choose—and she didn't want to have to do that—the winner would be James Aubrey. As head of MGM, he was quite a catch and might even turn her into a big-time movie star. But in hitching her wagon to Aubrey, she was giving up two of the world's most pursued bachelors—Steve McQueen and Elvis Presley.

Steve was stunned when Barbara informed him that she was pregnant. His first thought was that the child was his, perhaps conceived during their time together in Arizona. But, later that night, he began to wonder. He asked her if she'd told either Elvis or Aubrey, and she claimed that she hadn't.

Steve called both Casey and Darron at work and met them in a bar when they got off at five from their jobs at a garage in Palm Springs. "The bitch has got a kid in the oven," he told them over several beers. "But I don't know if it's mine. Maybe it belongs to Elvis. Or James Aubrey." Casey and Darron, of course, knew who Elvis was but didn't know who James Aubrey was.

Later, Barbara considered that her child might belong to Aubrey, but it could be Steve's as well. She claimed that it certainly wasn't Elvis' child, although if she were having intercourse with The King, why not? The suggestion was left that sex with Elvis must have always been protected sex or else oral sex, which Elvis indulged in more frequently than intercourse, according to his many girlfriends.

There was yet another possibility. In her memoirs, Barbara suggested that as Elvis had increased his dependence on drugs, his interest in sex had waned considerably. Perhaps she had not had sexual intercourse with him during the weeks she became pregnant. So Elvis was left out of the loop.

However, Steve was not aware of this, and one night he arranged for Elvis to visit him at his manse in Coldwater Canyon.

Elvis was two hours late, but he did manage to show up. One of Elvis' boys knocked on Steve's door, announcing, "He's here!"

Steve opened his front door in time to see Elvis emerge from the back of a long limousine. He walked toward Steve and shook his hand.

Once Elvis was inside, Steve offered The King a joint, which he gratefully accepted. As the two men talked and smoked, Steve wanted to get immediately to the point. He was never one for small talk. "I'm told by Barbara that me and you are about to become a daddy."

"What in hell does that mean?"

"I guess she hasn't told you, but our joint girlfriend is one pregnant chick."

At first Elvis didn't say anything, no doubt mulling over this startling news. Perhaps in his foggy state, he didn't even remember when he last had sex with Barbara. "I hear rumors about how you like sloppy seconds," he finally said. "Maybe you jumped on her one night when she didn't have a chance to flush out my sperm. Maybe my sperm mated with your sperm, and we're hatching McQueen Junior and Elvis Junior."

"I guess such a thing is possible," Steve said, "but it sure sounds far-fetched to me."

Before the night ended, the drugged and a drunken rivals had come to a decision. Both of them wanted Barbara to have her baby. "We'll see if it looks like Little Elvis or Little McQueen," Elvis said before heading out the door.

"If he's real good looking, we'll know the boy is my kid."

"Maybe it belongs to James Aubrey," Steve said.

"That old geezer," Elvis said. "Are you sure Grandpa can still get it up for Barbara?"

"Maybe not," Steve said. "See you around the block, Elvis."

When Barbara later confronted Aubrey with her pregnancy, he denied the child was his, even though they had been having unprotected sex. Then he revealed the real reason he was so adamant.

For the first time, he admitted to her that because he hadn't wanted any more children, he'd had a vasectomy. Since she was convinced that the child hadn't developed from Elvis' sperm, that left only one paternity possibility: Steve.

Aubrey came to Barbara's financial aid, and an abortion was performed. Barbara made the crucial decision to follow through with the abortion and avoid telling Steve that she was in essence killing his child. In "Monday morning quarterbacking," she later decided, it "was a rotten thing to do" to him.

Later on, she learned that Steve desperately wanted another child at the time of his marriage to Ali MacGraw, but she miscarried.

When Barbara had dinner with Steve after her recovery, she told him that she'd had the child aborted.

In a mystical mood, she later wrote that, "If there is a spirit beyond this Earth, I pray that the child's aborted spirit and Steve's spirit are together again, and I'm forgiven."

Steve called Elvis and told him that Barbara had aborted "Little Steve and Little Elvis."

Elvis paused. "That's just as well. I can't have anything to do with a woman who's given birth, or even a woman who's had one in the oven."

In 1976, at the Beverly Wilshire Hotel, a final meeting occurred between Barbara and Steve. Their reunion was eerily evocative of the last time she encountered Elvis, who at the time tipped the scales at 260 pounds. By then, he had another girlfriend, Ginger Alden, who would be with him until the time of his death.

Barbara's encounter with Steve was hideous. Years before, her boyfriends, Elvis and Steve, had been two of the most glamorous men in Hollywood. That, however, was no longer true.

When she arrived at Steve's hotel room and opened the door, the Steve she faced—in her words—"looked like a wild mountain man. His hair was long, shaggy, and disheveled, and he sported a full beard that was scruffy-looking at best." She said that his piercing blue eyes, however, were still the same.

Later, after a room service dinner, he pressed sex onto her, but she confessed, "It just wasn't there for me. No bells, no tingles." She preferred to remember him from his *Junior Bonner* days, when he was still virile and handsome. She thought the man looking back at her resembled "Heidi's grandfather from the Swiss Alps. The Steve McQueen mystique was gone."

As she moved to exit from his suite, he made one final play for her. She turned him down with a gentle peck on the cheek.

"Bye baby, I'll call you sometime," he promised her.

Heading for the elevator, she paused to look back for one fleeting glimpse. That would be the last time she saw her once beloved Steve McQueen alive.

Barbara, still alive today, still vibrant, an employee of *Playboy* for forty years, watched three of the most famous men in America—James Aubrey, Elvis Presley, and Steve McQueen—crumble before her eyes. She prefers to remember them as the sexy, vibrant, powerful, and attractive men they once were, not what they became.

***

The role of Doc McCoy, a fast-shooting convict/crook in *The Getaway,* had intrigued Steve from the beginning. He toyed briefly with playing an Arkansas hillbilly in *Roy Brightswood* before settling on *The Getaway* for Paramount, with Peter Bogdanovich directing.

When First Artists became involved, Bogdanovich was out. Despite his earlier involvement in the box office failure of *Junior Bonner*, Steve brought in once again the highly volatile director Sam Peckinpah, "Bloody Sam," for yet another feature film. When the news was announced that Steve and Peckinpah had reteamed, *Cosmopolitan* announced it as a mating of "two of the biggest studs and meanest bastards in moviedom."

The film was based on a crime novel, *The Getaway* by Jim Thompson, about a husband and wife bank-robbing team. The Oklahoma-born writer, a master of the hard-boiled crime fiction novel, was called the "Dime Store Dostoevsky." In the late 1980s and early 90s, after his death, the author and

In happier times, legendary cocksman **Robert Evans,** chief of Paramount Pictures, in the swim with his bride, **Ali MacGraw.** Evans became the first actor to run a major studio. The handsome hunk was a man of many liaisons until he mated with MacGraw.

The destruction of Evan's romantic life began with the arrival of Steve McQueen.

his body of work achieved something approaching cult status. Thompson hated Steve, who had crudely rejected his screenplay of *The Getaway*. "Too much dialogue, not enough action," Steve told him.

Though scriptwriter Walter Hill later was given sole credit for the version of the script that was eventually used, Thompson insisted that much of his original script ended up in the movie. He appealed to the Writers Guild for arbitration, but they ruled against him. As Stephen King once wrote, "If you have seen only the film version of *The Getaway*, you have no idea of the existential horrors awaiting Doc and Carol McCoy at the point where Sam Peckinpah ended the story."

Originally Dyan Cannon had been slated for the role of the romantic lead, Carol McCoy. After she was rejected, Angie Dickinson was suggested.

Steve had his own ideas about the film's casting, preferring either Katharine Ross, who had impressed him in *Butch Cassidy and the Sundance Kid*, or Tuesday Weld, whom he'd worked with, and perhaps did other things with, before.

But Peckinpah held out for the fast-rising Ali MacGraw, wife of Robert Evans, the chief honcho of Paramount.

The star of this dark-haired, olive-skinned beauty would shine only briefly in the Hollywood heavens. Once again, Steve could be blamed for derailing what seemed like a promising career.

Ali's dark features and her exotic look and inviting smile had made her a top fashion model. Playing a spoiled, immature girl from the suburbs, she shot to fame in *Goodbye, Columbus* with Richard Benjamin in 1969. The story was based on Philip Roth's stinging portrait of a successful Jewish family in the suburbs.

But it was *Love Story* in 1970 that put her over the top when she co-starred with the romantic heartthrob Ryan O'Neal. It was based on a best-selling short novel by Erich Segal. Upon its blockbuster release, it had half of America repeating its slogan and theme, "Love means never having to say you're sorry."

The film was produced by Robert Evans. After several months he took

Ali and Steve during a pivotal moment in *The Getaway*. The movie in which she played a murderous gangster was a far cry from the sappy *Love Story* that had made her famous. Originally, Ali had preferred Warren Beatty or Robert Redford as her leading man, but one night, Steve showed up at her condo, shirtless, in blue jeans, and without underwear, winning her over.

notice of Ali, and they were married in October of 1969. Evans installed her in his Beverly Hills mansion where two dozen pink phones rang day and night. Back in 1957, the handsome Evans had played a bullfighter in *The Sun Also Rises* with Errol Flynn, Ava Gardner, and Tyrone Power. At the time, Darryl F. Zanuck had labeled Evans "the hottest young man since Valentino," but Evans didn't turn out to be much of an actor.

From the beginning, the Evans/MacGraw marriage showed signs of strain. As the head of a powerful studio, Evans was gone many days and many nights. At the peak of her sexual desires, she didn't enjoy having an absentee husband, as she spent hours alone in a deluxe black marble bathtub or watching the latest films screened in Evans' projection room. Wandering around the Evans mansion, she pictured herself as a movie widow.

When the couple gave birth to a son, Joshua, in January of 1971, that blessed event provided some momentary distraction for Ali. But the strains in her marriage had become obvious months even before she was cast opposite Steve in *The Getaway*.

When she was told that she'd gotten the role, Ali's enthusiasm for Steve's screen performances had dimmed. She'd once thrilled to his image on the screen, but after the fabulous success of *Love Story*, she told Peckinpah that "I would have preferred Robert Redford or Warren Beatty as my leading man." Fortunately, word of that didn't get back to Steve, who no doubt would have exploded in rage. He also would have refused to work with her.

Steve, with outstretched hand, gives shooting lessons to Ali MacGraw on the set of *The Getaway*. She'd later tell a reporter from *The New York Times*: It was not my finest hour, and I'm sorry I wasn't better in the movie. But I'm not about to break into tears.'

"I guess McQueen will do," she added weakly.

When Ali actually met Steve for the first time at a party hosted by her then-husband, Evans, she changed her tune. "It was like a thunderbolt," she later said. "I saw him two thousand feet away and almost passed out. It was the strongest electric connection I've ever experienced in my life."

"When Evans was back in Hollywood, and Ali and Steve came together in Texas to shoot *The Getaway*, the stars at night shone a little brighter over the Lone Star state," Peckinpah said. "The attraction was immediate."

The following day, when members of the press asked Ali what she thought of her co-star, she claimed he "is no bullshitter like most Hollywood phonies. Really, he's a fascinating man."

On location, sex between Steve and Ali occurred on the second night. Steve appeared before the door of her condominium and knocked loudly with a certain macho swagger. Shirtless, he wore only a pair of sandals and blue jeans with no underwear.

Once invited in, he didn't wait to consume the drink offered, but began pulling off her clothes and his jeans. "I schtupped her right on the carpet," he later told his friends. "We couldn't wait to go to the bedroom."

She later claimed that getting seduced by Steve was like a "drug high."

From the beginning, Steve admitted his affair with Ali to Neile, who envisioned the possibility of her alimony payments disappearing if Ali's husband, one of the biggest honchos in the movie industry, ever took revenge on the man who was undermining his marriage. Neile worried that Steve's future would be limited to spaghetti westerns in Spain or Italy, or perhaps playing a detective like *Bullitt* in some underfinanced German film.

Only forty-eight hours into the shoot, epic battles were raging between Steve and Peckinpah, often in front of Ali. In one violent argument, Steve nearly bashed in his director's head with a magnum of champagne. The champagne on the set had been ordered to celebrate Peckinpah's birthday.

In contrast, Steve and Ali worked well together except for one problem. She'd been cast as the driver of the getaway car, and Peckinpah had just assumed that a Los Angeles woman knew how to drive. Ali did not.

"Skiddin' left, then right, she barely missed killing all the extras," Steve told Peckinpah. "Let me drive. I'm a world champion."

Peckinpah refused the request. "As for you being a great driver, kid, you've never met a car you didn't wreck. Who did you fuck to get a driver's license?"

Lovers both on and off the screen, **Steve** and **Ali MacGraw** in *The Getaway* never, as a couple, became a screen legend, even though that had been their goal. Script after script arrived in attempts to team them again, but Steve rejected all such offers, insisting, sometimes violently, that he didn't want "any other actor with a hard-on" appearing opposite Ali.

Steve's by now legendary homophobia reasserted itself in one of the opening scenes of the movie. For greater authenticity, actual prisoners were used from the local penitentiary at Huntsville, Texas, in which Steve plays a convict. He was required to strip down to shower with his fellow prisoners, who were real, not actors. It was only later that he learned that he'd been assigned to "the faggot section of the cellblock." Even though his genitals were not shown on the screen, he was furious to learn that he'd stripped completely nude and showered "with all those faggots."

For his role of Doc McCoy, Steve used Humphrey Bogart's performance in *High Sierra* (1941) as his role model.

To round out the cast of character actors, Peckinpah brought in old favorites such as Ben Johnson and Slim Pickens.

In a bit of surprise casting, the film also co-starred Sally Struthers, Archie Bunker's little girl, Gloria, cast in the slutty role of Fran, playing the wife of a rural veterinarian (Jack Dodson).

As an indication of the era's rapidly changing values, in the relatively permissive 1970s, Steve and Ali get away with their crime, violating the long-held rule that crimes do not pay. For the Spanish language version intended for viewing in Fascist Spain, the ending was changed, with additional footage showing Steve apprehended six weeks later and being hauled off to jail.

Even from the beginning, Ali and Steve had arguments off screen, as she seemed to resent his attempt to control her life. "With me and Steve, confrontation was the norm," she later said.

He got jealous after hearing stories about her former lovers, who had included Ryan O'Neal during the making of *Love Story*. He was even jealous of her first husband, Robin Hoehn, a Harvard man, Class of 1960, whom she quickly married and divorced in 1960. Oddly, in her autobiography, *Moving Pictures*, she referred to him by the pseudonym of "Alex."

One night at a party Ali infuriated Steve when she told a story about having had her toes sucked by surrealist

Blasting their way out of a trap in *The Getaway*, **Steve and Ali** were wed in Cheyenne, Wyoming, with the kids looking on. "I sensed from the minute I met Steve McQueen that I might might turn my life upside down for him. And I did."
It might indeed have been love, but he wrecked her financially.
She was left with nothing.

artist Salvador Dalí in his suite at the St. Regis Hotel in New York. "After that little encounter, Dalí sent me a fat, live iguana in a flower box," Ali said. "Its long tail was covered with imitation pearls."

In her memoirs, Ali wrote about her six-year marriage to Steve, asserting that he was stoned "almost every day."

Right from the launch of their affair, she knew that Steve would not be a faithful husband. "On days when he was angry with me, he would very flagrantly pick up one or more of the stream of bimbos who were always around the set. One night I could hear him in his apartment next door with two girls. It was excruciating."

"You have a great ass," he told her early in their relationship, "but you'd better start working out now, because I don't want to wake up one day with a woman who's got an ass like a seventy-year-old Japanese soldier. To me, a woman's ass is important. Jane Fonda always works out and keeps her ass in A-1 condition."

"Then why don't you go and fuck Fonda's ass?" Ali reportedly yelled at Steve.

If his love scenes with Suzanne Pleshette and Jacqueline Bisset lacked conviction, Steve heated up the screen in his scenes with Ali. "They weren't play-acting," Peckinpah claimed. "It was the real thing. The screen sizzled."

"I've found someone to replace Neile," he told Casey and Darron. They felt that they were losing the close bond that had existed between them and Steve before Ali, and were frankly jealous of their new competition. "He'll be back," Casey predicted to Darron.

Released just before Christmas of 1972, *The Getaway* was a box office hit, earning twenty-six million dollars at movie houses across the country. In 1994, it was remade in a rather lackluster fashion. Still called *The Getaway*, it starred Alec Baldwin and Kim Basinger.

Steve and Peckinpah would never work together again.

At the wrap party for *The Getaway*, Ali was madly in love with Steve, and he was in love with her, as much as he could love anyone. She prepared herself for a return to Hollywood, where she planned to tell Evans that their marriage was over.

Still in the throes of post-divorce trauma, Steve was looking for love, even if with a married woman.

***

The Getaway did not open to rave reviews, and "the dream couple," Steve McQueen and Ali MacGraw, would not be viewed as a charismatic duo with the magnetism of Clark Gable and Carole Lombard or Spencer Tracy and

Katharine Hepburn.

Pauline Kael, of *The New Yorker*, even pointed out in one of her reviews that Ali's head was bigger than Steve's. She also said, "His low-key professionalism is turning into minimal acting, and is indistinguishable from the blahs, while she is certainly the primmest, smuggest gangster's moll of all time."

Kael got in a final dig. "Last time I saw Candice Bergen, I thought she was a worse actress than MacGraw. Now I think I slandered Bergen."

Even Ali herself didn't like the movie. She told *The New York Times*, "It wasn't my finest hour. I'm sorry not to be better in it, but I'm not about to break into tears."

When Ali returned to Los Angeles, and made her husband completely aware of her affair with Steve, Evans thought that the marriage might still be saved.

He asked her to fly to New York with him for the premiere of his massive hit, *The Godfather*. Pictures of the two of them, called "The Happy Couple," were splashed across the frontpages of newspapers around the nation. It appeared that a reconciliation was underway. After all, the French actor, Alain Delon, in Rome, had assured Evans that, in his opinion, it was no more than "a location fuck."

"The greatest thing since Valentino," **Robert Evans**, in a bullfighter's costume, posed for this picture on location while filming Hemingway's *The Sun Also Rises (1957)* with Tyrone Power, Ava Gardner, and Errol Flynn. When the studio wanted to fire him, producer Darryl Zanuck bellowed famously, "The kid stays in the picture. If anyone doesn't like it, they can quit..."

When Ali came back to Hollywood, Evans booked her into a desert health spa "to think everything over before you ruin your life." Soaking in a world of eucalyptus steams and salt-glows at Murrieta Springs, she was constantly plagued with unwanted calls from both Steve and Evans.

Evans later admitted that at first he had no idea of the affair. "She was looking at me and thinking of Steve McQueen's cock."

Later, as he became more combative, Evans claimed that Ali was an unfit mother since she'd been "living in sin" with Steve.

Resisting his pressure, she moved out of his mansion and

found a secluded house off Mulholland Drive. It looked down on Steve's rented villa on Coldwater Canyon. The two houses were only twenty-five yards apart on foot, and the pathway between the two houses became well worn.

Adding to the pain and insult of losing his wife, Evans soon perceived that even custody of his son, Joshua, was in danger after Steve foolishly and belligerently called him. He claimed that Evans did not provide a proper home environment for the boy. "Your butler's a homosexual," Steve argued. "Your surroundings, the way you live, is not the environment that's right for Joshua."

Fighting back, Evans hired "the toughest Irishman attorney west of Chicago," Arthur Crowley, who promised Evans that Joshua would remain his kid, and that "this actor punk's gonna get a second asshole" when he finished with Steve.

On the day of confrontation, Crowley showed up with a dossier on Steve—he called it "his passport to oblivion"—that was almost a foot in height. Steve had been a very bad boy, and apparently much of his notorious past was documented in that dossier.

When Steve was confronted with this tsunami of evidence, it would be his career that was ruined. The claim that Evans' butler was a homosexual paled in comparison to what detectives had assembled on Steve.

Fearing a public exposure of his past, Steve caved in after facing this compendium of evidence of acts which, in many cases, had been illegal. He had no alternative but to give in to Evans.

As Steve was leaving with his own lawyer, Evans called to him, "Mr. Macho, in the future when you address me, call me *Mister* Evans."

During the filming of *The Getaway*, Steve had continued to place telephone calls to Neile, mostly to talk about Chad and Terry. Increasingly, she had noticed a hoarseness in his voice which soon developed into a cough. She urged him to get a total physical check-up and to give up smoking weed. "Without weed, Steve McQueen has no life," he told her.

Neile's fears proved right. After *The Getaway* was wrapped, and after an exami-

One of Steve's most memorable films, *Papillon*, was based on the life story of **Henri Charrière**, who may have taken liberties with the facts of his incarceration and eventual escape from Devil's Island. Despite its horrific and gritty plot, the story was a romanticized version of one man's quest for freedom following his imprisonment for a crime he didn't commit. Charrière is pictured here in a snapshot taken just a few days before his death.

nation, Steve was operated on at Mt. Sinai Hospital for removal of polyps in his throat. Excessive smoking was blamed.

Significantly, Neile showed up at the hospital to wait out the operation on Steve's throat. On the other hand, Ali sent flowers and a get well card. Perhaps that was the discreet thing to do. At the time, she was still living with Evans. Even so, Steve never really forgave her for what he perceived as a lack of involvement.

Although at the time, doctors announced that Steve's throat operation had been successful, Neile still had her doubts, writing in her memoirs that she was convinced "that this was the start of the insidious cancer that would in time destroy him. It was as if it had announced its presence to this almost perfect body and had said unceremoniously, 'Beware, I am here.'"

***

Steve needed cash, and he accurately guessed that appearing as Henri Charrière in the movie *Papillon* (1973) would get him a bonanza. This time around, Steve was correct in following his hunch, as *Papillon* brought him $2.3 million, which was a record for that era. In contrast, his co-star, Dustin Hoffman, walked off with only $1.25 million.

Papillon, which translates from the French as "Butterfly," takes its name from a tattoo on the chest of Henri Charrière, a petty criminal who in 1931 was convicted in a Paris court for the murder of a pimp, which he did not commit. He was sentenced to life imprisonment in the notoriously brutal penal colony of French Guyana.

The Odd Couple: **Steve McQueen** and **Dustin Hoffman** as French colonial prisoners led the cast of *Papillon.* When Steve saw Hoffman in *The Graduate,* he lamented, "The day of the Hollywood pretty boy, guys like Newman and me, is over."

During the filming of *Papillon,* Steve dreaded scenes with Hoffman, fearing that the actor might upstage him, especially through use of props that included those coke bottle glasses.

The story, based on the sometimes-dubious autobiography, published in 1968, of the real-life Henri ("Papillon") Charrière, concerns the prisoner's treacherous, yet failed, attempts to escape from his notorious prison. Finally, when sentenced to Devil's Island, from which no prisoner had ever escaped, and after years of being brutalized, he figures out a way to float away to freedom.

After reading Charrière's best-seller, Steve

knew that he had a prize property. It was a shocking, gripping, brutal, but ultimately uplifting odyssey of how far a human spirit will go to find the freedom that was wrongly denied him.

In real life, Charrière escaped in 1945 to Venezuela, where he later married and opened a restaurant in Caracas. He died in 1973.

Steve flew to Spain to film early scenes of *Papillon*.

In Europe, he learned that he hadn't been the original choice to star in the film. The French backers of the movie had wanted Jean Paul Belmondo, then the reigning star of the Continent. But the producers decided that to make a hit in the American market they needed a Hollywood star. Steve fitted the bill perfectly because he was also France's favorite foreign movie star.

Impressed with the sale of the book *Papillon*—five million copies in America and seventeen million abroad—director Roman Polanski wanted to film the movie starring Warren Beatty, but could not raise financing.

Steve met Franklin J. Schaffner, his director and one of the most innovative and creative minds in the movie business. Ten years older than Steve, he had been born in Tokyo, Japan. He had already directed such films as Gore Vidal's *The Best Man* in 1964, *Planet of the Apes* in 1968, and *Patton* in 1970. On meeting Steve, he told him, "Your role has Oscar written all over it."

The screenplay had been written in part by Dalton Trumbo, the blacklisted writer who also appeared in the film as the Commandant.

More and more, Steve hated the press and photographers, who after the release of *La Dolce Vita* were known as *paparazzi*. He referred to them as a "shitbag of cunts."

When Ali flew to see Steve on location, her arrival created a tabloid feeding frenzy. Her "illicit" romance with Steve almost spawned more headlines than those of Richard Burton and Elizabeth Taylor when they were filming *Cleopatra* in Rome.

In a wimple that resembles a shroud, the Mother Superior, a nun descended directly from Hell, calls for police to haul **Steve** back to prison. She informs him that if he's innocent, God will save him. If not, he deserves his punishment. In the meanwhile, she'll keep his precious pearls to feed the poor.

Ali wasn't the only one who showed up on location. Henri Charrière also arrived and was amazed at how the prison set looked very much like the one

369

where he'd been interred for so many years. He had many long talks and drinks with Steve, telling him tall tales of his adventures.

After he'd gone, Steve told Schaffner, "Henri is a major bullshitter. His book is filled with lies and exaggerations. But, what the hell. We're not making a God damn documentary. Let the cameras roll. Ali calls it poetic license."

After Steve had seen Dustin Hoffman in *The Graduate* in 1967, he left the theater in total confusion. Had ugly actors taken over the screen in an attempt to achieve greater naturalism and reality in films? Were the handsome Rock Hudsons and Tab Hunters of the 1950s on the way out the door? On the way home, Steve asked Neile, "What's going to happen to two pretty boys like Paul Newman and me? That Hoffman is one ugly cat, real homely."

Despite the fact that they were living apart from each other at the time, Steve wanted to remain with Neile after watching that movie. He pulled off his clothes and stood nude in front of her full length mirror. Turning to Neile, he reportedly asked her, "Look at this face and body. Ok, babe, which one would you pick? Hoffman or yours truly?"

Steve admired Hoffman's acting but, with the exception of *The Graduate,* not necessarily his choice of movies. In 1969, he'd been shocked when Hoffman's *Midnight Cowboy* had been voted Best Picture of the Year. "Can you imagine," he asked Neile, "a picture about two fags becoming Best Picture of the Year? I saw the stinking thing. It's a God damn dirty movie and should never have been written, much less filmed. To think that both Elvis Presley and Paul Newman wanted to play a male hustler selling his dick on Times Square."

High on Jamaican *ganja,* **Steve** appears (left photo) with this striking exotic beauty, **Ratna Assan,** who would later pose topless for a three-page spread in *Playboy.* There were rumors of a romance. In the right-hand photo, character actor **Victor Jory**, as an Indian chief, demands that Steve tattoo a butterfly (*papillon*) onto his chest.

Casey and Darron speculated that *Midnight Cowboy* raised old traumas in Steve associated with his early days as a male hustler. As he grew older, he tried to remove himself as far as possible from his early life.

When Hoffman first arrived on the set of *Papillon* wearing Coke-bottle spectacles, Steve greatly feared that such a prop would upstage him in their joint scenes.

Hoffman seemed perfectly cast as Louis Dega, a short, slender, and stoop-shouldered convict sent to the penal colony of French Guyana for forgery.

A scholarly, trepidant weakling, the character of Dega was known to have money, no doubt forged, which he had secreted in his rectum. "Men are the only animals that shove things up their ass for survival," wrote Charrière.

During the shoot, even though Hoffman was a better trained actor, Steve dared to give him some advice. He interrupted one of Hoffman's long-winded speeches by saying, "Less, man, less. Toss that shit out, you don't need it. Keep it simple."

Originally budgeted at four million dollars, the eventual cost of shooting *Papillon* skyrocketed to more than fourteen million. A lot of the extra cost was based on location shooting in both Spain and Jamaica. The film's budget, or so it was estimated, was six times the net worth of Allied Artists, which planned to release *Papillon*.

From the beginning, the producers of the film did not have enough financing. At one point the crew went for six weeks in Spain without a paycheck. When Steve found this out, he refused to work any more until the backers raised the needed cash.

In an emergency, they flew cans of the film to Paris where they met with "angels" willing to put up yet more money. Flying back to Spain, they paid the crew and gave both Hoffman and Steve their missing per diem allowances. Shooting resumed, but Steve's shut-

After the character he played spent five years in solitary confinement (left photo), **Steve** never looked worse than he did when he appeared on camera in rags, his face pale, his eyes sunken, his mask one of despair. Gone was his image as the screen's leading male sex symbol.

In a boat (right photo), he'll make a bid for his precious freedom, only to fail. But in the end, as part of yet another attempt, he will at last succeed.

down of production cost the company an extra $250,000.

***

Flying to Jamaica for the final location shoot, Steve as Papillon was to recreate life and incarceration on Devil's Island. As a screen tradition, he was following in the footsteps of Bogie in *Passage to Marseilles* (1944), Clark Gable in *Strange Cargo* (1940) and Boris Karloff in *Devil's Island* (1940).

He was in love with Ali, who wanted to remain in Hollywood, but she flew back and forth to Jamaica so Steve wouldn't feel abandoned or wouldn't "become involved with someone else if I stayed away too long."

In Jamaica, she discovered that Steve was putting on weight. He'd developed a taste for the island's Red Stripe beer. In contrast, Hoffman subsisted on half a coconut a day to keep his skeletal look.

Steve also took to a diet of heavy Jamaican specialties, which he came to love. He devoured not only curry dishes and refried beans, jerk pork, "dip and fall back" (a salty stew with bananas and dumplings), and "manish water" (a soup made from goat offal and tripe said to increase virility). Wardrobe had to keep making his prison uniforms bigger and bigger.

When not eating and drinking, Steve smoked *ganja*, pronouncing it the best marijuana in the world.

Steve's longtime friend, Don Gordon, played the role of Julot in *Papillon*. He spoke to author Penina Spiegel about the way Steve treated Ali on location in Jamaica. "Hey, cunt, come over here," Steve would call to Ali and she came. He'd grab her and kiss and even pinch her ass. 'Ooooh, what a great ass you got! Look at this ass, Don!'"

Schaffner later revealed that when Ali was back in California, Steve sampled "a lot of beautiful brown belles. Let's face it: Jamaica has some of the most gorgeous women in the Caribbean. He was no longer married to Neile. I'd never seen anything like it. These beauties practically lined up to get seduced by Steve. After flying out of there, I decided Jamaica was the sexiest island in the Caribbean, not that I've visited all the ports down there."

Steve expressed bitterness that some reviews called *Papillon* "a male love story."

"I don't shoot faggot pictures," he responded angrily. There was, however, a homosexual subtext in the film, where Steve's character urged a handsome young man to prostitute himself with another man in hopes of mugging him to expedite their escape from prison.

The only woman of note in the film was actress Ratna Assan, who also posed for a three-page topless spread in *Playboy* in February of 1974.

Cast as Zoraima, she played Steve's love interest in the movie. Born in

Torrance, California in 1954, she was the daughter of the 1940s MGM contract player, Devi Dia. Rumors in Jamaica linked her in a romantic liaison with Steve, but these cannot be confirmed.

To movie-goers, the face of the Indian chief looked familiar. It was the Canadian actor, Victor Jory. He is remembered chiefly today for his appearance as the Yankee-collaborating tax collector who taunted Vivien Leigh in *Gone With the Wind*. Based on his attempt to take a devastated Tara from her, Scarlett O'Hara tossed dirt into his face.

Steve had never looked so grotesque in a film, especially during the final thirty minutes, when he is made up to look like a gray-haired prisoner emerging from five years of solitary. "So what?" he told the director. "Fuck 'em. So the Memphis belles will no longer vote me the sexiest male animal alive."

Allied Artists premiered the 150-minute film on December 16, 1973. Pauline Kael dipped her pen in acid, writing in *The New Yorker* that, "If ever there was a wrong actor for a man of great spirit, it's McQueen."

Variety was more mesmerized by the film: "The atmosphere bored into the brain like it does to its victims, leaving them as well as an audience stunned, disoriented, incredulous, and nearly catatonic. It takes literally hours to come out of *Papillon*."

Film critic Casey St. Charnez graphically described some of the gory details presented to shocked audiences on the screen. "A prisoner's decapitated head splashes blood on the camera lens, a rifle wound pumps blood arterially, a centipede is sectioned with a spoon edge and dumped into a vomitous soup in solitary, a cut throat dribbles on beach sand, bug-gnawed corpses populate jungle underbrush, an escapee is impaled on a spring-driven Punjab stick, and sad, rotting lepers hide in huts and scarify with makeup heavy on horror and empty of pathos."

Despite the nasty reviews, *Papillon* became Allied Artists' highest grossing film, $25 million in the United States and more than $30 million worldwide. It is still shown today.

The film got a PG rating after some legal hassles. Some "blue noses" objected to an opening shot of one hundred bare-assed men or extended scenes with bare-breasted Indian women in the tropics.

Many critics, in contrast to the negative reviews, claimed that both Steve and Hoffman gave the single best performances of their careers. However, neither of them received even a nomination by the Academy. The Best Actor Oscar that year went to Jack Lemmon for *Save the Tiger*.

In trying to explain Steve's loss, Schaffner speculated that "a lot of actors didn't like Steve. If they worked with him, he upstaged them and stole scenes from them. If they didn't work with him, he probably had fucked their wives. Among the women, he'd probably fucked half of them and then dumped them rather crudely. If he hadn't fucked them, then they resented that fact. In talking with people over the years, when the name Steve McQueen came up, it was almost invariably followed by 'arrogant prick.'"

Steve's curt response to hearing how much his fellow actors loathed him? "I never went in for Hollywood ass kissing."

Since Steve McQueen still lives today on television, in DVDs, and in McQueen merchandise such as T-shirts and watches, his epitaph might well have been uttered in the closing lines of *Papillon*. "Hey, you bastards," he shouted at the sky, "I'm still here."

***

Even though he'd fallen in love with her, Steve didn't want to be with Ali all the time. He tried to escape whenever he could with Casey and Darron. One such weekend in May of 1972 found him in a rented Oldsmobile Toronado driving recklessly through the streets of Anchorage, Alaska.

"Raising hell on wheels and laying down rubber" (the words of one witness), he was stopped by a policeman.

"Hi, I'm Steve McQueen, and I'm having a hell of a time in this one-moose town."

"Pull over and get out," the policeman said. Steve staggered from the car with a beer in hand. When he was ordered to walk along a straight road line, he failed a sobriety test. Instead of walking, he somersaulted his way along.

Handcuffed, he was taken to the local jail, where a quick phone call led to his posting bail. While handcuffed, he signed autographs for the police staff. Fleeing town after he was freed, he was later convicted in absentia for reckless driving. The charge was later dropped.

As the months went by, Steve got along better with Neile than Ali. He often met Neile for private dinners in Malibu, and once he asked Neile if he could move back in with her in her new home on Amalfi Drive.

She turned him down, claiming, "I am not your wife any more."

To that, he replied, "You will always be my wife."

Robert Evans recalled waking up one morning and making love to his wife before heading out to direct Paramount. When he returned that night, she was gone, fleeing his mansion for Steve's arms. But it wasn't until June 7, 1973 that her divorce from Evans became final.

Ali did not ask for alimony from her millionaire husband, although, considering how her career later collapsed, she regretted that decision. Moving from one of the most luxurious mansions in Hollywood, she went to live in a modest rented villa at Trancas Beach on the far frontier of Malibu.

Terry McQueen preferred to live most of the time with her mother, Neile, although Chad wanted to spend most months with Steve and Ali.

On July 12, 1973, Alice MacGraw Hoehn Evans married Terrence Stephen McQueen. The ceremony was performed under the cottonwoods on the tranquil shores of Lake Minnehaha in Cheyenne, Wyoming.

From the beginning of their marriage, Ali made it clear that she wanted Steve to cut back on his drinking, drug taking, and "lost weekends," most of them spent running off on wild adventures with Casey and Darron.

Ali never met Steve's two companions, and they were relieved that Steve continued to see them. When Steve remarried, both Casey and Darron feared that they would be dropped.

After marriage, Ali more or less turned her back on Hollywood and her career. "All I want is to be with my son, Joshua, and Steve."

With the financial success of *Papillon*, Steve was flooded with new scripts. Ali had dreamed of starring in *The Great Gatsby*, based on F. Scott Fitzgerald's jazz age novel, opposite Steve himself. But because of her divorce from Evans, that was no longer possible. In one of filmdom's most horrible miscasting decisions, the part went instead to Mia Farrow. Mia, not Ali, got Robert Redford as her leading man.

Steve was sent selected scripts, including *Fort Apache, The Bronx*, but he turned down the role of a beat cop working the mean streets of the Bronx. In 1981, Paul Newman signed for the role on the dotted line instead.

The most bizarre offer of all came for him to play Rhett Butler in *Tara: The Continuation of Gone With the Wind*. "I can't pull that one off," Steve said. "Clark Gable's shoes are too big for me."

Many actors were waiting to grab Steve's rejects, including Sylvester Stallone in *First Blood* (1975), Jack Nicholson's Academy Award-winning performance in *One Flew Over the Cuckoo's Nest* (1975), and Marlon Brando in Francis Ford Coppola's *Apocalypse Now* (1976).

At one point, Steve and Ali were offered *Gable and Lombard* (1976). Wisely, both of them rejected the offer. "I'm no Gable and Ali has nothing to do with Carole Lombard."

The script for *The Betsy* (1978) arrived on Steve's doorstep, based on another Harold Robbins' novel. He'd already starred in two films portraying Robbins characters. This time he said no, and subsequently, Robert Duvall signed on. He also nixed the *Sorcerer* (1977), the role going to Roy Scheider.

Steve let it be known that in the future, Ali would star only in films with him. "And at the moment I'm not starring in anything," he said. Soon he wouldn't even read a script unless it arrived with a check for $50,000. After that announcement, the number of scripts sent to him dwindled.

It was then that he made one of the most shocking announcements from any star in Hollywood history. He ordained that in the future, any producer who wanted to star him in a film had to include a check for one and a half million dollars with the script.

If, after that, Steve agreed to star in the movie, the producer would then have to send yet another check for one and a half-million dollars. If a producer was unable to write a second check for the remainder of the money, Steve would then seize the first million and a half as his personal property.

That proclamation meant that Steve was virtually removing himself from the scene of action. Very few producers wanted to accept such terms.

In contrast, however, studio chiefs at both 20th Century Fox and Warner Brothers gave a green light to Steve's outrageous demands and sent over both checks and a script. It was called *The Towering Inferno*.

Debating whether he wanted to play the architect or the firefighter, Steve agreed to head the cast.

"There's only one problem," said the film's co-director, Irwin Allen. "Paul Newman's also starring in it. He wants top billing."

"Wanting and getting are two different things," Steve shot back. "My dick is bigger than his, so I get top billing. Not only that, but my eyes are bluer."

In his hooded prisoner's cap, **Steve** was Henri Charrière's personal choice to impersonate him on the screen. Roman Polanski had wanted to direct Warren Beatty in his own version of the film, but the director who eventually presided was Franklin J. Schaffner, who preferred Steve. Even so, the acerbic film critic Pauline Kael asserted that Steve was "a wrong actor for a man of great spirit."

Chapter Ten
The Last Mile

Despite his recent marriage to Ali MacGraw, Steve still wanted to possess his first wife, Neile Adams McQueen. Whenever he learned that she was dating some other man, he became almost insanely jealous, wanting to physically attack her suitor.

Such was the case when Neile had a harmless date with John Gavin, whom she does not name in her memoirs but refers to as "Don Juan." Power agent Sue Mengers arranged a date between Neile and Gavin, who stood 6'4", towering over her. He was a fifth generation Angeleno. At the time she dated him, Gavin was being groomed as "the next Rock Hudson" in case the original "got too big for his britches."

Tall, dark, and handsome, Gavin showed up on time at her doorstep.

The date was a disaster. When Neile lit up a cigarette on the way to the restaurant, he told her he forbade smoking in the car. At the restaurant, he asked her not to order garlic bread, as he could not stand the smell on a woman's breath. She couldn't wait for the evening to end. After giving her the obligatory peck on the cheek, he disappeared from her doorstep forever.

She was surprised that years later, his friend, Ronald Reagan, appointed him ambassador to Mexico in May of 1981. Gavin is known to movie audiences today primarily because of his appearance in Alfred Hitchcock's *Psycho* (1960). He almost became James Bond in the series, losing the part, of course, to Sean Connery.

By proxy, Gavin came between Steve and Neile in spite of their nothing date. When her for-

Long before he became Ronald Reagan's ambassador to Mexico, tall, dark, and handsome **John Gavin** was groomed to become the next Rock Hudson. His sexual taste differed from Hudson's, however, and he dated Neile Adams McQueen, which led to a punch in the nose from Steve. Gavin is known to movie audiences today because of his appearance in *Psycho* for Alfred Hitchcock.

mer husband arrived to divvy up some of their possessions, he demanded the pool table, which he'd been given when making *The Cincinnati Kid*.

Suddenly, perhaps to be stubborn, Neile decided to take a stand. For some reason, she was determined to keep the pool table. "You don't want that table," she told him. "John Gavin and I made love on that table the other night."

At first he looked at her in stunned disbelief, and she feared he might kill her for sure. Instead, he stormed out of the house. "Keep the fucking table," he called back at her.

In a chance encounter, Steve confronted Gavin at El Padrino in the Beverly Wilshire Hotel, where he proceeded to denounce him. "You son-of-a-bitch! You fucked my old lady on my pool table." Steve's punch landed squarely in the stunned face of Gavin, who didn't know what he'd done.

Not knowing the full story, Gavin later told friends, "That Steve McQueen takes a lot of drugs. He gets violent when he does. Stay away from him. A man can lose his front teeth around a guy like that."

***

After the death of Bruce Lee, Steve took karate lessons from Chuck Norris, an Oklahoma-born martial artist and former U.S. Air Force man. He founded a school, Chun Kuk Do, but was lured into films in 1972 when he co-starred with Bruce Lee, playing his nemesis in the movie, *Return of the Dragon*.

This film launched him into stardom. Taking advantage of his new-found fame, he pumped money into a chain of karate schools, one of which Chad McQueen attended.

Today Norris is a Right Wing conservative, turning out Born Again books for Christians, including *The Justice Riders*. He became the first show business personality to defend California's notorious Proposition 8, a ban on same-sex marriage.

After Norris went on his way, Steve trained with Pat E. Johnson, who remained one of his closest friends until the actor's death. A 9th degree Black Belt in Tang Soo Do, he learned the art in 1963 during his military stint in South Korea.

Karate champion **Chuck Norris** looks like he's gearing up to take on gays who want to get married in California. This Born-Again Christian right-winger was an Oklahoma-born martial artist who faced off against Bruce Lee in *Return of the Dragon*. He taught the McQueens (father and son) how to defend themselves.

Johnson later fought nearly 200 matches, losing just once.

He was a firm instructor, believing in hard-nosed karate. Once, when Steve showed up without ironing his uniform, he was forced to do push-ups.

Gradually Johnson and Steve, both distrustful men, became intimate buddies. When Steve needed an alibi during his marriage to Ali, he claimed he was going over to Johnson's house. Often he ended up in a motel with a bimbo he'd picked up. He always registered under the name of Pat Johnson.

While registered as Johnson at the Vagabond Inn on Santa Monica Boulevard with some unknown pickup, Steve received a call from Johnson, who always knew where he was staying. "Warner Brothers is trying to reach you. They're offering you a movie called *The Towering Inferno*."

Steve arrived at the studio four hours late wearing a Groucho Marx mask. After a rather bitter discussion, he signed a contract to make *The Towering Inferno*, his last big hit, a movie that would net him twelve million dollars. That deal would define him as the world's highest paid movie star.

***

Installed in his new home at Trancas Beach with Ali and his son, Chad, Steve one day encountered his new neighbor. Naked from the waist down, Keith Moon and Steve met in the rear of their houses as both were walking to the beach.

"It's about to blow," Moon shouted at Steve. "Duck!" Without knowing what was happening, Steve was knocked to the ground. In seconds a blast came from the rear of Moon's house. Exploding shards of porcelain shot through the yard. Picking himself up from where he'd thrown himself onto the lawn, the neighbor said, "Hi, I'm Keith Moon. I just moved in. I blow up toilets. It's a hobby of mine."

Once he heard the name, Steve knew at once who he was: The English drummer of the rock group "The Who." He indeed had gained a reputation for blowing up toilets, and that's why he wasn't welcomed at any hotel in the world.

"Hey, man, I heard about your gig of

"Moon the Loon," or **Keith Moon,** as he was known, was the lead drummer of the rock group "The Who." When not smoking a "fag," as pictured above, he spent time blowing up toilets in whatever hotel he stayed in. He became Steve's neighbor from hell when he moved into the house next door and began launching cherry bombs against the walls of Steve's house.

blowing up toilets, but I thought they belonged to other people," Steve said. "If you blow up your toilet, where are you going to take a crap?"

"In the ocean," Moon said, looking at the water in the distance. "I always like to shit in the ocean. Wanna join me?"

"No thanks," Steve said, retreating toward his house. "I've already crapped this morning."

That wasn't the last Steve would see of "Moon the Loon." Two weeks later, when Steve came outside to get into his car, he saw pieces of furniture being tossed from Moon's second floor terrace. Moon leaned out the window and called to him, "Good morning, McQueen."

"What in hell are you doing, man?" Steve called up to him.

"I'm tired of this fucking furniture, and I'm getting rid of it," Moon said. "Could you come up and help me with the big pieces like the bed?"

"Gotta go," Steve said, roaring off into the morning on his motorcycle.

Steve tolerated Moon until the following week when he began to lob cherry bombs from his window against Steve's house. The following night, Moon's Rolls-Royce exploded in his garage.

In the days ahead, Steve noticed electricians working on Moon's house, seemingly rewiring it. Five nights later, at midnight, massive spotlights were turned on, flooding Steve's villa with light. Racing nude down the stairs, Steve grabbed his rifle and rushed out into his front yard with a round of ammunition. One by one he took out each of those spotlights.

To get revenge, Moon arranged with somebody to purchase a dozen deadly rattlesnakes, which he had released in Steve's front yard. The plot didn't work. By the time the McQueens woke up and went outside, all the snakes had slithered away, although there were a lot of screams coming from the beach later that morning.

Both Steve and Ali were gone one afternoon when Moon showed up at the McQueen's front door, demanding to see Steve. Chad told him that his father wasn't home. The drummer forced himself into the house, not knowing that Chad had been trained in karate. Within five seconds the boy had punched Moon, knocking him out cold.

Steve pulled up on his motorcycle about three minutes later. Seeing what Chad had done, he said, "I've never been prouder of you, son." Both of them dragged Moon over to the side of his house and dumped him in his garbage can.

***

Inspired by the box office returns of *The Poseidon Adventure* (1972), starring Gene Hackman, both 20th Century Fox and Warner Brothers pooled their resources to make *The Towering Inferno*, a disaster movie with an all star cast. Scheduled for release on December 18, 1974, it would include location shooting in San Francisco where Steve had filmed *Bullitt*. Veteran producer Irwin Allen was the main director, with John Guillermin in charge of dialogue directing.

The two lead roles included that of an architect, Doug Roberts, who designed the skyscraper, and the fire chief, Michael O'Hallorhan, who faced the impossible task of putting out a major fire in the monstrously tall building.

From the beginning, Allen had envisioned Steve in the role of the architect, with Ernest Borgnine as the fire chief. When Steve read the script, one of the few he actually read, he wanted to play the fireman, after he correctly perceived that it was the more heroic of the two roles. "Steve was always the greedy pig when it came to scripts," Allen said. "He wanted the cream off the milk at the detriment of his fellow actors."

When Paul Newman, Steve's longtime friend and longtime rival, read the script, he agreed to play the role of the architect. Immediately, Steve demanded top billing, but Paul maintained that he was an international star with far more credentials than Steve. Freddie Fields, the agent, intervened and created the concept of equal billing.

Steve's name would appear on the left while Newman's name would be billed slightly higher on the right. At the time, this layout was referred to as "equal billing," and both Steve and Newman finally agreed to it after some bitter arguments. Steve caved in when Ali pointed out to him that most people, at least in the English language, read from the left to the right; therefore, they would read his

Longtime rivals and lovers from the 1950s, **Steve** (top photo, on the right) reunited with **Paul Newman** on the set of the disaster movie, *The Towering Inferno*. Steve was offered the role of the architect, but opted instead for the role of the fire chief because it was more heroic. Newman then assumed the architect's role.

The poster (center photo, above) promised blazing suspense, as it depicted party goers trapped in the world's tallest building.

Bottom photo (left to right): **Steve, Faye Dunaway,** and **Newman** share a joke to relieve their tension during the filming of this white-knuckle film. Audiences later debated who had the bluest eyes: McQueen or Newman.

name first.

Screenwriter Stirling Silliphant was hired to fashion a script based on two similar and roughly equivalent novels, *The Tower*, which was purchased for $390,000 and *The Glass Inferno*, which went for $400,000.

For his participation in the project, Steve received a million dollars up front with fifteen percent of the gross.

From the beginning of the negotiations and throughout the filming, Steve was obsessively jealous of Newman. He demanded that he have equal lines to Newman's. "Not one more word of dialogue, but not one word less," he told Silliphant.

The film reunited Steve with Faye Dunaway, his co-star in *The Thomas Crown Affair*, although they didn't have any scenes together. Playing the film's female lead, her love interest this time was Newman. Susan Blakely was cast as the wife of the film's larcenous electrical contractor, as played by Richard Chamberlain.

McQueen told Allen that, "I don't want to work with Chamberlain. Rumor has it he's gay, and I like to give gay men wide berth."

Allen later mocked Steve, "That's not what I hear about McQueen. He gives them wide berth until midnight in his bed, when they're welcome. What a closet case. Hollywood's full of those."

Chamberlain had no idea of the depth and range of Steve's homophobia and pronounced his performance as the fireman "a stunner."

"My character was the villain responsible for the catastrophic fire," the actor said. "I made the big mistake of playing him like a jerk from the beginning instead of keeping his nefarious nature disguised in good-guy clothes until his evil deeds were finally exposed."

The most likable guy in the cast was an athlete, O.J. Simpson. "Unlike most tough guy blacks, O.J. is the sweetest black boy I've ever encountered," Steve said. "Nice disposition. Wouldn't hurt a fly. We should have given him more to do in this flick."

Steve insisted that his friend, Don Gordon, be cast as a character called

Two seasoned film veterans, **Fred Astaire** and **Jennifer Jones,** played a couple conducting a December/December affair just before disaster strikes. When Astaire became too old for dancing parts, which were disappearing from the movie scene anyway, he accepted dramatic roles instead. **Jennifer,** with yellowing teeth on full display, ended her once-glorious film career by falling out of a crippled elevator eerily evocative of the World Trade Center tragedy more than 20 years later. Actually, it was a stuntwoman who impersonated Jennifer during the fall.

"Kappy," and it was arranged that Scott Newman, Paul Newman's son from his first marriage (to Jackie Witte), would play the role of a nervous fireman. Steve was reunited with his *Bullitt* co-star, Robert Vaughn, who was cast as Senator Gary Parker.

From the dusty archives of Hollywood's Golden Age, Jennifer Jones and Fred Astaire came together in this film for a geriatric romance. Steve was also united once again with Robert Wagner, with whom he'd last appeared in *The War Lover*.

Another golden oldie, William Holden, played the third lead as the billionaire real estate developer whose reputation goes up in smoke with the rest of his building. Although Holden demanded top billing over Paul Newman and Steve McQueen, Allen bluntly rejected his request, informing him, "Your star has set on *Sunset Blvd.*"

The film was shot during an era of well-publicized anxiety among fire safety advocates about the design of the World Trade Center, which at the time was rising 110 stories over New York Harbor. The press reported that there was no fire-fighting equipment in the world that can operate above the seventh floor.

Newman and Allen argued before every scene. But Dunaway finally concluded that it wasn't really anger. "It seemed to be their way of getting their juices flowing."

The gang's all here, ranging from those who put out the fires (**Steve McQueen,** far left) to the villain who caused it (**Richard Chamberlain**). Before this photo was snapped, there'd been a fight for star billing. In a complicated arrangement hammered out by their agents, Steve and **Paul Newman** eventually arrived at a "Mexican standoff."

Left to right: Steve, Robert Wagner, Faye Dunaway, William Holden, Jennifer Jones, Fred Astaire, Paul Newman, Richard Chamberlain, Robert Vaughn, and *(OH NO!)* O.J. Simpson in his pre-murder days.

In fact, Allen later recalled that "Newman was a real sweetheart throughout the whole shoot."

As for Steve, Allen had a different opinion. "He was a fuck-up pig, demanding everything, telling me how to direct and fighting over every word of dialogue, every close-up, even down to wardrobe's choice for his fireman uniform."

"Some of his demands included a stretch limo, only in black, driven by a chauffeur who had to wear a uniform of elephant gray, no other color," Allen said. "He also demanded a stand-in and a personal valet like Prince Philip had, but only an English one. He called for us to get him the best make-up man in Hollywood. We were told to find a hairdresser as good as Jay Sebring. Steve wanted his private gym and a steam room. Newman liked to sweat off his three six-packs of *cerveza* in a steam room, but McQueen issued orders that 'I don't want that queer checking out my dick in the baths. Off-limits.' From what I'd heard, Newman had already checked out McQueen's dick long ago. Believe it or not, the studio caved in to all of the piggy's demands. We even bought the mother-fucker a Cortez."

That Cortez motor home, a brand that was defined during the brief period they were manufactured (between 1963 and 1979) as the most deluxe and best-engineered in the world, was promised to Casey and Darron. They never received it.

"Both Steve and Paul insisted on being personally involved in scenes that placed them in the middle of the fire and the man-made flood we created in a desperate effort to put out the flames," Allen said. "As the action director, I was pleased by their willing cooperation. But as the producer, I was aware of the great risk and the fact that a single misstep could cause injury and shut down production if either Steve or Paul became unavailable."

"If anybody approached Steve on the set, he had only three little words for them, and I don't mean I love you," Allen said. "Go fuck yourself!" was heard on our sound stage throughout the day. If he ever gets around to writing his memoirs, I think it should be called GO FUCK YOURSELF. One day I asked him to stop calling some of our women workers cunts. Guess what he told me I could do?"

Tragedy struck in June of 1974 when Ali visited the set of *The Towering Inferno*. She sat in his director's chair labeled Steve McQueen. Not really feeling any pain at first, she suddenly became aware of something. As she looked down, she noticed blood on the floor. She'd been dripping blood until it had formed a small pool.

A blood-curdling scream brought Steve in a fireman's uniform rushing to her side.

In the ambulance, Ali held tightly to Steve's hand. "I think I'm having a

384

miscarriage."

"I didn't know you were pregnant," he said.

"I didn't know it either," she said weakly.

Devastating reviews did not keep audiences away from *The Towering Inferno*.

Vincent Canby of *The New York Times* weighed in with his opinion: "A suspense film for arsonists, firemen, movie-technology buffs, building inspectors, worry warts. It appears to have been less directed than physically constructed. Overwrought and silly in its personal drama, but the visual spectacle is first-rate."

Pauline Kael awarded *The Towering Inferno* with the "Dumb Whore Award of 1974," calling it a "junky fairground show."

As for his own performance in *The Towering Inferno*, Steve told Casey and Darron, "I called in my performance. But so did Fuckwit," as he privately called Newman.

Author Erica Jong, who wrote *Fear of Flying*, weighed in on the controversy of whether Steve had bluer eyes than Newman. "It is difficult to say, but McQueen's twinkle more. He makes me think of all those leathery necked cowboys at remote truck stops in Nevada. Does he wear pointy boots? And does he take them off when he screws?"

Allen recalled that following the huge success of *The Towering Inferno*, he drove out to visit Steve in Malibu with an offer of $3 million up front to star in *The Towering Inferno II*. "Guess what he told me I could do? Go fuck myself."

In spite of those reviews, the film enjoyed a world-wide gross exceeding $100 million dollars.

As the tallies from around the world came in, Steve once again found himself the biggest movie star in the world. His agent assured him that he could have almost any role he wanted in Hollywood.

So what did he do for his career?

He became a recluse, disappearing from the radar screen. He sat in front of a TV set most of the day, drinking Old Milwaukee and smoking grass. Naturally, he gained weight. To make himself even more unattractive, he grew a scruffy beard. Some people who encountered him during his exile from the screen didn't even recognize him. Some former girlfriends were turned off.

His weight ballooned to 220 pounds.

To attacks on his appearance, he publicly responded, "If I want to become bloated, that's my own fucking business. It's like I ain't exactly planning to enter any beauty pageants. I don't think I'm Miss California material."

At one point Ali let slip to a friend, "I'm married to a drunken, stoned beach hermit."

To those who were surprised at his appearance, Steve had a pat answer. "I *used* to be Steve McQueen."

He refused all interviews with reporters. Once, when a journalist spotted him on one of his infrequent forays, his copy would not be kind. Seen at the Polo Lounge in Beverly Hills for a business meeting, the *Los Angeles Times* wrote, "McQueen strolls through the room in a faded work shirt tucked into dirty beige jeans, his feet in Chukka boots, his beer gut leading the way."

The home front was a disaster. Steve had cut himself off so completely that he even had mail, including scripts, delivered to a nearby garage.

Ali was growing restless, and wanted to work again, perhaps in a vehicle tailor made for Steve and herself.

A script called *Fancy Hardware* caught her interest, but Steve nixed the idea after he broke his foot. "I've got all the fucking money in the world, bitch. Why would I want to work?"

Ali **MacGraw**'s breasts never put her into the category of Marilyn Monroe or Jane Russell, so she wasn't asked to pose for cheesecake very often. However, a photographer from *People* magazine caught Ali in this rare pose in a feature article published on July 24, 1978.

She hadn't appeared in a movie in three years, and she was well aware that the attention span of audiences was short. Even when *Fancy Hardware* was tailored for Barbra Streisand and John Travolta, they didn't like it either.

The rumors that Ali never got any film offers during her marriage are not true. Her agent, Sue Mengers, called with several deals, but Steve would take the telephone from Ali's hand and confront Mengers personally. "She works *only* with me and *only* on a project I select for the both of us!" He usually ended by slamming down the phone.

One of his justifications for rejecting movie offers for Ali was that, "I don't want some God damn horny movie star in a close-up with a hard-on kissing my wife." Memories of how he stole Ali from Evans came flooding back.

Throughout their marriage, Steve always felt inferior to Ali's intellect. To shoot her down, he constantly belittled her, listing her imperfections. When he found her sunbathing topless on their terrace, he asserted, "You've got no tits,

386

sweetie. I should have married a boy."

"Maybe you should have," she allegedly told him. "Perhaps those rumors are true."

He reportedly attacked her, drawing blood. She ran into the house.

Imitating one of his Hell's Angels friends, Steve would humiliate Ali in front of his male friends who happened to drop in. He'd order her to get him a beer and "to keep your fucking mouth shut."

"I'm a big movie star," he yelled at her one night. "I get offers of scripts every day. You get nothing. You know why? Because no one wants you."

"But I *do* get offers," she protested.

"No you don't. You're a fucking has-been. Better yet, a never was. *Love Story*. What crap! I bet Ryan O'Neal has a tiny dick."

At their Malibu home, objects were constantly flying through the air like missiles. Movie stars Steve McQueen and Ali MacGraw were not a happy couple.

When Steve barged out of the house, he often fled to the safety of his friends Casey and Darron. "We'd smoke grass for hours while he told us what a bitch MacGraw was, and how he was sorry he'd ever married the cow," Darron said. "He claimed that sex was far better with Neile than the cow. He told us that one night in Palm Springs he got so mad at the cow that he tossed her from the terrace into the swimming pool."

"Time after time we urged Steve to divorce Ali and let us move in with him in some new house," Casey said. "We promised we'd take care of him. Get him all the dope, all the girls, anything he wanted."

Ali McGraw and Steve deliberately selected a redneck restaurant for their dinner with **Ronald and Nancy Reagan.** The evening evolved into a complete disaster, and the two couples opted to never again meet over steaks, canned beans, and rotgut wine.

Having already served as governor of California, Reagan confided that he was seriously considering a run for president of the United States. Later, Steve told Ali, "He's out of his mind. No divorced Hollywood actor could ever get elected president."

"He stood up one night, completely stoned, in Palm Springs," Darron said. "He was totally nude. He shook his dick at us." 'Now tell me, guys,' he said, 'does Ali MacGraw deserve a dick like this?' We told him she didn't. Both of us offered to oil him down and give him one of those sensual San Francisco massages. We knew our boy needed to shoot off that night to relieve his tensions."

Pat Johnson was quoted as saying, "Ali MacGraw was the love of Steve's live."

Darron claimed that was bullshit. "He told us that Neile was the love of his life, and I believe that was true. He said he should never have divorced Neile."

"Sometimes Steve would stay with us for two whole weeks," Darron said. "Those were happy times. We liked just hanging out together and getting stoned. Sometimes we'd go for days without picking up some bimbo. Steve claimed he'd had so many bimbos in life that he didn't think he could tolerate another whining bitch. He also claimed that if something was wrong, MacGraw would find out about it and nag him."

Stoned, Steve once called Neile and proposed that she drive to Malibu. "I want to fuck both you and Ali in the same bed."

Neile rejected the offer.

"If me and Ali break up, she won't get a fucking cent of my money," Steve boasted to his friends.

He had asked Ali to sign a prenuptial agreement. She agreed to do it because at that time the idea that they would divorce was out of the question. She envisioned that they would live together through old age.

Today, she feels differently. "My gigantic gesture of abandoning my career and my means of financial support was stupid. On every level it was one of my more expensive lessons to learn. Steve got our house and everything in it, down to the frying pan and the salad server. I kept the books and clothes I came into the marriage with."

One night Steve announced to Ali that they'd be having dinner with Ronald and Nancy Reagan. He had just finished his term as governor of California, and was having a vacation on the beach with Nancy and some state troopers. Steve said that the ex-governor, ex-actor, was spending time under a large rainbow-hued umbrella embroidering, a favorite hobby of his.

Katharine Hepburn (top photo) wanted Steve to co-star with her in her pet project, *Grace Quigley*. He was horrified at the plot, the story of a lonely, elderly woman who hires a hit man to kill her-- and then others of her set who would all rather be dead. He politely rejected her offer. Nick Nolte wasn't that smart. Falling into her trap, he agreed to play the hit man. When the film's official movie poster was released, Hepburn was furious. Her name was misspelled as "Katherine" instead of Katharine.

Ali and Steve invited the Reagans to a battered tavern called Old Place, which was hidden away in the Santa Monica mountains.

The evening was a bit of a disaster, as various local yokels stopped at their table to gape. MY GOD, SHIT IN THE FAN, IF IT'S NOT RONALD REAGAN AND STEVE McQUEEN!

The Reagans and the McQueens never got together again for a meal after having bean salad out of a can, rotgut wine, and stale bread. But the steaks were good.

In his garage, Steve tore up any scripts that didn't contain a $50,000 reading fee. On some days he even tore up the scripts that contained the reading fee. He told Ali, "How in the fuck would some producer know if I read his rotten script anyway?"

Systematically depositing these easy $50,000 payments in his bank account, Steve had Ali send producers a generic rejection letter stating that he'd be unavailable for an appearance in their movie, pleading prior commitments, although there were none.

STEVE McQUEEN
in

HENRIK IBSEN'S
AN ENEMY
OF THE PEOPLE

The story of a man of courage.

Warner Brothers spent a half million dollars trying to figure out how to promote Steve's cinematic disaster, *An Enemy of the People,* based on a story by the 19th-century Norwegian playwright, Henrik Ibsen. In desperation, the studio decided to surround the long-haired, bearded Steve with handsome images from his hit films from yesteryear, hoping thereby to lure movie audiences into theaters. Finally, they decided that the film wasn't worthy of release at all. As shown by the photo on the upper right, **Steve** had never looked uglier and less appealing than he did in this ill-conceived project. In the photo on the lower right, **Steve** (left) is pictured with his co-stars, Swedish actress **Bibi Andersson** and **Charles Durning**.

"When Katharine Hepburn called and asked to meet with him to discuss co-starring with her in *Grace Quigley*, he agreed to see the great diva who drove to Malibu," Ali said. "Before she got there, Steve took off on his motorcycle. I didn't even know if he were coming back. She was hungry, and I made her a fresh salad and gave her a cup of soup from a can. Before Steve arrived, Miss Hepburn complained the soup tasted bad."

He turned down her project. The movie, eventually shot in 1985, was a box office disaster.

Casey and Darron knew that Steve's marriage to Ali was for the most part over when he rented a bachelor bad, a private suite atop the Beverly Wilshire Hotel in Beverly Hills. He filled up two levels of the hotel's garage with his collection of cars and motorcycles.

James Coburn didn't recognize him in the hotel elevator one day. "He looked like he hadn't bathed in a month."

John Foreman, the producer who had known Steve since the day he roared up on his motorcycle to the MCA offices in New York, arranged to meet with Steve and director John Huston. Both of them were interested in Steve playing an Ernest Hemingway character in *Across the River and into the Trees*.

"We didn't recognize this man who came up to us at first," Huston recalled. "Finally, we figured out it was McQueen disguised as a pot-bellied, aging Ernesto with a beard. We later learned he looked this unkempt and disheveled all the time. He was one fat slob. Needless to say, the picture never got off the ground."

A bellhop reported that Steve insisted he accompany all visitors to his room. "I had never seen such a parade of bimbos. Many a gal wanted to fuck Steve McQueen even if he looked like shit, and was old and fat."

***

Never in his life had Steve let himself go to seed the way he did after *The Towering Inferno*. For what was tantamount to a comeback, he chose a script in 1977 that shocked Hollywood. He wouldn't have to slim down to "fighting weight," as he called it, to appear in Henrik Ibsen's 1882 classic, *An Enemy of the People*, playing the crusading doctor, Thomas Stockmann.

It was unlike any other movie he'd ever made. The film was all dialogue, almost no action. "I hate dialogue," Steve had always said. Once he agreed to film *An Enemy of the People*, he would have to memorize many pages of dialogue.

First Artists pleaded with him not to return to the screen with Ibsen. But, according to his agreement with the company, he had the legal right to select whatever script he wanted. He reminded Barbra Streisand, Sidney Poitier, and

Paul Newman of the "vanity projects" they'd selected that had failed to find audiences.

As director, he hired George Schaefer, who was well versed in the classics, having crafted a version of Ibsen's *A Doll's House* for TV in 1959. Between 1954 and 1971, he'd been the director of 58 televised episodes of the *Hallmark Hall of Fame*. Those Hallmark Hall of Fame episodes had been the source for Schaefer of a dozen Emmy Awards.

There was speculation around Hollywood studios that Steve had deliberately chosen a noncommercial film as part of a vendetta against First Artists, a final revenge against its president, Phil Feldman. McQueen hated Feldman, who constantly reminded him that if he did not meet his contractual obligations to the company, a lawsuit would ensue.

Steve confided to Pat Johnson, "It's a wonderful part for me, but it's not going to make one damn cent at the box office."

Steve even approved of Alexander Jacobs' draft of a screenplay based on the Arthur Miller translation of Ibsen. When Steve heard that Miller's text was being used, he said, "We have something in common. I've fucked his wife, Miss Marilyn Monroe herself."

Schaefer, who had served in the Pacific in the U.S. Army during World War II, told the author that, "I was shocked at Steve's choice of Ibsen. Other directors warned me that he was a pain in the ass, but it was relatively smooth sailing with him in spite of our limited two million dollar budget. He worked for no salary, according to his agreement with First Artists. He gave me the freedom to select a cast, even though Steve warned, 'Your actors will probably overshadow me.'"

For Steve's co-star, the brilliant actor Charles Durning was cast as Peter Stockmann, with Bibi Andersson playing Catherine Stockmann. Durning, as predicted, emerged from the movie bombastically splendid as the town's mayor who is bitterly opposed to Steve's character.

The diversely talented Durning, an ex-boxer, ex-World War II veteran, and former dance instructor, was surprised to be cast opposite Steve in an Ibsen drama, "but we decided to give it hell," he claimed. "I'd already played opposite Charles Bronson, so why not McQueen? I'd later be asked to play a light-footed dancing governor opposite Burt Reynolds and Dolly Parton in *The Best Little Whorehouse in Texas*, so as an actor I was up for anything so long as those paychecks kept flowing."

"Naturally, I was a natural for the role of Big Daddy in the revival of Tennessee Williams' *Cat on a Hot Tin Roof*," Durning said. "'Bring 'em on and I'll act them,' I told my agent. As the only member of my unit to survive the Omaha D-Day invasion of Normandy, I knew I could survive McQueen, even though I'd heard he was a bastard. He wasn't exactly my idol. My idol was James Cagney, who showed the world you could be tough and dance too. But contrary to all expectations, McQueen and I became good friends."

"What did Steve McQueen and Charles Durning have in common?" Schaefer asked. "Durning got his start working as an usher in a burlesque house, and McQueen got his start working in Caribbean whorehouses."

Schaefer claimed that Steve particularly liked the play's closing statement, "The strong must learn to be lonely."

Originally Steve had wanted Ali to star opposite him in *An Enemy of the People*, but they broke up before production began.

Born in Stockholm, and five years younger than Steve, Bibi Andersson was cast as the female lead. She remains famous today because she starred in films directed by Ingmar Bergman: *The Seventh Seal*, *Wild Strawberries*, and *Brink of Life*.

Bibi had worked with Steve's friends, James Garner and Sidney Poitier, and one of them might have recommended her to Steve for *An Enemy of the People*. Among her many credentials were John Huston's *The Kremlin Letter* in 1970. After her appearance with Steve, Robert Altman would cast her in *Quintet* in 1979.

When Steve first met her, he jokingly called her "Jailbird." Police in Stockholm had arrested her and held her in custody on a charge of failing to pay income taxes earned from Ingmar Bergman's German production of *Persona* (1978). Steve had seen only one film of hers when he cast her, having watched *I Never Promised You a Rose Garden* in 1977.

When Steve appeared in public again, he explained to people working with him on *An Enemy of the People* that he'd put on weight to make the character he was playing, Dr. Thomas Stockmann, more believable. "Dr. Stockmann was definitely a portly Norwegian," he said "as are most middle-aged Norwegians. Because of Marilyn Monroe's Norwegian background, she probably would have become fat if she'd lived. Many actors have put on pounds to fit a certain role, although usually they have to lose weight to play a part before filming begins."

He even suggested to Schaefer that he wear a prosthetic pot belly to look even heavier, but the director turned down the idea. "You're fat enough, Steve, believe me."

"The theme ties right into the problems we face today with polluted lakes and poisoned air and chemicals in all our food," Steve said. "That's what attracted me to this play, the message it carries—that we need to take personal responsibility for what is happening around us."

Attending the wrap party for *An Enemy of the People*, a heartsick Ali MacGraw told Schaefer. "I gave up Robert Evans' mansion with its two dozen pink telephones, a glamorous lifestyle, chauffeurs, limousines, a potential big-time movie career, all for that guy sitting over there." She pointed to Steve who was the only man wearing jeans. "What he gave me was the back seat of a motorcycle and a ride into the night to eat bugs."

"But you loved him," Schaefer said. "Surely you did."

"I must have at the time," she said with a certain melancholy in her voice. "Was it possible? Could I have loved such a demanding person? He never respected our marriage vows. I did. But he was a philandering husband. Never true to me. Neile could take that part of his character better than I could."

Warner Brothers spent half a million dollars test marketing the film, with disastrous results. An executive said, "During most of our test screenings, the audience walked out. One woman wrote the truth on a card. 'I thought I was attending a Steve McQueen movie. I didn't even recognize him. What a juice-less movie. Long haired, bearded, spectacled, who does this asshole think he is? Lionel Barrymore?'"

One executive at Warner Brothers said, "It's a God damn embarrassment, a piece of junk! Who wants to see Steve McQueen—at 210 pounds for Christ's sake!—running around in granny glasses and a Santa Claus beard?"

During the first five minutes of viewing *An Enemy of the People*, Neile didn't even recognize Steve. He looked bloated. "This attempt to do Ibsen seemed as though he were deliberately trying to destroy the image he had carefully cultivated over the years."

"I'm horror struck," Paul Newman said.

Neile, who in most cases had been a brilliant judge of scripts suitable for Steve, also thought it was a dumb idea. In spite of warnings from in-the-know people, Steve stubbornly plunged ahead. The character in one sense was close to Steve's heart. In spite of all the perceptions of everyone else, the Stockmann character doesn't waiver but forges ahead. In his heart, he knows he's right, the story of Steve McQueen himself.

"Where is Jay Sebring now that we need him?" Marlon Brando asked when he saw Steve's long mop of bushy hair in the film. "I never fucked Farrah Fawcett, but her hairdo seems to be on every cover of every magazine. Steve's hairdo seems excessive even by her standards."

"*An Enemy of the People* had been an abject failure at the box office, but Steve suddenly pictured himself as a classical actor," said Freddie Fields.

***

Even though many in-the-know film industry insiders had viewed *An Enemy of the People* as a dillettantish disaster, Steve moved on to an equivalently esoteric project, plotting the details of a movie called *Old Times*.

Artsy, acerbic, and chilling, and permeated with a sense of bitter competition among its three characters, it was based on a dark drama by Harold Pinter, whose theme evaluates the reliability of human memory and the very nature of reality itself. Steve personally selected his co-stars for this existentialist three-actor drama, each of them A-list: Audrey Hepburn and Faye Dunaway.

McQueen thinks he's the next Laurence Olivier," said an executive at Warners.

Sensing another disaster in the making, top executives at Warner Brothers vetoed the entire project, and Steve's film version of *Old Times* was never made. Steve sued Warner Brothers for failing to honor its agreements, but the case never actually went into a courtroom. After weeks of legal wrangling, Warners eventually agreed to reimburse Steve for the expenses he'd generated during his development of *Old Times,* and the proposal quietly died.

"Steve had his moment in the sun," Fields said. "He was the hottest thing in Hollywood. But his star shone so brilliantly it quickly burned out. He could have been the box office champ of the '70s. But he made one stupid decision after another. That's what happens when you take a hog farmer from Missouri and catapult him into such international fame. Ibsen, my ass!"

***

"After he turned her into a housewife, Ali over the years became a dull fixture around the house," Fields claimed. "When he married her, she was the wife of one of the most powerful men in Hollywood. After *Love Story*, she was one of the most sought-after movie stars n the world. Steve grabbed The Prize. But as the years went by, and Ali moved toward middle age, she dimmed in Steve's eyes. He had his eyes out for younger dames."

"I'm not exactly a spring chicken myself," Steve told Casey and Darron. "The bitch was born in 1938. I was born in the 30s as well. Women born in 1960 are beginning to look good to me."

Throughout their marriage, if Ali didn't have dinner on the table at six o'clock, he shouted at her. With Robert Evans, she had known elegant late-night dinners with sophisticated friends at fabulous restaurants such as Chasen's.

With Steve, all she'd get might be an 11pm visit to a greasy hamburger joint. But on most of those forays, he preferred to let her stay home with the kids while he went beer drinking with his biker friends.

To the world, Ali put up a brave front, denying that Steve had been abusive to her in his marriage or that he had beaten her.

At one time he suspected Ali of having crushes on both Warren Beatty and Robert Redford, and refused to allow her to attend pictures starring those two super handsome men.

"I really hate to say this," Fields claimed, "but I think Steve was walking down the stairway to a dark gulf. I'm not sure how sane he was. He was always paranoid, but as the years went by and the lines in his face deepened, he grew increasingly ill mentally. I don't know how Ali put up with him. She should never have married such a freak in the first place. Could she have loved him that much? To me, Steve had become a maniac. He was unlovable. But then I'm not a woman."

"Even if he let himself go, he wanted a woman with a perfect body," Fields said. "The slightest bulge could turn him off a woman. I think he imagined himself as some old Arabian sheik who wanted only the most perfect bodies delivered to him. Bodies that hadn't been spoiled by other men. Frankly, if he had his wish, I think he wanted two or three virgin teenagers delivered to him every night on a silver platter."

"In every movie he liked to take off his shirt," Fields said. "He told me, 'even if the picture is lousy, horny women and those fucking gays can get off seeing me half dressed.' To maintain that perfect body, he worked out every day. But by the late 1970s, he was letting himself go. He gave up the gym altogether. What he didn't give up was his beloved weed. He increased his consumption of marijuana."

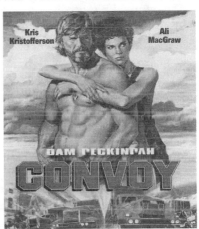

One day Ali, a bored and lonely housewife, received a call from director Sam Peckinpah. He wanted her to star opposite Kris Kristofferson, then at the height of his screen fame, in a trucking movie called *Convoy*, to be filmed in Texas. Kris had been cast as a long distance trucker with the nickname of "Rubber Duck."

When Steve finally did come home, she told him she wanted to play in Peckinpah's latest movie, knowing that Steve respected the director, having worked with him before. He adamantly refused and went one step more. "If you sign for that fucking film, I will divorce you. That's a very serious threat." Steve barged out of the house that night and drove to his hotel suite.

Steve called Ali from his suite early the next morning. "I heard from Sue Mengers that you've been offered a dyke movie."

"That's true," she said softly. "But I

Director Sam Peckinpah (Bloody Sam) cast **Kris Kristoffersson** and **Ali MacGraw** in one of the worst movies of 1978. It was a stupid script with blah acting. Kris never had pecs like those depicted in this poster, whose artist seemed to think he was depicting Michelangelo's *David*. Steve warned Ali that if she went to Texas to shoot this film, he'd divorce her. He was a man of his word.

turned it down. But I have not turned down Peckinpah. Remember a movie in which he directed us? It was called *The Getaway*. Surely you remember that."

He slammed down the phone on her.

Before facing Peckinpah's cruel cameras, Ali had silicone injections to smooth out the wrinkles in her forehead, those worry lines no doubt caused by Steve and his promiscuity.

Despite Steve's threat to divorce her if she made another movie, Ali spent the summer of 1977 working in New Mexico with Peckinpah. "It was a very bad movie, not really worth ruining my marriage over," Ali said. "But my marriage was already ruined. I knew that."

She granted an interview to a reporter from *Ladies Home Journal*. She was not exactly accurate when she claimed. "If you put a freeze frame on my life right now, I'd say I'm leading exactly the sort of life I want."

Just as that magazine hit the newsstands, Steve's attorney contacted her. "Your husband wants a divorce," one of his lawyers bluntly told her.

Steve kept getting unconfirmed reports from the set in Texas that Ali was engaged in a torrid affair with Kris Kristofferson. These rumors have never been confirmed. It was Steve himself who was engaged in a torrid affair with a beautiful model.

After reading the divorce notifications from Steve's lawyer, Ali knew she had to find a place to live for herself and her son by Robert Evans, Joshua. She had little money of her own, but found a house nearby. She wanted to live near Steve so Joshua could visit him. Her son had grown to love Steve and was very attached to him.

Days later, she called Steve and asked if he'd reconsider getting back together again. His voice was icy cold. "I love you, but I am not in love with you anymore," he told her.

She hung up, knowing the marriage, and with it their love affair, was over.

She was warned not to take anything from their Malibu house because of the prenuptial agreement she'd foolishly signed with Steve. "Just take your clothing," the attorney warned.

"But my Moroccan rugs," she protested.

"Mr. McQueen says those rugs actually belong to him," his lawyer wrote her.

Without even a bed, much less sheets to put on it, she moved nearby into a badly maintained house.

She sat crying in her new home. In spite of what she'd told *Ladies Home Journal*, she was the unhappiest she'd ever been in her life. "What have I done?" she sobbed out loud. She was moving into middle age. No husband. No money. No career except for a horrible movie that she didn't even want to see released.

"My soon-to-be ex-husband has a beautiful cover girl model to keep him company at night," she said. "I have no one, except my son, whom I love very much."

After a night of tears and despair, she went to the post office the next morning. She no longer wanted her mail to be sent to that bleak garage. Maybe there would be some movie offers. She changed her name at the post office. Steve had insisted that she be registered as "Mrs. Steve McQueen." She changed that back to Ali MacGraw.

"No one could blame Ali for finally taking steps to divorce Steve," said Fields. "What the hell! He was living outside the home. And the tabloids were screaming that he was shacked up with a beautiful model. A gal named Barbara Minty. What else could poor Ali do?"

"Leave the fucking bastard," Sue Mengers was alleged to have shouted into the phone.

"He ruined her movie career, he ruined her life, and he's now fucking another *puta*, said Robert Evans. "I warned her that this would happen."

Her ex-husband came to the rescue and cast Ali in *Players*, released in 1979 and co-starring of all people, Maximilian Schell, Neile's former lover. News of the casting caused "road rage" in Steve, as he headed up the Pacific Coast Highway roaring at 150 miles per hour. Months later, members of a preview audience in New York broke into laughter at Ali's screen utterances. That was a final humiliation for her.

***

"One night when we were having ribs and apple pie for dinner miles from Palm Springs, Steve told us something I'll never forget," said Casey. "'I rode a lot of horses in films,' he said, 'but I never developed an affection for these animals, although I think they're noble creatures. But I prefer my horses under the hood.'"

"By 1976 something had seriously gone wrong with Steve," Casey said. "His old throat problem came back. Darron and I no longer slept in the same bed with him. We began to fear we might catch something. We'd lay there in the bed hearing him cough all night. We begged him to see a doctor, but he told us to mind our own business."

Steve finally gave in and listened to his friends, consulting a series of eight different doctors over the next few weeks, trying to find out what was wrong with him. A final doctor suggested "fungus on the lungs," which was aggravated by the damp air blowing in from the ocean.

Seeking a dryer climate, Steve left the beach and partially moved to a ranch in Sun Valley, Idaho, where he hired builders to construct a log cabin.

He gave up cocaine and heroin and went back to eating organic foods. After all these years, he finally quit smoking except for about fifteen marijuana cigarettes daily. As Casey said, "That really wasn't giving up smoking, now was it?"

"Even though he'd abandoned car racing, Steve still joined us in cycle riding," Darron said. "Sometimes we'd sit in the desert for hours and never say a damn word. When racing, if Steve spotted a rabbit, he'd chase after it and we'd follow along over the rough terrain. He'd always stop if he spotted any Indian petroglyphs on rocks."

"One night, sitting around a camp fire, Steve admitted to us that he thinks his daughter Terry is smarter in book learning than his son is," Darron said. "'It's like me and Ali,' he said. 'She has more book learning than I do, but when it comes to machinery, me and Chad boy have those women beat by a country mile. Unlike me, I think my kids will grow up without all the hate I still have in me.'"

"As he grew older, Steve's hatred of bitches became more intense," Darron claimed. "One night at a cheap diner, a waitress got his order all wrong, and he jumped up and slapped her hard, not once, but two times. We had to pull him back off the cow. We had a total of three hundred dollars on us—thank God it was Saturday payday—and we paid the heifer off. Otherwise, she might have sued Steve for assault and battery. He was getting more and more out of control."

Steve still remained sensitive to homosexual slurs. Casey recalled that one night in a trip through Nebraska they entered the Crazy Horse Saloon. Deep into the evening, a drunk called out to Steve from the bar. "Hi there, faggot! Why don't you drop your jeans and show us just how small your dick is?"

"Walking over to the guy, Steve knocked the creep out in one punch," Casey said. "He later told us, 'All actors in bars get called a faggot. It comes with the territory.'"

When Neile was told by Steve's therapist that he was struggling against facing the possibility that he was a homosexual, and he heard about that, he went ballistic.

"Steve plotted to kill that therapist," Darron said. "He wouldn't actually do it himself, but he'd get somebody to do it for him. We really feared for his sanity. We were able to convince him that killing someone, or ordering someone killed, might not be such a good idea."

"I warned him that he might wind up in jail," Casey said. "What did the trick was when Darron told him he might get gang-raped by black dicks, maybe fourteen in one night. Steve had painful memories of getting gang-raped when he was a boy. There was no more talk of killing the therapist."

"But he still wanted revenge," Darron said. "Another idea came to him.

One night as we were leaving Palm Springs, we saw this young boy hitchhiking. Steve slammed on the brakes. He called to us, 'That boy's a queer. I just know it.' He stopped and asked the kid to get in the front seat with him. We were ordered to get into the back seat."

"For one brief second I thought Steve planned to take the boy somewhere and kill him," Darron said. "In some way, that would get his revenge on queers. We soon found out he had other plans. He knew this abandoned cabin a few miles in the distance. He tricked the boy into going there with us. I don't want to go into all the details. I'm ashamed. We took the boy there and Steve ordered us to strip him down."

"The kid really struggled but we overpowered him," Darron said. "He was just a frail boy. We held him down. Steve ordered us to rape him. I went first, then Darron, then Steve who always loved sloppy seconds. We left the kid crying there and bleeding. Steve ordered us just to walk off and get back in the car. Nothing was said about that night ever again."

Steve switched "shrinks" after a therapist brought up a diagnosis of homosexuality. Steve hired another therapist who, after a few sessions, articulated the same prognosis. After threatening him, Steve stormed out of the psychologist's office.

"Steve came through the door to our new mobile home about three o'clock one morning," Casey said. "He had a key, but at first me and Darron thought somebody was breaking in. He switched on the light in our tiny bedroom and pulled the covers from our bodies. We were sleeping naked like we always did."

"We couldn't believe this madman," Darron said. "He started pounding us with his fists, even trying to kick us in the balls. 'You fucking pervs,' he shouted at us. 'You faggots have tried to turn me queer.'"

"We never struck him once, but we were able to subdue him," Casey said. "We actually had to tie him up and keep him from killing us. We kept him tied up

A beautiful model (see her likeness on the covers of two separate editions of *Cosmopolitan*, above), **Barbara Minty** became Steve's third and final wife. He met her under false pretenses, promising her a role ("an Indian princess") that at the time didn't exist. It was she who would nurture him through the cancerous end of his life.

all night. When morning came, he seemed filled with remorse. He apologized and we understood. God knows what a bad acid trip he was on. He fell asleep in our bed and slept all day. But he scared the shit out of us. That was one tormented man. Somebody important must have called him queer. He just couldn't stand for anybody to think he was a fucking homosexual."

"There was something worse happening to Steve than being called a homosexual," Darron said. "We feared that our friend had come down with something big—maybe he caught it from one of those bimbos he was always fucking. Steve had started to spit up blood. I mean, a lot of it."

***

When Barbara Minty's agent, Nina Blanchard, called her and told her that Steve had seen her picture in a magazine and wanted to audition her for a future movie role, she confused him with Paul Newman. "I guess that means I'll have to try his famous salad dressing."

"No, you moron," said Blanchard. "Steve McQueen, not Paul Newman."

"I saw them both in *The Towering Inferno*, and I don't know which one was which."

"Steve was the fireman," Blanchard said.

"Ok, I got that," Barbara said. "Now I remember McQueen. He was that blond guy I used to watch on television, *Wanted: Dead or Alive*."

Blanchard accompanied Barbara to meet "the wolf" at El Padrino at the Beverly Wilshire where Steve had a suite. At first, she didn't realize that "this Charles Manson look-alike was the same actor she'd seen on *Wanted: Dead or Alive*.

Barbara's intimate introduction to Steve's lifestyle came as a shock. When she accepted his invitation to visit his suite, she was startled to discover "two of the tallest, most beautiful, huge-breasted blonde women I'd ever seen." He assured her that these women in tight jeans were just leaving.

Unlike Neile and Ali, Barbara was Steve's kind of girl. Born on an Oregon farm, she rode horses and motorcycles and even flew antique planes. She could wear grungy clothes like Steve and drink Old Milwaukee, and look beautiful while she was doing all of the above.

Gracing covers of *Harper's Bazaar* and *Vogue*, Barbara, in her early 20s, could have been Steve's daughter.

"I was killing myself with Ali," he told James Coburn. "Now I'm losing weight. Drinking lots of juice. I'm working out again. If I tell Barbara to get on the back of my bike, she jumps on right away. Doesn't even bring her lipstick. We ride into the desert. Sleep anywhere there aren't too many rattlesnakes."

"A man should change women every decade," Steve told Freddie Fields. "To me, Neile represented the 50s, Ali the 60s. But, for me, I want a woman of the 70s. It's Barbara Jo Minty for me."

With another woman in his life, he developed a new sexual fantasy. He had dreams of Neile, Ali, and Barbara all in bed with him at the same time, and of himself satisfying each member of the trio with multiple orgasms.

Phil Parslow, a former athlete turned TV and film producer, became a close friend of Steve's. He would later become known for producing such TV hit series as *Dynasty* and *Falcon Crest*. He had once headed Steve's Solar Productions.

When Phil met Barbara, he told Steve, "She is better looking than Neile and Ali put together. She's perfect for you."

Phil was one of the few people who knew about Steve's relationship with Casey and Darron. He advised him to "drop both boys—pure white trash. They'll get you into trouble—and I mean big trouble, maybe even sell something to the tabloids for all I know."

Steve advised Phil, "I'll associate with whoever I want to."

One of the joys Steve associated with "bagging" Barbara was his perception that she was actually Warren Beatty's main squeeze. He'd always been jealous of Beatty, and often they were up for the same roles. Steve told Freddie Fields, "Jane Fonda and I should have done *Bonnie and Clyde*. We would have been so much better than Faye Dunaway and Beatty."

One night, after the tabloids got wind of Steve's affair with Barbara, he received an anonymous call from a strange man. "McQueen, Warren Beatty got to the bitch before you, but I hear you like sloppy seconds." Steve slammed down the phone.

His other chief rival was Robert Redford. He'd never forgiven himself for turning down the role of Sundance in *Butch Cassidy and the Sundance Kid*, the part eventually being awarded to Redford.

When many producers at the time cast a film, they'd say, "This is a part for Steve McQueen. But he's so expensive and such an asshole, let's offer it to Redford—that is, if Newman doesn't take the bait first."

Other than being up for the same parts, Redford had never done anything personal to harm Steve. Even so, out of pure jealousy, Steve wanted revenge. It came one night when a group of Hollywood insiders at a party were talking about what a wonderful actor Redford was, and what an extraordinarily handsome man he was.

Steve joined in the conversation. As revealed by the author Marshall Terrill, Steve spread a rumor about Redford that still persists to this day. "Aw, you know what I heard? I heard a nasty rumor that Redford has a really small dick. His nickname is Needle-Dick. I don't know how he could please a woman. I don't know why a woman would see anything in him if the guy's got a needle dick."

In about ten days, the rumor had reached Ali who reported it to Steve. Even Marlon Brando asked Paul Newman, "Is it true what they say about Redford? Is his dick really that small?"

"How in the fuck do you think I would know the answer to that?" Newman said.

"I thought during the shooting of that Butch and Sundance movie, you two guys bumped pussies one night," Brando said.

Eventually Steve convinced Barbara to leave her home in Idaho and come to live with him at his beach home at Trancas Beach, a house he'd shared with Ali.

Barbara moved in with Steve in the late autumn of 1977 "to share my life with him. He needs me, he cares about me."

As Steve's relationship with Barbara deepened, the press was harsh, calling her "squaw woman," a type portrayed in his film *Nevada Smith*, or else "the Stepford Wife," although Barbara and Steve weren't married at the time.

When Ali saw a photograph of Barbara Minty, who looked like a fresh-faced Jacqueline Kennedy, riding on the back of Steve's motorcycle, Ali claimed, "I'm happy for Steve. He's lucky to have her." What she didn't say was that Steve looked like Barbara's father.

***

After filming *The Towering Inferno*, Steve stayed in touch with O.J. Simpson. It was a friendship of sorts, but not a very deep one, although the two men often called each other. Both of them had shared something in common, and that was an interest in blondes.

When O.J.'s football team, the Buffalo Bills, came to Los Angeles, Pat Johnson invited Steve to go with him to see the game.

After the game, Steve went to the locker room to greet O.J. No one seemed to recognize Steve McQueen, movie

Robert Redford had always been a rival of Steve's, who regretted turning down the role of The Sundance Kid that made the handsome blond star world famous. To embarrass his rival, Steve spread a rumor claiming that Redford had a "needle dick" and couldn't satisfy any woman. That (false) rumor spread like wildfire through Hollywood. Steve gloated in his triumph.

star, because he wore an old John Wayne cowboy hat, perhaps the one left over from John Ford's *Stagecoach*, and a pair of sunglasses that Barbara had given him to cover his blue eyes. Even though Steve was bearded, with little of his face showing, O.J. spotted him at once.

The football great was talking to reporters and signaled Steve to come over and join him in front of the press. Since O.J. had called out "Man" to Steve, no reporter seemed to take notice that it was Steve McQueen in person. As O.J. answered questions, Steve was completely ignored by the press.

After the reporters left, Steve went in the back as O.J. stripped down, showered, and got dressed. Steve walked him to the team's sumptuously equipped bus, where he shook his hand and told him good-bye.

Before that happened, O.J. was mobbed by autograph seekers, at least four dozen of them. Amazingly, in the rush to get to O.J., none of the fans recognized this old cowboy from Missouri.

"Steve's ego took a beating that night," Pat Johnson said. "One old lady spotted Steve and asked for his autograph. He was very gracious and signed her pad, and this from a man who never gave autographs. But I think on that night he really appreciated a fan."

The next day Steve talked to his friends at Santa Paula about meeting O.J. in the locker room. "Haven't you always heard that black men have big dicks? Well, I think God passed over O.J. when the peckers were assigned. All that beef but not where it counts."

***

After that awkward encounter with O.J., Steve drove to Palm Springs to meet his new agent. Soft-spoken, genial, and conservatively dapper, Marvin Josephson had represented some of the biggest clients in the world, often political. These ranged from President Richard Nixon to Jimmy Carter and Henry Kissinger, even Barbara Walters, Laurence Olivier, and Tennessee Williams.

On one of the main streets of Palm Springs, Steve was introduced to Josephson, finding him a rather boyish, freckle-faced guy who was smoking a cigar. Already he

During his glory days, **O.J. Simpson** befriended Steve when they starred together in *The Towering Inferno*. The friendship was challenged when Steve showed up to greet O.J. after a game and only one fan recognized him, the rest crowding around the football hero for autographs. Steve had seen O.J. nude in the shower and wasn't impressed at all.

was managing such CBS personalities as Dan Rather and Walter Cronkite.

"Steve liked to test people, or so Freddie Fields told me," Josephson said. "Testing me involved taking out his prick and pissing in front of me. I just didn't pay attention."

Josephson later regretted all the films that Steve turned down, including such high-grossing classics as *Close Encounters of the Third Kind*.

"You can't believe all the great scripts he wouldn't even consider," the agent said.

Many movie roles eluded Steve, including *The Gauntlet*, which had been written specifically with Marlon Brando and Barbra Streisand in mind. Later when Brando pulled out, it was offered to Steve, but Streisand nixed the idea of Steve's participation. *The Gauntlet* finally ended up starring Clint Eastwood and Sondra Locke. Allegedly, one of the last pictures Steve rejected was an Andy Warhol-inspired horror about mutant lesbians.

Steve left strict orders with his agent that he was never going to appear in a film that Paul Newman had turned down.

He also told Josephson that he wanted to make really big bucks before he turned fifty. "After all, I have to leave a few million for Chad and Terry."

Steve almost couldn't stand to see a Paul Newman picture. "Fuckwit is the ageless wonder," he said. Unlike Steve, whose face grew more lined, the trenches deeper with each passing year, Newman seemed to grow handsomer as he aged. "I can't stand the idea that I'll no longer be an action hero and pin-up boy of thousands of beautiful broads," Steve said. "I'll be playing daddies. Even worse, a grandpa."

Wife **Tina** and husband **Marvin Josephson** attend a gala, an almost daily occurrence in the life of this super agent. He represented some of the biggest clients in the world, including U.S. presidents Carter and Nixon. He became Steve's agent after they first met on the main street of Palm Springs, where Steve had stopped to take a leak.

"My youth is passing," Steve confided to Casey and Darron one night. "I'm gonna make one last stab at it. Have one big-time fling before it's all over."

Steve was very protective of "my little girl," Terry, especially when she dared show up on his doorstep with a boyfriend. However, he felt very differently about Chad. For his Christmas present in December of 1976, he took him out by the pool. "Jump in, kid," he said. "You've got to learn sometime."

In the pool were three naked

young women.

Once, when Barbara was out of town, Steve called Ali again and invited her for a drive up the coast. She admitted in her memoirs that she felt the "power of attraction" for him, and she sensed he felt the same way toward her. Even though he asked her to make love to him in an orange grove near Oxnard, she didn't feel she could accept the proposition. After he deposited her back at her house, she never saw him again.

In summing up her life with Steve, Ali wrote, "How tragic it was that a man who had—or nearly had—absolutely everything could have spent a lifetime feeling weary of his friends, vindictive toward his enemies, and certain that the whole world was out to do him in. I have ached for him, for the hugs and support he never had as a child. I am sorry for all the times that my own selfishness prevented me from looking beneath his thoughtlessness for the battered creature within. We met and fell in love at the wrong time in each of our lives. I am sure we are linked in some way together, forever."

***

As happens so often in Hollywood, two competing studios announced simultaneous plans for films based on the same subject. Steve wanted to film a script called *I, Tom Horn*. Down the corridor on the same floor of a building at Warner Brothers, Robert Redford's Wildwood Productions announced that they were going to produce *Mr. Horn*, based on the same Wild West character.

As was his nature, Steve adamantly refused to give up his plan. "For a while it was a Mexican standoff," said director William Wiard, who eventually produced Steve's version, the title reduced to *Tom Horn*. "It was Redford who eventually blinked and gave up his plan to play Tom Horn himself."

During the two years that *Tom Horn* was in production, Steve signed to star in *Tai-Pan*, James Clavell's epic novel of dynastic China. He was given one million dollars upon signing. It was contractually agreed that the fee for his involvement in the project would be four million dollars, plus a percentage of the profits.

When the producers didn't keep up with their payments to him, Steve pulled the plug. He kept the money granted so far. "It was the easiest million I never made in my life," Steve told Barbara.

When Hollywood was shocked that Marlon Brando took in $3.7 million for his brief appearance in *Superman*, Steve upped the ante.

Years had gone by and he'd made only one film, *An Enemy of the People*, that was judged as so uncommercial that it couldn't be released. In spite of that, he announced to Hollywood producers that "in the future, Steve McQueen's base salary will begin at five million dollars a picture."

At this price, there were few takers, especially in view of Steve's repetitive series of previous box office disasters. In spite of that, Carlo Ponti, husband of Sophia Loren, offered Steve $4 million to star with his wife in the terrorist melodrama, *Manhattan Project*. Steve turned down the offer, and Ponti made no counter-offer.

Steve faced the possibility that he'd evolved into a has-been. Perhaps no producer wanted him at any price. The 1960s were his heyday, but in the movie business that had been a long time ago. A whole new generation of movie-goers was attending film houses across the country, and Steve McQueen was already a distant name to them, if they'd ever heard of him at all.

Ostensibly because of his commitment to filming *Tom Horn*, which was eventually released in 1980, Steve also turned down *Missouri Breaks*, about a bounty hunter and an outlaw, the role going to Marlon Brando.

The historical figure of Tom Horn tracked down the Apache chief, Geronimo, and arranged his surrender, and he also served with Theodore Roosevelt's Rough Riders. In addition, he was a Pinkerton detective, a champion rodeo rider, a boxer, a cavalry scout, and the owner of a silver mine before becoming a gun-for-hire.

In Steve's film version he is hired by a consortium of Wyoming land barons to wipe out cattle rustling in their territory. Horn tracks the rustlers down and kills them. Afraid that he is doing his job too well, and perceiving him as a threat to their power, the barons frame him for a murder he did not commit. At the end of the movie, Tom Horn faces the hangman's noose.

The character played by the strikingly sexy **Linda Evans** looks down on **Steve** the morning after a night of sex during the filming of *Tom Horn*. Wearing a gold tooth for her role in the movie, Linda was deglamorized for her role in a film about a renegade from the Old West. During the shoot, Linda was alleged to have also had an off-screen affair with Steve.

Many actors prepare for a role, but Steve went a bit far in his research on *Tom Horn*. He spent a night sleeping on Horn's grave, where he claimed he was visited by the ghost of the dead hero of the Old West, who begged him to "do my story."

At the time, Steve was nearing fifty years of age, and he looked every year of it. Before filming began, he had lost nearly sixty pounds, and the toll of that accelerated weight loss clearly showed.

The character of Horn, on his last legs, called for a haggard, pained, leathcry face, and Steve's fit the bill. His days of being a sex symbol had come to an end.

Linda Evans appeared in the film, but she was a long way from stardom on TV's *Dynasty* on ABC. She wore a gold tooth but no makeup. Though a lovely girl, she looked decidedly unglamorous. During the shoot, Steve was rumored to have had an affair with Evans. If that were true, it was so brief that neither of them seemed to particularly notice.

At the time, Evans, a graduate of Hollywood High, was a relatively unknown MGM starlet. Regularly listed as one of the most beautiful women in America, Evans had appeared in *Playboy* magazine, at the behest of her then-husband John Derek, in 1971.

Steve was happy to work with his friend Slim Pickens, who had been a real cowboy. Steve's nickname for Pickens was "Shit-Kicker."

After firing all other directors, Steve tried to helm *Tom Horn* himself. But, according to the Directors' Guild charter, an actor can't take over a picture once shooting has begun. William Wiard, who had directed *M*A*S*H* and *The Rockford Files*, was hired, but he mainly sat in the chair while Steve helmed the rest of the picture.

Shot in Mexico and the Coronado National Forest of Arizona and New Mexico, *Tom Horn* was produced by Fred Weintraub, with Steve serving as executive producer. The screenplay was by Thomas McGuane and Bud Shrake.

Actually Steve would make very little, if any, money off *Tom Horn*. When the production budget was cut from $10 million to $3 million, there was no room in the budget for Steve's $5 million salary. Agreeing (uncharacteristically) to a drastic cut in compensation, Steve stubbornly pushed on, even though he was not a well man.

His health became alarming to him. Before beginning work on *Tom Horn*, he had caught pneumonia, and it took a staggering four months before he got well. He was left with a lingering cough. "If a breeze would blow in from the sea, I'd catch cold," he told his first wife Neile.

Steve would often visit Neile to make love to her. At one point he had promised her that he'd divorce Ali and remarry her, but she turned him down.

"Since I told you you will always be my wife, I intend to keep fucking you until the day I die," he told Neile.

That was all right with her. "I enjoyed the sex. Why deny myself that pleasure just because we were divorced?"

Although Ali was gone from Steve's life, Neile still showed up sporadically.

She remembered "the last time I made love to my former husband was in a seedy motel on the outskirts of Las Vegas when he was working on the script for *Tom Horn*."

After making love to her and after eating one of her tuna fish salads that he dearly loved, he made his pitch. "Can we get back together again?"

There was no way at that point that she'd accept such a proposal. She'd moved on and had to turn him down. He made a final proposal that involved a plan for Ali and Neile to live with Barbara and him in a log cabin in Idaho.

"Can't you just imagine that?" Neile asked. "*Oooweee!*"

No longer Mrs. Steve McQueen, Neile was still a beautiful vibrant woman. At a luncheon for Princess Grace of Monaco, Neile was invited. At the buffet table, she ran into Cary Grant, who introduced her to Alvin Toffel, a handsome man of charm. As it turned out, Toffel was assigned to sit beside her at the luncheon.

A former Air Force fighter pilot, he had been in the Strategic Air Command. After working for Richard Nixon in the White House, he had been urged to settle in Los Angeles by Norton Simon, who had offered him a position as president of several of his foundations, including the Norton Simon Museum.

"From that luncheon I decided that Mr. Toffel was mine," said Neile.

Steve had a hard time adjusting to the fact that Neile had fallen in love with this rather dashing man. Toffel was also a major activist in the Democratic Party of California.

He'd had a glamorous background as an engineer for NASA, working on the *Apollo* and *Gemini* programs. He'd dreamed of becoming an astronaut. "I want to be the first Jew on the moon," he announced to friends.

Toffel eased into the role of stepfather to Terry and Chad. He announced, "I'm here if you need me. No one can replace Steve McQueen in your lives, and I won't even try."

Toffel and Neile were married on January 19, 1980. Steve was unable to attend, but Neile didn't really want him there. "A wedding should have only one star, and that's the bride," she said.

Although in the hospital, Steve had asked Neile to remarry him. Wisely, she had refused. Perhaps in an attempt to beat her to the altar, he wed Barbara on January 15, 1980.

***

Instead of sports car racing, Steve developed an interest in aviation, picturing himself as another Howard Hughes. He purchased two World War II dual-wing Stearmans.

"I want to follow in my father's footsteps," he announced to Barbara. "Become a pilot."

"We were shocked by Steve's wanting to get airborne," Darron said. "When we first met him, he told us he had a fear of flying."

"I like my planes old and my women young," he told his friends.

Santa Paula, lying some fifty miles northwest of Los Angeles, is a small town of farmers and expats from L.A. who wanted to give up an urban existence.

Steve moved to Santa Paula because he heard that it was the antique plane capital of the world. He persuaded Sammy Mason, who was retired, to become his flight instructor. A fearless acrobatic flyer, Mason was legendary, the first pilot ever to execute an intentional loop in a helicopter. He had once been an engineering test pilot with Lockheed.

Steve wanted Mason to give him flying lessons, but the veteran pilot was a hard man to persuade. Finally he was won over by Steve's charm. *The Great Escape* had been one of Mason's favorite movies, but he didn't remember the name of its star until his son, Pete Mason, assured his father that Steve had indeed been one of the heroes of that film.

In time, Mason became a kind of father figure to Steve, something he'd never had in real life.

Steve adjusted easily to the little town of Santa Paula, where everybody was laid back. He even took to chewing Apple Jack tobacco instead of smoking cigarettes. From the elegant digs he'd once occupied at "The Castle" in Brentwood, he had descended to sleeping with Barbara on a mattress near his airplane. Life was simple, surrounded with a noteworthy collection of mechanical accessories, everything from Buck Rogers guns to vintage gasoline pumps.

Memories of living in a mansion with Neile were far, far away. At the

Abandoning car racing, Steve became an airplane pilot like his father, who had abandoned him early in life. His favorite was a dual-wing Stearman left over as surplus from World War II. It was a plane like this that carried an urn of Steve's ashes for scattering over the Pacific Ocean

hangar, he stored his growing collection of airplanes.

In May of 1979, Steve made his first solo flight. Eight weeks later he was granted his pilot's license.

Also that July, he purchased a ranch that was located within a fifteen-minute drive from the airport. The house that came with it was built in 1896, a classic Victorian which he filled with antiques which he and Barbara had collected from road trips throughout the West. His prize was a bar counter that had been a stage prop in *Bus Stop*, the 1956 film that starred Marilyn Monroe, the one Elvis Presley had wanted to appear in.

Unlike Steve, Barbara was a devotee of horses, and on the new ranch she was able to have a stable of them. She and Steve made a deal. If he'd go horseback riding with her, she'd go motorcycle riding with him. As with his two previous wives, Steve insisted that Barbara give up her career as a model and devote herself to him and her horses.

She was an amateur photographer when she met Steve, and he allowed her to snap candid shots of him. (In each of them, he looks like an aging relic.) Long after his death in 2006, she accumulated those photographs into a picture book which was published as *Steve McQueen: The Last Mile*.

It forms a rare glimpse of a once-handsome star in decline. In many of the pictures, he is shaggy haired and bearded, looking like an old desert rat.

She snapped a few pictures of him before he'd had his favorite breakfast of a cup of black coffee with an Old Milwaukee for a chaser, plus a piece of chocolate cake. In those pictures, he looks as if she'd dug him up from the grave.

In his final years Steve almost always dressed in his Marlboro Man drag—the inevitable blue jeans and flannel shirt with a denim jacket, cowboy hat, and a turquoise belt buckle. Turquoise was his favorite color.

In August of 1979, Steve went into Los Angeles to consult with specialists who performed a biopsy on his lung. The results did not uncover any malignancies. Back at the ranch, and in spite of the tests, his cough lingered. It disturbed him immensely. He pronounced his doctors quacks. "Those fuckers wouldn't even know how to remove a wart."

***

In September of 1979, Steve began work on his last film, *The Hunter*, based on the true life story of a bounty hunter named Ralph Thorson.

He remembered all too well how he'd gotten his start in a TV series, *Wanted: Dead or Alive*, playing a bounty hunter.

During the shooting of *The Hunter*, in the bitter cold of a Chicago winter, Steve refused to give in to sickness. His cough continued. Even when many members of the crew were bedded with colds or flu, he always showed up on time, determined to see it through. Perhaps he knew that it would be the last film he'd ever make. He did some of his own stunt work, even though he was already on the long road to death and was constantly short of breath.

Steve had been born in 1930, but in *The Hunter* he looked as if that year had actually been 1918. His blond hair had turned berry brown, and he had a tough, leathery, deeply lined face. The golden boy of the 50s was a distant memory. His face looked even worse when blown up on the screen.

After Sally Field turned down the lead female role, it went to actress Kathryn Harrold, who would later go on to become Arnold Schwarzenegger's leading lady in *Raw Deal* (1986). More recently, she played Helen Rowland in *Desperate Housewives*. When Steve first met Harrold, he told her she looked like Grace Kelly.

The man who signed on as director of *The Hunter,* Buzz Kulik, had been for the most part a producer of television shows, including various episodes of *The Twilight Zone, Gunsmoke, Playhouse 90,* and *Studio One. The Hunter's* screenplay had been composed by Ted Leighton.

With a cast who included Eli Wallach and Ben Johnson, Steve was cast as the famed bounty hunter Ralph (Papa) Thorson. In real life Thorson had stood 6'2", weighing 310 pounds. Steve at the time he shot the movie stood 5'6", weighing 150 pounds.

A fourteen-minute chase is the centerpiece of the movie, evocative of *Bullitt.*

For the role, Steve took home $3 million, plus 15% of the gross, of the movie's $10.5 million budget.

The Hunter would be Steve's last motion picture. But after the failure of his previous two films, he was eager for another action movie. He told Kulik, "I want to crawl back on top again."

***

Right before Christmas in 1979, Steve, along with Barbara, flew to Los Angeles. There, registering under the name of Don Schoonover, he underwent a battery of medical tests. When he recovered consciousness after being anesthetised, his doctor was waiting. The prognosis was a disaster.

"I'm sorry, Steve, to tell you this. But you have mesothelioma."

"Does that mean I'm pregnant or something?" Steve asked.

"It's a deadly form of cancer. There is no cure."

Mesothelioma is almost always caused by an exposure to asbestos, and Steve had lived with asbestos throughout most of his life. Malignant cells develop in the mesothelium, that protective lining that covers most of the internal organs of one's body. He'd been told that symptoms of mesothelioma may not appear until 20 years or a lot more after the initial exposure.

After the doctor's news was delivered, Steve collapsed into a coma. When he woke up, his daughter, Terry, was beside his bed. In a very weak voice and in between coughs, he told her, "I don't have cancer. I'm going to get well."

Of course, she didn't believe that, especially when he immediately went into a coughing spasm.

Steve's dream of keeping his name out of the tabloids came to an end because of a leak from the medical staff at Cedars-Sinai.

Steve denied even to most of his friends and to his children that he had inoperable cancer. The press was on his trail, but he still denied it.

Finally, because of a headlined story (STEVE McQUEEN'S HEROIC BATTLE AGAINST CANCER) in the *National Enquirer*, the world knew the truth on March 18, 1980.

The story read: "Frantic last-ditch efforts by doctors have failed to halt a vicious and inoperable lung cancer that is killing Steve McQueen. The end could come within two months, believes one of his doctors. But the steely eyed screen hero is battling back bravely."

To combat the rumors, Steve called his old manager, Hilliard Elkins, and agreed to lunch with him at Ma Maison, where seemingly half of *tout*

Steve's last film was *The Hunter,* in which he played a bounty hunter. Although still ruggedly handsome, he looked even older than his actual age of fifty. Not known to him at the time, he was being eaten up with cancer. Actress **Kathryn Harrold** not only was Steve's girl friend in the movie, but would later become Arnold Schwarzenegger's leading lady in *Raw Deal* before becoming one of the *Desperate Housewives.* In the photo on the right, the hulk **Karl Schueneman** portrays a bail jumper who tangles with **Steve**, who's aiming a gun at him.

Hollywood would see him looking well and taking care of business. To Elkins, Steve denied that he had cancer, and told him to spread the word.

Steve pulled himself together to attend the premiere of *Tom Horn* on March 28, 1980. No one was interested in the picture, the movie later bombing. Reporters crowded around Steve, asking him if he had lung cancer. He stood back, showing off his heavily made up face. "Do I look like a man who's dying? I'm in the peak of health."

Tom Horn ran for 98 minutes. It marked the sorry ending of First Artists Productions, for which its founders had once had such high hopes.

*** *** ***

Loyal until the end, Barbara lived where Steve wanted her to. Her residences included, for a while, a motor home parked behind a medical center in San Fernando Valley.

He was at the center for chemotherapy treatments, which seemed ineffective for patients suffering with mesothelioma. He received the treatments within the motor home so he wouldn't have to be seen in the corridors of the hospital.

The doctors in Los Angeles repeatedly warned him that conventional forms of therapy would not work in the case of mesothelioma.

At the San Fernando Valley Medical Center, Steve was given intravenous doses of huge amounts of vitamins and put on a rigid new diet. Later, tests showed that none of this had stopped or even delayed the advancing cancer.

The Hunter was released on July 28, 1980, but it quickly evolved into yet another box office failure. Barbara tried to keep the reviews away from Steve. *The Village Voice* in New York's Greenwich Village referred to Steve as "a tired daredevil."

As much as he had tried to disguise his pain during the shoot, it showed through on the screen, perhaps most obviously in the way he walked with a slight limp. Old friends who'd known Steve from healthier and perhaps happier days were shocked by what they saw onscreen. Freddie Fields was the first to say what was on a number of minds: "Steve McQueen is dying."

One of the last pictures ever taken of **Steve** in 1980, before his death. He is snapped by a paparazzi with his new wife, the glamorous **Barbara Minty,** who has been linked with other A-list stars, including Clint Eastwood and Warren Beatty. Steve appears dazed and startled to have been caught by the photographer.

413

In desperation, Steve flew to Spokane, Washington to meet with Dr. William D. Kelley, who wasn't really a medical doctor but a dentist, one who had been barred from his practice in the State of Texas.

Kelley would in time become the most controversial figure in Steve's life. He was actually an orthodontist, but claimed that he had developed a pioneering cancer therapy based on the ingestion of huge doses of pancreatic enzymes, fresh fruits and vegetables, plenty of juices, and coffee enemas. The doctor made a claim that he had cured himself of pancreatic cancer using this form of therapy, along with massages and shampoos. His self-help book, *One Answer to Cancer*, published in 1967, was banned in the United States.

Already the press was portraying him as a "celebrity-chasing, money-driven, greedy quack," as related in an article in the *Townsend Letter* by Dr. Nick Gonzalez.

In spite of the media's criticism, Steve was intrigued with the doctor and his unconventional methods, since the mainstream medical profession held out no cure for him.

Back at the ranch at Santa Paula, all the fruit juice and vitamin C didn't seem to do any good. Steve's coughing spasms continued.

Dr. Kelley had urged him to check into a clinic he'd recently established in Mexico. "We will completely cure you of cancer South of the Border," the dentist faithfully promised.

"Grabbing for straws," as Steve put it to Barbara, "we're heading for Mexico in the morning. It's my last chance to save my life."

Dr. Kelley, practicing his "cures," had established the Plaza Santa Maria Clinic outside Tijuana, about 76 miles south of San Diego. Once it had been a mountain resort, hanging over a bluff overlooking the Pacific.

Steve drove with Barbara to check into the clinic. He used the name of Don Schoonover and was assigned a two-room cabana with Barbara as his faithful guardian.

Defined by the doctor as an "ecological therapy," the treatments were said to summon the body's forces like an army to fight off the invading cancer cells. Specialists in the United States, however, dismissed the treatments as quackery.

Steve was subjected throughout the day to rectal enzyme implants and those endless

"The Cancer Outlaw" as he was called, **Dr. William D. Kelley** became one of the most famous doctors in America, basking in his notoriety for allegedly having found a cure for cancer in his clinic across the U.S. border in Mexico. Steve flew to Kelley's clinic in a desperate attempt to save his life through Dr. Kelley's unorthodox methods. The doctor faithfully promised Steve, "I will grab you from the arms of death."

coffee enemas. The first of these rectal invasions occurred every day at 4am, with another following at 6:30am.

He received injections of cells from cows, and he went on special diets and swallowed bottles of vitamins. Conventional cancer treatments then prevalent during the 1980s— surgery, chemotherapy, and radiation—were abandoned.

The treatments cost about $15,000 monthly.

Resisting painkillers, Steve suffered the agony of the damned. But he told Barbara, "If the fucking cure works, it will have been worth the suffering."

Neile called and begged him to enter a top hospital in Los Angeles, but he refused.

Ali, learning of the disease, phoned him and pleaded with him to let her come to Mexico, but he refused her. Preferring that she remember him as he had been, he didn't want her to see him in this condition.

Many of his medications, including injections of sheep embryos and thymus, caused him to vomit. He seemed to be allergic to at least one of these medications. His suffering increased.

Tabloids offered $50,000 for any *paparazzo* that would sneak into the hospital and snap a picture of a devastated Steve McQueen in his death throes.

Neile complained to friends who called, including George Peppard, James Garner, and Don Gordon "They're giving him endless shampoos—yes, shampoos and enemas. It's all so stupid. But no one ever told Steve McQueen what to do."

For nourishment he was fed ground raw beef liver mixed with pineapple juice day after day.

He put up a brave front, but one afternoon as Neile was departing from Mexico, he grabbed her arm and revealed the truth. "Frankly, I think they're

Steve McQueen
THE LAST MILE
By Barbara McQueen
with Marshall Terrill

Riding a motorcycle, **Barbara Minty** and **Steve** enjoyed a brief respite in the desert before he began his long battle with cancer that would ultimately take his life. On this day, he promised her, "I won't die! I won't leave you!"

This is the cover of the photo-essay Barbara co-authored about her life with Steve. Featuring candid shots she took of Steve in his last year (1980), she called her autobiographical book *The Last Mile.*

415

all full of shit. I'm not gonna make it!"

He was telling her something she already knew.

On October 8, 1980 it became official. Steve issued a statement to the press that he did indeed have cancer but was responding to treatment at the clinic. "Mr. McQueen's tumors have shrunk and no new ones have been detected," the statement read. It was a lie, of course.

Steve sent his love to all his fans and a "God bless you."

Dr. Kelley told the press, "I believe that Mr. McQueen can fully recover and return to a normal lifestyle."

Steve's public broadcast on Televisa, the national TV network, praised his treatment at the clinic. "Mexico is showing the world this new way of fighting cancer through metabolic therapy. Congratulations—and thank you for saving my life."

Newspapers all over the world headlined the "miraculous" cure for cancer along with the "disappearance" of Steve's malignant tumors. Thousands of cancer sufferers were given renewed hope during their final hours of despair.

Neile remained unconvinced. She publicly attacked the clinic's doctors, calling them "charlatans and exploiters." She feared that many dying cancer patients, believing Steve's message, would throw away their life savings and rush to Mexico in a vain attempt to save their lives.

Despite the media hype, the reality on the ground at Tijuana was grim.

Steve woke up Barbara one morning, "I can't take a piss. Help me! I can't take a piss, and I need to desperately."

The doctor was summoned. It was ordered that day that Steve should undergo an operation to remove that ever-growing tumor from his body. Apparently, too much pressure was being put on his kidneys, preventing proper urination.

On October 22, Steve asked Barbara to drive him back to Santa Paula. Without actually saying so, it was obvious that he wanted one final visit with his planes and his ranch.

***

On October 24, Steve checked himself out of the Tijuana clinic under the cloak of night. Dr. Kelley approved his departure provided he kept to his regime once back in California.

A camper that had been modified into a mobile sick room was the vehicle that transported him across the border and northward to the town of Santa Paula.

Hearing he was back on the ranch, Neile asked if she could drive over for a final visit, and Barbara invited her to come.

At the ranch, while Barbara was otherwise occupied, Neile climbed the stairs to Steve's bedroom. She found him lying nude and asleep on the bed, except for a blue T-shirt. After a few minutes, he opened his eyes and was startled to find her in the room.

"I thought I'd never see you again," he said weakly.

"I'll always be around," she falsely promised him.

"It could have been so different for us," he said. "If only I could have kept my pecker in my pants."

When he complained that he was tired, she kissed him goodbye. He quickly fell asleep again. Taking one last look at her husband of so many years, she headed down the stairs. She would never see him again.

Steve called Casey and Darron to come to see him but he didn't want Barbara to meet them. He scheduled their arrival for when she was sleeping or out on an errand. When they arrived in Santa Paula, they didn't recognize Steve. "He was sitting shirtless in the yard in this great big chair that dwarfed him," Casey said. "He was all skin and bones and had grown a beard. He looked real scary. We were almost afraid to come close to him."

"Believe it or not," Darron said. "He asked us to bring him a cigar. Just what a dying cancer victim needs, right? A cigar."

"We awkwardly embraced him," Casey said. "It made me feel all creepy inside. His stomach looked like he was about to give birth to some fucking monster. I guess that was the tumor growing inside his gut."

"When we saw him after an absence of several weeks," Casey said, "he was a ghost of himself. Not the Steve McQueen we knew. He looked like he was seventy years old. His face was sunken. His once-vibrant blue eyes were a dull gray. He'd lost a lot of weight. His cancer was eating away at his flesh."

"He stayed with us only an hour or two, claiming he had to get back to Barbara," Darron said. "She was his nurse. We asked him to come and live with us, but he turned us down."

"It was rather awkward," Darron said. "He told us that we shouldn't expect him to leave us anything in his will. He said we were grown, healthy men and were able to take care of ourselves. We told him that was okay with us."

"We didn't really tell him the truth," Casey said. "Of course, we expected something. He owned all those cars. He could have given us something, three cars at least which we could have sold for a little money. Even something to remember him by. He was a millionaire. We'd been his faithful servants for years, and he was cutting us off without a penny. He knew that all the future we had was to become two old desert rats with a rotting mobile home."

"We talked it over and decided we wouldn't leave him now," Darron said. "But we were plenty pissed off. We'd been his closest friends in life. That just proved he was ashamed of us. I guess we always knew that."

Privately, Casey and Darron believed that Steve would never recover. "I know a dying man when I see one," Darron said, "and I've seen enough of them. We felt sorry for Steve, but we knew there was nothing we could do for him."

"I think he didn't want us around any more," Casey said. "We knew that he was saying good-bye. We asked if he'd let us go to Mexico, but he didn't want us there. He'd found a place for us in his life with his other wives, but Barbara seemed to have taken over. Steve could tell that we were hurt at his rejection. He told us that he wanted us to remember him as strong and virile, rattling our cycles across the desert and running over a rattlesnake to skin for dinner."

"They want me dead," Steve told Casey and Darron, even though he never really defined who "they" were. Darron figured out that he was referring to drug cartels hawking their wares to thousands of cancer victims, or to doctors performing operations even though they had little or no chance of saving a patient's life. "They're out to get me, because through Dr. Kelley I'm the poster boy for showing the world that cancer can be cured through nature's natural means."

"We begged him not to go back to Mexico, but he was determined," Casey said. "He wouldn't listen to us. If the operation to remove that big tumor didn't work, he had this big scheme of flying to Germany. There was a clinic there. He'd read that they'd developed an experimental cure for cancer. It was very hush-hush and wasn't legal in the United States. The treatment had worked on animals, but hadn't been thoroughly tested on human beings. Steve planned to volunteer as a guinea pig. The whole thing sounded crazy to me, but he grabbed my hand. He seemed to summon all his strength as he gripped me."

"Don't you understand?" he asked. "It's my last chance. Who can deny me that?"

"Go for it!" Darron told him. "We're right behind you in whatever you decide to do."

"I remember the last time we saw him," Casey said. "We both hugged him in the yard. His body felt real bony. He told us he'd call us soon but warned us that he didn't expect to live through 1980. We still loved the guy, but he could be such an insensitive bastard."

"We knew that his life was all but over," Casey said. "He tried to smoke a cigar but was too weak to inhale. Before we left him, he asked each of us to kiss him on the mouth for a final good-bye. We really weren't into that, but we went through with it. His breath smelled like something was rotting inside him."

"As we were leaving, he spoke to us in a very weak voice," Darron said. "'It's been a hell of a ride, boys.' He called to us one more time and we came to his chair. He held each of our hands. 'Never tell my secrets. The world doesn't have a right to know.'"

***

There was one more surprise visitor at the ranch. To his friends' amazement, Steve wanted to meet with the Rev. Billy Graham, at the time, the most famous televangelist in the world, and spiritual advisor to several U.S. presidents.

In the past when Steve was asked if he believed in God, he'd delivered a pat answer. "I believe in me. God will be number one as long as I'm number one."

All his life Steve had more or less despised the church. "It's an attempt to control people," he used to say. Many of his old friends, including Don Gordon, were stunned when he turned to religion, becoming a Born Again Christian.

"It was probably a last desperate attempt to hold onto life," Gordon said. "Maybe he was making a final bargain 'Okay, God, if you'll let me live, I'll believe in you. Show me!'"

Von Dutch reportedly said, "Now a Jesus freak with crosses dangling around his neck. What next?"

Elmer Valentine claimed that Steve was an atheist, but didn't want to take a chance just in case there really was a God.

Whether he nurtured a belief in God or not, his condition steadily worsened. His new wife Barbara lived in agony. She'd married a fantasy man of the screen who in real life wasn't that at all.

When the Rev. Graham first met Steve, the evangelist asked the actor what his religion was. Steve answered him as honestly as he could: "It's the desert, the grass, the sun in the sky, my wife, the kids—and my wheels."

Appearing like a fire-and-brimstone preacher, which he wasn't, **the Rev. Billy Graham** was summoned to Steve as he was dying. Graham arrived by his bedside to help Steve come to terms with his death and to find some sort of spiritual peace at the end.

The Rev. Graham spent three hours in prayer with Steve, giving him spiritual guidance. Steve desperately wanted to know the answer to some questions: "What was Heaven like? What do people do there?" He was especially interested in finding out if people in

Heaven were allowed to make sexual love with each other.

The preacher's answers to these intriguing questions are not known.

Graham's last words to Steve were, "I'll see you in Heaven."

"I look back on my experience with Steve with thanksgiving and some amazement," Graham said. "I had planned to minister to Steve, but as it turned out, he ministered to me. I saw once again the reality of what Jesus Christ can do for a man in his last hours. It was also interesting to me that Steve had accepted Christ some weeks before he even knew he was ill. Otherwise people might have thought it was a deathbed decision."

***

Before leaving Tijuana, Dr. Kelley had told Steve that in a last ditch effort he could book him into a hospital in Juaréz to remove the large tumor in his stomach and others in his neck. His clinic was not equipped for such delicate operations. Steve agreed that he would go to Juaréz.

On his final night in Santa Paula, Steve lay awake all night thinking about an alternative plan for death.

Come twilight he would board one of his planes. Just as the sun started its descent into the Pacific, he would fly west with it.

As its dying rays were reflected off the coast of California, he would fly into the Pacific as far as his plane would carry him. When the fuel ran out, he'd crash into a watery grave.

By dawn, though, he had abandoned this idea. "Too much like a film script," he said.

From his Santa Paula ranch, Steve wanted the tumors removed from his stomach and neck. On November 3, Steve and Barbara flew back to Mexico on a chartered plane for him to face the operation.

Back in Mexico, on November 4 Steve checked into the Clinica de Santa Rosa in Juaréz. This brought back memories, as the town lay across the wide Rio Grande from El Paso, where many years previously he and Ali MacGraw had filmed *The Getaway* and had fallen in love.

In Juaréz the hospital's cardiologist pronounced Steve's heart "strong as an ox," claiming he was physically able to undergo this very dangerous surgery. Both of his children, Terry and Chad, were with him. Barbara was also by his side.

Steve's last words to Terry were, "I've done everything one can do on Earth, but I've wrecked most of my life. If you live to have a long and happy life, then I will have succeeded at something."

A large nurse had appeared on Steve's final night on Earth and, because security was lax, had entered his room unchallenged. It was later speculated that she'd bribed someone to gain entrance to Steve's room.

Apparently, she administered coagulants, shooting Steve with a fibrinogen extract, which could trigger an embolism, as indeed it did.

Leaving the room, the nurse was reported to have entered a large van and drove off into the moonlit night. A hospital staff member claimed that he didn't know who she was, only that he spotted an Arizona license plate.

Steve was cut open between eight that morning and one o'clock the following afternoon when he was sewed up. Five pounds of inflammatory tumor were removed from his abdomen. Dr. Kelley was at the operation and was told that tumors had formed around Steve's liver.

The operation revealed that Steve's right lung was dangerously cancerous, as were all of his intestines.

Both Chad and Terry were allowed to watch the operation.

Back in recovery, Steve regained consciousness. Barbara was at his side. He looked into her eyes and in a very weak voice said, "I came through. I knew I would."

Before giving in to the final sedation, his last words were, "I did it."

Fourteen hours after surgery, Steve suffered a massive heart seizure while under sedation. Five minutes later, a second attack rattled his body. The last seizure proved fatal. He died at 3:40am on November 7, 1980.

The Rev. Billy Graham's Bible was clutched in his hands.

Awakened from her sleep, a nurse informed Barbara of her husband's death. "Steve is in God's hands now," Barbara told the nurse.

After Barbara called Chad to wake him with the sad news, he dressed hurriedly and rushed to the clinic for a final goodbye with his beloved father. He asked to have a few quiet moments alone with Steve's body.

In the room, lit by a soft bulb, he found his father's blue eyes open. No longer gray, they were a bright blue again like they had been in the movies. With his fingertips, he gently closed Steve's eyes.

Impulsively Chad bent over and kissed Steve's heart. To his surprise, it was still warm. "So long, dad," he said, "I'll love you forever."

Terry called Neile who was in bed with her new husband. Her mother didn't want to answer the phone. She already knew what had happened. "Our Daddy's dead," Terry sobbed.

Neile later said, "When I said goodbye to Steve, I knew I'd never see my husband, my friend ever again."

Since his body was cremated and no autopsy was performed, the mysterious circumstances of Steve's death caused rampant speculation that he'd been murdered.

That mysterious Arizona license plate, piloted by a "nurse," provoked lurid conjecture.

A question mark still hangs over his death, and perhaps always will, unless in future years someone delivers a death bed confession.

Steve was taken to the Prado Funeral Home in Juaréz where his nude body was prepared for shipment back to Santa Paula for his funeral.

A photographer from *Paris Match* bribed an attendant to let him slip into the funeral home. He entered the morgue where Steve's body lay in state. He removed the sheet from the corpse and snapped a picture of Steve's nude, shrunken body in death. In full color, the grotesque picture made the front page of *Paris Match*. *The New York Post* published a censored version.

"It was the final indignity for a very private man," Ali said. "Steve would have been mortified to be exposed in this horrible way. He looked ghoulish. No more the screen legend that had thrilled hearts around the world."

The suspicions linger to this day: STEVE McQUEEN MURDERED headlined an underground paper in Hollywood.

It could well have been true. Dr. Kelley had agreed to take the five-pound tumor removed from Steve's body to a pathology lab in Mexico City where it could be analyzed. He flew to Mexico City where a lab examined the monstrous tumor, finding it a mass of dead tissue.

While he was in the laboratory talking with a pathologist, Kelley received a call from Santa Rosa. He was told that Steve had died of cardiac arrest four hours earlier. Kelley immediately rushed back to Juaréz, but learned that the corpse had been flown to Ventura.

For years after Steve's death, Dr. Kelley strenuously maintained that his treatment had been working and that Steve would have survived had this mysterious woman not entered and administered that lethal injection.

***

Even in death, Steve didn't escape from this world without one final entanglement with a *paparazzo*. A photographer for *Paris Match* bribed his way into the morgue where Steve's nude body lay under a sheet. The shrunken corpse was photographed in this hideous condition, the picture published in the pages of *Paris Match*.

Grady Ragsdale, Steve's foreman at the Santa Paula ranch, transported the corpse to the El Paso Airport. A private Lear jet flew him back to the States for the final time. The plane landed in Ventura, where Steve's body was removed by an ambulance to a mortuary for cremation.

Many of Steve's friends said that there had never been any hope of his recovering from the Kelley program. However, Dr. Dwight McKee, who

422

worked at the Santa Rosa Clinic, presented Steve's X-rays to Ragsdale when he landed in Mexico. "The X-rays clearly show that Steve, if he had held in there, could have beaten his cancer," McKee said. "The tumors in his body had died. Remember, he didn't die of cancer. He died of a blood clot."

As unlikely as it seemed, other experts claimed that if Steve had not succumbed to an embolism, which is known to sometimes happen after major surgery, he might have had a chance.

News of this advanced the theory that pharmaceutical cartels from the United States, in ways not fully explained except for the mysterious visit of a "nurse" from Arizona, took Steve's life from him.

Freddie Fields went to his grave claiming, "Steve was murdered."

Steve's simple funeral services were held at the ranch in Santa Paula, with old friends showing up. They included George Peppard, James Garner, Elmer Valentine, and Bud Ekins.

Steve's aviator friends flew over the ranch in a cross formation to honor him. His flying companion, Larry Endicott, piloting Steve's yellow Stearman, dipped the wings in a final salute to their fallen comrade.

Of all of Steve's celebrity friends, only four issued laments in the press about their grief: Faye Dunaway, Slim Pickens, James Garner, and Jacqueline Bisset.

Steve was granted one final wish. He had long told some of his male friends that his ultimate sexual fantasy was to have all three of his wives—Neile, Ali, and Barbara—in his bed at the same time.

When his friend, Elmer Valentine, went upstairs at the ranch, he discovered all three women sitting on Steve's bed. "His dream fantasy came true, except he wasn't there to take advantage of this mother lode. If he'd been there, and had been in top form, he would have seduced all of them. What a guy! We'll not see the likes of him around Hollywood ever again."

Five days later, Sammy Mason, his veteran flight instructor, took Steve's urn containing his ashes. He loaded them aboard Steve's favorite yellow Stearman and then flew south toward Santa Clara and out over the Pacific.

He scattered Steve's ashes over the vast ocean.

The sky that night seemed so much more vast than the ocean. When he returned, Mason told Barbara that Steve's ashes had been buried with "a John Wayne sunset."

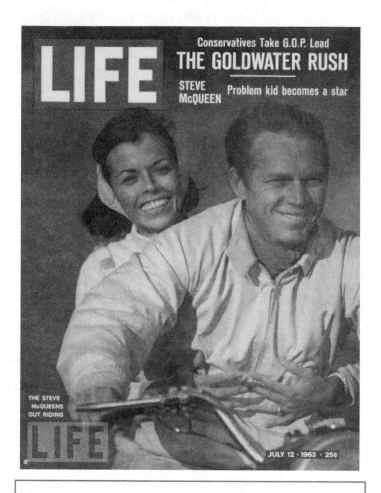

The McQueens (Neile and Steve)
in happier times:

Life Magazine, July 12, 1963

Epilogue

Terry McQueen, Steve's daughter, later spoke to some friends who'd gathered to express their sympathy. "My Dad was full of paradoxes, but he was a loving father, although totally paranoid. As a husband, he was never faithful. He was a free spirit like the coyote. He was always searching for legitimacy, even though I don't know what he meant by that. He sought international fame but once he got it, like Greta Garbo, he wanted to be left alone. As long as I live, his aura will always be with me. I think new fans in 2080 and beyond will discover his screen image anew, and that my Dad will live forever."

Steve died with assets worth twelve million dollars. Terry and Chad were bequeathed three million each. Barbara was left one million.

Upon his death, Steve owned fifty-five antique automobiles, plus two hundred and ten motorcycles. Terry and Chad auctioned off this armada, netting two million dollars.

Terry herself died on March 19, 1998 at the age of thirty-eight. She was diagnosed with haemochromatosis, a hereditary iron imbalance that attacks one's internal organs, especially the vulnerable liver.

It is said that both Neile and Steve carried the dangerous gene for this malady, though it did not attack either of them.

Steve left $200,000 in his will to his "alma mater," Boys Republic. At the reformatory, a commemorative plaque was erected. It read: "When Steve McQueen arrived here, he was

Steve McQueen's daughter, Terry, pictured here with her bearded father, once claimed, "I think Steve hated all women except me."

Like her father, Terry, too, would go to an early grave.

a troubled boy; when he left, he was a man. Although he was a great film star, he often came back to tell us about himself and his success. His example is a source of hope and inspiration for our pupils now and in the future."

Before Barbara's remarriage, her name was romantically linked to Clint Eastwood. In an ironic twist of fate, Chad McQueen was linked with Eastwood's daughter, Alison.

In time, Barbara remarried. David Brunsvold became her new husband. The couple follows somewhat the same lifestyle that Steve and Barbara did, enjoying an adventurous existence in their decked-out bus as they travel to their Montana ranch in summer or head south to Arizona for the winter.

On reflection, Barbara claimed that the three and a half years she lived with Steve were "the most beautiful learning experience of my life, and it was a gift. He was a great teacher and a beautiful man. I loved him very much."

In 1986, Dr. Kelley retired and sold his practice. Holistic methods are still used in the 21st century to battle malignant cancer.

As he neared the end of his life in 2005, Kelley became increasingly despondent, even paranoid about the mention of his controversial cancer therapy. He had grown old, his mental and physical health deteriorating as he did. "My attempt to save Steve McQueen cost me everything because of the relentless attacks of the media," he said shortly before he died. "It brought me financial ruin. I'm completely broke. I could have saved him. It was the American drug cartels who murdered him. As for me, I realize now that no good deed goes unpunished."

Casey and Darron revealed a strange story after the death of their friend. "One night Steve told us that he'd already left a deposit of himself in a sperm bank," Darron said. "He'd left it in care of his daughter, Terry, and she was to tell no one, not even her mother. He saw this as a chance to raise extra cash for 'my little girl.' He didn't even want his wife Barbara to know about this."

"He hoped that Terry would be able to sell his sperm for five million dollars to a rich woman who wanted another Steve McQueen, one who would live in the 21st century," Darron said. "We don't know if Steve was bullshitting us or not, but knowing him it would be just like him to do something like that."

Since records of sperm donors are confidential, it is not known if some woman—or possibly a husband—purchased Steve's sperm, if such a deposit does indeed exist or did exist at one time.

If a Steve McQueen dead-ringer turns up on the screen one day, movie fans might know who his daddy was.

Steve McQueen
1930-1980
REST IN PEACE

Acknowledgments

Any biography of a recently deceased person who lived during the latter half of the 20th century, as opposed to historical figures from earlier eras for whom a body of already-published sources might be available, out of necessity has to be the work of collaboration with others. As such, many contributors helped me, at least in some small way, in solving the puzzle that was Steve McQueen.

Either through personal interviews, published quotes, or private comments they made to colleagues, I am grateful for the information provided by the people cited here and on the following pages. I am also in debt to many unnamed sources who were willing to provide information about Steve McQueen, but who didn't want their names acknowledged.

I acknowledge my deep gratitude to Steve's three wives--Neile Adams, Ali MacGraw, and Barbara Minty--who have each gone on public record by writing three radically different memoirs, each sharing their experiences of what life was like with the charismatic star. At least in the case of Ali and Neile, Steve is partly responsible for derailing what might have been brilliant careers on the stage or in the movies.

I am also grateful for Steve's two friends, Darron McDonald and Casey Perkins, for revealing what they shared with those of us who were publishing at Manor Books at the time. And whereas their own book never got off the ground, their memories will live on in this biography. Casey died of AIDS in 1984, with Darron's death, also from AIDS, occurring the following year.

To Steve's three wives, to Darron and Casey, and also, to those persons, either living or dead, whose names are listed on the following page, I transmit my heartfelt thanks. And especially to Steve McQueen, whom I admired and respected, many thanks, from

Darwin Porter
New York City
November, 2009

Acknowledgments (continued)

Nick Adams
Edie Adams
Irwin Allen
Elga Anderson
Brigid Bazlen
Candice Bergen
Vivian Blaine
Joan Blondell
Tom Bosley
Rogers Brackett
Marlon Brando
Robert Bray
Fulton Bryant
Yul Brynner
Horst Buchholz
Vincent Bugliosi
Philip Buloff
Leroy Calder
Truman Capote
Brooks Clift
James Coburn
Frank Corsaro
Aneta Corseaut
Joan Crawford
Richard Crenna
Maggie Daly
Bobby Darin
Belle David
Sammy Davis, Jr
Dr. Matthew Dennehy
Crahan Denton
Brad Dexter
Charles Durning
Peggy Feury
Freddie Fields

John Foreman
Jack Garfein
John Gilmore
Jackie Gleason
Suellen Gordon
Frank Graves
Uta Hagen
Stanley Mills Haggart
Jack Harris
Henry Hathaway
Rock Hudson
Kim Hunter
John Huston
Dean Jeffrey
Norman Jewison
Christine Jorgensen
Betty Kaiser
Stan Kamen
Arthur Kennedy
Veronica Lake
Peter Lawford
Philip Leacock
Claire Lemmon
Lorna Luft
Karl Malden
Samuel Miller
Sal Mineo
Robert Mulligan
Ralph Nelson
Anaïs Nin
David Niven
Woody Parrish-Martin
Phil Parslow
Sam Peckinpah
Ralph Porter

Dick Powell
Robert Relyea
Lee Remick
Harold Robbins
Mark Rydell
Mildred Sacker
George Schaefer
Franklin Schaffner
Don Siegel
Maureen Stapleton
Rod Steiger
Cliff Stevens
Robert Stevens
Lee Strasberg
John Sturges
Warren Talbot
Olga Tamayo
Lana Turner
Lita Valachi
Robert Vaughn
Robert Wagner
Eli Wallach
Ethel Waters
Sonny West
William Wiard
Mary Wilke
Tennessee Williams
Henry Willson
Floyd Wilson
Shelley Winters
Robert Wise
Jack Wittaker

Selected Bibliography

Andersen, Christopher. *Barbra: The Way She Is.* William Morrow, 2006.

Bacon, James. *The Jackie Gleason Story.* St. Martin's Press, 1985.

Baker, Carroll. *Baby Doll: An Autobiography.* Arbor House Publishing Co., 1983.

Bergen, Candice. *Knock Wood.* Ballantine Books, 1985.

Brown, Peter Harry. *Kim Novak: Reluctant Goddess.* St. Martin's Press, 1986.

Bugliosi, Vincent, with Gentry, Curt. *Helter Skelter The True Story of the Manson Murders.* W.W. Norton & Company, Inc., 1974.

Carne, Judy. *Laughing on the Outside, Crying on the Inside, The Bittersweet Saga of the Sock-It-To-Me Girl.* Rawson Associates, 1985.

Chamberlain, Richard. *Stattered Love.* HarperCollins, 2003.

Charrière, Henri. *Papillon.* Harper Perennial, 2006.

Clarke, Gerald. *Capote: A Biography.* Simon & Schuster Books, 1988

Dalton, David. *James Dean: The Mutant King: A Biography.* Straight Arrow Books, 1974.

Davis, Ronald L. *Zachary Scott Hollywood's Sophisticated Cad.* University Press of Mississippi, 2006.

Donati, William. *Ida Lupino.* The University of Kentucky Press, 1996.

Dunaway, Faye, with Sharkey, Betsy. *Looking for Gatsby.* Simon & Schuster, 1995.

Evans, Robert. *The Kid Stays in the Picture.* Hyperion, 1994.

Finstad, Suzanne. *Natasha: The Biography of Natalie Wood.* Harmony, 2001.

Fury, David. *Chuck Conners: The Man Behind the Rifle.* Artist's Press Publishers, 1997.

Gifford, Barry, & Lee, Lawrence. *Jack's Book: An Oral Biography of Jack Kerouac.* St. Martin's Press, 1978.

Gilmore, John. *Laid Bare: A Memoir of Wrecked Lives and the Hollywood Death Trip.* Amok Books, 1997.

Harris, Warren G. *Natalie & R.J. Hollywood's Star-Crossed Lovers.* Doubleday, 1988.

Haygood, Wil. *Black and White: The Life of Sammy Davis Jr.* Aurum Press

Ltd., 2004.

Henry, William A. III. *The Great One: The Life and Legend of Jackie Gleason.* Doubleday, 1992.

Hudson, Rock and Davidson, Sara. *Rock Hudson: His Story.* William Morrow & Company, 1986.

Hunter, Allan. *Faye Dunaway.* St. Martin's Press, 1986.

Jeffers, Paul. *Sal Mineo: His Life, Murder, and Mystery.* Carroll & Publishers, 2000.

Jorgensen, Christine. *Christine Jorgensen: A Personal Autobiography by Christine Jorgensen.* Cleis Press, 2000.

Lambert, Gavin. *Natalie Wood A Life.* Alfred A. Knopf, 2004

Leigh, Barbara with Terrill, Marshal. *The King, McQueen and The Love Machine.* Xlibris Corporation, 2001.

Lenburg, Jeff. *Dustin Hoffman: Hollywood's Antihero.* St. Martin's Press, 1983.

Levy, Shawn. *The Last Playboy: The High Life of Porfirio Rubirosa.* Fourth Estate, 2005.

Louvish, Simon. *Mae West: It Ain't No Sin.* Thomas Dunne Books, 2006.

Luck, Richard. *Steve McQueen.* Pocket Essentials, 2000.

Luft, Lorna. *Me and My Shadows Living with the Legacy of Judy Garland.* Simon & Schuster, 1998.

MacGraw, Ali. *Moving Pictures.* Bantam Books, 1991.

McCoy, Malachy. *Steve McQueen: The Unauthorized Biography.* Henry Regnery Company, 1974.

McQueen, Barbara with Terrill, Marshall. *Steve McQueen The Last Mile.* Dalton Watson Fine Books, 2006.

Merrill, Gary. *Bette, Rita and the Rest of My Life.* Yankee Books, 1988.

Nolan, William. *McQueen.* Congdon & Weed, Inc. 1984.

_____ *Steve McQueen: Star on Wheels.* Berkley Publishing Corporation, 1972.

Porter, Darwin. *Paul Newman The Man Behind the Baby Blues.* Blood Moon Productions, 2009.

Ragsdale, Grady Jr. *Steve McQueen The Final Chapter.* Vision House, 1984.

Riese, Randall. *All About Bette: Her Life From A to Z.* Contemporary Books, 1993.

Robbins, Jhan. *Yul Brynner: The Inscrutable King.* Dodd Mead, 1987.

Rose, Frank. *The Agency: William Morris and the Hidden History of Show Business.* HarperCollins, 1995.

St. Charnez, Casey. *The Films of Steve McQueen.* Citadel Press, 1984.

Sandford, Christopher. *McQueen The Biography.* Taylor Trade Publishing, 2003.

Server, Lee. *Ava Gardner: Love Is Nothing.* St. Martin's Press, 2006.

Spiegel, Penina. *The Untold Story of a Bad Boy in Hollywood McQueen.* Doubleday & Company, Inc., 1986.

Stone, Matt. *McQueen's Machines The Cars and Bikes of a Hollywood Icon.* Motorbooks, 2007.

Terrill, Marshall. *Steve McQueen Portrait of an American Rebel.* Plexus Publishing Limited, 1993.

Toffel McQueen, Neile. *My Husband, My Friend.* Antheneum, 1986.

Valentine, Tom, & Mahn, Patrick. *Daddy's Duchess.* Lyle Stuart, Inc., 1987.

Van Doren, Mamie, with Aveilhe, Art. *Playing the Field: My Story.* Putnam, 1987.

Vaughn, Robert. *A Fortunate Life.* Thomas Dunne Books, 2008.

Wagner, Robert, J. with Eyman, Scott. *Pieces of My Heart.* Harper Entertainment, 2008.

Wallach, Eli. *The Good, The Bad, and Me: In My Anecdotage.* Harcourt, 2005.

Weatherby, W.J. *Jackie Gleason: An Intimate Portrait of the Great One.* Pharos Books, 1992.

West, Sonny. *Elvis: Still Taking Care of Business.* Triumph Books, 2007.

Wilson, Mary. *Dreamgirl—My Life as a Supreme.* St. Martin's Press, 1986.

Index

436

437

438

439

441

442

BLOOD MOON PRODUCTIONS

Entertainment About How America Interprets
Its Celebrities

Blood Moon Productions originated in 1997 as *The Georgia Literary Association*, a vehicle for the promotion of obscure writers from America's Deep South. Today, Blood Moon is based in New York City, and staffed with writers who otherwise devote their energies to *THE FROMMER GUIDES*, a trusted name in travel publishing.

Since 2004, Blood Moon has generated nine different literary awards. They've included both silver and bronze medals from the IPPY (Independent Publishers Assn.) Awards; four nominations and two Honorable Mentions for BOOK OF THE YEAR from Foreword Magazine; and two Honorable Mentions from the Hollywood Book Festival.

Our corporate mission involves researching and salvaging the oral histories of America's entertainment industry--those "off the record" events which at the time might have been defined as either indecent or libelous, but which are now pertinent to America's understanding of its origins and cultural roots. For more about us, click on **www.BloodMoonProductions.com,** or refer to the pages which immediately follow.

Thanks for your interest, best wishes, and happy reading.

Danforth Prince, President
Blood Moon Productions

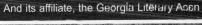

PAUL NEWMAN

The Man Behind the Baby Blues
His Secret Life Exposed
by Darwin Porter

The most compelling biography of the iconic actor ever published:

Drawn from firsthand interviews with insiders who knew Paul Newman intimately, and compiled over a period of nearly a half-century, this is the world's most honest and most revelatory biography about Hollywood's pre-eminent male sex symbol, with dozens of potentially shocking revelations.

Whereas the situations it exposes were widely known within Hollywood's inner circles, they've never before been revealed to the general public.

If you're a fan of Newman (and who do you know who isn't) you really should look at this book. It's a respectful but candid cornucopia of information about the sexual and emotional adventures of a young man on Broadway and in Hollywood.

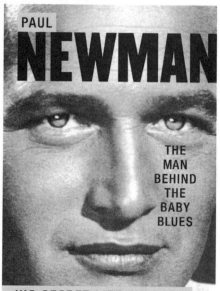

PAUL NEWMAN

THE MAN BEHIND THE BABY BLUES

HIS SECRET LIFE EXPOSED
BY DARWIN PORTER

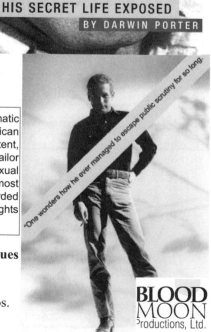

"One wonders how he ever managed to escape public scrutiny for so long."

A pioneering and posthumous biography of a charismatic icon of Tinseltown. His rule over the hearts of American moviegoers lasted for more than half a century--a potent, desirable, and ambiguous sex symbol, a former sailor from Shaker Heights, Ohio, who parlayed his ambisexual charm and extraordinary good looks into one of the most successful careers in Hollywood. It's all here, as recorded by celebrity chronicler Darwin Porter--the giddy heights and agonizing lows of a great American star.

Paul Newman, The Man Behind the Baby Blues
His Secret Life Exposed
ISBN 978-0-9786465-1-6 $26.95
Hardcover,   520 pages, with dozens of photos.

BLOOD MOON Productions, Ltd.

MERV GRIFFIN
A Life in the Closet

by Darwin Porter

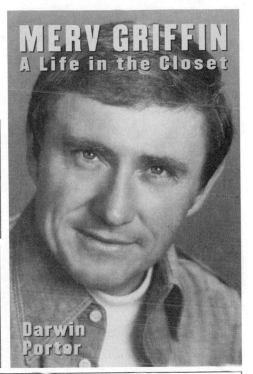

Merv Griffin, A Life in the Closet

Merv Griffin began his career as a Big Band singer, moved on to a failed career as a romantic hero in the movies, and eventually rewrote the rules of everything associated with the broadcasting industry. Along the way, he met and befriended virtually everyone who mattered, made billions operating casinos and developing jingles, contests, and word games. All of this while maintaining a male harem and a secret life as America's most famously closeted homosexual.

In this comprehensive biography--the first published since Merv's death in 2007--celebrity blographer Darwin Porter reveals the amazing details behind the richest, most successful, and in some way, the most notorious mogul in the history of America's entertainment industry.

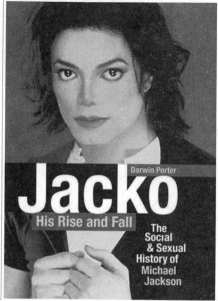

This "entertainingly outrageous" (FRONTIERS MAGAZINE) biography provides a definitive,
blow-by-blow description of the "hot, provocative, and barely under control drama" that was the life
of America's most famous Postwar actor.

Brando Unzipped

by Darwin Porter

"Lurid, raunchy, perceptive, and certainly worth reading ...One of the ten best show-biz biographies of 2006."   *The Sunday Times (London)*

"**Yummy**. An irresistably flamboyant romp of a read." *Books to Watch Out For*

"Astonishing. An extraordinarily detailed portrait of Brando that's as blunt, uncompromising, and X-rated as the man himself."
Women's Weekly

"This shocking new book is sparking a major reassessment of Brando's legacy as one of Hollywood's most macho lotharios."
Daily Express (London)

"As author Darwin Porter finds, it wasn't just the acting world Marlon Brando conquered. It was the actors, too "
Gay Times (London)

"*Brando Unzipped* Is the definitive gossip guide to the late, great actor's life."
The New York Daily News

BRANDO
Unzipped

Bad Boy • Megastar • Sexual Outlaw

Book of the Year
AWARD FINALIST

Hardcover, 625 indexed pages,
with hundreds
of photos.
ISBN 978-0-9748118-2-6.
$26.95

This is one of our most visible and most frequently reviewed titles. A best-seller, it's now in its fifth printing, with French, Portuguese, and Dutch editions selling briskly in Europe. Shortly after its release, this title was extensively serialized by THE SUNDAY TIMES in the UK, and in other major Sunday supplements in mainland Europe and Australia

Katharine the Great
(KATHARINE HEPBURN)
A Lifetime of Secrets Revealed

A softcover that fans of old Hollywood find fascinating.

by Darwin Porter
569 pages, with photos $16.95
ISBN   978-0-9748118-0-2

Katharine Hepburn was the world's greatest screen diva--the most famous actress in American history. But until the appearance of this biography, no one had ever published the intimate details of her complicated and ferociously secretive private life. Thanks to the "deferential and obsequious whitewashes" which followed in the wake of her death, readers probably know WHAT KATE REMEMBERED. Here, however, is an unvarnished account of what Katharine Hepburn desperately wanted to forget.

"Behind the scenes of her movies, Katharine Hepburn played the temptress to as many women as she did men, ranted and raved with her co-stars and directors, and broke into her neighbors' homes for fun. And somehow, she managed to keep all of it out of the press. As they say, *Katharine the Great* is hard to put down."
*** The Dallas Voice***

"The door to Hepburn's closet has finally been opened. This is the most honest and least apologetic biography of Hollywood's most ferociously private actress ever written."
*** Senior Life Magazine, Miami***

"In Porter's biography of Katharine Hepburn, details about the inner workings of a movie studio (RKO in the early 30s), are relished.
*** The Bottom Line, Palm Springs***

"Darwin Porter's biography of Hepburn cannot be lightly dismissed or ignored. Connoisseurs of Hepburn's life would do well to seek it out as a forbidden supplement."
*** The Sunday Times (London)***

Katharine Hepburn was the most obsessively secretive actress in Hollywood. Her androgynous, pan-sexual appeal usually went over big with movie audiences-- until those disastrous flops when it didn't.

Humphrey Bogart

The Making of a Legend

by Darwin Porter

A juicy saga of a film icon's early love affairs, revealing what really lay under the trench coat of history's most famous movie star.

Whereas Humphrey Bogart is always at the top of any list of the Entertainment Industry's most famous actors, very little is known about how he clawed his way to stardom from Broadway to Hollywood during Prohibition and the Jazz Age.

This radical expansion of one of Darwin Porter's pioneering biographies begins with Bogart's origins as the child of wealthy (morphine-addicted) parents in New York City, then examines the scandals, love affairs, breakthrough successes, and failures that launched Bogart on the road to becoming an American icon. Drawn from original interviews with friends and foes who knew a lot about what lay beneath his trenchcoat, this exposé covers Bogart's life from his birth in 1899 till his marriage to Lauren Bacall in 1944. It includes details about behind-the-scenes dramas associated with three mysterious marriages, and films such as *The Petrified Forest, The Maltese Falcon, High Sierra,* and *Casablanca.* Read all about the debut and formative years of the actor who influenced many generations of filmgoers, laying Bogie's life bare in a style you've come to expect from Darwin Porter. Exposed with all their juicy details is what Bogie never told his fourth wife, Lauren Bacall, herself a screen legend.

This revelatory book is based on dusty unpublished memoirs, letters, diaries, and often personal interviews from the women—and the men—who adored him. There are also shocking allegations from colleagues, former friends, and jilted lovers who wanted the screen icon to burn in hell. All this and more, much more, in Darwin Porter's newest celebrity exposé,

A DEMENTED BILLIONAIRE:

From his reckless pursuit of love as a rich teenager to his final days as a demented fossil, Howard Hughes tasted the best and worst of the century he occupied. Along the way, he changed the worlds of aviation and entertainment forever. This biography reveals inside details about his destructive and usually scandalous associations with other Hollywood players.

Howard Hughes
Hell's Angel by Darwin Porter

Set amid descriptions of the unimaginable changes that affected America between Hughes's birth in 1905 and his death in 1976, this book gives an insider's perspective about what money can buy--and what it can't.

"Darwin Porter's access to film industry insiders and other Hughes confidants supplied him with the resources he needed to create a portrait of Hughes that both corroborates what other Hughes biographies have divulged, and go them one better."

-Foreword Magazine

"Thanks to this bio of Howard Hughes, we'll never be able to look at the old pin-ups in quite the same way again."

-The Times **(London)**

A BIG comprehensive hardcover,
Approx 814 pages, with photos
Available in May, 2010
$32.95
ISBN 978-1-936003-13-6

Hughes--A young billionaire looks toward his notorious future

Billie Dove--duenna of the Silent Screen. She gave him syphilis.

Did Howard Hughes murder David Bacon?

"The Aviator flew both ways. Porter's biography presents new allegations about Hughes' shady dealings with some of the biggest names of the 20th century"

New York Daily News

The Secret Life of the U.S. Emperor
LOVE! SEX! POWER!
"The Aviator flew both ways."
New York Daily News

The Richest Man in America
SEXUAL PREDATOR
LUSTFUL VISIONARY

50 Years of Queer Cinema

500 of the Best GLBTQ Films Ever Made

An indispensable reference source for films about

The Love that Dare Not Speak Its Name

(Available April 2010)

As late as 1958, homosexuality couldn't even be mentioned in a movie, as proven by the elaborate lengths the producers of Tennessee Williams swampy *Cat on a Hot Tin Roof* took to evade the obvious fact that its hero, Paul Newman, was playing it gay. And in spite of the elaborate lengths its producers took to camouflage its lavender aspects, in-the-know viewers during the late 50s realized all along that Joe E. Brown was fully aware that Jack Lemmon wasn't a biological female ("nobody's perfect") in *Some Like it Hot* (1959).

That kind of baroque subterfuge ended abruptly in 1960, when cinema emerged from its celluloid closet with the release of *Boys in the Band.* Decades later came *Brokeback Mountain, Transamerica,* and *Milk.*

This comprehensive anthology documents it all, bringing into focus a sweeping rundown of cinema's most intriguing Gay, Lesbian, Bisexual, Transgendered, and "Queer Questioning" films that deserves a home next to the DVD player as well as on the reference shelves of public libraries. Crucial to the viability of this book is the fact that new DVD releases have made these films available to new generations of viewers for the first time since their original release.

More than just a dusty library reference, this book shamelessly spills 50 quasi-closeted years of Hollywood secrets--all of them in glorious Technicolor.

A comprehensive paperback designed as a reference source for both private homes and libraries.   Approx. 450 pages, with 400 photos
ISBN 978-1-936003-09-9 $24.95

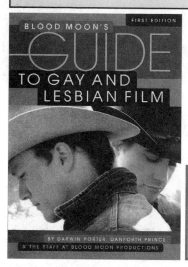

> "If you're gonna tell a story,
> you'd better get to the punch line fast,
> and you'd better make it sexy."
>
> Groucho Marx

Midnight in Savannah

Sexual Eccentricities in the Deep South.
Perversity in Extremis
Trade Paperback   498 pages   **$16.95**
ISBN   978-0-9668030-1-3

After its publication in 2000, Darwin Porter's *Midnight in Savannah* quickly established itself as one of the best-selling gay novels in the history of the Deep South.

Eugene Raymond, a filmmaker in Nashville, writes, "Porter disturbs by showing the world as a *film noir* cul-de-sac.   Corruption has no respect for gender or much of anything else.

"In MIDNIGHT, both Lavender Morgan (at 72, the world's oldest courtesan) and Tipper Zelda (an obese, fading chanteuse taunted as 'the black widow) purchase lust from sexually conflicted young men with drop-dead faces, chiseled bodies, and genetically gifted crotches. These women once relied on their physicality to steal the hearts and fortunes of the world's richest and most powerful men. Now, as they slide closer every day to joining the corpses of their former husbands, these once-beautiful women must depend, in a perverse twist of fate, on sexual outlaws for *le petit mort*. And to survive, the hustlers must idle their personal dreams while struggling to cajole what they need from a sexual liaison they detest. Mendacity reigns. Physical beauty as living hell. CAT ON A HOT TIN ROOF's Big Daddy must be spinning in his grave right now."

"If you're not already a Darwin Porter fan, this novel will make you one!   We've come a long way, baby, since Gore Vidal's *The City and the Pillar.*"

-Time Out for Books

459

Hollywood's
Silent Closet

by Darwin Porter

ISBN 978-0-9668030-2-0   Trade Paper 7" x 10"
746 pages. 60 photos $24.95

"The Little Tramp" Charlie Chaplin (above) was one of the most recklessly debauched players in Hollywood

An anthology of star-studded scandal from Tinseltown's very gay and very lavender past, it focuses on Hollywood's secrets from the 1920s, including the controversial backgrounds of the great lovers of the Silent Screen.

Valentino, Ramon Novarro, Charlie Chaplin, Fatty Arbuckle, Pola Negri, Mary Pickford, and many others figure into eyewitness accounts of the debauched excesses that went on behind closed doors. It also documents the often tragic endings of America's first screen idols, some of whom admitted to being more famous than the monarchs of England and Jesus Christ combined.

a novel by
Darwin Porter

The first book of its kind, it's the most intimate and most realistic novel about sex, murder, blackmail, and degradation in early Hollywood ever written.

"The *Myra Breckenridge* of the Silent-Screen era. Lush, luscious, and langorously decadent. A brilliant primer of **Who was Who** in early Hollywood."
-Gay London Times

A banquet of information about the pansexual intrigues of Hollywood between 1919 and 1926 compiled from eyewitness interviews with men and women, all of them insiders, who flourished in its midst. Not for the timid, it names names and doesn't spare the guilty.   If you believe, like Truman Capote, that the literary treatment of gossip will become the literature of the 21st century, then you will love *Hollywood's Silent Closet.*

Millions of fans lusted after Gary Cooper (background) and Rudolph Valentino (foreground) but until the release of this book, **The Public Never Knew**

BLOOD MOON
A sexy, horrifying spellbinder

by Darwin Porter

In 2008, this title was designated as one of the ten best horror novels ever published in a survey conducted by *Boiz Who Read*

ISBN 978-0-9668030-4-4

A controversial, compelling and artfully potboiling paperback $10.99

Blood Moon exposes the murky labyrinths of fanatical Christianity in America today, all within a spunky context of male eroticism. If you never thought that sex, psychosis, right-wing religion, and violence aren't linked, think again.

In the gay genre, *Blood Moon* does for the novel what Danielle Steele and John Grisham have been publishing in the straight world for years
---**Frank Fenton**

Rose Phillips, Blood Moon's charismatic and deviant evangelist, and her shocking but beautiful gay son, Shelley, were surely written in hell. Together, they're a brilliant--and jarring--depiction of a fiercely aggressive Oedipal couple competing for the same male prizes.

"*Blood Moon* reads like an IMAX spectacle about the power of male beauty, with red-hot icons, a breathless climax, and erotica that's akin to Anaïs Nin on Viagra with a bump of meth."
Eugene Raymond

Rhinestone Country
by Darwin Porter

**All that glitter, all that publicity,
all that applause, all that pain.**

<small>WHAT COUNTRY MUSIC LEGEND INSPIRED THIS NOVEL?</small>

ISBN 978-0-9668030-3-7   Trade Paper   569 pages. $15.99

The *True Grit* of show-biz novels, *Rhinestone Country* is a provocative, realistic, and tender portrayal of the Country-Western music industry, closeted lives south of the Mason-Dixon line, and three of the singers who clawed their way to stardom.

Rhinestone Country reads like a scalding gulp of rotgut whiskey on a snowy night in a bow-jacks honky-tonk.

-Mississippi Pearl

"A gay and erotic treatment of the Country-Western music industry? Nashville has come out of the closet at last!"

The Georgia Literary Assn.

Beautifully crafted, *Rhinestone Country* sweeps with power and tenderness across the racial, social, and sexual landscapes of the Deep South.

This is a daring and dazzling work about trauma, deception, and pain, all of it with a Southern accent.

--Peter Tompkins

BUTTERFLIES IN HEAT

by Darwin Porter

A compellingly retro softcover expressing some eternal truths about love, hate, greed, and sex.   ISBN 978-0-9668030-9-9 $14.95

Tennessee Williams, who understood a thing or two about loss, love, and drama, had this to say about **Butterflies in Heat:**
"I'd walk the waterfront for Numie any day."

"The most SCORCHING novel of the BIZZARE, the FLAMBOYANT, the CORRUPT since *Midnight Cowboy*. The strikingly beautiful blond hustler, Numie, has come to the end of the line. Here, in the SEARING HEAT of a tropical cay, he arouses PASSIONS that explode under the BLOOD-RED SUN."

-Manor Reviews

"A well-established cult classic. How does Darwin Portor's garden grow? Only in the moonlight, and only at midnight, when man-eating vegetation in any color but green bursts into full bloom to devour the latest offerings."

-James Leo Herlihy, author of *MIDNIGHT COWBOY*

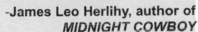

This title, a cult classic now in its *16th printing*, has sold steadily to a coterie of Darwin Porter fans since its inauguration in 1976, when it was the thing EVERYBODY in Key West was talking about, and the inspiration for the movie that EVERYBODY wanted to be in.

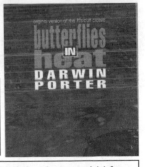

"Darwin Porter writes with an incredible understanding of the milieu--hot enough to singe the wings off any butterfly."
James Kirkwood, co-author of *A CHORUS LINE*

"We know from the beginning that we're getting into a hotbed that has morbid fascination for potential readers. The novel evolves, in fact, into one massive melée of malevolence, vendetta, and e-v-i-l, stunningly absorbing alone for its sheer and unrelenting exploration of the lower depths."

BESTSELLERS

463

About the Author

This tell-all exposé of Steve McQueen was authored by **Darwin Porter**, whose earlier portraits of **Paul Newman, Merv Griffin, Marlon Brando, Humphrey Bogart, Katharine Hepburn, Howard Hughes,** and **Michael Jackson** generated widespread reviews and animated radio and blogsite commentaries worldwide. Some of Porter's biographies have been serialized to millions of readers in THE SUNDAY TIMES of London and THE MAIL ON SUNDAY.

Porter is also the author of ***Hollywood Babylon-It's Back!***, a prize-winning anthology of celebrity indiscretion that was defined by some critics as "the hottest compilation of inter-generational scandal in the history of Hollywood," and "The Ultimate Guilty Pleasure." A sequel, ***Hollywood Babylon Strikes Again,*** is planned for release in the late spring of 2010.

After seeing *The Blob* with school friends in 1958, Darwin became the president of the Steve McQueen Fan Club in Miami. Over the years, and in preparation for this book, he gathered data on McQueen from various sources, especially from eyewitnesses to McQueen's career living in Hollywood and New York. Included in his research were ongoing dialogues with actors, directors, and producers, friends, lovers, and enemies of McQueen. Often they supplied only a paragraph of information, an insight here or there, but in the end, those interviews contributed to a rich mosaic.

In this pioneering overview, Darwin attempts to answer the question never really addressed in any previous biography: Who was the man behind the myth known as Steve McQueen?

Darwin is also the well-known author of many past and present editions of *The Frommer Guides,* a respected travel guidebook series presently administered by John Wiley and Sons Publishers.

When not traveling, which is rare, Darwin lives with a menagerie of once-abandoned pets in a Victorian house in one of the outer boroughs of New York City, with frequent excursions to California and various Frommer-related parts of Europe and the Caribbean.